THE RELIGIOUS QUESTS OF THE
GRAECO-ROMAN WORLD

THE RELIGIOUS QUESTS
OF THE
GRAECO-ROMAN WORLD

A STUDY IN THE HISTORICAL BACKGROUND
OF EARLY CHRISTIANITY

BY

S. ANGUS, Ph.D., D.Lit., D.D.

PROFESSOR OF NEW TESTAMENT AND HISTORICAL THEOLOGY
ST. ANDREW'S COLLEGE, UNIVERSITY OF SYDNEY

LONDON
JOHN MURRAY, ALBEMARLE STREET, W.

FIRST EDITION . . . 1929

TO

MY MOTHER

ἰδοὺ καινὰ ποιῶ πάντα

FOREWORD

CHRISTIANITY arose as an historical religion, historically
conditioned in a definite environment. It was based on
certain historical facts; it was preached by and to men
who held a view of the world which differs radically in
many respects from the views of the present. Christianity not only made history but was modified and
shaped by history. No genetic study of Christianity
will ever explain Christianity, yet ignorance of its antecedents and of the contemporary spiritual forces and
mentality renders a true appreciation impossible. There
is a more excellent way of magnifying Christianity than
by ignoring or decrying Paganism, or disparaging the
rival systems which Christianity overcame and laid
under tribute.

During the last generation there has been an increasing
recognition of the effect of environment on early Christianity and of the necessity of envisaging Christianity
in its complete cultural and religious background. The
Graeco-Roman world was the soil on which the Sower
went forth to sow the Christian seed; the growth
depended not only on the vital forces inherent in the
seed but on the preparation and fertility of the soil. We
must know the ancient habits of thought and intellectual
postulates with which Christianity came into contact and
which it partially at least adopted, to understand
adequately its task.

To the question, ' Is God the God of the Jews only? '
students of ancient history must affirm that He is also
the God of the Greeks and the Orientals and the Romans.
There was a rich Pagan preparation for Christianity as
there was undoubtedly a rich Jewish contribution to
' the fullness of the times.' The spiritual values of

Hellenistic-Oriental syncretism cannot be overlooked by students of the history and evolution of Christianity. The Christian *Ecclesia* is best appreciated when observed at work in an intensely religious world in competition with the Synagogues of the Dispersion, the Guilds of the Mystery-Religions, and the Schools of Greek philosophy.

In Paganism there was a ' groping after God if haply they might find Him,' and such aspirations are of direct interest to us as enabling us to appreciate better the Gospel which satisfied them. In every age Wisdom, ' entering into holy souls,' makes men ' friends of God and prophets,' eager to apprehend and live the Truth. ' Those who lived with the Word and were Christians before Christ,' those who delivered their *testimonium animae naturaliter Christianae,* prepared the way of the Lord. And among those who later opposed the irresistible progress of our Faith, when spiritual issues were often confused in political and sectarian zeal, there are found sincere ' men who were lovers of wisdom both in their characters and in their discourses,' and believed that ' we must absolutely by no means let go our hold of God by day or night.' Christianity proved unable to discover a method of coming to terms with or appropriating ancient culture without rending the rich fabric of Graeco-Roman civilization. We observe its champions often so conscious of moral perils that in their alarm they rooted up wheat with the tares, refusing to let both grow together till the harvest.

In the hope of contributing, in however modest a fashion, to a knowledge of the conditions in the Mediterranean world at the rise and during the spread of our Faith, this volume is published. It consists of lectures given in Yale University during October and November of last year ; delivered also in part in Chicago University ; Toronto University ; Oberlin College, Ohio ; and Hartford Seminary Foundation, Connecticut. In revision of the work for the press, the original lecture form has been adhered to, even at the risk of occasional repetition.

An attempt has been made not only to interpret the Graeco-Roman period, but also to present it speaking for itself in its own words. Considerations of space, however, rendered compression and selection necessary and made only brief citations possible; numerous other citations and references accumulated from ancient records have been regretfully omitted.

Quotations from ancient sources are indicated by single quotation marks; those from modern authors in double quotation marks. Translations from both are, unless otherwise specified, by the writer.

Thanks are due to my colleague Professor Edward E. Anderson for having read the manuscript and for helpful suggestions.

S. A.

St. Andrew's College, Sydney.
December 22, 1928.

CONTENTS

xiii

CHAPTER IV

GREEK MORAL AND GREEK MYSTICAL PHILOSOPHY

CHAPTER V

THE MYSTERY-RELIGIONS

CHAPTER VI

CHRISTIANITY

CHAPTER VII

CHRISTIANITY AND THE ANCIENT CULTURE

THE RELIGION OF MAGIC, SACRAMENT AND SYMBOL

CHAPTER VIII

ANCIENT SACRAMENTARIANISM

CHAPTER IX

ENTRY OF SACRAMENTARIANISM INTO CHRISTIANITY

CHAPTER X

THE EVOLUTION OF MAGICAL-SACRAMENTAL IDEAS AND USAGES

CHAPTER XI

THE PERSISTENCE OF ANCIENT SACRAMENTARIANISM

CHAPTER XII

RELATION OF ST. PAUL AND THE FOURTH GOSPEL
TO SACRAMENTARIANISM

CHAPTER XIII

THE PLACE AND FUNCTION OF SACRAMENT

and the Sensible; (2) human nature sensitive to impressions of the external world—sacraments as meeting-places of finite and Infinite—symbols natural or conventional—religious use of the economy of Nature; (3) the inarticulate in religion—the Absolute in symbols; (4) difficulty of maintaining high levels of spirituality—many channels of the Infinite to the soul—subjective receptivity—differentiation between symbol and sacrament—" uncovenanted mercies "—sacraments and character—varieties of sacramental experiences—the Real Presence—rite and Love—abuses of sacraments (1) as surrogates for Reality—confusion of sensible sign and sacrament; (2) isolation from general sacramentalism; (3) overlooking other modes of revelation—especially in personality; (4) obligatory, or " generally necessary to salvation "—other types of mystics .   .   .   .   .   . pp. 219–238

CHAPTER XIV

SACRAMENTS TO-DAY AND THEIR FUTURE

Three essentials of a sacrament: (1) predisposing psychological condition, (2) objective means or material channel, (3) spiritual insight—examples of use of tangible objects—Joan of Arc—Mary of Scots—R. L. Stevenson—Keats—Robert E. Lee—through sense to spirit—practical tests of sacraments—congregational value—use of symbols and images—legitimate use of external means of grace: (1) *ex opere operato* credence strengthens magic—possible incongruity between rites and morals; (2) sacraments not exclusive or chief gateway to reality—' the Soul has its sense '; (3) abolish difference *in kind* between ecclesiastical rites and the symbolism of human life; (4) and between Christian and Pagan sacraments—cleavage between popular and reflective religion in every age—For future (1) the sacramental principle to be carried all through life, (2) advance toward healthy mysticism—subjectivity and objectivity in religion .   .   .   . pp. 239–253

ASTRALISM, OR THE RELIGION OF ASTROLOGY

CHAPTER XV

ASTRAL RELIGION AND ITS CATHOLIC APPEAL

Cosmic and astral *Zeitgeist*—persistence of astrology—a science-religion—wide appeal—four postulates of astralism: (1) Element-mysticism—' like by like '—' sun-like eyes '; (2) Cosmic unity—Stoics on cosmos—universal harmony; (3) Ensouled universe; (4) Microcosm-macrocosm—Astralism (1) a practical religion—fatalism and freedom—Providence—correspondences; (2) sidereal mysticism and cosmic emotion; (3) ethical aspects—(*a*) Providence, (*b*) commerce with heaven, (*c*) inward cleansing—testimonies—Philo; (4) Solar monotheism—Sun-cult and philosophy—importance of the Solar worship .   pp. 254–278

2

CHAPTER XVI
ASTRAL IMMORTALITY

CHAPTER XVII
THE ASCENT OF THE SOUL

ANCIENT GREEK THEOSOPHY AS A RELIGION
CHAPTER XVIII
CHARACTERISTICS OF HERMETICISM AS A RELIGION

CHAPTER XIX
THE HERMETIC 'UPWARD WAY'

THE WAY OF GNOSIS

CHAPTER XX

MOTIVES AND AIMS OF GNOSTICISM : ITS ENTRY INTO CHRISTIANITY

CHAPTER XXI

REACTIONS OF GNOSTICISM AND CHRISTIANITY : GNOSTIC PIETY

RELIGION AND MEDICINE

CHAPTER XXII

RELIGION AS A THERAPEUTIC IN PAGAN AND CHRISTIAN CIRCLES

THE RELIGIOUS OUTLOOK OF THE GRAECO-ROMAN WORLD

CHAPTER I

HISTORICAL IMPORTANCE OF THE GRAECO-ROMAN PERIOD

THE study of the Graeco-Roman world, stretching from Alexander the Great to Constantine or Julian, will always be of great historic interest for the intrinsic value of a period profoundly civilized and pulsating with religious life; for its striking modernity and its relevance to modern problems; but chiefly as the cultural background of that religion which has won its way to be the religion of our Western civilization. Study of the New Testament and of the popular enthusiastic movement which became conquering Christianity has suffered through being pursued apart from its historic background and religious environment. Much New Testament study is of the same order as if Shakespeare were studied largely in the background of Victorian Britain or in the atmosphere of the Enlightenment instead of in that of " the spacious times of great Elizabeth." Or— since Christianity is an Oriental religion and the New Testament has reached mostly Western readers—our New Testament has suffered much in the same way as if it were looked upon and interpreted largely in the light of present-day Japan rather than first in that of peasant Galilee, the Jewish Diaspora, and Hellenistic culture.

Moreover, this ancient Mediterranean basin, where civilization reacted on civilization and ideals came into conflict with ideals, is of immediate relevancy to us, inasmuch as there are three main elements in our modern

Western civilization, or, to change the figure, three main strands in its warp and woof, and all three have come to us from that Graeco-Roman world—Hellenism, Hebraism, and Christianity.

One can scarcely exaggerate the importance and value of the Greek contributions and of the momentous decision of Greece to consecrate her matchless genius to Christ instead of to Mithra. Shelley exaggerates when he says " we are all Greeks ; our laws, our religion, our art, have their roots in Greece," as does Francis Thompson on the other hand when he says " Paganism is lovely because it is dead," since Hellenistic-Oriental Paganism was not without high moral and spiritual values. Hellenism, or " the thirst for richness and harmony," is an essential for fullness of life. Why does Greece live ? Because of that inspiring ideal of a full and integral manhood—" Hellas the nurse of man complete as man " ; because in the Greek schools of Ionia and Athens and Magna Graecia European philosophy took its rise and saved the West from the inchoate thought of the Orient and from submission to the external authority of sacerdotalism ; because her philosophy was the first to embrace complexity in unity, and to refuse to rest in half truths ; because in ethics and religion and in all else the typically Greek outlook was the rare attitude of *Sophrosyne,* a moderation of perfect poise without exaggeration and without weakness ; because she was the mother of rational civilization and the first advocate of the supremacy of reason which posited no limit to inquiry ; because she was the first to assert the right of " man's meddling intellect " to raise questions and to pursue their solution to the utmost horizon ; because of her sanity in religion, Greece being the first to expel fear from religion and the first to subject religion to fearless criticism ; because Greek religion " proclaimed the divine consecration of the intellectual life " [1] ; because, in a word, Greece is " the mother-country of

Farnell, *Higher Aspects of Greek Religion,* p. 124.

the mind " [1] to which every man instinctively points when he would illustrate the indefeasible claims and inherent destinies of human nature.

Hebraism has made its perennial contribution, especially to the religious life. If Shelley exaggerated regarding the Greeks, Romanes has exaggerated still more regarding the Jews when he says, " If it had not been for the Jews the human race would not have had any religion worth our serious attention." Matthew Arnold has more truthfully affirmed, " As long as the world lasts, all who want to make progress in righteousness will come to Israel for inspiration, as to the people who have had the sense for righteousness most glowing and strongest, and in hearing and reading the words Israel has uttered for us, carers for conduct will find a glow and a force they could find nowhere else." " Judaea, pregnant with the living God," bequeathed a stern morality as the basis of both social and individual life, a tenacious social consciousness such as no other race in antiquity knew, an indomitable faith in a personal God which made her defiant in defeat, a belief in an increasing purpose in history, an attitude to suffering which has left the sublimest interpretation in all literature of the redemptive power of suffering.

The third element in our civilization, Christianity, was " the revelation of personality and depth " in a deepening of conscience and in appeal to experience. Its message of the infinite worth of personality with all its subtle modulations of individuality is our peculiarly Western pride. It satisfied best the two dominant passions of our self-hood, the passion for love and the passion for knowledge; it discovered the mysterious depths, range, and complexity of human personality and the privileges and awful responsibilities of freedom.

With no more accuracy than should be expected from general statements we may summarize by saying that Greece contributed philosophy, Israel morality, and

[1] Butler, *Hist. of Ancient Philosophy,* I, p. 268.

Christianity personality; that the watchword of Greece was Freedom, of Israel Law, and of Christianity Love; that Hellenism stressed Beauty, Hebraism Duty, and Christianity Selfless Service; that the first was anthropocentric, the second theocentric, and the third Christocentric; the first issued in individualism, the second developed a social and corporate consciousness, the third is a synthesis of both; the method of the first was inquiry, that of the second trust, that of the third faith-knowledge.

These three extensive views of life from that Graeco-Roman era have been superimposed upon an alien racial and cultural basis—the character and genius of our Western, especially Teutonic, race. Our Western civilization is an attempted, but as yet very imperfect, synthesis [1] of these three great heritages of the things of the spirit. The West has not yet been wholly converted to Christianity, only nominally, and with all the perils of a superficial adaptation. It has not yet adjusted itself to the full religion of Jesus, nor assimilated these three heritages, nor taken them in their healthful proportions.

In making an incursion into this ancient world we are, therefore, making a practical study of our spiritual antecedents and of the near and the remote associations of Christianity. We should be less than human and lacking in historic imagination did we not hear the appeal of our distant predecessors.

> " The souls of now two thousand years
> Have laid up here their toils and fears
> And all the earnings of their pain."

Every effort made by the human spirit in its pursuit of reality is of perennial worth. Had these ancients made no mistakes and proved infallible, they should be dis-

---

[1] " If the Church had fully understood and accepted the purpose and spirit of Christ, the great rational Graeco-Roman civilization, so far as we can see, need not have been swept away " (Lilian Dougall, *Modern Churchman*, XII, p. 327).

qualified as our predecessors. We must attempt to relive their perplexing experiences, to face life as they did, to capture their mentality, and to develop a sympathetic humanism. Unprejudiced historians are no longer unequivocally oblivious of the inner conditions of the soul as the real creators of the external facts of history, nor are they ashamed to acknowledge the recurrent and inevitable reactions of the spirit as the epoch-making factors, whether these reactions operate on economic, philosophical, or religious problems. History has always an inner side in the secret happenings of the soul; it presents also the external aspect of happenings chronicled in outward events. There is nothing more humanly interesting than to contemplate man making his experiments in different ways and directions after satisfaction—his ignorance and blind strugglings, his disappointments, his renewed efforts to find the light, and his unquenchable thirst for truth—' *veri avidus.*' Every endeavour to secure " news from the inner court of things " and to bring man into touch with the Eternal is of worth in our human story. Without undue generosity we may have patience with men who set out for a goal which they never reached, as we realize that the failures of former generations are as interesting and often more instructive than their successes. Deep calls to deep and spirit to spirit speaks across the intervening centuries, levelling with its humanism artificial and external and chronological differences. We may enter into the reverence of those who knelt not at our altars. We may gratefully appreciate bygone strivings. Humanity speaks a common language, and it is essential to the historian who would read the lessons of the past to hear it and to ponder reverently the varying expressions from age to age of the unchangeable truths. " Sorrow sobs in all the languages of the world," and " the martyr souls of heathendom " deliver their courageous message only to martyr souls to-day. In the flux of things oftentimes ' with the course of time the ancient things again become

new,' [1] and, as another ancient thinker [2] observed, God is
' ever substituting new blessings for the older.' Despite
Tertullian's petulant ' what has Jerusalem to do with
Athens? ', there were saints and martyrs of Athens and
Alexandria and of the Orient as well as of Palestine and
Italy. There were regenerating and cleansing forces
then as in every society and culture. Satan did not cast
out Satan in the Graeco-Roman age. If what was said
about Truth and Happiness and Beauty two thousand
years since is not final for us, neither is our apprehension
of these adequate. ʹWe are at one with the Graeco-
Roman age in moving about in worlds not realized.

Considering the innate conservative tendency of man
to cling to venerable customs and stale beliefs, we must
the more admire the daring experiments made during
these seven wonderful centuries. Men were then as now
divided between the charm of the old and the appeal of
the new. Experience is ever setting up and casting
down human theories and values. In the process of
progress much that is Reason becomes un-Reason, and
much that was both precious and useful to man at one
stage loses its value in face of new values and fresh
aspects of truth, but this does not relieve the student of
history of the duty of discovering how and why what
may have now become antiquated and nonsense was
once reason and science to the most enlightened contemporaries, and of recognizing how some ancient formulas of truth have been corroborated by the passing
generations. In the unresting striving of the human
spirit toward an ever far-off, realizable and unrealizable
goal, we may thankfully receive the torch of truth from
the runners who have finished their course; we may
enter sympathetically into the experiences of those who
have laboriously and unfalteringly climbed

> " Upon the great world's altar-stairs,
>   That slope thro' darkness up to God."

---

[1] πάλιν χρόνῳ τἀρχαῖα καινὰ γίγνεται, Stobaeus, *Ecl.* I. 8, 12.
[2] Philo, *De post. Caini*, 43, C.-W. 145; M. I. 254.

So doing we shall appreciate why Plotinus called his great master ' the divine Plato.' Only those who, amid the rush and commercialism and superficiality of our modern world, have leisure and love for ' the things of yonder world,' as had Plotinus, can confess his greatness and power and yield to his appeal. Only those who have paused to hear the throbbings of the human heart and to know ' the yearning and love of the soul ' and ' the soul's frequent rapturous joys ' [1] can find in Philo, amid grotesque exegesis and antiquated cosmology, a perennial testimony to the things in life that endure. Philo's aspiration,[2] ' Strive then, O Soul, to become the house of God, His holy temple, His loveliest abode,' is but too rare in the breathlessly organizing Christianity of the twentieth century.

Well might Lactantius [3] on the ' admirable sentiment ' of Seneca, ' There is some great Deity, and greater than can be imagined; and for Him we endeavour to live. Let us approve ourselves to Him. For it is of no avail that conscience is confined; we lie open to the sight of God,' write, ' What can be spoken with greater truth by him who knew God, than has been said by a man who is ignorant of the true religion? '

Origen,[4] the stalwart defender of Christianity, could not withhold his complete assent from the following words of his anti-Christian adversary, which he admitted were spoken when ' his judgement was not disturbed by demons ': ' We must absolutely by no means let go our hold of God, neither by day nor by night, neither in public nor in private; constantly in every word and deed, nay with and without these [words and deeds] let the soul ever be directed towards God.'

Though our Christian predecessors in the fifth century sought out and burned all accessible works of Porphyry

---

[1] *Leg. Alleg.* III, 60; C.-W. 173. / [2] *De Som.* I. 23; C.-W. 149.
[3] *Div. Inst.* VI. 25; tr. by Fletcher, I, p. 417. Seneca is *saepe noster*, Tert. *de anima*, 20.
[4] *C. Celsum*, VIII. 63.

as a shrewd critic and writer against Christianity, no unprejudiced reader can fail to be uplifted by the sincerity and contagious enthusiasm of this philosopher's exhortation in the beautiful *Letter to Marcella*, his wife, of which only the briefest extracts are possible:

' Prayer accompanied by vicious deeds is unclean, and therefore not acceptable to God; prayer with good works is both clean and acceptable. In our relations to God let these four things be made strong as the foundation—faith, truth, love, hope. Faith we must have that there is no salvation except conversion to God, and, believing, we must use all possible diligence to know the truth about Him, and, when we know, we must love Him who is known, and, having come to love Him, we must nourish the soul throughout life by good hopes, for it is by good hopes that good men are superior to base men. These are the foundations, the A B C, and let these things be made strong.' [1]

In the reference to prayer, though from the pen of a doughty defender of Paganism, many Christians will recognize a genuine personal experience:

' To spend a long time in prayer nourishes our spiritual understanding, makes a far wider room in our soul for the reception of the Gods, opens the things of the Gods to men, gives us familiarity with the flashings of the Light, little by little perfects us internally for the Divine contact, till it leads us upward to the highest height, gently uproots the habits of our own minds and plants instead those of the Gods, awakens trust and communion and indissoluble friendship, increases the Divine Love, kindles what is Divine in the Soul, purges away from the Soul everything of contrary quality, eliminates so much of the shiny aether-stuff round about the Soul as disposes us to physical reproduction, perfects good hope and faith in the Light: in sum, Prayer makes those who employ it, if one may use the word, familiars of the Gods.' [2]

---

[1] Ch. 24; tr. by Bevan, *Later Greek Religion*, p. 218, with insertion of a clause omitted by him. Or tr. by Alice Zimmern, *Porphyry to Marcella*, p. 71.

[2] Iamblichus, *De Mysteriis*, V. 26, tr. by Bevan, *ib.* p. 227.

And we may infer something of the genuine religious feeling, sincere piety, and aspiration of waning Paganism from the prayer—which we may term the last prayer of Paganism—with which Simplicius, the Aristotelian commentator (who was driven from his chair of philosophy at Athens when Justinian by edict closed the Pagan schools of philosophy), concludes his commentary on the *Encheiridion* of Epictetus:

'I beseech Thee, O Lord, our Father and Guide of our reason, make us mindful of the dignity of which Thou hast deemed us worthy. Grant unto us moral freedom, that we may be cleansed from the contagion of the body and of all irrational passions; may we overcome and master them, and, as is fitting, use them properly as our instruments. Assist us to a proper direction of the reason within us and its harmony with all Reality by means of the light of Truth. Thirdly, I beseech Thee, my Saviour, remove completely the mist from our eyes that, as Homer says, we may know God and man.' [1]

We may even learn from Augustine, who was none too generous to contemporary Paganism, to whom the 'virtues of the ancients' were nothing but 'splendid vices' and who also owed more than he knew to Plotinus and Plato, when in his *Confessions* [2] he thanks God for a book, now lost, of the Pagan Cicero, 'that book changed my whole disposition and directed my prayers to Thyself, O Lord, and it transmuted my desires and wishes. Suddenly every vain hope lost its charm for me, and with an incredible warmth of heart I began to yearn for the immortality of wisdom, and I began to arise to return to Thee.' [3] Truly 'in every people and nation I [Wisdom] got a possession.' [4]

[1] Ed. by Enk (Vienna, 1866); or Prussian Acad. ed. by Heiberg; or pp. 331-2 of Wolff-Salmasius ed. (Leyden, 1634).

[2] III. 4.

[3] Cf. his advice as to the Christian use of Pagan culture and training in *De doctr. Christiana*, II. 18: " profani si quid bene dixerunt, non aspernandum."

[4] *Ecclesiasticus* xxiv. 6.

If our experience in investigating the voluminous
literature, the thousands of inscriptions and papyri
and archaeological remains of the Graeco-Roman
period is that described by the philosopher-mystic of
old, ' those who seek gold dig much earth and find
little gold,' [1] it is but the same experience in wending
one's way through the present-day productions of the
press.

Yet this incursion into a far-off period with its conflict
of religions is not a purely academic affair: " all of
great, Or Good or lovely, which the sacred past In truth
or fable consecrates " may still send to our hearts
" choicest impulses." Race-memory persists and religious instincts repeat themselves. In spite of all the
changes of time, the differentia of nationality, and
divergence of culture, the fundamental needs of the race
remain the same to-day on the shores of the Pacific and
the Atlantic and the North Sea as on the shores of the
Mediterranean lake. In a sense men are to-day what
they have always been, endowed with inquiring minds,[2]
hungry hearts, and uncertain wills. To-day as of old
' great is the conflict and divine the task ' [3] of winning
the ' kingdom of self-control and moral freedom.' We
may be thrilled by ancient enthusiasms, quickened by
ancient faiths, and instructed by old beliefs. With the
aid of our predecessors we may make more articulate
what they could merely suggest in symbol. Spiritual
needs, like our own, may have long ago sought and
found satisfaction in rituals and prayers strange to us
and outgrown, but once palpitating with life. Ancient
worship, at first sight weird and grotesque, may be
eloquent with universal yearnings and aspirations, joys
and sorrows. " I have no longer any antagonism," says

---

[1] Heraclitus, Byw. fr. 8 (in Clement, *Str.* IV. 2; 4, 1).

[2] ' Mobilis enim et inquieta homini mens data est; nusquam se tenet,
spargitur et cogitationes suas in omnia nota atque ignota dimittit vaga
et quietis inpatiens et novitate rerum laetissima ' (Seneca, *Ad Helv.
matrem*, VI. 6).

[3] Epictetus, II. 18, 5.

George Eliot,[1] " towards any faith in which human
sorrow and human longing for purity have expressed
themselves," an attitude of intelligent sympathy that
commands our reverence.

There are certain aspects in which it is easier to
estimate a bygone epoch than to judge the contemporary
epoch; others in which it is decidedly more perplexing.
If it can be said of the present, " This huge complicated
world, the sum of countless interacting tendencies,
driven by forces that are often dark till they issue in
apparently abrupt explosions incalculable, changeful,
exhaustless—which of us can see more than a little way
into its working? ",[2] how much more pertinent are those
words to the Graeco-Roman world?

The extant literature is a mere fragment of the whole,[3]
and Augustine's testimony to the *Hortensius* proves that
the survival of ancient literature did not depend on its
worth and beauty. Posidonius, whose influence on great
writers like Cicero, Virgil, Seneca, Philo, and on the
leading religious systems was so permeating, is represented only in quotations. And this literature, again,
was on the whole a product of a small and élite coterie.
But this is not so serious as might appear, as in all ages
the prophetic spirits have caught the best ideals of their
day, and genius has ever anticipated the path along
which the common pilgrim slowly moves. Yet the
ordinary man is not quite disfranchised. The rustic
stonemason carved his sorrow with ungrammatical
eloquence into sepulchral stones in many a forgotten
graveyard, and many such memorials survive. Numerous papyri convey to us the interests and occupations
of the average man. And a considerable proportion of
our New Testament belongs to the same popular
literature.

---

[1] Letter to John Blackwood, May 18, 1860.

[2] Bevan, *Hellenism and Christianity*, p. 251.

[3] ' O quam multarum egregia opera in obscuro iacent ' (Seneca,
Ad Helv. XIX, 5).

Vast indeed were the differences in the expression of the moral and religious life in these centuries which offer an amazing medley of contrasts. On the one hand magic, and theurgy, and terror, and degrading forms of superstition; on the other a lofty mysticism with keen critical insight and clear philosophical alignment, and a high and unselfish morality. On the one hand asceticism in its unlovely disproportions; on the other the culture of self-knowledge, self-reverence, self-control: on the one hand a nervousness about the disturbance of past orthodoxies and the repudiation of picturesque and venerable myths; on the other a recognition that myths are the poetic wrappings and symbolic veils of religious truth. This latter view is so excellently represented by Julian and by Sallustius that it is worth while to cite some extracts, e.g. from Sallustius:

' We may well inquire, then, why the ancients forsook these doctrines and made use of myths. There is this first benefit from myths, that we have to search and do not have our minds idle. That the myths are divine can be seen from those who have used them. Myths have been used by inspired poets, by the best of philosophers, by those who established the mysteries, and by the Gods themselves in oracles. But why myths are divine it is the duty of philosophy to inquire. Now, the myths represent the Gods themselves and the goodness of the Gods. . . . Just as the Gods have made the goods of sense common to all, but those of intellect only to the wise, so the myths state the existence of Gods to all, but who or what they are only to those who can understand. They also represent the activities of the Gods.' [1]

Julian holds that myths are part of philosophy and due to Nature's desire for concealment of her secrets. It is accordingly that which is most incongruous and paradoxical in them that furnishes the key to the truth. Myths dealing with sacred subjects must be beautiful both in diction and in thought:

[1] *De Diis et Mundo*, chs. 3, 4; tr. by Gilbert Murray.

'Our language must be wholly dignified and the diction must be as far as possible sober, beautiful, and entirely appropriate to the gods . . . therefore there must be no incongruous element in diction thus employed, but all must be dignified, beautiful, splendid, divine, pure, and as far as possible in conformity with the essential nature of the gods. But as regards the thought, the incongruous may be admitted, so that under the guidance of the gods men may be inspired to search out and study the hidden meaning, though they must not ask for any hint of the truth from others, but must acquire their knowledge from what is said in the myth itself. . . . Do you not perceive that the myth is obviously an allegory?' [1]

In these concurrent tendencies (which are those of every age in the evolution of a religion) men proved, as Plutarch shrewdly remarked, ' in some things too credulous, and in others too incredulous.' And as in our own age, so of old thoughtful spirits turned wistfully toward the rising sun and welcomed the new with all its mental discomfort and moral readjustments, while their contemporaries turned their gaze fearfully toward the setting sun, blindly preferring the antique in religion, plausibly declaring ' no man having drunk old wine asks for new, for he says the old is better.' Religious men look on in every age, some in dismay, others with increasing faith, at that incessant process whereby all human things are shaken ' that the things which cannot be shaken may remain.'

That ancient world passed through crisis after crisis and weathered tempests which would have wrecked any less virile civilization. The Graeco-Roman age was a period of profound transition and of the blending of East and West. It witnessed vast changes, revolutions in material, social, political, and religious conditions, the extent of which we can scarcely measure. The spirit of

[1] *Oration*, VII. 216b-219b, Wright's tr.; *v*. Macrobius's defence of the use of myths by philosophers, *Com. in Som. Scip*. I. 2; Maximus Tyrius, *Orat*. IV (Hobein).

man was awakened to new demands and fresh vital issues. Society was dashed again and again from its moorings and compelled to voyage on uncharted seas, upon which many, like the Trojan women, *pontum adspectabant flentes*. Politically the collapse of the Greek city-state (*polis*) formed a crisis of the first magnitude [1] in the Mediterranean world, accompanied by the shifting of the moral centre of gravity from rigorous collectivism to perplexed individualism. Then came the new world of Alexander with his ' marriage of East and West,' with the consequent meeting both in collision and in alliance of Oriental and Western ways of interpreting life, and the rise of cosmopolitanism [2] and the acceleration of religious *theocrasia*: then the break-up of the Diadochian kingdoms and the passing of these one after another under the domination of Rome. The devastating Republican wars of conquest reduced provinces from a high state of civilization to a condition of misery and depopulation. Greece entered upon her long career as educator of her conquerors, both Macedonian and Roman, the first result of which was a disintegrating criticism. Then with the establishment of the Roman peace and the Roman Empire nationalism disappeared ; racial barriers were thrown down and the world reduced to such a unity as hardly obtains to-day even with rapid transit of goods and ideas. Under the aegis of Rome, Hellenistic and Oriental propaganda produced a unique blending of religious thought and philosophic speculation, which with its syncretism emphasized what had once been essential differences. If the Empire solved some problems, it accentuated others. Finally, that Damocles sword of aggressive barbarism, which was menacingly suspended over every ancient civilization, and fell successively on each when over-ripe, fell upon

---

[1] Cf. Kaerst, *Gesch. d. hell. Zeitalters.*

[2] " La vie cosmopolite remplaça la vie nationale, la vie privée remplaça la vie publique " (Chantepie de la Saussaye, *Manuel,* Fr. ed. p. 586).

' eternal Rome ' itself. The State religions of Greece and Rome were dead, though enchoric cults retained their hold in country districts, especially in Greece, and the imperial cult was merely a religious badge of loyalty.

In this religious and social upheaval the West increasingly gave ear to the new gospels offered by the missionary zeal of the Orientals, with their sacramental grace, cathartic rites, with their enthusiasm and their ecstasies, with their definite promise of a rewarding immortality through deification, with their esoteric properties and traditions of sacerdotal infallibility eminently suited to the mentality of the age disposed to accept truth on authority rather than seek it through the painful process of inquiry. The Jewish Dispersion formed an important intermediary in the contact of East and West which was pregnant with vast issues for that Mediterranean civilization and for its heir, our own civilization. There were other *diasporae* —of the Syrians with their stellar religion; of Persians and the populations of Pontus and Commagene with their Unconquered Mithra; of Egyptians with Lord Serapis and Queen Isis of the many names; of Babylonians with their astralism; of Hellenes with their philosophy. All these people were living together, generally on friendly terms, and meeting in the markets, in clubs and trades-unions and in religious guilds, and on town councils. Their more inquisitive members foregathered at great university centres, such as Athens, Alexandria, Tarsus, or Rhodes.

These centuries of baffling crises, change, and convulsions produced a new and personal interest in religion and corroborated the remark of one of the shrewdest observers of the phenomena of religion who lived in that era, that ' in the days of adversity the minds of men turn more eagerly toward religion.' [1] One could not point to any other centuries in which religious interests were more universal and dominant than in these seven

---

[1] ' Multoque in rebus acerbis acrius advertunt animos ad religionem ' (Lucretius, *De rerum nat.* III, 53 f.).

centuries, or in which adherents of religious institutions were more actuated by the spirit of propaganda. The cry for *Soteria* (salvation) became persistent, and only Saviour-gods [1] could command a hearing. Inquiry was raised as to the causes of irreligion and the cessation of oracles in what appeared a process of disintegration. Tiberius, we are told, was so concerned about the story of the Egyptian pilot, Thammous, who was commanded by a mysterious but unmistakable voice from the isle of Paxis to announce when passing Palades that ' the Great Pan is dead,' that he summoned the pilot to Rome and instituted inquiries as to this Pan.[2] The prophetic soul of Virgil was more oracular than he knew when in the year 40 B.C. he wrote

" Magnus ab integro saeclorum nascitur ordo."

It has been remarked by Rittelmeyer [3] that " twice in the history of the world under the common experience of great inward premonitions has the yearning for redemption (Erlösungssehnsucht) become the potent and fundamental sentiment of wide circles," first in ancient India of about the sixth century B.C., and again at the beginning of our era in the Roman Empire, when the dissonance between the external and imposing

---

[1] Cf. Harnack, *Soter* in *Reden u. Aufsätze*; E. B. Allo, *Les dieux Sauveurs du paganisme gr.-rom.* (in *Rev. d. Sciences phil. et théol.* 1926, p. 5 ff.); H. Lietzmann, *Der Weltheiland*; J. Weiss, *Heiland* in *Relig. in Gesch. u. Geg.*; Wendland, Σωτήρ in *Zeits. f. d. neut. Wiss.*, V, pp. 335-53.

[2] Plutarch, *De def. orac.* 17.

[3] *Relig. in Gesch. u. Gegenwart*, II, art. *Erlöser*, col. 474 : " Zweimal in der Weltgeschichte ist jedoch unter dem allgemeinerem Erlebnis grosser innerer Spannungen die Erlösungssehnsucht zur mächtigen Grundstimmung weiter Kreise geworden . . . wurde um die Wendung unserer Zeitrechnung im röm. Reich die Wertlosigkeit des Lebens empfunden in der Form einer Spannung zwischen den hochentwickelten äusseren Verhältnissen und der wahren menschlichen Bestimmung, die mann in Anlage und Ahnung zu fühlen glaubte und trotz aller Kultur nicht erreichen könnte. Von der Aermlichkeit und Beflecktheit seines Lebens suchte mann sich in immer neuen Weihungen und Sühnungen zu befreien."

religion and that human need which no culture could satisfy was keenly felt, and when " in ever-new rites and propitiations release was sought from the misery and stain of human life." This expectation was intensified by the fervid Messianic hopes of the Jews and their ineradicable belief that God would intervene in world-history for a brighter future.

This age can as little be reduced to a formula or summarized in a quotation as any age, especially an age of transition. Then, as ever, the Spirit as life manifested itself more surely and readily in change and motion than in stereotyped forms, prescriptive beliefs, and arrested developments. There was an almost pathetic eagerness for new religions with promises of salvation and guarantees against failure. Man was continuing his moral pilgrimage; he was setting the eternal verities against the temporal seemings; he was striving as in all ages for the truth, conscious that he must find the truth and live by it or perish. Reason was persisting in its onerous task of grappling with the irrational and liberating man, notwithstanding the growing distrust toward unaided reason and the strong disposition in many quarters to elevate revelation above reason and to substitute authority for argument,[1] both in Pagan and in Christian thinking. This age was a wistful, yearning, even prophetic age when men were—

> " Wandering between two worlds, one dead,
>   The other powerless to be born."

It was a serious, brooding, emotional, even sentimental, introspective age, but not an age of darkness and despair as it is too often depicted; it was sad and disillusioned, but not hopeless. We may say of it what Tasso said of another epoch:

---

[1] " The authority of the past became the watchword in all departments of spiritual and intellectual activity " (Bevan, *Hellenism and Christianity*, p. 111). Thus Julian (*Or.* V. 162d) holds that the theories of Aristotle must be harmonized with those of Plato, ' or rather harmonized with the oracles given by the gods.'

" Il mondo invecchia,
      E invecchiando intristisce." [1]

In growing old it became sad,[2] but it was not within the Graeco-Roman era that the Dark Ages fell like a pall upon the human spirit.

[1] Dafne to Tirsi, in *L'Aminta*, II. 2, 71.

[2] The close of this period when syncretism was most active Wendland summarizes thus : " Eine alte, reiche Kulturwelt im Sterben und in der Agonie, im Sehnen nach einer Neuschöpfung und Wiedergeburt, in einer nicht zum Ziele kommenden Unruhe des Gottsuchens—so stellt sich uns das niedergehende Heidentum dar " (*Hell.-röm. Kultur,* 2nd-3rd ed., p. 186).

CHAPTER II

THE VARIETY OF RELIGIOUS INTERESTS AND THE DOMINANT CONCEPTIONS OF SALVATION

THERE arose from these intensely religious centuries a universal cry for release [1] and ' safety ' or salvation as diverse and comprehensive as human needs. The external and political upheavals had reacted on the spirit, and amid the welter of new systems and in the perplexities of a new world-order, men were disposed to give a ready hearing to confident gospels such as that of Orphism, which in the happier days of Greece had failed in its message concerning the fall of man and the need of grace. The Orphic and Pythagorean revivals bear witness to the intense interest of the Greek world in the salvation of the soul. From the break-up of the City-state system and the rise of the individualistic subjective post-Aristotelian philosophies there grew a more persistent inquiry : ' What must I do to be saved ? '

The longing for *Soteria*, salvation, was more prevailingly negative than positive—for release from the burdens of finitude and the contradictions of the world, and exaltation from the cloying weight of bodily existence into the raptures of ecstasy, from the dread tyranny of the Seven Archons and the oppressive fatalism of astralism, from the universal power of *Fatum inexorabile* [2] and the caprices of inscrutable Fortune, *Fors inopinata,* from the terrors of the magician who with his science-religion had as much supernatural power to bind or loose as the mediaeval priest, from the fear of death

[1] Cf. Kattenbusch, " Das wundersame tiefe Sehnen jener Zeit nach einem ' Heile,' einem heilenden, rettenden Gotte, nach einer σωτηρία, einem σωτήρ," *Real-Ency.* 3rd ed. XVII, p. 351.

[2] Cf. prayer to Isis, translated in Angus, *Mystery-Religions,* p. 240.

' which affects practically all men ' [1] regardless of youth
or age,[2] from the malefic agencies of the demons to
inoculate with disease, to thwart the best laid plans of
men and grant or prevent answers to prayer, from the
sense of degeneracy, from the ills and sorrows of life
accentuated by the new individualism and heightened
sensitiveness to personal suffering and pain, from
economic insecurity, from social and political convulsions, from the aggravated sense of guilt and moral
failure, from the perils threatening the bravest soul on its
upward path to its home, from the discouragements encountered in following the heroic spirits of a classical past.

Nevertheless the negative demands were only a means
to an end, symptoms of a positive outlook. Thus the
concern about death is the verso to which the recto is
that ardent desire of these centuries for immortality,
' the hope of immortality and the hope of existence is
the most venerable and the mightiest of all affections.' [3]
The sense of moral slackness has as its positive expression the earnest search for a moral dynamic. The burden
of pain and suffering produced that clamant desire for
sympatheia with the Divine which made *philanthropia*
(the love of human kind) the chief attribute of a God.

The soul had its moods then as now, its high levels of
faith and love and its depths of distrust and despair, its
revealing insights and its recurrent doubtings. In that
eclectic epoch in nothing were men so catholic as in their
religious affairs so far as the character of their religion
permitted. Pagan tolerance fostered eclecticism, variety,
and catholicity, but even the marked intolerance of
Judaism and Christianity could not prevent either their
ablest representatives from availing themselves of workable views from elsewhere or withdraw their masses from
the influences operative around them. Thus even Philo,
while professedly loyal to Moses, acknowledges the greatness of his Greek master, Plato, and his whole writings

---

[1] ' Fere sic afficiuntur omnes ' (Cicero, *De Fin.* V. 11).
[2] Seneca, *Ep.* XXII. 14.   [3] Plutarch, *Non posse suav.* 26.

are interspersed with Stoic, especially Posidonian, and Platonic ideas. Similarly the writer of the Fourth Gospel recognized the advantage or the necessity of reinterpreting his religion under the influence of the Hellenistic spirit.

In the process of the unification of civilization and the cross-fertilization of cultures and religions brought about by Alexander, by his successors, the Diadochi, and by the Romans, there obtained varied types of religion, the characteristics of which were by no means exclusive, their peculiar nature being determined by the combination and adjustment of several elements and the relative emphasis on one phase rather than on another. Thus, for example, the *disciplina arcani* was admitted in some degree by every religion from Orphism in the sixth century B.C. to Hermeticism in the fourth or fifth centuries A.D., and speedily effected an entry into Christianity, greatly to the advantage of sacerdotalism. The importance and necessity of sacral acts were not so universally accepted, such a belief being absent from Stoicism, the religion of Plotinus, and Hermeticism, but appearing elsewhere with such prominence that Christianity lost no time in adopting such an attractive practice. Asceticism [1] was a postulate for practically

---

[1] The Orphics introduced to the West asceticism and continence as an ideal of holiness for all, and their Pythagorean successors made asceticism necessary to salvation. The extent to which this ideal gripped Christianity and the scorn with which the sex instinct was repudiated is amazing. Tatian was as opposed to all sex relations as to the dangers of philosophy. Cf. the Beatitudes in the *Acts of Paul and Thekla* (II. 5, tr. in James, *Apoc. New Testament*, p. 273):

' Blessed are they that keep the flesh chaste, for they shall become the temple of God.
Blessed are they that are continent, for unto them shall God speak. . . .
Blessed are they that possess their wives as though they had them not, for they shall inherit God. . . .
Blessed are the bodies of the virgins, for they shall be well-pleasing unto God and shall not lose the reward of their continence.'

Clement exalted married life to the level of celibacy and defended the liberty of Christians to marry. He even defended the marriage of the

every religion of the period which made salvation consist in deliverance from the world rather than in the deliverance of the world from itself by the realization of the Divine Spirit in it.[1]

Generally speaking, we may say that the following types of religion were operating in the Graeco-Roman period in easy juxtaposition and in looser or compact alliances, as also in conflict.

(1) The political religion of the imperial cult and the State religions of Greece and Rome, the latter of which had lost their vitality and were maintained as merely venerable institutions of the past. The imperial religion, or Caesar-worship,[2] cannot, properly speaking, be termed a religion. It was a badge of loyalty, just as if to-day a man's only compulsory duty consisted in standing up, respectfully uncovering, and singing " God Save the King " or " My Country, 'tis of thee," and forthwith were free to accept any religion or as many religions in as many proportions as he wished, or to repudiate all. It was the cosmopolitan form of the national Roman religion. The Caesar-cult was a test of uniformity and an outstanding example of religion being forced to do duty as a political bond of coherence as practised by the Seleucids or by the Tudors of England.

(2) The ritualistic-sacramental religions, represented

Christian Gnostic as superior to celibacy and attacked heretical asceticism (*Str.* VIII. 12; 70, 7; III. 6; 48, 1). Tertullian with much reluctance permitted marriage, but advocated virginity as of superior spiritual value. Jerome regarded matrimony as little short of disobedience to God. Encratism, based on dualistic views, tended to become the hall-mark of sincere piety, both among Pagans and Christians, and in certain Jewish sects such as the Essenes and the Therapeutae, but the Jews in general and the Stoics advocated procreation within marriage. A Pagan poem (Stob. IV, 22-32, cited Scott, *Hermetica,* III, p. 139) addressed to a young lady exalts virginity in language more refined than that of, e.g., Jerome. Cf. Fehrle, *Kultische Keuschheit im Alt.*; Swain, *Hellenic Origins of Christian Asceticism*; Scott, *Hermetica,* III, pp. 135-43.

[1] Cf. Caird, *Evolution of Religion,* II, p. 284.

[2] " Caesar-worship was an attempt to perpetuate the theocracy under the changed conditions of society " (Bigg, *The Church's Task,* p. 37).

chiefly by the Mystery-Religions and by later Christianity. (3) Religions of divine revelation, *Gnosis*, and sacrament—the Gnostic type. (4) Religions of *Gnosis* without sacrament or with a minimum of sacramental practices, chiefly the Hermetic brotherhoods of Greek theosophy. (5) The individualistic-ethical type, of which the best representative is Stoicism. (6) Social-ethical type, chiefly Judaism and primitive Christianity. (7) The ethical-mystical type, found chiefly in Neo-Platonism, Neo-Pythagoreanism, and in some of the latest phases of Stoicism, as also in such a phase of Christianity as became articulate in Dionysius the Areopagite. (8) Astralism, or the religion of astrology, which was less distinctive but penetrated all other religions and philosophies.[1]

Our term " salvation " has long retained a rather negative, individualistic, and apocalyptic connotation as implying the rescue of the soul from serious disaster hereafter, to be consummated catastrophically at some impending or distant world-ending and society-terminating spectacular event on a last day. In the more enlightened circles, which do not seek signs in the heavens from a God who writes his sign-manual within, the term has acquired a more positive and present significance as the realization of the highest manhood and the enrichment of personality in communion with an immanent God and expressed in Christlikeness. If within one religion there is such a disparity between the popular chiliastic conception of salvation and that of the more reflective spiritual experiences, and if within our own religion there obtain two distinctive types of soteriological outlook corresponding to the " miserable sinner Christianity " and that which appeals to the divine powers resident within and to the God-implanted love which draws man to its source, we may expect wide varieties as to the way of salvation in the Graeco-Roman world

[1] Cf. Boll, *Die Erforschung der antiken Astrologie* (*N. Jahrb. f. d. klass. Alt.*, XXI, p. 112).

not only between one religion and another, but within the same religion, e.g. in the Mystery-Religions, in Stoicism, in Judaism, and in Hermeticism.

Thus again, in a general way, salvation, *Soteria,* in its ancient comprehensive sense was conceived in the Graeco-Roman world:

I. Politically and socially. It is difficult for those who live in the more stable centres of Western civilization even after the confusion and ravages of the world-war to realize the universal yearning in the ancient world for that social and political security which affords leisure for the higher interests. Perhaps a resident in Soviet Russia or in Mexico or in China would be best qualified to enter into sympathy with the harassed Roman provinces which had served as battlefields for the Roman armies and to appreciate the universal acclamations of joy with which the *pax romana* [1] was hailed. Soteria, salvation, must include security of life and property, economic stability, and the opportunity of conducting one's business with a fair degree of protection. Part of the duty of the Man-God was to afford such opportunities for life and its necessary occupations. The Oriental usages of prostration before kings and rulers as the incarnate presences or representatives of deity facilitated the increasing connexion of political safety with religion. The close connexion of economic conditions and religious conditions has often been manifested at historical crises, as, e.g., at the Reformation and in the present day. The appearance of colossal personalities like Alexander and Caesar suggested to the ancient imagination supermen endowed with a mission of *philanthropy* from heaven. Such ' philanthropic ' men and the more useful and successful Gods acquired with a growing prominence the epithet of ' Saviours,' which the Greeks had been accustomed to address to Zeus.

---

[1] The *immensa Romanae pacis majestas* brought, as it were, ' a new dawn to humanity,' *velut alteram lucem* . . . *rebus humanis* (Pliny, *H.N.* 27, 1).

Demetrius the Besieger was lauded by the Athenians in 307 B.C. as ' the only true God ' when the gods of mythology were asleep: ' the other gods are remote or are not and hear us not, but we see thee face to face, not in wood and stone, but in living form. Therefore we pray thee, Beloved God, grant us peace, for thou art our Lord.' [1] The Rosetta inscription of March 27, 196 B.C., declares of Ptolemy Epiphanes:

' Having restored the life of humanity . . . to whom the Sun gives the victory, the living image of God, son of the Sun, Ptolemy of eternal life, loved of the God Phtha . . . in manifold aspects he rendered service to the temples and the priests and to all his subjects, being God of God and Goddess, as Horus son of Isis and Osiris . . . and by all his powers he proved his philanthropy.' [2]

' Saviour ' and ' manifest ' (God) became titles of Hellenistic kings. Seleucus himself after death was honoured as ' God the Conqueror ' (*Zeus Nikator*) and his son as ' Antiochus-Apollo the Saviour.'

After the break-up of the Diadochian kingdoms and the ruinous wars of succession and the still more ruinous wars of Roman conquest, this habit of recognizing peacebringers and stabilizers of society as ' gods manifest ' and as special revelations of heaven was given new impetus with the appearance of the Romans. The triumvir Antony is hailed as ' God and Benefactor ' in an Alexandrian inscription [3] of 33 B.C. Likewise an Athenian inscription [4] designates Julius Caesar as ' Saviour and Benefactor,' while an Ephesian inscription [5] of 48 B.C. recognizes the same Julius as ' God manifest and the universal Saviour of human life.'

[1] Athenaeus, VI. 253c, Hymn in honour of Demetrius at the Eleusinia procession, September 290 B.C. Metrical tr. in Bevan, *Later Greek Religion*, p. 60. Cf. Plutarch's caustic remarks, *Vita Demetrii*, X ff.

[2] Dittenberger, *Or. gr. inscr.* 90.

[3] *Ib.* 195.

[4] Dittenberger, *Sylloge*, 3rd ed. 759; *I.G.* 428.

[5] *Ib.* 3rd ed. 760; *C.I.G.* 2957.

It was under Augustus and with the establishment of
' the Roman peace ' [1] that religious thanksgiving, not
without an admixture of flattery and servility, was
directed to the emperor as the personal cause of all the
world's rest. ' It is a God who has given us this peace,'
says the devout Virgil. ' The Fates have bestowed
nothing better or greater on earth than him,' says a court
poet, interpreting the popular sentiment.[2]

The inscription of Halicarnassus,[3] about 2 B.C., testifies
' since the eternal and deathless nature of the universe
has bestowed upon mortals the greatest boon in abound-
ing benefits by bringing to our happy life Caesar
Augustus . . . tutelary God and Saviour of the whole
human race, whose Providence has not only fulfilled but
surpassed our prayers, for land and sea enjoy peace,
and the cities bloom under good government, internal
peace, and prosperity.'

A decree of the Greek cities of Asia in 9 B.C. on the
introduction of the Julian calendar reads:

' What could be more pleasant or more fraught with
blessing than the birthday of the most divine Caesar,
which we might rightly regard as like the first beginning
of all things? . . . He gave a different aspect to the
whole world that would otherwise have readily fallen a
prey to ruin. . . . It is difficult to give thanks commensurate with such acts of blessing by him . . . whom
Providence filled with virtue to do good to mankind. . . .
The birthday of the God was the beginning for the world
of the good tidings (*evangelia*) which he brought.' [4]

Naturally in the court poets we find abundant expression of this sentiment, not merely from the distant provinces accustomed to accord divine honours to worthy
rulers, but from the very heart of Rome itself. To
Propertius, e.g., Augustus is ' saviour of the world '
(*mundi salvator*).[5]

---

[1] On the celebration of this peace, cf. Virgil, *Geor.* I. 500 ff.
[2] Horace, *Carm.* IV. 2, 38.
[3] *Ancient Greek Inscriptions in the British Museum*, No. 894.
[4] Dittenberger, *Or. gr. inscr.* 458.   [5] IV. 6, 36.

In a twofold fashion the religious aspects of this new era of social salvation appear; first, in the equation of Augustus with divinities such as Jupiter Augustus, Apollo-Augustus; in his equipment with divine attributes such as saviour, benefactor, eternity, divine descent; and in the erection of a temple [1] and elevation to divine rank in heaven on account of 'philanthropy' toward mankind; secondly, in the direction of prayers to him as the 'God manifest.' Visibility of deity [2] was a weakness of ancient religion as of modern superstition, and the ability of the visible manifestation to satisfy all kinds of external wants of men was taken for granted. Ovid in praying for the favour of the gods significantly adds, 'than whom he (Augustus) is more tangible.' [3] Similarly Horace: [4]

> 'praesenti tibi maturos largimur honores
> iurandasque tuum per numen ponimus aras,
> nil oriturum alias, nil ortum tale fatentes.'

There were certainly many who felt with Valerius Maximus [5] that preference should be given to the Caesars as visible incarnate deities above the invisible and distant Olympians.

The spontaneity of this religious outburst of thanksgiving for tangible blessings much needed for human life was of course imitated later and expressions of real sentiment became forms of mere conventionality or even of servility. Tiberius, none too lovable, is 'the common Benefactor of the world,' [6] and Claudius 'saviour of the world' [7] and 'God visible' [8]; to the Alexandrines he is 'our God Caesar.' [9] In A.D. 37 an inscription of Assos [10]

[1] Cf. Virgil, *Geor.* III. 16.
[2] 'Praesens Divus habebitur Augustus' (Horace, *Carm.* III. 5, 2).
[3] *Ex Ponto*, I. 1, 63; cf. *ib.* IV. 9, 111.   [4] *Ep.* II. 1, 15.
[5] *Prol.*   [6] *I.G.* XII. 2, 206.   [7] *I.G.* XII. 2, 541.
[8] *Inscr. Graec. ad res rom. pertinentes*, III. 328.
[9] Papyrus 1912, p. 23 in Bell & Crum, *Jews and Christians in Egypt* : note the title θεός here used in an official document for a living emperor.
[10] Dittenberger, *Sylloge*, 3rd ed. 797; or, *Graeci inscr. sel.* 666. Similarly *Oxyrh. Pap.* VII. 1021, 1, 9.

declares of Caligula: ' The world knows no limit to its joy, and every State and people has turned eagerly to gaze on the face of the God as if now the happiest age had dawned for mankind.' An altar dedicated to Nero in A.D. 67 reads, ' To Nero God the deliverer for ever,' [1] who is likewise ' the Good Daemon of the world.' [2] Trajan is in Greek eyes ' God, the invincible son of God.' [3]

II. Another path along which salvation was sought by multitudes of earnest men was that of self-realization by self-reliance here, represented chiefly by Stoicism, and particularly Stoicism of the Roman type. This quest was based on the conviction, first, that man can do all the things necessary for his highest life, and secondly, that all other things *extra potentiam humanam* can be accepted in resignation to the will of God, with which one's own will can and ought to be brought into conformity, so that man can rise superior to all ineluctable circumstances. The individual is placed as a responsible actor under divine law, and he gains his freedom by recognizing his place in the scheme of things and playing his part manfully. The system was wholly anthropocentric. Its ethics were stern and its cosmic speculations [4] involved a pitiless determinism, from which, however, it departed as conscientiously as the most rigid Calvinist in asserting man's freedom and his capacities for every lofty demand together with his awful responsibility. It was partially in its inconsistencies, its adaptability, and its inclusiveness that the strength of Stoicism lay; it was thereby equipped to be not only a philosophy of an élite coterie but a way of life for the ordinary man. Like many another excellent system, including Christianity, it retained enough of the past to

---

[1] Dittenberger, *Syll.*, 3rd ed. 814.
[2] *C.I.G.* II. 4699.
[3] *C.I.A.* 462.
[4] " To its support more than to any other single cause was due the long reign of astrology " (Halliday, *Pagan Background of Early Christianity*, p. 160).

appeal to the populace; too much for its own advancement and progress. It could with almost equal truth be presented as a materialistic monism, or as pantheism with God immanent in the universe, or as a lofty monotheism, as in Cleanthes' *Hymn to Zeus,* from which Paul cited. Its citadel was the will; it regarded the emotions as something indifferent, to be eradicated or at least to be severely disciplined. Nevertheless, so subtle and strong is the *Zeitgeist,* Stoicism was gradually drawn into the emotionalism and sentimentality of the later Graeco-Roman age. It learned to make concessions to the weakness of men, and it ultimately became the home of a mature mysticism and conceded a place to the intuitive motions of the soul. The Stoics modernized, or at least removed the offence of ancient religious classics by a liberal use of allegory,[1] which could make Homer, for example, the text of an up-to-date philosophy and could render the Homeric poems a Greek Bible in the same way in which allegory and imagination can constitute *Leviticus, Numbers,* and the *Song of Solomon* part of the Christian Bible and rich in homiletic material. They also returned to the Socratic insistence on the imperious authority of conscience and agreed with the Pythagorean requirements of self-examination in the interests of the moral progress of ' God's athletes.' [2]

The ethical ideal of Stoicism was the ideal Wise Man whose personality is—

' dignified, magnificent, consistent, since reason declares that moral good is the only good, he alone must be happy . . . he will more properly be termed king than Tarquinius . . . richer than Croesus . . . rightly will all things be said to be his who alone knows their use; rightly too will he be styled beautiful since the lineaments of the soul are more beautiful than those of the body; rightly is he alone free, under the domination

[1] E.g. in Cornutus, *Theologiae graecae compendium.*
[2] Epictetus, IV. 4, 32.

4

of no one and obeying no appetite; rightly is he invincible whose body may be fettered but whose soul is not to be enchained.' [1]

There was no unhealthy delusion about the difficulty of discovering such a man or attaining such a lofty ideal, but ideals however remote are in no age inoperative. Stoicism was at a disadvantage in not being able to point to its wise Man incarnate [2] as Christianity could point to the historic Jesus. Nevertheless it was a potent ideal that guided and uplifted many, and it presented a worthy phase of human life which is necessary in every age.

On the burning question of immortality, Stoicism, strictly speaking, consistently with its physics was obliged to deny this faith, and many noble Stoics were heroically content with a return to the elements, such as Panaetius, Epictetus, and Marcus Aurelius. But here again Stoicism proved inconsistent and allowed human yearnings to have the right of way over their logic, and '' an assimilation of the religious ideas attaching to Babylonian cosmology enabled Stoicism to develop a theory of astral immortality which harmonized with its general account of the universe.'' [3]

This system, for which inner freedom alone was of supreme worth, proved a veritable gospel and afforded a strong spiritual support [4] to thousands of tried souls

---

[1] Cicero, *De Fin.* III. 22, 75; with which cf. 2 Corinthians vi. 9 f.

[2] Cf. Seneca, *Dial.* IX. 7, 4 (*de tranquillitate*); Cicero, *Acad. pr.* 145. Plutarch, *De com. not.* 33 (' He is nowhere on earth, nor has ever been ').

[3] Halliday, *Pagan Background*, p. 162.

[4] Halliday (*ib.* p. 162 f.) gives as reasons for the dominant position of Stoicism in the thought of the empire: '' It provided a complete and intelligible account of the universe, adequate to satisfy minds which were neither preoccupied with, nor peculiarly endowed for, subtle metaphysical speculation. The virtues of conduct which it particularly inculcated were eminently those which appealed to the sympathy and admiration of Rome's inherited tradition. But, above all, its elasticity and adaptability enabled it to reconcile existing religious practice with its tenets and to absorb into itself alien philosophic theories.''

who lived unselfishly and died fearlessly under its inspiration. It appealed to all classes of earnest men,
from the Phrygian slave to the solemn Roman emperor
writing his inmost thoughts as he guarded the frontiers
against threatening barbarism. Its asseveration of
character as man's only and inalienable possession was of
far-reaching importance for ancient society and for the
spreading Christian Church. Its insistence that the only
way of overcoming the world is self-conquest cannot be
antiquated; rather this thought was taken up afresh in
Christianity under the new and more favourable environment of love, a moral passion the rights and powers of
which were inadequately revealed to these path-finders
for the Christian preachers. Stoicism heartily accepted
the religious submissiveness of ' Thy will be done,' but
failed to enter into the complementary or resultant experience of ' rejoicing in the Lord.'

III. Religion of the *unio mystica,* which manifests
much the same characteristics in every age and culture,
and which was then represented chiefly by the mystical
Christianity of Paul and the Fourth Gospel; the
Platonism of Philo and Plotinus, and in the speculative
asceticism of revived Pythagoreanism.

Ancient mysticism, generally speaking, rested upon a
dualistic basis, on an antithesis between soul and sense,
between spirit and matter, between this world and
yonder, between the promptings of intuition and the
evidence of sense perception. The general outlook was
an other-worldliness which assigned to the evanescent
things of this terrene world a negligible or inconspicuous
place. Its starting-point is the divine spark within,
whether this be the *anamnesis* (recollection) of Plato, or
the intuition of Plotinus, or the indestructible *pneuma*
(spirit) of Paul, or the congenital Logos in man to which
the universal or divine Logos makes its appeal. Like
Stoicism, this mystical religion would discipline the will
to do right, but its main inspiration was Love, or an
imperious desire for the things that are real and abiding

and of transcendent worth. Like Stoicism it was pre-
eminently a practical religion of reformation of life and
integrity of conduct. Like later Stoicism it preached the
identification with the Divine as the aim of all religious
striving, but unlike Stoicism it refused to regard this
identification as merely absorption into the cosmic forces
or into the rational element of the universe, but viewed
it rather as the identification of love with its object, of
the lover in the beloved. It frankly recognized that
there is more in man than can be satisfied by conceptual
knowledge; that there are aspects of truth and reality
irreducible to formal logic; that there are other avenues
to the higher knowledge than sense perception or ratiocinative deductions. It would neither wholly distrust
nor trust the emotions, but it learned increasingly to
appeal to personal experiences as validating a way of
life that approved itself by its uplift and by its standards
of ineffable values. The leaders of this quest of reality
by the *unio mystica,* though proving in no way inferior
intellectually,[1] accepted contemplation and vision,
ecstasy and enthusiasm, as modes of union with the
Divine.

The most catholic factor in this high and timeless
religion was naturally Platonism, which in its transcendental idealism is the ageless refuge from the tyranny
of the material, and which is everlastingly summoning
men to make all things according to the pattern shown
on the mount of vision. It affected every philosophical and religious system until Stoicism blended
into Platonism in the conflict with Christianity, and
Neo-Platonism became the main source of Christian
mysticism.

This could never naturally in any age be a popular
religion. Within some of these same circles, probably

---

[1] " The Neo-Platonists are from first to last rationalists . . . and they
are as ready as any philosophers who have ever lived to expound their
reasons for their convictions " (Taylor, *Proc. Arist. Soc.* XVIII,
p. 605 f.).

no more or no less universally experienced, there was another form of rich idealism, the Christ-mysticism of Paul and of all those who were drawn to this central experience of his religion as against the multitudes who found in him a legalistic system, and also that suggestive and more mature Hellenistic mysticism of the Fourth Gospel which constituted God and Christ and believers who were ' not of the world ' into a mystical organic unity. Such Christian circles could not fail to recognize a spiritual kinship with the Pagan religious experience expressed by Plotinus :

' God, says Plato, is not far from every one of us, but is near to all without their knowing it. It is they themselves who flee away from Him, or rather they flee away from their own true selves. Hence they cannot seize that from which they have fled, and cannot, having destroyed their own true self, seek for another : as a child which has become insane and has become beside itself does not recognize its own father. But the man who has learnt to know himself will also know whence he comes. . . . We are not cut off from God or severed from Him . . . but we breathe and consist in Him, since God does not give and then withdraw, but He ever lifts and carries us, so long as He is what He is. . . . There too in union with Him the soul rests after she has fled away from Evil to the place which is pure from evils. And the true Life is there ; for the life here and without God is but a trace of life in imitation of that Life. . . . The good of the soul is there, and a Longing Love (Eros) is innate in the soul. For, since the soul is indeed other than God and yet from God, she loves and longs for Him of necessity ; and when she tarries there she possesses Heavenly Love, whereas straying here below she becomes, as it were, a common courtesan (*Aphrodite Pandemos*).' [1]

A conspicuous example of the *unio mystica* is found in the philosophy of Philo, which forms an interesting

[1] Plotinus, *En.* VI. 9, 7 ff.; tr. from von Hügel's *Essays and Addresses*, cited by Bevan, *Later Greek Religion*, p. 202 f.

stage between the original and the later Platonism. As in Plato and Plotinus, Philo's mysticism went hand-in-hand with deep religious and perhaps with stronger ethical motives. His dualism is more pronounced than that of Plato, and therefore an unnecessary stress is put on *askesis*, ascetic discipline. In regard to ecstasy, Philo magnifies its function as a means to the highest knowledge and union beyond any parallel in Plato [1] and far beyond the rôle assigned by Plotinus to this fugitive psychical experience.[2] Faith appears as a new factor in Philonian mysticism which was to prove of great moment in the history of religion.[3] This faith, like the Plotinian intuition, was not to be exercised in such isolation or exaggeration as to conduce to mysteriosophy or credulity: it was ' the work of an Olympian understanding ' and demanded the utmost concentration and ratiocination.

In another aspect Philo prepared the way for Christian Mysticism; his mystic quest was for knowledge of and a union with a personally-conceived God, with the One God,[4] and not merely with the metaphysical and Abstract One, which is likewise the All, to which Plotinus surrendered his pure spirit on his agonizing death-bed.

Philo, like Plato and Plotinus, was a practising mystic in a workaday world of flux and change and political concerns, despite his yearning for retirement and contemplation in the desert.[5] Something of the health and

---

[1] Plato recognized the sudden flash of transcendental ecstatic experience as in Diotima's prophetic and glowing language (*Symp.* 210e).

[2] Inge, *Phil. of Plotinus*, II, pp. 142 f., 152, 158.

[3] " For the first time in the history of religion we find the thought of faith in the centre of religion. Philo is the first great psychologist of Faith " (Bousset, *Religion des Judentums*, 2nd ed. p. 514. Cf. H. A. A. Kennedy, *Philo's Contrib. to Religion*, p. 121 f.).

[4] " Philo ist der erste Mystiker und Ekstatiker auf dem Boden spezifisch monotheistischer Frömmigkeit. Als solcher hat er seine bleibende Bedeutung in der Geschichte der christlichen Mystik " (Bousset, p. 520).

[5] Bousset, p. 511; Drummond, *Philo Judaeus*, I ff., 24.

humanism of Greece clung to his mysticism and so set
it in relief against much of the cloistered and morbid
mysticism of the Christian recluses.[1]

Of the numerous references in Philo to direct mystical
experiences, a few meagre quotations must suffice:

' I am not ashamed to relate the way in which I am
myself affected, which I know I have experienced countless times. Intending sometimes to come to my usual
occupation of writing the doctrines of philosophy, and
having seen exactly what I ought to compose, I have
found my mind fruitless and barren and left off without
accomplishing anything, reproaching my mind with its
self-conceit and amazed at the power of Him who is,
by whom it has turned out that the wombs of the soul
are opened and closed. But sometimes, having come
empty, I suddenly became full, ideas being invisibly
showered upon me and planted from above, so that by
a divine possession I was filled with enthusiasm, and
was absolutely ignorant of the place, of those present,
of myself, of what was said, of what was written, for
I had a stream of interpretation, an enjoyment of light,
a most keen-sighted vision, a most distinct view of the
subjects treated, such as would be given through the
eyes from the clearest exhibition (of an object).' [2]

His soliloquy when ' any yearning comes upon thee,
O Soul,' is quoted on p. 293, and on p. 273 that on the
Nous or Spirit ' raised aloft on wings ' and ' conducted
by Love ' ; it outsoars all the senses and attains ' a sober
intoxication ' in the splendour of the Divine presence.

Again, a revelation of the nature of God came to him
in such an immediate experience:[3] ' I heard once a
more earnest argument from my soul that had been
accustomed to be much enraptured by the Divine and
concerning things of which it did not know how to sur-
mise the meaning. I shall tell you about it so far as I can

---

[1] Inge, II. 153-4.
[2] *De migr. Abr.* 7, C.-W. 34 f.; tr. from Drummond, I, p. 15.
[3] *De Cherubim,* 9, C.-W. 27.

remember,' and the revelation was that there are in the
One God two supreme powers, Goodness and Might, with
Reason as a third harmonizing these.[1]

IV. Another escape sought was from cosmic necessity.
A scheme of cosmic ' safety ' was absolutely indispens-
able to every religion which would make a successful
and popular appeal in that age. Each religion must
aim at making men comfortable in an uncomfortable
universe overwhelming to the detached individual.[2] So
much was this need felt that Christianity itself in its first
contact with the outer and larger world was compelled
to equip itself with cosmic apparatus and to impose
cosmic functions upon the person of Jesus, who, indeed,
was better able to bear them than His mythical competitors. Christianity supplied the lack partly by a
modification and intensification of Jewish apocalyptism
of the two-aeon theory of history in the dénouement of
which Jesus played the supreme rôle under God, and
partly by the adoption and assimilation of current
Hellenistic cosmic speculations. To the Gentile Christians the new religion was not only an escape from the
curse of the Law, but a release from ' slavery to the
Elements,' that is, the star deities. A modern Christian,
for whom the geocentric view of the Universe has yielded
to a view of countless universes, for whom the demons,
good and bad, have become a dead category, and for
whom the dread ' world-rulers ' have become chemical
bodies operating with mathematical precision, can hardly
appreciate the good news ' that neither the Ascension of
the stars nor their Declinations ' should be able ' to
separate them from the love of God in Christ.'

Christianity and its competitors and all the philosophies were summoned to lift the cosmic burden and
to offer a way of escape. Some minds, finding the
Universe too great and inevitable, cast in their lot with

---

[1] Cf. also *De Cherubim*, 14, C.-W. 48 f.
[2] " To make men at home in the universe " is Bevan's summary of
the activity of Posidonius, *Stoics and Sceptics*, p. 98.

it and with its laws by a pantheistic identification; they accepted the universe, as Carlyle remarked that the lady " had better." Accept fate and work with it was a mode of winning cosmic freedom, at least of a kind. A dread uncertainty dogged men's steps. Tyche, or Chance, was a capricious goddess as compared with the fixed Fate. The ' tempests of Fortune ' might wreck the strongest life and turn for the individual his world upside-down. The only refuge was in fellowship with a Deity superior to Chance.

The demons [1] remained to be dealt with by some supernatural means. Plato's elaboration of the doctrine of demons in the *Banquet* as intermediaries between gods and men had proved very fruitful in the early centuries of the Christian era. Through contact with the Orient these beings occupied an increasingly conspicuous place. It never occurred to Pagans or Christians to wipe them out as a category. The Pagans as a whole inclined to regard the majority of demons as good and useful, though they still believed in the existence of evil demons. Christians treated them all as evil; the bad demons were as real to them and as busy as the good angels, despite the fact that in the preaching of the missionary of Gentile Christianity angels and intermediary hierarchies occupied no flattering place.

In Pagan thought the demons exercised much the same function as their angelic counterparts, especially in supplying the demand for intermediaries created for both Pagans and Christians by the conception of a transcendental deity; by the dualism between *Stuff* and Mind, and the need of an adequate theory of the origins both of the world and of evil. There must be to Pagans, Jews, and Christians an ordered hierarchy of superhuman beings, demons, saints, angels, seraphim, *logoi*,

---

[1] Cf. J. A. Held, *Étude sur les démons dans la littérature et la religion des Grecs* (Paris, 1881); Oakesmith, *The Religion of Plutarch* (London, 1902); Tambornino, *De antiquorum Daemonismo* (Giessen, 1909).

to carry out the will of the Deity in a world unworthy
of His presence. Demons acted as ' satraps of the
Gods.' [1] They carry up the prayers of men to the gods
and bring back the answers and blessings.[2] They also
executed the behests of the Deity in protecting the
righteous and punishing the wicked both here and hereafter. They may also act as guardian genius [3] or as the
voice of God or the conscience of men, an example of
which was the demon of Socrates, about which there
arose so much interesting speculation.[4] They are not
wholly beneficent; evil demons still exist, for they
deceive men by forging oracles, they cause divorces [5]
and other evils. The Deity can be justified or exonerated
from evil on the theory that it is the demons that perform evil, and so a solution is offered of the existence
of evil under a good Deity.

By one of the many surprising developments within
Christianity the much-maligned Pagan demons became,
with their Jewish compeers, the predecessors of the
Christian angels and saints, to whom they bequeathed
their more useful and popular functions. As in

---

[1] Origen, *C. Celsum*, VIII. 35.

[2] ' Per quas (potestates) et desideria nostra et merita ad deos com-
meant. . . . Inter terricolas caelicolasque vectores hinc precum inde
donorum qui ultro citro portant hinc petitiones inde suppetias ceu
quidam utriusque interpretes et salutigeri ' (Ps.-Apuleius, *De deo
Socratis*, VI. 133).

[3] For the demon as the moral imperative, cf. Marcus Aurelius, V,
10: ' It is possible for me to do nothing contrary to my god and demon.
No one can force me to transgress this '; ' He lives with the gods who
constantly shows them his soul pleased with what they appoint and
obedient to the will of the demon,' 27; and Epictetus, *Diss.* I, 14:
' God has placed by each one a guardian, every man's demon, and He
has committed him to the guardianship of one who never slumbers and
who cannot in any wise be deceived. To what better and more careful
guardian could he have committed us? When therefore you have shut
your doors and darkened your room, remember never to say that you
are alone. God is within you and your demon is within. What need
have they of light to behold your actions? To this Deity you should
swear such an oath as soldiers do to their emperor.'

[4] Cf. Ps.-Apuleius, *De deo Socratis*; Plutarch, *De genio Socratis*, 9 ff.,
580 Bf.; Maximus of Tyre, VIII and IX (Hobein's ed.).

[5] As in Grenfell and Hunt papyri, *New Classical Frags.* 76.

Catholicism the path to sainthood is open officially to the most meritorious members, so demonology held out to Pagan saints the possibility of becoming demons after death charged with the honourable privilege of shepherding their fellow-men or even of becoming deities in full sympathy with mankind. Cleombrotus affirms [1] that the better class of souls undergo a transformation from men to heroes, from heroes to demons, and of the demons some few by thorough purification in virtue attain to participation in the divine nature. Elsewhere [2] Plutarch cites Isis and Osiris as examples of demons raised to the rank of deities. When an Egyptian priest went to the Iseum on the Campus Martius to interview the demon of Plotinus, he found to his amazement that he was no longer a demon but had become a god.[3] Thus the doctrines of demonology furnished to the most convinced believers a religious idealism [4] by becoming the vehicle of expression for the faith that there is no limit to the spiritual attainment of mankind, that we know not yet what we shall be.[5]

In Christian apologetic the demons were put to all kinds of uses to prove the superiority of Christian exorcism and the Name of Jesus. The demons hate the Christians and stir up rulers against them.[6] Jesus and His followers as well as the Pagans attributed diseases to demoniacal activities, an attitude against which Plotinus [7] vigorously protested when attacking the Gnostics. He attributed ailments to natural physical causes and denounced the use of magic in medicine or invocations in healings. Anything of truth expressed

---

[1] Plutarch, *De def. Orac.* 10, 415 C.

[2] *De Is. et Osir.* 27, 361 E.

[3] Porphyry, *Vita Plotini*, 10.

[4] Cf. Oakesmith, *Religion of Plutarch*, p. 173 f.

[5] " The doctrine created an eschatology by which vistas of moral perfection were opened before purer spirits in worlds to come, and the infinite responsibilities of this life were terribly enforced by threats of endless degradation " (Dill, *Roman Society from Nero*, p. 426).

[6] Cf. Justin, *Apol.* II. 1.

[7] *Enn.* II. 9, 14.

by Pagans was done when the demons had temporarily left their minds free.[1] The Pagan miracles, too patent to be denied, were the work of demons. When the demons learned that Jesus would be a physician of all diseases and raise the dead, they anticipated Him by bringing Aesculapius on the scene.[2] Christians sometimes called for test cases [3] of demon-possessed to prove the superior Christian way of dealing with them. Christians held that images of the Deities and Pagan temples were the favourite abodes of demons. Christian ecclesiastics [4] did not doubt that demons could enter even Christian bodies through eating foods consecrated to idols. According to Tertullian, the demons are all the more dangerous because they are equipped with wings like the angels ; they are everywhere at once, and know all that is taking place in every quarter. The demons also forced polytheism on the heathen, mimicked the Christian sacraments, and hardened men's minds against the force of evangelical arguments. They were more afraid of Christians than of the heathen.[5] Gregory of Nyssa tells in his Life of Gregory the Thaumaturge how the latter banished the demons from a Pagan shrine and by the Name of Christ and the sign of the Cross purified the air. Subsequently at the challenge of the local priest, who had returned and found his temple empty of demons, Gregory caused the demons to come back in obedience to the permission ' Gregory to Satan, enter.' [6] And just as in our oldest Gospel written for the Church at Rome the evangelist descries a valuable argument for the pre-eminence of Jesus in representing the demons as confessing His Messiahship, so in later days the demons reluctantly departed from human bodies, confessed the truth, and

---

[1] Cf. Origen, *C. Celsum*, VIII. 63.
[2] Justin, I. 54.
[3] As Tert. *Apol.* 23.
[4] Cf. Angus, *Mystery-Religions*, p. 256.
[5] Tert. *Apol.* 27.
[6] Migne, *P.L.* XLVI, p. 913 D.

brought converts to Christianity, and this was ' no unusual occurrence.' [1] It was not forgotten that the demons compassed the crucifixion as they had compassed the execution of Socrates.[2] In fact, a Christian Platonist asserted that Jesus became man to destroy the demons,[3] to whom His very name was terrible.[4]

As the Mystery-Religions were rich in cosmic pretensions and secured safety by union with cosmic deities, they were very popular. Thus Attis was ' the Most High and bond of the Universe ' [5]; Serapis [6] ' the Coryphaeus of the Universe, holding the beginnings and the ends ' and ' for all things everywhere through thee and on account of thee happen to us '; Mithra ' the Demiurge and Lord of Creation ' [7]; Isis the *rerum naturae parens, elementorum omnium domina,* the *Una quae est omnia* ;[8] or ' the Aeon makes the world ' and ' holds this Universe together.' [9] Dolichenus is *aeternus conservator totius poli.*[10]

Philosophy collaborated with religion to ease this cosmic burden. Stoicism in one mood would solve the problem by an emotional application of its pantheism ; in another mood it would transmute its pantheism into theism to satisfy personal longings and bestow personal assurances. Even in the same Stoic these moods might alternate. Cleanthes, for example, while holding that the world is divine or even a god, immediately dictates his famous theistic *Hymn to God,* or he could practically correlate God and Destiny as in the prayer :

---

[1] Tert. *Apol.* 23.

[2] Justin, *Apol.* II. 5, 7, 8; 1 Cor. i. 6, 8; Col. ii. 15.

[3] Justin, II. 6.

[4] *Dial. with Tryphon,* 30.

[5] *C.I.L.* VI. 509; Hepding, *Attis,* p. 83. Cf. Julian, *Or.* V. 161 C.

[6] Aristides, *Or. Sacrae,* VIII. 53. Dind. I, p. 91 and p. 87.

[7] Porphyry, *De ant. nym.* 5, 6.

[8] Apuleius, *Metam.* XI. 5; Orelli-Henzen, 1871; Dessau, *Inscr. lat. sel.* 4362, from Capua.

[9] *Corp. Herm.* XI (1), 2 and 5 (adopting W. Scott's reading in 5).

[10] *C.I.L.* VI. 406.

' Lead me, O Zeus, and lead me, Destiny.
Whither ordained is by your decree.
I'll follow, doubting not, or if with will,
Recreant I falter and I shall follow still! ' [1]

Philosophy would also remove the terror from the universe and so lighten the burden of daily living for thousands by the conception of a benign and loving Providence which guarded against the implacable blind ' Powers.' In reading the later philosophies one is constantly reminded how these are preparing men for the attitude and confidence of approach of ' Abba Father ' and how earnestly they grappled with the problem of raising men above the fear of relentless and incalculable cosmic forces. Amid the deepening pessimism and evils of dualism and the travail of the material world the servants of philosophy offered a guiding light—*o vitae dux philosophia*.[2]

V. Another way of escape was the religion of ritualistic *henosis* or union with God by rite and sacrament, represented chiefly by the Mystery-religions and subsequently by the magical-mystical Christian sacraments. Such union was secured not so much ethically as ceremonially and emotionally. The correct ritualistic process released the divine element to make its ascent to the higher world. The Mystery furnished the initiated soul with the pass-word to bliss. By sacramental efficacy akin to contemporary magic the material man was in rebirth transmuted or remade into immaterial and therefore immortal substance. A guarantee of immortality so passionately longed for was given here to each member of the Mystery fraternities. Initiates were ' demortalized,' and thus rendered divine were endowed with deathlessness. (See Ch. V.)

[1] Matheson's tr. in Bevan, *Later Greek Religion*, p. 15. Arnim, *Fr.* 527.

[2] '' Sed et huius culpae et ceterorum vitiorum peccatorumque nostrorum omnis a philosophia petenda correctio est. . . . O virtutis indagatrix expultrixque vitiorum ! quid non modo nos sed omnino vita hominum sine te esse potuisset? . . . ad te confugimus, a te opem petimus . . . est autem unus dies bene et ex praeceptis tuis actus peccanti immortalitati anteponendus '' (Cicero, *Tusc. Disp.* V. 2, 5).

VI. Religious aspiration takes two general forms. First, release from the thraldom of the external world and its transiency, necessity, death, and perplexing enigmas; and, secondly, from the constricted or rebellious self. Hence another conception of salvation which accompanied the increasing religious emotion was that of deliverance from moral stain and the forgiveness of sins. In passing from the classical to the Hellenistic age one is arrested by this heightened sense of sin [1] and the consciousness of need of divine grace in the upward struggle and the new attitude of self-abasement.[2] The reaction had been equal to the previous Promethean position and inaugurated an outlook on man which found its culmination in the Augustinian doctrine of grace and in the mediaevalism against which the Renaissance claimed the dignity of man and the worthiness of all human interests and efforts.

Orphism [3] first heralded in the West this new doctrine of the weakness and sinfulness of man and his need of grace and of cathartic ritual which a thousand years later in Augustine's *Confessions* found its classic expression. The Pythagoreans took up the Orphic pessimistic anthropology and furthered it by emphasizing the necessity for holiness and by dwelling on the awful retribution awaiting the unforgiven sinner beyond. The Neo-Pythagoreans in the first and second centuries carried on the intensification of the consciousness of sin and the need of atonement. In all the later phases of Pagan religion we are made acutely aware of the urgent demand for reform of life and purity of soul, and the fragmentary remnants of Pagan religious literature are eloquent on the theme of the manifold privileges and joys of the cleansed soul and Godward-directed spirit.

[1] Cf. J. Lebreton, *La Connaissance relig. à la fin du II*ᵉ *siècle dans le monde hellénistique et dans l'église chrét.* (*Rev. d. sciences relig.* 1926, 4); Réville, *Religion à Rome sous les Sévères*, p. 152.

[2] ' Bonus vero vir sine deo nemo est ' (Seneca, *Ep.* 41, 2; cf. 28, 9).

[3] Pausanias, IX. 30, 12, speaks of the Orphics as discovering purifications and means of placating deity.

The quest on which Socrates set the West brought unpleasant discoveries of helplessness and guilt which wrung from agonized souls the *Miserere Domine*. By the failure of collective responsibility in the city-state the individual responsibility was augmented to an extent perplexing to the average man. The emergence of this brooding sense of failure, the consciousness of sin and its ineluctable moral issues, the bewilderment of individualism, were the moral counterparts of the great social upheavals. A religious crisis of universal magnitude was the loss of faith in Occidental ways of securing atonement. Self-sufficiency gave way to a cry for help in oppressive weakness. Such was the " failure of nerve " that introspection became morbid and means of purification were eagerly sought in asceticism and sacramentarianism and in esoteric knowledge. Consciences became hypersensitive. Lucian's parodies of such consciences, the attitude of the Superstitious Man in Theophrastus's *Essay* seeking monthly absolution on monthly confession, Plutarch's *On Superstition,* and Lucretius's sublime protest against superstition, are depicted from life. The need and accessibility of grace for atonement grew only more clamant with the increasing inwardness and the new religious value of the individual. Demands for self-examination are made by all the moralists. With the rise of the Roman Empire and the leisure for personal concerns possible in the Roman Peace the soul turned still more for refuge to compassionate Saviour-gods. Penance, confession, and purgatorial rites and pilgrimages became more prominent.[1] The pathological morbid reaction and the accepted dualism [2] with its concomitant doctrine of the

[1] " Throughout the world of St. Paul we see a mighty wandering of pilgrims desirous to wash away their sins at the great shrines and to be delivered of their need " (Deissmann, *St. Paul,* p. 44).

[2] " Dualism, with the asceticism inseparable from it, was, so to speak, in the air; it was the strongest spiritual tendency of the time, almost equal to Christianity in power " (Dobschütz, p. 112), but in several aspects it proved stronger than Christianity by distorting Christianity.

evil of matter issued in an extravagant asceticism in Pagan circles, the severity of which is astonishing. Social life was decried [1] in favour of some form of flight from the world or monasticism, an interesting example of which are the recluses in the Serapeum [2] of Memphis, who formed an order of a very rigorous kind. From the first generation onwards the early Church found the regnant asceticism as a mode of religion so strong that, in forgetfulness of the sanity of its Founder, but exaggerating suggestions of Paul, it took over Pagan asceticism in such a wholesale fashion as to magnify the merits of fasting, to make celibacy and virginity a higher life than the obligations and duties of married life, to encourage the practice of ' brothers ' having ' sister ' wives, and to find its expression in the unlovely asperities of the scholarly Jerome and the self-tortures of Stylites. Christianity recognized that if it adopted asceticism it must surpass the Pagans in their excesses and discomforts. The devotion of the Isiac devotee crawling on bleeding knees to break the ice in winter and bathe in the icy waters, the self-flagellation of the Galli, the gashing with knives, the long fasts, the monastic life, the insensibility to pain, and such exercises as sometimes issued in the death of the penitent must be surpassed. If the Phrygian priest offered his virility to his Lord, Origen inflicted upon himself a similar emasculation. An historian of early Christianity rightly assesses the " two influences which worked with disintegrating effect " in the first centuries as " the divergence between the intellectual and moral side of Christianity " and " the effect which

---

[1] Asceticism and resignation resulted " from exaggerated attention to the individual consciousness at the cost of social and political life " Arnold, *Rom. Stoicism*, p. 258).

[2] Cf. *Rev. des études grecques*, XXXVI, p. 82. K. Sethe, *Sarapis u. d. sogen. κάτοχοι des Sarapis* (in *Abt. ges. Wiss. Göttingen*, XIV. 913), decides for *reclus* rather than religiously *possessed*, for which J. Wilcken (*Archiv f. Pap.* VI. 1913, pp. 184-212) contends. Cf. Bouché-Leclercq, *Les Reclus du Sérapeum de Memphis*, and Preuschen, *Mönchum u. Sarapiskult*.

5

the ascetic tendencies of the age had on its morals."[1]
It is no exaggeration to say that " it was not so much
immorality as the excessive chastity of many Christians
which was the danger which threatened the congrega-
tions "[2] in the sub-apostolic age.

[1] Dobschütz, *Christian Life in the Primitive Church*, p. 251.
[2] Wernle, *Beginnings*, II, p. 320.

CHAPTER III

IN the first century religiously-minded men responding to the ubiquitous religious appeal might have recourse for religious support and the communion of sympathetic souls to one of four main religious refuges—Judaism, Greek moral and Greek mystical philosophy, the Mystery-religions, or Christianity. This enumeration by no means implies that there were only four religions or that each of these proved impervious to the others and to outside influences. Even the conspicuously exclusive of the Graeco-Roman religions—Judaism and Christianity—proved unable, to their own enrichment, to erect effectual barriers against encroachments from without. Moreover, these religions were interpreted in categories of that day and with acquiescence in the philosophical-religious postulates, for example, individualism, dualism, demonology, asceticism. The contemporary cosmologies and scientific views made lasting impacts upon each. Thus each religion was compelled to the task of making man comfortable in the universe, and this naturally led to comparison and contrast with the cosmic pretensions of its competitors. Again, Astralism compelled the attention of Greek philosophy and at certain points entered into dangerous competition with it, and at others, for example, on the ascent of the soul, it entered into alliance with it. It forced recognition from Judaism. It compelled Christian preachers to counteract its appeal and to outbid its claims, and it secured a place in canonical writings in the *Apocalypse*. It obliged Origen in the most comprehensive early Christian philosophy of history to treat of the ensouled heavenly

47

bodies and to hold that the sun, moon, and stars pray to God.[1] Its largest scope was probably in the Mysteries.

Again, we may not look for mysticism in any one corner. We find it in one quarter confused with occultism and theurgy, in another operating with the exalted experiences of the Mysteries, in another proclaiming the triumphant faith that " our destiny, our being's heart and home, is with Infinitude and only there," in another finding the world sacramental and issuing in a soul-purifying cosmic emotion.

Or the political associations of religion were not wholly neglected by any of the above four forms of religion. The religious standing of Israel was constantly jeopardizing her peace with the political powers, and in a real way her religion constituted an *imperium in imperio* in the Empire. Her faith in providence had a keen eye for the embarrassments of Seleucid or Roman overlords. Christianity at first was indifferent to political life, but learned to imitate the Mystery priesthoods in seeking political power:[2] at first it learned to pray for the powers as ordained of God; then challenged them to a mortal conflict for two and a half centuries, after which it became the State religion, when Christ succeeded to the place vacated by Serapis and Mithra, and the Madonna gradually to the place vacated by Isis and the Great Mother.

Finally, as an illustration of the working of a general belief, magic may be mentioned, which was regarded as too dangerous to neglect. In this field the Jews were experts, and their scriptures and divine titles were put to frequent magical working. Greek philosophy in its clarity and power opposed magic, yet we note the tragic declension of the system of Ammonius Saccas into a theurgy in Iamblichus, Proclus, and Maximus. The Christians at first attributed magic to demons, but

---

[1] *De Prin.* I. 7; *C. Celsum*, V. 11, VIII. 67.
[2] E.g. *C.I.L.* IV. 787, 1011.

learned in larger commerce with an alien world to assign
to their own rites the pernicious or the blessed efficacies
of the rites of the magician. Philosophy and Christianity
had close contacts. The first great reinterpretation of
Christianity as a timeless religion—the Fourth Gospel—
was the achievement of a mind which was attracted by
Greek mysticism. Pantaenus, the founder of the Cate-
chetical school of Alexandria, and Clement were both
brought to Christianity through Greek philosophy.
Ammonius, the master of Plotinus, was a Christian
before he became a philosopher and teacher of the
philosopher Origen. Justin Martyr was a devoted
Platonist before he became a Christian, and as a
Christian asseverated that ' the teachings of Plato
are not different from the teachings of Christ ' and
saw no incongruity in wearing the philosopher's mantle.[1]
Though Augustine abandoned Plotinus because there
was no Incarnation in his doctrine,[2] he could
not withdraw himself from the spiritual influence of
Plotinus, whose philosophy through his Christian
follower has found a permanent place in Christianity.
And from Proclus the Areopagite drew his mystical
inspiration. Jerome in his preface to the *De Viris
illustribus*—the earliest Christian " Who's Who "—
contends that there are men among the Christians whose
culture confutes the arguments of Celsus, Porphyry, and
Julian.

To multitudes in quest of a religious refuge, Judaism
offered a spiritual home. The prophecy of Baruch [3] was
abundantly fulfilled, ' I will scatter this people among
the Gentiles, that they may do good to the Gentiles.'
And ' the Father and Creator of the universe did not
abandon mankind. He gave a Law and sent holy
prophets to proclaim and to teach the race of men that
each of us might awaken and come to know that there

[1] *Apol.* II. 12-15.
[2] *Conf.* VII. 10.
[3] *Apoc. of Baruch*, I. 4.

is one God.[1] The Synagogue deserved better of that
ancient world Pagan and Christian than has been generally acknowledged. Too long has Judaism been set
in stark contrast to Christianity and judged by the hostile
references of the Gospel narrative and by the detrac-
tion of Judaism that early became fashionable in the
triumphant Gentile Christian communities. On the other
hand, Judaism has been so presented as to detract from
Christianity. But the researches of Jewish and Christian
scholars have revealed the fact that there was a type
of Judaism inward and spiritual, prophetic and un-
conventional, preparing the way in Palestine for the
prophetic preaching of John the Baptist and of Jesus,
and in the Diaspora for the propaganda of Philo and the
missionary career of Paul, just as Lindsay has shown
that the Reformation movement which culminated in
Luther was in gestation in the quiet religious family life
of the German people. This more spiritual Judaism,
though pessimistic about man's nature and loud in
lamentation that ' a corruptible body weigheth down the
soul ' (*Sap.* ix. 15), gave rise to a profounder sense of sin
such as is found in the *Wisdom of Solomon* or in Paul,
and intensified the desire for a Redeemer from sin and
from the conflict of flesh and spirit and for a Saviour-
God to ensure victory in that supra-mundane conflict
against Principalities and Powers, against the World-
rulers of Darkness, and so to deliver men from the
Powers of Darkness. This type of Judaism, while
rendering religion an inner and personal concern, also
lifted it into the plane of universalism co-extensive with
human needs.

From the days of Alexander the Great the Jews took
their place in world-history in closer contact with the
movements, political, intellectual, and religious, of the

[1] Theophilus, *Ad Autolycum*, II. 34. Cf. ' thy sons through whom
the incorruptible light of the Law was destined to be given to the world
(*aeon*),' *Sapientia*, xviii. 4. Cf. Moore, *Judaism in the First Centuries*,
I, p. 115 f.

Mediterranean world. They participated in the missionary zeal [1] of the religions which in Alexander's Empire and that of Rome were carried beyond their geographical and racial boundaries and came daily into collision and contact. To an amazing degree the Jews, while obstinately maintaining their racial characteristics and cult, were affected by the regnant syncretism [2] or blending of religious ideas and usages in the congeries of peoples. In a world craving spiritual power and moral reformation they attracted converts by the appeal of a venerable antiquity—an important item of apologetic in the Graeco-Roman world; by an austere and virile morality which gave them pre-eminence among the laxer morals of Paganism; by a resolute and robust theism and an invincible personal faith in God as the omnipotent Dispenser of the happenings of history; by regular

---

[1] For the popularity of Judaism cf. Josephus, *C. Ap.* II. 39; Seneca in Augustine, *De Civ. Dei*, VI. 11, ' major pars populi facit quod cur faciat ignorat.' Cf. the legislation on circumcision, vide Schürer, I, p. 677 ff.; III, p. 117 f.

[2] The Jews, particularly of the Diaspora, were active commissaries of syncretism or eclecticism in religion; cf. Gunkel, *Zum religionsgesch. Verständnis d. N.T.*, p. 25 ff.; Bousset, *Religion des Judentums*, 2nd ed. p. 542 ff.: " Das Judentum war die Retorte, in welcher die verschiedene Elemente gesammelt wurden," p. 594. It is surely an underestimation to say " alles in allem aber ist, wenn wir von der Zauberei absehen, die jüdische Religion für den heidenischen Synkretismus nicht von grosser Bedeutung geworden, weil es ihr an Toleranz und Anpassungsfähigkeit gebrach " (art. *Synkretismus in Alt.* in *Relig. in Gesch. und Geg.* V. 1053). A truer estimate of the Diaspora is given by A. Causse (*Quelques remarques sur les origines de la Diaspora*, Paris, 1924, p. 12 ff.), who points out that since the Exile Israel had begun to forget her native tongue: " c'est assurément une heure grave quand un peuple change de langue. Avec la langue nouvelle de nouvelles pensées pénètrent l'âme d'Israël. . . . C'est le moment où l'iranisme et le sémitisme tendent à fusionner; et non seulement iranisme et sémitisme, mais aussi les religions et les superstitions de tous les peuples d'Orient. Déjà commencent à se propager certains cultes mystiques. . . . Israël dispersé sur la terre ne devait pas échapper à la contagion. Il était particulièrement bien placé aux carrefours des nations pour la subir. C'est un fait significatif que les grands centres de la diaspora étaient justement les grands centres de culture syncrétique."

congregational worship in democratic religious brotherhoods; by the scrupulous attention to the religious
education of children;[1] together with a general educational policy for the people;[2] by the denunciations and
promises of the synagogue pulpit; by the assurances of
moral self-control and moral progress; by their superior
holy books translated into the *lingua franca,* and by an
energetic and competent literary apologetic. The prayer
with which, according to Philo, the translators of the
Hebrew scriptures into the Greek Septuagint version
approached their historic task, received an abundant
answer in that this Greek version not only " kept millions
in the old faith, to win fresh millions for whom the
Hebrew text would have remained a buried treasure," [3]
but became the first, and remained for a considerable
time the only, Bible of missionary Christianity:[4] ' He
heard their prayers that not only the majority but rather
the whole human race might be benefited by giving heed
for reformation of life to wise and noble ordinances.'
Add to this the amazing ability " of this grimly earnest
people " to comprehend the nature of Hellenistic-
Oriental mysticism, which they not only adapted with
great success to Judaism and made a means of modern-
izing their scriptures, but which they also associated with
stronger religious and moral purposes and motives than
in its native environment. It was this larger, eager,
aggressive Judaism of the Diaspora that sponsored
Christianity in the Gentile world—*sub umbraculo insig-
nissimae religionis certe licitae* ;[5] and after the catastrophe
of A.D. 70 and the end of the sacrificial system, and

[1] Cf. Philo, *De Sept.* 6, C.-W. 60; Moore, *Judaism in the First Centuries of the Christian Era,* I, p. 308 ff.

[2] Cf. Moore, *ib.* I, pp. 284 f., 308 ff. The Synagogue had features
in common with a Mystery *collegium,* a school of philosophy, a mutual
benefit society, and a court of civil jurisdiction.

[3] Hausrath, *New Testament Times,* I, p. 142.

[4] " Greek Judaism with the Septuagint had ploughed the furrows for
the Gospel seed in the Western world " (Deissmann, *New Light on
the New Testament,* p. 95).

[5] Tertullian, *Apol.* 21.

particularly after the final rupture with Christianity in the Bar Cochba war, it was the Diaspora that saved Judaism as a spiritual force in the world.

That Judaism proved a religious home to numerous converts, including those of high rank and culture, we have abundant evidence. The success [1] of their propaganda is as certain as the difficulties in its way were real. The Jewish mission was confronted with the *odium generis humani* hurled against a people who were represented as a *genus hominum invisum deis,* and this pronounced anti-Semitism [2] was aggravated by the uncompromising attitude of the Jews toward the current *theocrasia* [3]—mixture of rites and deities—and toward the imperial cult [4] as the symbol of loyalty and by their disdain of many of the social customs of their neighbours. In the Roman period they also fell under the deep suspicion of disloyalty and of readiness to take advantage of every crisis threatening the Empire. They also stood aloof in their spirit of intolerance which Christianity inherited from them. They were adamant on the question of monotheism and on the observance of the sabbath, on dietary regulations and on aniconic worship, and above all on the rite of circumcision by which alone outsiders could receive the full benefits of the special covenant mercies, thus cutting themselves off from their former social and religious alliances. The utmost concession made was the recognition of a class of God-fearers or *Metuentes* who were adherents of the Synagogue without becoming full Jews by circumcision. Judaism exemplified the strength and weakness of a

---

[1] Cf. Schürer, *Gesch d. jüd. Volkes,* 4th ed. III, p. 155 f.

[2] Cf. Bousset, p. 86.

[3] " The separateness of the Jews, their ἀμιξία, was one of the prime causes of the animosity toward them, especially in the miscellaneous fusion of people and syncretism of religions in the Hellenistic kingdoms and the Roman world; but it accomplished its end in the survival of Judaism, and therein history has vindicated it " (Moore, I, p. 21).

[4] Cf. Juster, *Les Juifs dans l'empire romain,* I, p. 340 ff.

nationalistic [1] religion with catholic pretensions. There was, however, a universalism latent even in Mosaism, and the prophets undermined particularism and privilege in religion. On such an important question there was much heart-searching and intense conflict within the ranks of Judaism between the liberals and the orthodox. Two tendencies became manifest, the one issuing in the exclusiveness of Ezra and Rabbinism in the supposed interest of self-preservation, the other stressing the inwardness of a denationalized religion and its independence of outward forms and expressing itself in love of God and Man. [2]

The Jewish mission [3] for righteousness and morality and monotheism and for a social religion with an individual responsibility captured many not only from among the masses, but from the higher circles.

The literary remains of Alexandrine Judaism, such as the *Wisdom of Solomon, Ecclesiasticus,* and the works of Philo, show how the Jews could hold their own in the academic groups of the University of Alexandria and how they could adapt and assimilate new and foreign thought to strengthen their propaganda without sacrificing any essential of their faith. They learned to present their faith as a sacerdotal or a legalistic or a prophetic or a mystical religion. [4]

Christianity inherited the lofty ethical ideals of Judaism. The Apostle of the Gentiles found it easier to win converts to the new Christian society than to

---

[1] " The strength of Judaism rested on its ethical and spiritual content, its weaknesses on its national political aspirations " (G. la Piana, *Harvard Th. Rev.* XX. 4, p. 384).

[2] Cf. *Archiv f. Religionswiss.* XXV, p. 218 ff.

[3] Cf. Harnack, *Expansion,* I, p. 15.

[4] " Dennoch bleibt *das alexandrinische Judentum eine Erscheinung von allerhöchster Wichtigkeit. . . .* Es hat in her Tat die Brücke geschlagen, auf dem das Evangelium in die Welt einziehen konnte. . . . Hier wurden die Formen geschaffen, die das Evangelium braucht, um sich der Welt verständlich zu machen. Hier entstand die Logostheologie, hier wurden die Mittel bereitet, mit denen die christliche Apologetik arbeitete " (Bousset, *Religion des Judentums,* 2nd ed. p. 502).

mprove their morals. It was the Jewish system of thics intermingled with Stoic principles and suffused with the new enthusiasm of Christian love which Paul ought to impose upon the Gentiles. The poorer Jewish-Christian Churches more than repaid the Gentile-Christian contributions in money by the wealth of their thical heritage. The former were agitated by questions f legalism, while the latter were endeavouring to restrain ibertinism by the adoption of the ethical code of Judaism nd Christianity. Because Christianity sprang from udaism, its birthmark was morality. " The Jewish Christianity of Palestine trained by the Law was, so to peak, the backbone, which supported the moral con-cience of the whole. . . . And the Judaistic agitation n his (Paul's) churches, in spite of the injury that it did, still achieved the result of laying more stress on the moral side of Christianity." [1]

Judaism offered the ancient world all the advantages f a religion of authority, appealing to weary minds eeking for a sure word in days of religious doubt. The authority of its proclamations rested on the fact that it was professedly an exclusive revealed religion which, hough consonant with the highest philosophy, was beyond the will of men and permitted no questioning of its claims.[2] A scheme of redemption satisfying to numerous proselytes was offered. The unequivocal message of a divine purpose working itself out in the events of time and advancing surely towards a goal upplied an inspiring world-view to those who were dis-atisfied with the Hellenic, especially Stoic, view of the world-process as a never-ending recurrent series of cycles

[1] Dobschütz, *Christian Life in the Primitive Church*, p. 172; cf. p. 139; Wernle, *Beginnings of Christianity*, I, p. 20 f.
[2] Judaism was " a revealed religion, which did not ask man's pproval but demanded obedience to the whole and every part, reason nd inclination to the contrary notwithstanding; an exclusive religion which tolerated no divided allegiance; a religion which made a man's ternal destiny depend on his submission of his whole life to its law, or is rejection of God who gave the law " (Moore, *op. cit.* I, p. 324).

which merely repeated the past without any very definite
aim or consummation, the same events occurring, and
the same acts of baseness and of heroism transpiring on
the same stage. And Israel would not be balked of the
conviction that God and good shall triumph, if not here
in this order then in another and better succeeding order
This heroic message—for it was of faith—likewise sup
plemented and acted as a wholesome corrective to the
world-view of those who under later Platonic influence
removed the world of reality into the supernal realm and
belittled the mightiest events of history as symbols of
the eternal world or as ideas. Thus the Jews gave to
these centuries in the throes of change and renewal a
concrete present value to the very history, with all its
perplexity, of which they were a notable part. To the
Greek, God reveals Himself, at least supremely, in pure
' form ' or sublime ideas; to the Jew, God reveals Him
self in history, in the temporal happenings of the years
The Greek interpreted history as philosophy teaching
by examples; the Jew as a continuous concrete vindica
tion of right over wrong, as a moral system of rewards
and punishments.[1]

The supreme interest of the Greek was in philosophy
he philosophized his religion; the supreme interest of the
Jew was in religion, he moralized his religion. Jewish
character was rooted in Jewish religion. '' The people
whose religion forms the foundation of Christianity and
Mohammedanism, the people whose religion is the source
of that of nearly half the population of the world, must
be peculiarly endowed with the genius of religion—more
over, the people who have given to the world the Old
and New Testaments must needs stand out as pre

---

[1] Cf. Bevan's excellent contrast of the Hebraic and the Hellenic
world-views in *Legacy of Israel*, p. 50. Inge speaks of " the most
formidable problem of Christian theology—how to make room for the
Jewish philosophy of history by the side of the Platonic philosophy of
eternal life " (*Phil. of Plotinus*, II, p. 19; cf. Carpenter, *Phases of Early
Christianity*, p. 9).

eminently endowed with the spirit of religion." [1]   And yet the time came when ' it is absurd to use the name Jesus Christ and play the Jew.   For Christianity has not believed in Judaism, but Judaism in Christianity.' [2] But by one of the most astonishing reactions in history, Judaism, which had so thoroughly prepared the way for Christianity and had contributed so liberally to its missionary equipment, began to look askance at the readiness with which the Greeks accepted, enlarged, and universalized the primitive Gospel; then as a whole Judaism rejected Christianity and thereby practically rejected Hellenism,[3] and so turned its face toward Asia rather than toward Europe, in which Paul had found such a response to a vitalizing message.

[1] Oesterley & Box, *The Religion and Worship of the Synagogue*, p. 20.
[2] Ignatius, *Ad Magn.* X. 3.
[3] Cf. H. H. Schaeder, *Der Orient und das griech. Erbe* in *Die Antike*, V. 3, p. 245 ff.

CHAPTER IV

GREEK MORAL AND GREEK MYSTICAL PHILOSOPHY

AMONG the religious refuges of the Graeco-Roman world
Greek philosophy, moral and mystical, occupies a con
spicuous place because of its pre-eminent services to
ancient seekers after truth who strove to attain a syn
thesis of life's varied activities. It enabled earnest men
to determine their bearings in face of the contradiction
of the universe. Greek moral philosophy made its appeal
to virile morality and love of truth; it advocated the
high potencies resident within man, making him les
dependent on external or supernatural help and fostering
moral self-respect. Greek mystical philosophy, con
tinuing Plato's mystical quests and deeply influenced by
Oriental mysticism, granted increasing recognition to the
soul's intuitions.

Socrates, " almost the ideal of humanity itself," fully
conscious of a divine call, diverted inquiry from physic
to logic, from the objective to the subjective, to in
vestigate human nature itself and its ethical concerns, to
determine the good and the evil in conduct. Against
the dogmatism of his predecessors he introduced the
system of ' humble inquiry,' ' always doubting and
causing others to doubt,' that they might have convic
tions and attain knowledge rather than hold mere
opinions, and that they might know things as they are
The discovery of conscience (' the wife from whom there
is no divorce ') by Socrates and all the deepening of
personality and moral responsibility based on inner
freedom gave rise to a high sense of the supreme worth
of the individual and of the value of moral integrity and
autonomy, of which the martyr death in the Athenian

58

prison became the supreme expression. Socrates gave a new and defiant security to moral strivings.[1] This type of moral philosophy taught men to look within and find salvation there in the realization of the inherent divinity of man and of the true nature of the soul to aspire on high in love of the things that are true and noble.

Plato, following up the method of Socrates to discern the true nature of things, discovered a new mode of knowledge, or rather he found a way of escape from the world of uncertainty inherent in the Heraclitean doctrine of the flux of all things, about which opinion only is possible, by setting over against this shifting successive world of sensible things a world of eternal forms which neither ' become ' nor perish and by claiming that of these latter alone true knowledge is possible—the forms or ideas are the proper and only objects of the understanding, that is, only real things can be completely known.[2] Thus he delivered the spirit of man from the puzzling multiplicity of things and from depressing instability.

Plato and his master both believed that men have only to contemplate virtue to be enamoured of it so as to pursue it, and to behold Beauty (in its large Greek sense) to be attracted by it. Plato enthroned Goodness in the centre of the Universe by making the Good the source or ultimate cause of the Universe as also the goal of the whole world-process. The world itself with all its fullness is the overflow of the Good, as argued by Timaeus

[1] " From them [Socrates and his followers] in effect comes the connected scheme of virtues and duties within which the educated conscience of Christendom still moves when it is impartially reflecting on what ought to be done. Religious teachers have no doubt affected the hopes and fears which actuate us in the pursuit of virtue or rouse us from its neglect. Religious societies have both strengthened men in the performance of recognized duties and taught them to recognize relations of duty . . . but the articulated scheme of what the virtues and duties are, in their difference and in their unity, remains for us now in its main outlines what the Greek philosophers left it " (Green, *Proleg. to Ethics*, V. 249).

[2] Cf. *Repub*. 477 A.

in the dialogue of that name, and this overflow is not
due to any compulsion or even to free choice, but arose
wholly from the constitution of the Good to give forth
itself without jealousy or niggardly motives. Something
of the Good persists in all its emanations or self-
expressions, because it imparts its own characteristics.
Plato accordingly made the Good the universal quest or
nisus of all things: he would have approved as heartily
as did Aristotle of the famous declaration of the
astronomer Eudoxus: ' It is the Good for which all
things strive.' He therefore asseverated unequivocally
that man always seeks the Good; being ' a plant of
heavenly origin ' he can rest in nothing short of the
Good, nor accept, save for a time and under illusion,
any substitute. This doctrine of the inherent worth of
the soul, its inalienable goodness, and its equipment with
wings for heavenly flights was a message very much
needed as a wholesome corrective during subsequent
ages of pessimism as to man's nature. The juggernaut
of the fatalism of astralism was for many deprived of its
terrors by Plato's lofty faith that the things of the eternal
world are found within and are realizable in daily
experience. That immortality is man's constitutionally
and yet something to be gained through the forth-putting
of the moral powers resident within, and that the rationality of man rests on the activity of the divine element
within him which alone renders him truly human, was
a healthful gospel.

It is impossible to estimate the incalculable blessings
to the ancient world accruing from Greek philosophy.
It remained the strongest bulwark against the sentimentality and emotionalism, and, though it too was over-
taken by a desire for Revelation, the tradition of inquiry
and the brilliant achievements of the Greek genius were
too strong to yield easily to traditions of sacerdotal learning. It delayed for centuries the advent of the Dark
Ages of credulity and miracle. It is possible to-day to
realize its attraction and respond to its timeless appeal.

No earnest reader can to-day study Plato's disciples, Philo and Plotinus, without his soul expanding in sympathy with those who so lived in the reality of the spiritual and eternal, and without being elevated toward the height of their pure loves. And the more Christian the reader the more sensitive he will be to their deep intuitions of truth and their experiences of joy. He will gratefully acknowledge the *anima naturaliter Christiana*.

It is also impossible to estimate the contribution of Greek philosophy to Christianity both nascent and later.[1] Little wonder that the Christian teachers who knew Greek philosophy best, such as Justin, Clement, Origen, esteemed it highly as a preparation for and ally of Christianity in supplying standards of values. Clement protests that ' philosophy is not false,' and even conceding that ' philosophy was discovered by the Greeks by human understanding,' such understanding was God-sent, so that Greek philosophy is a revelation from God ; it was God's ' peculiar covenant with the Greeks as a basis for the philosophy according to Christ.' [2] Clement quotes the influential *Preaching of Peter* as proving that the one eternal God ' known to the Greeks in a Gentile fashion and to the Jews in a Jewish fashion and to us in a new and spiritual fashion ' was ' the Giver of Greek philosophy to the Greeks,' [3] which he recognized as one of the two divine antecedents of Christianity. Justin [4] was ' delighting in the teachings of Plato ' when the

---

[1] " The philosophy of Greece provided the inward conditions whereby its [Christianity] ideas could be interpreted and brought into that systematic form which was necessary to secure their permanent influence upon the human mind . . . Greek philosophy supplied the form in which the reflective thought of the time was cast, the intellectual weapons with which it worked, the categories or general conceptions by means of which it sought to deal with any new matter. . . . Greek philosophy may be regarded as the germ out of which Christian theology sprang, or as the great adverse force which it had to combat " (Caird, *Theology in the Greek Philosophers*, I, p. 49, II, pp. 363, 369). ' Hellas has dominated the creed as she has dominated the intellectual history of Christendom " (Farnell, *Evolution of Religion*, p. 81).

[2] *Str*. VI. 8 (62, 4; 67, 1).

[3] *Ib*. VI. 5; 41, 6.   [4] *Apol*. II. 12-15.

6

heroic testimony of Christian confessors induced him
to become a Christian, ' not that the teachings of Plato
are different from those of Christ, though not wholly
similar,' but because the doctrine of the incarnate Logos
as ' Son and Apostle ' rendered Christianity ' superior
to all human philosophy.'

The insistence of Platonism on hearkening to the
intuitions of the soul as a source of true knowledge
additional to ratiocination and the carrying of all things
for meaning to their eternal idea, the demand of Neo-
Pythagoreanism for holiness and renunciation and kindness and the unambiguous testimony of Stoicism to
autonomous personality as man's only inalienable
possession, cannot be antiquated in the strivings of mankind, though much in each of these systems has been
antiquated and become even grotesque. But the mystic
the ritualist, and the moralist abide.

The most potent strain in Greek philosophy was
Platonism, which penetrated or affected every sub
sequent system of thought, especially Neo-Pythagorean
ism, Stoicism, and Neo-Platonism. Platonism entered
Christianity largely through Neo-Platonism, and Neo
Platonism mostly through three channels—from Am
monius Saccas through Origen, from Plotinus through
Augustine, and from Proclus through Pseudo-Dionysius.
The supreme value and abiding appeal of Platonism to
the world and especially to aggressive Christianity is it
amazing combination and fusion of the keenest critica
search of truth intellectually with the moral and religiou
contemplation of truth itself. In fact the Platonic tem
perament is constituted of " the singular blend o

[1] " It is in the main from him [Proclus] that Christianity receive
the Neo-Platonic impress still distinguishable in orthodox theolog
under all the guise of a formal Aristotelianism. . . . The main source
of the unmistakable Neo-Platonism of the great scholastic philosopher
are two—the writings of the so-called Dionysius, themselves the wor
of some Christianized follower of Proclus, and the work *De Causis*
(of Proclus) (Taylor, *Phil. of Proclus*, in *Proc. Aristotelian Soc.* N.S
XVIII, p. 600).

humanism and asceticism, poetry and logic, the critical and the devotional spirit." [1] The Platonist is at once mystic and rationalist: he believes that the soul makes its ascent both by reason and by love and in this ascent the logical is joined with the emotional. Platonism has proved a vast enrichment of our faith. To-day we need not less but more Platonism to revitalize dogma and to quicken with a genuine mysticism which refuses to become synonymous with abnormal non-moral manifestations or to be restricted to exceptional individuals in cloistered calm or of towering greatness, but is workable by and accessible to such classes as fisherfolk, day-labourers and craftsmen and peasants, who first heard its loftiest expression and promise, ' Blessed are the pure in heart: for they shall see God.' If Clement of Alexandria reminded nervous and conventional Christians that philosophy was not a hobgoblin to frighten them, such Christians may still be reminded that in that practical and catholic practice of thinking on ' whatever things are true, honest, just, pure, lovely, and of good report,' Greek philosophy cannot be excluded. Christianity will be clarified and enriched and the greatness of its Founder enhanced by moving in the direction advocated by the Cambridge Platonists back to " her old loving nurse, the Platonick philosophy," to realize with one of them (Whichcote), " I oppose not rational to spiritual, for spiritual is most rational."

Cicero said of Plato *scribens est mortuus,* but his timeless message abides, and his prophetic voice will never cease to be heard while the problem of the transient and the immutable presses upon man. He will ever invite men to hearken to and identify themselves with the divine principle within. In every age the follower of Plato, borne far " above the howling senses' ebb and flow," will be able without confusion both to contemplate and to participate energetically in that ceaseless process whereby—

[1] Dodds, *Select Passages,* p. 9 f.

" Our little systems have their day;
They have their day and cease to be ";

his soul will find a sure anchorage in the realization (in
the most succinct statement of Platonism from Christian
lips and from one who professed no love for philosophy)
that ' the things which are seen are temporal, but the
things which are not seen are eternal.' Plato has taught
his own a more excellent way of building Eternity than
out of the ruins of Time: Eternity may be securely built,
even during its ' moving image,' out of the more precious
material of the heavenly mind loving and living now in
the ' eternal and immutable ideas.' Speaking thus of
Platonism, it is no more intended to deny the presence
of contemporary and antiquated elements in Plato than
in first-century Christianity. Platonism was the last
and loftiest refuge of noble souls who in the waning of
Paganism could not accept Christianity in an age, alas !
when the unhappy alternatives of Either—Or, of
Catholicism or Platonism, were thrown out by Christianity in its oblivion of Clement and Origen.

Greek thought has rendered one lasting service to the
universality and validity of religion, not only in banish-
ing fear and bringing criticism to bear, but in insisting
that the religion of rational and intelligent beings must
be at least rational and intelligible in its principles, and
in maintaining, in the words of Whichcote, that there
cannot be " an action of religion which is not an act of
the understanding ; for that is not a religious act which
is not human," so that religion is something embraced
with reverence both by the intellect and the emotions.
And Greek philosophy did this while recognizing increasingly in its epistemology the rights of intuition, and
the truths that wake, not by the ratiocinative faculty
" to perish never," and the aspiration of man to
" breathe in worlds To which the heaven of heavens is
but a veil."

If Platonism offered to the yearnings of the Graeco
Roman age an ideal world of eternal Beauty and Good

ness within, Stoicism preached eloquently a new ideal
humanity as a spiritual unity, permeated and held
together as a mystic organism by the Logos or Pneuma
and in which all are members of one another and akin.
Stoicism pursued the double aim of rendering the individual self-sufficient and independent of externals and
at the same time of qualifying him to act strenuously as
a member of society and a citizen of the world.   In
Stoicism there is neither Roman knight nor freedman
nor slave: ' this mind may belong as well to a Roman
knight, as to a freedman, as to a slave.'   ' Nature made
us kin when she produced us from the same things and
to the same ends.'   Nature ' gave me alone to all men
and all men to me alone.'   ' Virtue is barred to none:
she is open to all, she receives all, she invites all, gentle-
folk, freedmen, slaves, kings, exiles alike.' [1]   All are
' kinsmen, brothers by nature, children of God.' [2]
' Love the human race; follow God.' [3]

This rich humanism, called by the Romans *humanitas,*
was a clarion call in a caste-ridden world, and it was the
cause of much humanitarian legislation.[4]   With the stress
on the inwardness of virtue and the worth of the individual on the one hand and the social worth of each
in the ideal humanity of the *cosmopolis,* a potent stimulus
was given to high endeavour on the part of men as
' God's athletes.' [5]   While Stoicism was rigorous in its
logic, it learned increasingly to take account of man's
emotions and yearnings, and later Stoicism veered more
and more toward Platonism, until they practically blend.
While its ideal as represented by the Wise Man was
tantalizingly high, as ideals should be, it believed this
was within the reach of the humblest lover of virtue.   If
Platonism appealed most to the individual, Stoicism was
a gospel for the masses, which their street-preachers took
out of the schools and popularized.

[1] Lightfoot, *St. Paul and Seneca* in *Phil.* p. 304 f.
[2] Epict. I. 13.   [3] Marcus Aurelius, VII. 31.
[4] Cf. Arnold, *Rom. Stoicism,* p. 384.   [5] Epict. IV. 4, 32.

Immense indeed were the services rendered by Stoicism to the ancient world and to Christianity. But even in Stoicism at its best there was something lacking —something intensely human. The Stoics learned thoroughly, wrestling without tears and cries, the lesson of self-renunciation, but they never fully or adequately achieved their ideal of self-realization, despite their firm belief in the unity of man and God and an interpenetrating Reason. This unity was one in which the difference, as found in devotion and in religious experience, was not duly noted. They placed the individual under divine Law, but that Law offered not the sympathy for which the heart craved. Further, Jesus had given the primacy to Love among the virtues, which produced among His followers an " enthusiasm of humanity." Beside the Stoic " ideal of Detachment " [1] the Christian " ideal of Love " stood out in its superior uplifting and humanizing power: the Stoic self-discipline bore its fruit in Christian self-sacrifice. Stoicism, like Christianity, was called upon in its humanism to deal with the perennial enigma of suffering, and in the attitude to suffering we find the true heroic fibre of the Stoic soul. The Stoics did not deny suffering, but they steeled themselves to hardness against sensibility thereto. The Stoics could not consistently weep with those that weep, and sympathy must be more assumed than real. The Stoic calm, endurance, self-discipline, and the consciousness of the throes of the cosmic-process gave moral victory to the strong athletic souls. But all men are not of the heroic temperament and few are capable of becoming experts in philosophy, and fewer still are able to bring their philosophic convictions to bear upon the conduct of life. The problem of pain and suffering is perhaps insoluble, but Christianity offered to the average man not an idealized Wise Man nor an abstract ideal of perfection, but an historic Leader who Himself, ' having learned obedience from His sufferings,' invited men ' into the

[1] Bevan, *Stoics and Sceptics*, p. 67.

fellowship of His sufferings ' that they might ' have My joy fulfilled in them.' [1]

It would not be just to compare Stoicism with the thought of the present day, which has not even yet actualized the two great Stoic ideals of inwardness and universal brotherhood, but its message can be understood only in the needs and circumstances of its day and may be compared with the Christianity contemporary with it. Thus we may recognize that the parochial and nationalistic form of the earliest Christian preaching was far inferior to the cosmopolitanism and universal humanity preached by Stoicism, and also that Paul's catholic gospel of a World-Society did not take its rise from Judaism or from the provincialism of his fellow-apostles, but from the wide horizons for mankind made familiar by Stoicism to his native Tarsus. We shall also recognize that the Pauline universalism was more dynamic and more humanistic than that of the Stoa.

" At length," says Lightfoot,[2] " the bond of coherence, the missing principle of universal brotherhood has been found . . . the magic words ἐν Χριστῷ (in Christ) have produced the change. A living soul has been breathed into the marble statue by Christianity; and thus from the ' much admired polity of Zeno ' arises the *Civitas Dei* of St. Augustine."

In assessing the indebtedness of Christianity to its antecedents the vital importance of the morality of Judaism causes the Stoic contribution to the moral education of the ancient world to be overlooked or written off as merely Pagan. But in the larger world of the early Christian mission the ' God-fearers ' were tutored in moral values by the codes of both the Synagogue and the Stoa, which in many respects supplemented each other. The Stoic insistence on Duty,

[1] " Stoicism throve because, like Christianity, it is a philosophy of suffering; it fell because, unlike Christianity, it is a philosophy of despair " (Bigg, *Christian Platonists*, p. 288).

[2] *Op. cit.* p. 306.

Providence, and *propria virtus,* and the unremitting
endeavour to render man independent of externals, produced a strength of character which qualified for the
martyr spirit of early Christianity and resulted in an
unshakeable conviction that a man's life consists not in
the abundance of the things which he possesses. If the
ethics of Stoicism were in some respects hard and too
regardless of the emotions, it cannot be asserted that
early Christian ethics can be imposed literally upon
Christian society to-day. For example, the attitude of
most Stoics toward suicide offends our moral sense, but
do not Paul's repugnance to marriage and the sex-
instinct and his morally questionable concession of
marriage for the incontinent (1 *Cor.* vii. 9) fall short of
moral ideals to-day and the spiritualization of the passion
of love? With all its defects but with its more abundant
excellencies, Stoicism may properly be termed a " root
of Christianity." [1] The influence of Platonism was
strongest in Christian theology and philosophy; that of
Stoicism in Christian ethics.

By an evolution that only at first sight appears strange
—for the whole trend of Greek thought was a quest for
unity and a resolution of the most obstinate philosophical
antitheses of the One and the Many stated so clearly by
Parmenides, a progression from concrete to abstract—
the latest phase of Greek philosophy took on the character of mysticism, not the anti-rationalistic quietism of
the Orient, but a wholesome mysticism which repudiated
neither dialectic methods nor logical articulation but
summoned the emotions [2] to collaborate with the reason

---

[1] As by Winckler, *Der Stoicismus eine Wurzel des Christentums.* For
other favourable estimates cf. Arnold, *Roman Stoicism,* pp. 408-36
(*The Stoic Strain in Christianity*); and especially P. G. Chappuis, *La
Destiné de l'homme, de l'influence du Stoïcisme sur la pensée chrét.
primitive* (Paris, 1926), on which de Faye remarks: " Tout le monde
reconnaît que la morale ecclésiastique est largement redevable à l'éthique
stoïcienne " (*Rev. de l'hist. des religions,* XCVI. 4, p. 83).

[2] Cf. *Intellektual u. Mystik in gr. Phil.* (*N. Jahrb. f. d. klass. Alt.*
XLIX-L, 1922, pp. 137-57.)

with a view to the apprehension of a larger and fuller truth. Greek contemplation was intensive concentration, like that of Plotinus. The amazing double strain in Socrates of rationalism and mysticism came to expression. The period of subjective and individualistic philosophies after Aristotle [1] naturally led to that of religious philosophy and introspection. This mystic quest was doubtless accentuated and fostered under contact with Oriental contemplative genius; nevertheless the highest form of this mystic philosophy—Neo-Platonism—remains essentially true to its Greek origin and Greek master.[2] Loyal to the genuine Greek tradition, it exalted vision above emotion. Greek thought in its wonderful comprehensiveness had sought unweariedly to explore man's rational and moral faculties, and during this process it discovered and tried to do justice to the boundless aspirations and to the deep thirst of the spirit. It discovered that ' our greatest difficulty is that consciousness of the One comes not by knowledge, not even by such an intuitive Intellection as possesses us of the lower members of the Intellectual Orders, but by an actual Presence superior to any knowing.' [3] It discovered, too, the land that is very far off from the prosaic man, but is none the less real because visited by the few and sincere travellers: ' the Supreme is not absent from anyone—and yet is absent from all; present everywhere, it is absent except only to those who are prepared to receive it, those that have brought themselves into harmony with it.' [4] The moral factor [5] in the cognition of reality is projected into the foreground; a man must be good and love the Good to know the Good, for—

---

[1] Cf. Caird, *Evol. of Theology in the Greek Philosophers*, II, pp. 178, 248 f.

[2] Cf. Caird, *ib*. II, p. 238 ff.

[3] Plotinus, *En*. VI. 9, 4 (Mackenna's tr.).

[4] Plotinus, *ib*. (Mackenna).

[5] ' For without virtue God would never have appeared to men ' (Proclus, *In remp*. I, p. 255 (Kroll)).

' If the eye that adventures the vision be dimmed by
vice, impure, or weak, and unable in its cowardly
blenching to see the brightness, then it sees nothing even
though another point to what lies plain to sight before it.
To any vision must be brought an eye adapted to what
is to be seen and having some likeness to it. . . . Let
each become godlike and each beautiful who cares to
see God and Beauty.' [1]

Thus a *katharsis*, purification, is necessary before
knowledge as for initiation into the Mysteries.

Moreover, with this new epistemology a new court of
appeal for the testing of reality was opened, the appeal
to the self-consciousness and religious experience—to
those secret movements and disturbing experiences of the
inner life. Dialectic thought and teaching pointed the
way, but only vision disclosed the reality. ' Anyone that
has seen [the Good] knows what I intend when I say
that it is beautiful. Even the desire of it is to be desired
as a Good. . . . One that shall know this vision, with
what passion of love shall he not be seized, with what
pang of desire, what longing to be molten into one with
this, what wondering delight ' [2]; or ' those who have
seen will know of what I speak when I affirm that both
in her approach to the Divine, and again when she is
come near and has fruition of it, the soul lives with
another life ; so that by her own condition she is assured
that the Dispenser of true life is present to her. Beside
this consciousness man has need of nothing else.' [3] Love
opened wide the gate of deepest knowledge. Plato's
beautiful myth of Eros and Psyche was frequently used
in Neo-Platonism to suggest in regions inaccessible to
ratiocination.[4]

This philosophy of mysticism was one phase of the

[1] Plotinus, I. 6, 9 (Mackenna). [2] Plotinus, I. 6, 7 (Mack.).
[3] *Id.* VI. 9, 9 (Dodds' tr. in *Select Passages illustrating Neo
Platonism*, p. 122).
[4] ' Following Love, the guide to Wisdom ' (Philo, *De Opif. Mundi*
23, C.-W. 70). Cf. Plotinus, VI. 7, 23.

sustained endeavours of later Paganism to become like God, to live in the communion with the Divine, and to enjoy immediate union with God. The prolonged concentration of interest in the welfare and salvation of the individual soul was sure to raise a demand for the discovery of the means of access of the individual to God and of personal union with Deity. The Stoic pantheistic conception of an all-pervasive Spirit or Reason as the principle of the world conduced to a mystic yearning for union therewith as experienced in cosmic emotion.

Moreover, viewed in perspective of centuries of Greek speculation, Mysticism is recognized as the culmination [1] of Greek thought. If Platonism and Neo-Platonism failed to discover a complete harmony of the phenomenal and the ideal, of soul and sense, in some divine counterpoint, they at least impelled the spirit to the quest for a synthesis or reconciliation and lent a burning intensity to religious and philosophical life. The tense idealism of Plato, the strong antithesis both in Plato and Aristotle between Form or Reality and Matter or Phenomenality, the pronounced subjectivism of the Stoics with their emphasis on unity and their desperate mode of escape from Dualism by the practical identity of mind and matter, and their immanence, find a meeting-place in Plotinus's mysticism and a synthesis as complete as thought can render.

Numenius, writing under the influence of Philo and Plato, recommends the following method to attain knowledge of the Good:

' So must a man go far away from sensible things to converse with the Good, alone with the Alone, where there is no other man, no other living thing, nothing corporeal small or great; only a vast divine solitude, unutterable, indescribable, the region where the Good

---

[1] Cf. Caird, *ib.* II, p. 250—the philosophy of Plotinus is " a kind of summary, or concentrated expression of the whole movement of Greek philosophy "—also p. 236 ff.

ranges, Its playing-meads and pleasances ; and the Good Itself abides in peace, in loving-kindness.' [1]

Plotinus is pre-eminently [2] the exponent of mystical philosophy and the psychologist [3] of this mode of union with the Divine. Four times during Porphyry's sojourn with him he enjoyed the consummate experience of becoming uniate with God.[4] Brief quotations cannot convey any adequate idea of the richness and beauty of Plotinus's thought in treating of the divine potentialities inherent in the Soul, and the ineffable joy of the Soul in immediate contact with reality and of the supreme duty of man to bring all his conscious life into identification with God. In the tractate on Beauty he gives expression to this striving :

' The soul includes a faculty peculiarly addressed to beauty—one incomparably sure in the appreciation of its own, never in doubt when any lovely thing presents itself for judgement. . . . Such vision is for those only who see with the Soul's sight—and at the vision they will rejoice, and awe will fall upon them and a trouble deeper than all the rest could ever stir, for now they are moving in the realm of Truth. . . . This is the spirit that Beauty must ever induce, wonderment and a delicious trouble, longing and love and a trembling that is all delight.' [5]

The discursive intelligence is recognized as preparatory or propaedeutic, but the intuitive intelligence or ' Spirit

[1] In Eusebius, *Praep. Ev.* XI. 22, 1; tr. in Bevan, *Later Greek Religion*, p. 150.

[2] Caird designates Plotinus as " the greatest of all mystics," and " Plotinus is one of the greatest names in the history of philosophy, the classical representative of one of the main lines of human thought; he is the Mystic *par excellence* " (*op. cit.* II, pp. 208-10). Dom Butler with less justification claims one who drew from Plotinus, Augustine, as " the prince of mystics " (*Western Mysticism*, p. 24).

[3] " He is not the originator of the doctrine of ecstasy. . . . But no Greek writer, perhaps no other writer of any period, has brought to the attempts to describe this remarkable psychical condition so much introspective ability as Plotinus, or to the interpretation of it so sane an imagination " (Dodds, *Select Passages*, p. 14).

[4] Porphyry, *Vita Plotini*, 23. [5] I. 6, 3-4.

in love ' which transports beyond intelligence gives an immediate and ineffable experience, as in VI. 7, 35. But Plotinus was too profound a philosopher and too sober a psychologist to set great store by abnormal psychopathic excitations or raptures or ecstasies. In those conditions he recognized that the percipient individual could not give any logical exposition of his experiences, and that therefore such raptures could not be the source of philosophical truth. And on issuing from " rapture " the subject could not recall with accuracy the details. These rare experiences were of a corroborative character, but could not pass as a substitute for philosophical inquiry. In fact in their philosophy the Neo-Platonists were essentially rationalists, as Whittaker remarked, and no school of philosophers was ever more prepared to give adequate reasons for their belief, while in religion advocating the value of personal experience. They were neither pure intellectualists nor emotional anti-rationalists. They generally remained genuine mystics in that they never really set feeling above reason as a means of knowledge.[1] They recognized various modes of apprehension [2] commensurate with the five grades of Being. At the one extreme stood the One who as ' being beyond reality ' is unknowable save in ecstasy or the uniate state; at the other, ' matter,' which could be known only negatively as non-being. Between these extremes the things of the sensible world admit only of ' opinion '; those of the Soul are apprehensible by discursive reason, while those of the Nous (Mind) are accessible to intuition.

It was the profound religious experience and earnestness of Plotinus which gave vitality to the Neo-Platonist movement. He made religious experience a criterion of truth. Like Jesus, he believed that his highest state-

---

[1] Cf. Burnet, *Greek Philosophy*, I, p. 168. The philosophy of Plotinus " is nothing more than the ecstatic experience rationalized " (Stewart, *Plato's Doctrine of Ideas*, p. 160).

[2] Cf. Dodds, p. 63 n.

ments about the possibilities of the life of the Spirit were referable to and verifiable by experience. By prompting man to taste the joys of possession by God now he would strengthen his endeavours to realize man's nature in actualizing the potentially divine within him. Plotinus would have his philosophy conceived as the most practical thing in the world for earnest men. He would enable the soul to enjoy foretastes of the blessedness of return ' to the Father and the dear dear Homeland.' He indicates a double method of leading fallen souls back to their source, by revealing to them the shame of their present desires and so bringing home to them their sorry plight, and then by reminding them of their race and primal high dignity, for ' our soul did not descend in its entirety: something of it always remains in the spiritual world.' [1]

Greek philosophy was the supreme and perennial Western contribution to religion as that of the East had been the redemptive Mystery-cults and the high morality and monotheism of Judaism. Yet this profound revelation to Greece was not qualified for a catholic destiny as a religion, not merely because of the obviously less extensive appeal of an intellectual and rational system with a mysticism going hand in hand with knowledge, but for two other reasons: (1) Because the Greek lovers of wisdom did not feel a moral necessity laid upon them of carrying the fruit of their search for knowledge as a message to the masses, and in fact they frankly confessed the impossibility of uplifting mankind at large by converting them into lovers of wisdom. The God of Platonism was difficult to find and more difficult to declare to all, and the God of Stoicism was too unsympathetic and too involved in the cosmic process himself. The missionary impulse never became a moral passion with the philosophers; few were the chosen, and the many were not called, save by the street-preachers of the Stoics and the mendicant friars of the Cynics.

[1] *En.* IV. 8, 8.

(2) Greek philosophy was one of the most eloquent expressions of man as seeking God near and within, and finding him because of his native kinship with God and the unity of divine and human, but it was relatively weak in that correlative aspect of religious comfort emphasized by Christianity that God is seeking and finding men. The Soul loves and seeks God rather than God seeks and loves the Soul.

CHAPTER V

THE MYSTERY-RELIGIONS

THE third main religious refuge was the type of religion known as the Mystery-Religions or Sacramental Religions, which stressed the approach to Deity through rite and liturgy after a severe probation and an oath pledging to secrecy. The Mysteries presented immense variety [1] both in detail and in outlook, but may be brought under a common denominator in their agreement on the view of man as having a divine element from a higher world imprisoned within, which must be released to ascend to its heavenly source, on the necessity of solemn initiation for salvation, the need of cathartic rites to wash away sin, the impartation of sacramental grace, the participation in or repetition of the experiences of the Deity, the uplift of communion or even identification with the Deity, the sure promise of immortality to the members of their religious fraternities, contrasted with the sad destiny awaiting those who neglected to avail themselves of their salutary sacraments. The gamut of differences among the Mysteries was as great as that obtaining in Christendom to-day, when adherents of the Greek Orthodox Church with its lovely symbolism and the members of the Society of Friends, or the members of the imperial Roman Communion, with its

[1] Cf. Anrich, *Das antike Mysterienwesen*, p. 24. Ch. Lécrivain (Daremberg et Saglio, *Dictionnaire*, III. 2137a) classifies thus: (1) " fêtes mystiques avec ou sans initiation," especially Dionysiac; (2) " mystères complets," especially the Kabiri, Isis, Eleusinian; (3) " mystères de thiases," the cults of Sabazios, Adonis, Attis, Cybele, Bendis, Cotytto; (4) " mystères orphiques." For a summary of the chief Mysteries see Nicola Turchi, *Le Religioni misteriosofiche del mondo antico*, chs. III-IX; R. Pettazzoni, *I Misteri*, pp. 41-281, Cumont *Religions orientales*.

elaborate ceremonial and appeal to the imagination through the sense, and the Presbyterians equally claim, and equally justify, their title to be called Christians. There were both public and private Mysteries, parochial and ecumenical. The pages of Pausanias, for example, abound in references to local Greek Mysteries. Each great type of Mystery admitted numerous developments and modifications both in East and West. Mithraism, for example, cannot be proved to have maintained in the West the rite of the *Mithrakana* which survives in Parseeism to-day. On account of the absence of an authoritative Mystery-Catholicism each Mystery permitted itself certain enchoric licences, as to-day in South Italy and Sicily many local Madonnas attract the devotion of the inhabitants because each is endowed with some special parochial miraculous power or territorial patronage. In some Mysteries the rites were orgiastic and bloody; in others they had become dignified sacraments. In some magic was more apparent and more in vogue than in others. Some Mysteries overstepped their primitive boundaries and entered upon universal dominion, and local secret societies evolved into universal religious institutions. For example, the local telluric secret society possessing the magic key to the fertility of the Rarian plain became the most eminent of the Greek Mysteries, ' the universal shrine of the world ' as Aristides names it, which for over a thousand years supported the faith in immortality and called forth eloquent expressions of gratitude from all parts of the Greek world.

Pre-eminent among these cults were the Orphic and Pythagorean fraternities; those of the Great Mother and Attis; the Egyptian Lord Serapis and Queen Isis; the Syrian Baals and Adonis; the Samothracian Kabiri; the Persian Mithra; the Greek Eleusinia; the Gnostic fraternities; the Phrygian Sabazios; the *Dea Syria* and her satellites; Dionysos; the theosophical Hermeticists. These and similar Mystery-cults were the most popular

7

means of satisfying the ardent desire for *soteria* and of maintaining the democratic spirit in religion. Like certain types of Christianity, chiefly African, they did not require men to reason or encourage them to ask questions, but only ' to enter into a certain frame of mind ' and to believe and to hold a vicarious faith by acceptance of assurances of infallible hierophants in a sacred succession. They had their message—and a comprehensive one—to the burdened minds of the age. To those moving nervously in a world disturbed by puissant demons they promised union with a deity to whom even the demons were servants. To those burdened by matter and the evils of dualism they vouchsafed a way of escape and of exaltation in ecstasy and enthusiasm and liberating psychopathic emotionalism. To those " servile to skyey influence " they effected *henosis* with a cosmic deity to whom the astral gods and the elements were in submission. To those overwhelmed by the sense of finitude they opened ' the path to the stars ' or secured participation in the life of the deity. To those oppressed by the dread of death they imparted demortalizing sacraments guaranteeing immortality through deification. To uneasy consciences they brought the assurance of divine favour [1] and indulgence or the comfort of a confessional.[2] For the dying a *viaticum* was provided and prayers and promises for the closing hours.

Among further services rendered to the ancient world by the Mysteries, mention should be made of the fact that they made the ancient world familiar with the possibility and necessity of a rebirth conceived as a quasi-spiritual, quasi-magical operation. Such regeneration bestowed upon the recipient a new divine substance. He underwent some mysterious change, a metamorphosis

[1] For the ram as a sin-offering in the Kabiri cult, vide Kroll, *Sam. Kabeiroi* in Pauly-Wissowa, *Real-Ency.* X, 1427.

[2] Cf. Steinleitner, *Die Beicht im Zusam. mit d. sakralen Rechtspflege in der Antike*, pp. 110-23.

whereby he was endowed with deathlessness and put on immortality. The Mystes became a supernatural being of immortal substance.

The Mysteries were the first religions to remove all gentile and social barriers and to declare that there is neither slave nor master, Greek nor barbarian, neither male nor female [1] in religious privileges. They enfranchised the masses religiously and fostered the democratic spirit in the Pagan world as the Synagogue did in the Jewish world. They not only denationalized religion, but they made religion a matter of personal choice, rendering it at once universal and individual, cosmic and personal. A man was no longer born into a religion, but entered it of his own volition, choosing his God and his cult. It is indisputable that the Mysteries in fostering personal religion intensified faith in the possibility of an intimate and mystic communion with the Deity, and made escape from sin a serious quest. They tutored men in the high faith that they might be ' partakers of the divine nature ' ; ' thou shalt be God instead of mortal.' They were the first to bring men together in mystic religious brotherhoods, and from the days of Alexander the Great voluntary associations for religious purposes have been a decisive factor in history.[2]

Stoicism had inculcated the idea of humanity as a mystic organism, all of the same origin and divine parentage sharing the same reason, but the Mystery-Religions limited this corporate idea and so qualified the solidarity of mankind through their exclusiveness, that is, they gave rise to a new conception of vast importance in the history of religion, the conception of a mystic exclusive supernatural society held together by sacramental bonds and drawing its life from common channels of grace, and the members of such a society

---

[1] Cf. Poland, *Gesch. d. griech. Vereinswesens*, p. 20 ff.; Foucart, *Mystères d'Eleusis*, p. 67.

[2] Cf. Legge, *Forerunners and Rivals*, I, p. 27.

were ' members one of another ' rather than of the brotherhood of Nature.[1]

The Mysteries also exercised an immense influence in the great syncretistic movement which blended East and West and prepared the ancient world for the most syncretistic religion, Christianity. They were of great historical significance in that " they provided an opportunity for the evolution of new religious ideas." [2] In the isolation of the individual the Mysteries through their social fellowship imparted a new dignity to the life of the humblest by the recognition of their personal worth and by the opportunities offered for self-expression. These Mystery fraternities were scattered all over the Graeco-Roman world and with the Synagogue furnished a model to the Christian house-churches; but as the converts after the first generation came overwhelmingly from the Pagan guilds rather than from the Synagogue, it was only natural that they should transfer the guild system into their new faith and adapt the guilds to Christian practices. These guilds were specially numerous and influential in the great centres of the Pauline mission-field. Indeed, the Christian Agape or ' love-feast ' was modelled more after the pattern of the guild common meals than after any other form of social religion. These fellowship meetings became centres of enthusiastic propaganda. They lifted the lowliest above the transiency and misery of the present order; they opened the highest offices to the humblest member; they were the harbingers of new social values. Like Christianity and Judaism, they were of immense significance in inculcating the dignity of labour, the duty of self-help and of mutual service. The Mysteries removed God from the realm of the transcendental to intimate fellow-

[1] " The Catholic conception of sacraments as bonds uniting religious communities and as channels of grace flowing from a corporate treasury was as certainly part of the Greek Mystery-Religions as it was foreign to Judaism " (Inge, Outspoken Essays, 2nd ser. p. 227).

[2] A. D. Nock, The Historical Importance of Cult-Associations, in Class. Rev. 1924, XXXVIII, p. 105b.

ship with man in his needs. The Mystery Deity granted theophanies and immediate assurance of salvation. Unlike the God of Jewish and Platonic thought, and unlike the God of the Greek *Compendium of Theology* who can as little suffer as rejoice, the Mystery Deities were conceived as suffering [1] and entering into fellowship with man in a *sympatheia*. By identification, deification, demortalizing, or mystic marriage the devotee could become one with the God in his death and resurrection.

The Mysteries were thus the popular allies of Greek mystical philosophy: they accomplished for the masses through their symbolism what the higher philosophy did for the élite. This intense desire for exalting union with the Divine accounts for the vogue of Dionysos as the most typical [2] Mystery God who had first offered to the West identification with himself. With this conception may be compared the Pauline doctrine of the Christ-Pneuma, which confers an indestructible character upon the Christian, but the Pauline doctrine is based on a faith towards which the Mysteries groped but of which they fell immeasurably short. Nearer to the conception of the Mysteries is that of Justin that the eating of consecrated bread and drink effects a change in our flesh and blood leading to incorruptibility, even guaranteeing the resurrection of the body. But we have evidence that in this mysterious borderland where the magical impinges on the spiritual and the boundaries between immateriality and corporeity are left indeterminate, there obtained as wide divergences in the apprehension of the new life of the regenerated and the means and mode thereof as in Christian reflection upon the relation of ritual transaction to spiritual results; as, for example, between the Pauline mystic doctrine of

[1] On a Gnostic gem, Orpheus is represented as stretched on a cross: Eisler, *Orpheus*, pl. xxxi.

[2] " Keinen Gott sucht der antike Mensch so innerlich zu erfassen " (Poland, *ib*. p. 67).

baptism and the post-Pauline laver of regeneration, or as between the Fourth Gospel conception of the Lord's Supper and that of Ignatius or Irenaeus.

These were religions of faith rather than of works; the ascent of the soul was guaranteed not by its native powers but by supernatural expedients in the hands of sacerdotal purveyors. The divine within man was released by correct ritual and gnosis, and communion with God was secured, on the whole, not so much ethically as emotionally.

Although the Mysteries were most tolerant and showed amazing hospitality to one another and their members were so catholic in their tastes that they made assurance of salvation doubly sure by undergoing initiation into several Mystery fraternities, these religions propagated in the ancient world the High Church principle or cult-exclusiveness [1] which was destined in its long career to exercise a malign and divisive influence in Christianity. The thesis of Cyprian,[2] ' without the Church no salvation,' was largely the adoption of the exclusiveness of the Mysteries that without initiation or incorporation by Sacrament in the membership of a sacred society which secured fellowship with its deity there could be no salvation. So far as our knowledge goes, the Orphics were the first to enunciate this principle of exclusiveness. All were not candidates for salvation, merely those who lived the Orphic life, observed the Orphic rites, and secured their passwords for the hereafter—for the rest, they were to lie in mud in Tartarus and undergo dreadful torments and suffer reincarnation. It should be added, however, that the Mysteries were more tolerant than Christianity. Since even in the twentieth century neither the ordinary members nor the priests of the more exclusive varieties of Christianity may be buried beside each other in the same " consecrated " ground, it is worth remembering that even the priests and high

[1] Cf. Lobeck, *Aglaophamus*, p. 272.
[2] But cf. Origen, *Hom. in Jos*. III. 6.

officials of the Mysteries feared so little the posthumous
contagion of their competitors in rival cults that they
could without offence be buried side by side and on
their epitaphs proclaim this fact to the world.[1] There
were also other graveyards apparently as exclusive as
the Christian, as, for example, for the Bacchic dead.[2]

This type of religion, like Christianity, divided mankind into the saved and the unsaved, the ' thrice blessed '
initiates and the uninitiated who die without the ' better
hope.' Part of the appeal was that common to a type
of Christianity in the same age, and even now—the in-
eluctability of punishment hereafter for those disobedient
to the preaching. Indeed the dreadful apparatus of the
Christian mediaeval hell pourtrayed so graphically in
Dante owed much to the ingenuity of the imagination
of Orphics, Pythagoreans, and other adherents of the
Mysteries in devising torments for the non-initiated.
The assurance of the initiates concerning their own
future was proportionate to their dreadful certainty concerning the uninitiated—a feature also of early Christian
apologetic which seems so strange to the modern reader.

In the Mystery-Religions outward signs and psychopathic outbreaks and ecstatic conditions were regarded
as indicative of religious experience, as in early popular
Christianity. The emotional exaltation brought about
as a result of tense expectancy, prudent sacerdotal suggestion, the contagion of other worshippers, fasting and
ascetic asperities and physical stimuli, was highly prized.
It was in competition with the psychic experiences and
miracles of these cults that Christianity appealed for
authentication to ' signs and wonders and powers ' and
' distributions of the Spirit.'

These sacramental religions are of direct interest to
every student of the history of Christianity. Not only

[1] Orelli-Henzen, *Inscript. lat. ampl. sel. collectio,* 6042; Réville,
Religion à Rome sous les Sévères, p. 92; Dill, *Roman Society,* p. 610,
n. 2.

[2] *Notizie degli Scavi,* 1905, p. 378; Leipoldt, *Religion in der Umwelt
des Urchristentums,* no. 173.

were they in the ascendant during the centuries of the struggles of early Christianity, but they attracted the largest number of religiously-minded men. / In the protracted conflict between national and universal religion and in the liberation of religion from political bonds to become a matter of personal choice, " all the religions advancing from the Orient rendered pioneer service to Christianity." [1] They have not only left their permanent mark upon our religion, but they so operated upon it and upon the mentality of the New Testament world that they effected the transformation of Christianity into a mystery-esoteric religion of their own order,[2] though, of course, with the vast difference arising from the connexion of Christianity with history through the person of Jesus, and the difference in the evolution between an historical religion and mythical cults. Yet they contributed to the preparation for and modification of Christianity as the religion of Europe, so that " it was as a Mystery-Religion that Europe accepted Christianity." [3] They formed one of the chief environmental

[1] Wendland, Hell.-röm. Kultur, 2nd-3rd ed. p. 254.

[2] On the vexed question of the extent to which Christianity took on the character of a Mystery-Religion cf., e.g., on opposite sides, Loisy, Les Mystères païens et le Mystère chrét., and Clemen, Einfluss d. Mysterienreligionen auf das älteste Christentum. Clemen, p. 82, cites with approval Heinrici, " Fragt man nach dem Gesamtcharakter des Urchristentums, so könnte es eher eine Antimysterienreligion genannt werden als eine Mysterienreligion," and concludes, " Ein tiefergehender Einfluss der griechischen Mysterienreligionen auf das Christentum beginnt erst im Gnostizismus."

We cannot adopt either extreme conclusion. Christianity from at least the post-Pauline period took on increasingly the character of a Mystery-Religion, but with the differences necessitated by its historical association with the person of Jesus. Pettazzoni is nearer the truth than Clemen or Loisy: " Il resultato fu che il cristianesimo, essenzialmente affine sotto certi rispetti ai misteri (ultranazionalismo, interiorità, individualismo, soteriologismo) finì per assumere formalmente l'aspetto di un mistero; e dai misteri tuttavia per altri rispetti essenzialmente diverso (fondazione storica, assenza di miti, monoteismo, spirito esclusivistico), si mise contro di essi e finì per vincerli " (I Misteri, p. 328).

[3] Inge, Outspoken Essays, p. 227. " Christianity was always, at least in Europe, a Mystery-Religion " (Lake, Earlier Epistles of St. Paul, p. 215).

factors of early Christianity. They were one of the main coefficients in the gradual Orientalization of the West, which persuaded the West to give its loyalty to an Aramaic gospel. They fostered new and profound religious cravings and stirred up high hopes which Christianity alone could adequately satisfy. Indeed the conquest of the Graeco-Roman world by the Mysteries was one stage [1] in the conquest of that same world by Christianity; the success of these Eastern cults was a promise of the success of Christianity. They supplied Christianity in its Hellenistic mission-field with a soteriological vocabulary and ideas which proved both fruitful and of lasting value. Christianity derived in a great measure from the Mysteries the ideas of secrecy and esoteric privileges in religion, and it was also tutored in the use of symbolism in worship. Christian baptism, at first the immersion of responsible adults, was soon extended in the form of sprinkling infants, so that the children of Christians should not suffer a serious disadvantage compared with the children of the members of the Mystery-Churches in which children [2] of tender years were permitted to receive the privileges of initiation with all the blessings for this life and beyond accruing to initiation. One chief source of that distorting asceticism, which from the first generation seduced Christianity away from the health and sanity of Jesus' religion, was to be found in cults which accepted the dualism of flesh and spirit, soul and matter, and required the most rigorous abstinences and self-torture. The

---

[1] "The change from old Roman to Graeco-Roman gods, the rise of the Eastern religions, and the triumph of Christianity, are thus successive steps in an orderly progression" (Showerman, *The Great Mother of the Gods*, p. 326).

[2] Cf. for Eleusinian usage, Foucart, *Mystères d'Eleusis*, p. 274 ff. For a child-priest of seven, cf. *I.G.* XIV, 1449. One of the paintings in the Villa Item outside Pompeii represents a child-priest officiating by reading from a roll in a scene of initiation; cf. De Petra, *Notizie d. Scavi*, 1910, p. 140 ff.; Macchioro, *Zagreus*, p. 117, and plates facing p. 134, or *Journal of Rom. Studies*, III. Cf. further instances in Anrich, *Das antike Mysterienwesen*, p. 55.

devotee of Isis, who on bleeding knees would wend her way through the Campus Martius to take her ritualistic bath in the waters of the frozen Tiber, was the forerunner of many a Christian penitent.

The immense success of the Mysteries may still be gauged by the numerous references in ancient literature, by the countless and ever-increasing archaeological remains, by the numerous places of worship still known, the relentless persecution by organized Christianity, and the unsparing terms of denunciation of the Christian apologists. The double appeal of the Mysteries both to the masses and to the cultured proves that they were more than mere pantomimic representations.

The millennial reign of these religions witnesses to their satisfying to some extent the needs of very different periods. Thus Orphism with its amazing powers of absorption and assimilation [1] had a history of about two thousand years.[2] The Great Mother was known in the Greek world from the fifth century B.C. and held her place till practically the collapse of ancient civilization, and when she passed she bequeathed her titles and honours to the Christian Virgin-Mother.[3] Adonis entered Athens before the end of the fourth century B.C., and was celebrated with great pomp in the cultured city of Alexandria in the second century A.D. Sabazios entered Greece during the Peloponnesian War and Men in the fourth century B.C. Mithra, after a long history in his

[1] " The greatest characteristic of this development [the Orphic movement] was always its readiness to incorporate elements possibly alien to the original Dionysos mystery, till it finally takes all Greek religious tradition within its scope " (M. Tierney, *A New Ritual of the Orphic Mysteries*, in *Classical Q.* XVI, p. 77). For this Orphic document from the recently discovered Gurob papyrus, vide also Kern, *Orphica*, p. 101.

[2] Dieterich, *Kleine Schriften*, p. 479.

[3] The similarities between the Mother of the Gods and the Mother of God were not unnoticed by the ancients. It is a striking fact that it was Ephesus, the chief capital of the Phrygian and Hittite Great Mother, that gave the formula ' Mother of God ' to the Church at the Council of Ephesus (431), and here too are found the earliest traces of the cult of the Christian Virgin-Mother.

native Iran, reigned in the Roman world for half a
millennium and challenged Christianity to conflict for
the throne of the Caesars. Isis entered the Peiraeus in
the fourth century B.C. and held her sway till the end of
the fourth century A.D. Serapis, the brilliant creation
of the first Ptolemy, with a view to uniting his Greek
and his Egyptian subjects in a deity including both as
' Serapis alone is Zeus (God),' won thousands of devoted
worshippers during the intervening centuries till the
destruction of the Serapeum of Alexandria, 391 A.D.
Gnosis was for over five centuries the path to salvation
sought by inquiring souls. Eleusis for over twelve centuries stood as the catholic shrine of the Greek world
and dispensed its sacraments of immortality till destroyed
by Christian fanaticism in 397. Another evidence of the
strength of the Mysteries was their ability to transform
Christianity into a religion of their own order and compel
it to use their terms and teach it to claim their strange
and inexplicable potencies for its rites. So influential
and popular was this type of religion that but for Paul's
resolute stand and catholic attitude on the foreign-
mission question in the first great cause of division in
Christianity one cannot see what other type of religion
could have won the allegiance of the West.

And this success is all the more arresting inasmuch as
it was achieved without the four incalculable advantages
enjoyed by Christianity in (1) the thrilling moral power
of the person of Jesus, (2) the decision of Greece to
consecrate her whole-hearted devotion and peerless
genius to Christ, (3) the organizing genius of the Bishops
of Rome, and (4) the fact that Christianity made a new
beginning untrammelled by naturalism and venerable
but perplexing rites, and without being held to strict
account with the past.

The Mysteries were passionately emotional cults which
did not always aim at or succeed in guiding emotion
into ethical channels, and in this respect were infinitely
inferior to Christianity. In their excessive sacrament-

arianism they ignored character and never produced an ethical code as did Judaism, Stoicism, and Christianity.

By intensifying feeling, however, they afforded an uplift [1] to man from his finitude and prepared him for the fuller and more healthy participation in the higher mysticism regnant in the first centuries among Pagans and Christians. The extant testimonies of the initiates with their warmth of devotional language deserve credence as expressions of intimate personal experiences. There were exultations of joy and raptures of religious emotion at initiation which were to the mystae corroboratory experiences and of which they could speak only in language akin to ' what eye hath not seen nor ear heard.' The psychopathic outbreaks and revivalistic phenomena familiar in primitive Christianity had their parallels among the initiates. The *glossolalia* or ecstatic speaking with tongues so prized among the early Christians had its counterpart in the *mania* of the Pythia of the Delphic Apollo, as also in the *enthousiasmos* characteristic of the Dionysiac worship. The visions [2] and trances familiar to the initiates are no longer denied in view of similar experiences among the Christians and in the light of the investigations of modern psychology. Some of these visions doubtless were rather hallucinations or were artificially induced, but delusions were not confined to the ancient mystae. St. John of the Cross knew of folk who fancied they were talking with God when they were merely holding a conversation with themselves. Origen knew of ' many ' instances in which dreams or visions caused by ' some kind of spirit ' produced conversions.[3]

[1] On ecstasy or tense exaltation of the emotions in the Mysteries cf. especially de Jong, *Das antike Mysterienwesen,* pp. 180 ff., 243 ff., 272 ff. *et passim; id., De Apuleio Isiac. mysteriorum teste,* p. 99 ff.; Graillot, *Culte de Cybèle,* p. 187; Rohde, *Psyche,* pp. 255-60, 285 etc.

[2] On epiphanies and visions in the Mysteries, cf. Dibelius, *Die Isisweihe bei Apuleius,* p. 25 ff.; De Jong, *Das antike Mysterienwesen,* 2nd ed. pp. 244 ff., 301 ff., 317 ff.

[3] *Contra Celsum,* I. 46.

Practically all men, according to Tertullian, receive their knowledge of God from visions. He narrates [1] how ' a sister amongst us ' enjoyed ecstatic visions at the weekly worship; she held conversations with the angels and even with the Lord Himself and saw and heard *sacramenta*. Cyprian also recognized the reality of visions in the direction of life. Eusebius records the conversion of Basilides, a pupil of Origen, owing to a dream-vision in which Potamiaena appeared putting a crown on his head.[2] The culmination of tense emotion at Christian baptism as the entry upon a new life was the Christian counterpart to the reassuring and exhilarating emotions of Pagan initiation. Indeed part of the Christian ritual and practices was taken over directly from Paganism.

As illustrating [3] the emotional exaltation in the Mysteries and also indicating the privileges possible to the spiritually prepared, the passage in Plutarch may be cited in which he compares the soul at death to the condition at initiation: [4]

' When it undergoes such an experience as those do who are initiated into great mysteries. Thus death and initiation closely correspond, word to word, and thing to thing. At first there are wanderings and laborious circuits, and journeyings through the dark, full of misgivings where there is no consummation; then before the very end, come terrors of every kind, shivers and trembling, and sweat, and amazement. After this a wonderful light meets the wanderer; he is admitted into pure meadow-lands, where are voices, and dances, and the majesty of holy sounds and sacred visions. Here the newly initiate, all rites completed, is at large.'

But all initiates did not attain the highest possible experience, as Proclus testifies:

[1] *De Anima,* 9.   [2] *H.E.* VI. 5, 6.
[3] For other testimonies cf. Halliday, *Pagan Background,* pp. 256-74; Angus, *Mystery-Religions,* p. 238 ff.
[4] Stobaeus, *Flor.* 120, 28; Meineke, IV, 107; Turchi, *Fontes Hist. Mysteriorum,* p. 81; tr. by Prickard, *Selected Essays of Plutarch,* p. 215.

' For who would not agree that the mysteries and the initiations lead the souls upward away from this life of matter and mortality and bring them into contact with the gods, that they cause to disappear the disturbance which has crept in from unreason, by intellectual illumination, and that they eject the undefined and the darkness from those who are being initiated, by the light of the gods? But nevertheless nothing deters the vulgar from not suffering all kinds of distortions of these things and from misusing the benefits and the powers of them according to their own disposition towards the worse, whereby they are set aside from the gods and from the true holy worship, and are borne into the life of sensation and unreason.' [1]

Beside the cultivation of the emotional life in connexion with religion, the greatest service rendered by the Mysteries was in their gospel of life and immortality to the multitudes who were little touched by philosophical arguments on behalf of the hope of man. ' Beautiful truly is the Mystery given us by the blessed Gods ; Death is for us mortals no longer a bane but a blessing,' is the confession of an Eleusinian hierophant.[2] Cicero [3] affrms that the Greek Mysteries have given ' not only good cause why we should live joyously but also a better hope in death.' The Great Mother and Attis were invoked as ' guardians of soul and mind.' [4] Attis becomes the assurance of a resurrection and appears as bursting the bars of death.[5] The Orphic dead passed to bliss as ' offspring of Heaven, of immortal race.' Their spiritual kin, the Pythagoreans, were assured of safe-conduct across the waters of death and a gracious welcome from the God of Light.[6] The *Taurobolium* guaranteed ' re-

---

[1] *Comm. in remp.* I, p. 75 (Kroll), tr. by Halliday, p. 274.

[2] *Ephem. Arch.* 1883, p. 82.

[3] *De Legg.* II, 14, 36; *In Verrem*, V. 72, 187.

[4] ' Animae mentisque custodes,' *C.I.L.* VI, 499; Pettazzoni, *I Misteri*, p. 137.

[5] *Bull. d. corr. hell.* 1895, p. 538.

[6] Cf. Carcopino, *La basilique Pythag.* p. 292 ff.; E. Strong and N. Jolliffe, *Journal of Hellenic Studies*, XLIV, p. 103 f.

birth for eternity.' On the tombs of those departed in the faith of the Egyptian Mysteries could be read, ' May Osiris give thee the water of refreshment,' and ' Be of good cheer with Osiris,' ' May Isis grant thee the holy water of Osiris.' [1] Mithra-Helios assured his devotee not only of ' a cable and sure anchorage during life,' but on departure ' thou shalt go with a good hope.' [2] As early as the seventh century B.C. the Goddess-mother of Eleusis imparted the faith: ' Happy is he of mortals on earth who has seen those Mysteries; but the initiate who has no part in these holy things cannot, when dead and down in the murky gloom, have like portion of such blessings.' [3] Initiation accompanied by righteousness had rich reward, ' for to us alone there is sun and cheerful light who have been initiated and lived piously.' [4]

The Mystery-Religions are certain more and more to engage the attention of students of the evolution of Christianity as being one of the chief channels whereby sacramentarianism [5] entered the Western world to dominate two millenniums of the religion which arose from the penetration of the spirit of Jesus into humanity. Christianity hastened, in a world taught to esteem sacral acts, to equip itself with such rites as requisite to enjoyment of communion with God. Contemporary magic was refined into sacramental efficacy. The robes of the Mystery-priest were worn and the privileges of the Mystery-hierophant appropriated by the Christian priest. The pontiffs of the Mysteries anticipated the Christian

---

[1] *I.G.* XIV, 2098. [2] Julian, *Caesars,* 336, C.

[3] *Hymn to Demeter,* 480 ff.; Turchi, *Fontes,* p. 79.

[4] Aristophanes, *Frogs,* 455.

[5] '' Just as Jewish Christians took with them the whole framework of apocalyptic Messianism and set the figure of Jesus within it, so the Greeks took with them the whole scheme of the Mysteries with their sacraments, their purifications and ' fasts,' their idea of a mystical brotherhood, and their doctrine of ' salvation ' ($\sigma\omega\tau\eta\rho\iota\alpha$ is essentially a mystery word), the membership in a divine society, worshipping Christ as the patronal deity of their Mysteries '' (Inge, *Outspoken Essays,* 1st ser. p. 227).

hierarchy in seeking political [1] power and in using religious associations for other than religious purposes. Christianity soon claimed magical potencies for its rites similar to those claimed by its most catholic competitors. The God of the Mysteries, like the Deity of the larger sections of Christendom to-day, was approached properly and most securely through sacral acts of immense but mysterious intrinsic value enhanced by the official character of the ministrants.

[1] Cf. one of the graffiti from Pompeii: " Cn. Helvium aed. Isiaci universi rog(ant) " (*C.I L.* IV. 787, and *ib.* 1011).

CHAPTER VI

CHRISTIANITY

INTO a world of seething hopes and impalpable yearnings
and religious ferment, into a mystery-laden atmosphere,
Christianity entered as a new religion, new not in point
of time only, but in character and power, ' the spirit of
life in Christ Jesus,' and with a startling claim to possess
truth not through an idea or a theory of knowledge, but
in a person who ' bestowed on us light, who addressed
us as a father his sons, and saved us when perishing.' [1]
To a world seeking divine help it immediately proved
itself the very ' power of God ' to countless souls. It
wrought such a transformation in character that it
attracted attention as the best means of lifting man
above himself. The new faith had reaches far beyond
its competitors in its transmuting influences. ' He
opened the gates of Light to them who had been the
sons of darkness and of night, but had devoted themselves to become sons of the Light,' [2] was a confession
gratefully and joyously made by many. Though at first
a religion with no missionary outlook—the apostles and
its first adherents remaining in Jerusalem awaiting
the end of the world—Christianity became the most
aggressive missionary religion, spreading a network of
vigorous propagandist brotherhoods over the Mediterranean world, succeeding to a higher place than the
religion from which it sprang, and within three centuries
driving all others off the field [3] and superseding the
mightiest empire of antiquity.

In Christianity the spiritual forces of the Pagan world
found a new rallying-ground. It was in Christianity
ultimately that the creative powers and assimilative

[1] II Clement, *Ad Cor.* 1.   [2] Origen, *C. Celsum*, II, 67.
[3] Vide Origen's striking words, *ib.* II. 79.

8   93

energies of Graeco-Roman civilization became most alive
as the forerunner of modern civilisation. It met the
needs and satisfied the demands [1] of that age in breathless search for a new religion with a redemption at once
personal and cosmic, based on authority and revelation,
conspicuously other-worldly, promising cleansing and
supernatural aid, and envisaging a mystic humanity.
' What the soul is to the body, Christians are to the
world,' [2] was the assertion of an early apologist.

Christianity was a view of the world (*Weltanschauung*)
and a way of Life with the inestimable advantage over
all its competitors of possessing an historical [3] and personal centre in the person of Jesus, which saved nascent
Christianity from evaporation in excessive apocalytic
emotionalism, and which later, in the life-and-death
struggle between history and metaphysics in Gnosticism
and in the Christological controversies, preserved for
all ages a concrete convincing reality. This unique
Personality proved potent to awaken moral enthusiasm
and release spiritual powers in many lives and remain
the perennial means of renewal through the course of
Christian history. Jesus could never be presented as
an abstraction or reduced to a beautiful myth.

In an eminently practical age when incarnate
examples [4] of human perfection were sought as guides
to conduct and inspirations to high endeavour, it is
obvious that Christians had an immense superiority of
appeal in the character, life, and ideals of one who had
actually lived within recent times and died a martyr
death, ' crucified under Pontius Pilate.' When an
earnest Stoic could despairingly ask of his ideal Wise
Man ' Where is he to be found whom we have sought
so many ages ? ' [5] the Christians could point to one who

---

[1] Cf. Wendland, *Hell.-röm. Kultur*, p. 235 f.

[2] *Ep. ad Diognetum*, VI. 1.

[3] Cf. Ignatius, *Phil.* 8. Loisy, *Les Mystères païens*, p. 343 ff.

[4] ' Quia longum iter est per praecepta, breve et efficax per exempl'
(Seneca, *Ep.* VI. 5).

[5] Seneca, *De Tranq.* VII. 4; cf. Cic. *De Fin.* IV. 65; *Acad.* 145.

was not only Lord in the cult, but the Elder Brother in a numerous divine family (Romans viii. 34). The difference in point of appeal and relativity to everyday life stands out in stark contrast in the statements of two contemporaries, that of Plutarch,[1] ' This [Wise Man] is nowhere on earth nor has he ever been,' and that of the Prologue to the Fourth Gospel, ' The Logos became flesh.'

The *mythus,* or story of divine passion and victory and of man's redemption, has played an important rôle in the evolution of religious thought. In Christian theology the *myth* with its symbolic expression has either been harshly expelled as mere superstition or more generally been treated with undue respect as literal fact. Christian apologists treated all myths of their competitors and contemporaries as false or grotesque, while their own mythopoeic activities undertook to match or outstrip Pagan myths. Christian apologists also, even Augustine, insisted that Pagans accepted their myths literally—in the face of abundant evidence to the contrary extant to this day—and popular Christianity has ended by accepting its own myths in the same literal fashion. A religious *myth* may be the poetical and imaginative expression of truth, and Greek mythology has been found wonderfully suggestive of timeless truth. There is the truth of myth, and there is the truth of historical fact. And it is just here that Christians could point with a sense of triumph to their historical Master, who in the universality of His personality was superior to their historical examples like Socrates, and who in His historical tangibility was superior to their mythical Heracles and the Great Mother, and Serapis.[2] In the

---

[1] *De Com. not.* 33.

[2] " The initiates into the Mystery-Religions might believe themselves rooted and grounded in trust begotten of incommunicable personal experiences; the followers of Christ could produce the title-deeds of historic faith " (Carpenter, *Phases of Early Christianity,* p. 5. Cf. Kennedy, *St. Paul and the Mystery-Religions,* p. 213 f.).

myth of redemption the passion of Dionysos was symbolism or legend, but the passion of Jesus was real.
In the last analysis Jesus was an historical person whose
character needed no burnishing and whose ideals were
beyond criticism, but there never was a Mithra, and he
never slew the mystic sacramental bull. In the cults
of His competitors it was the religion that made the
myth and the deity, but it was Christ who made
Christianity, not Christianity who made Christ, however
much mythical elements were superimposed upon His
person.

In addition to possessing a creative personality
Christianity made its appearance in history with other
incalculable advantages, chief of which was the fact that
it made a new start in the world without the encumbrance
of a hoary past, which proved intractable to Judaism
Stoicism, and even to Neo-Platonism. Christianity was
not interested in reproducing a past world in some
glorious prime, but in giving birth to a new world
Christianity suffered from none of the disadvantages o
survivals of naturalism, nor was it hampered by a com
promising past, nor was it called upon to find new
explanations for grotesque and absurd though venerabl
usages, of the difficulties of which Plutarch is so keenly
conscious in his essay on Isis and Osiris. Nor was i
burdened with an entail of myths, repulsive or puerile
which must be courageously allegorized, as the Stoic
and Orphics did myths of the past, so as to elicit th
esoteric or spiritual meaning amid a mass of incredibl
literalism.

Its emergence on the scene when the general tren
of religion was toward syncretism and the amalgamatio
of faiths constituted a peril indeed to a new religior
but a source of strength to a religion with such an idea
as Jesus Christ and imbued with such a moral earnes
ness. The religious syncretism, the blending an
borrowing, assimilations and alliances among the re
ligions of the Mediterranean world, was a wonderf

preparation for and a decided advantage to Christianity,[1] though in the closing conflict it was also the last despairing opposition to the rapidly spreading faith. Christianity was more vitally and healthily syncretistic than Judaism and its competitors, and therefore able to borrow lavishly without suicidal results and able to assimilate forms of thought and methods of social cohesion to hand. Similarly, even the fiery energy of apocalyptism, the evanescence of which constituted a crisis, lent to its preachers a propagandist zeal and spiritual passion which awakened men to the eternal issues and called them to witness a mortal combat in the skies which affected every man. The impassioned appeal, the tender urgency, the breathless expectancy, the other-worldliness, caused earnest men to give ear to the ' good-news ' concerning human destiny. The prayer repeated at every service, ' May grace come and let this world pass away: come Thou, Lord (*maranatha*),' was but one symptom of that world-renouncing spirit which gave rise to the heroic temperament in which Christianity accomplished a social and religious revolution against heavy odds. The Kingdom of God was in line with the religious cosmopolitanism. And the threatening Great Assize, at which the books will be surely opened, made the eternal things more precious. Enthusiasm with self-control and humanism can move the world.

[1] " Die neue durch die Synkretismus aufgenommene Religiosität mit ihrer schwärmerischen Innigkeit, gestattete eine völlige Hingabe an Christus, ein Sichversenken in das einzigartige seines Wesens, das schliesslich seiner Religion zum Siege verhelfen musste " (*Relig. in Gesch. u. Geg.* V. 1055). " *Das Christentum ist eine synkretistische Religion.* Starke religiöse Motive, die aus der Fremde gekommen waren, sind in ihm enthalten und zur Verklärung gediehen, orientalische und hellenistische. Denn das ist das Charakteristische, wir dürfen sagen, das Providentielle, am Christentum, *dass es seine klassische Zeit in der weltgeschichtliche Stunde erlebt hat als es aus dem Orient in das Griechentum übertrat.* Darum hat es Teil an beiden Welten. So stark auch später das Hellenistische in ihm geworden ist, so ist doch das Orientaische, das ihm von Anfang an eignete, niemals ganz verschwunden " (Gunkel, *Zum relig. Verständnis d. N.T.* 2nd ed. p. 95).

Yet the Christians handicapped themselves by this proclamation, as unwise as it was confident, of an imminent society-ending catastrophe, which on the one hand tended to foster a perilous religiosity, and on the other to raise such obvious questionings as ' Where is the promise of His Coming, for since the Fathers died, everything remains as it was? '; which necessarily drew upon themselves the hostile attentions of the political powers of the time and gave rise to suspicions as to their citizenship in an earthly state, for the end of which they hoped and prayed.

Christianity, though an Oriental religion, found its future in the West, and has proved the most successful fusion of East and West, the blending of Semitic and Aryan hopes and aspirations. It fell heir to a rich heritage of religious language and religious ideas and associations. It reaped the advantages of the protracted propaganda of Jewish prophetism and Greek philosophy for monotheism. It discovered ready to hand a world-language, the Greek *koiné*, an efficient vehicle for its message; within a surprisingly few years from its origin and before our Gospels were written it was divinely guided to adopt this language and so linked its destiny with Hellenism.[1] In an age seeking divine revelations and respecting hoary antiquity in its religion it found ready to hand a collection of holy books written by another faith which could be used at once as the authoritative Bible of the new faith, a *corpus* so venerable and authoritative that the greatest of all the missionaries of Jesus would clinch nearly every argument in his controversial letters with an appeal to this book. There awaited its message—which overflowed all the ordinary resources of expression—a rich mysticism cultivated by the

---

[1] " There is hardly any fact which deserves to be turned over and thought over so much as this, that the religion of Jesus has never been able to root itself in Jewish or . . . upon Semitic soil. Certainly there must have been, and certainly there must be still, some element in this religion which is allied to the greater freedom of the Greek spirit '" (Harnack, *Expansion of Christianity*, I, p. 74).

suggestive sympathy of the Mysteries, by the propaedeutic symbolism of contemporary Judaeo-Alexandrianism and familiar in the empyreans of joy and spirituality in the philosophy of Neo-Platonism. It found the Stoa and the Synagogue prepared with a mature ethical system to be adapted and furthered by the Ecclesia ; and Platonism was ready to tutor it in its first attempts toward a theology and a philosophy. A ' gentler spirit ' awaited its advent—a wonderful preparation for the social revolution and humanitarian message of Christianity. A profound deepening of religious life preceded and ran concurrently with its spread.[1] It found men groping for God and seeking truth, and yearning for comfort and experimenting in quest of satisfaction. It heard the oracular souls, its harbingers and contemporaries, proclaiming a new inwardness prophetic of a deepening spirituality and a more responsible sense of personality, and asseverating ' all that is best for man lies beyond human power ; it can neither be given nor taken away,' [2] as ' My peace ' is not given ' as the world gives,' and ' your joy no man taketh away ' because enshrined at the centre of the personality. Its competitors were its allies in the affirmation that there is one pure cult, that of the pure soul, as in the lovely *Letter to Marcella* by Porphyry, and only one supreme method of worship, *deum colit qui novit*.[3]

If no religion ever came in such ' fullness of time ' or was planted in a more favourable milieu, no religion braved such perils when cast upon the stream of evolu-

[1] " Niemals lauschte die antike Menschheit gespannter auf die Offenbarungen der Gottheit als in jener Periode, zu deren Ende Jammer und Not noch lauter und eindringlicher beten lehrte. Das ganze Wesen jener Zeit wurzelt in der Religion und in ihrer Äusserungen " (Geffcken, *Der Ausgang d. griech.-röm. Heidentums*, in *N. Jahrb. f. d. klass. Alt.* XLI, p. 96).

[2] ' Quicquid optimum homini est, id extra humanam potentiam iacet; nec dari nec eripi potest ' (Seneca, *Ad Helv*. VIII. 4).

[3] ' He worships God who has come to know God ' (Seneca, *Ep*. 95, 47).

tion to become a world-religion. The waning of the enthusiastic apocalyptism and the delay of the Parousia, to the witnessing of which the apostolic preachers had pledged their converts, created a moral crisis of the first order, and had Christianity not been more than a revivalistic outbreak it should have perished with the crisis. Christians with some consternation realized that instead of being ' metamorphosed ' to glory, they were called upon to live in an uncomfortable world which they had hoped to abandon; that instead of witnessing a transcendent combat of spiritual forces in the air and hailing the victory of the conquering Christ over His superhuman adversaries, they were called upon to wage an incessant conflict within and with human foes without. Moreover, as a spiritual movement Christianity was called upon to experience the most acute internal opposing tendencies contending for mastery: to decide whether it was to remain a Jewish sect and out-Judaize Judaism in its exclusiveness, or to offer a religious home to mankind; whether to hearken to the bigotry of those who had known Jesus in the flesh, or to the larger visions of those who had not seen Him with the eyes of sense, but had believed and loved. When the question of the Gentile mission was forced upon it by the hard logic of facts or by the incidents of persecution, it was rent over the question as to the terms of admission of Gentiles to the privileges of the Messianic society. One of the outstanding features in Church history is the regularity with which the Church chose the *via media* between extreme positions. One of the earliest of such decisions was the choice between the chiliastic literalistic Ebionite gospel and the Gnostic gospel, and the Church chose neither, though it repudiated much of value from each. At least it decided against restricting itself after primitive precedent to being a Jewish sect, as also against becoming the most comprehensive and alluring theosophy. The principle of life maintained its continuity in evolution and identity of essential spirit, but the form changed almost beyond recognition. Indeed, as Harnack re-marks,[1] " primitive Christianity had to disappear in order that Christianity might remain."

In the universalism which Christianity attained through Paul [2] it offered no pre-eminence to the race and religion from which it sprang; in point of fact it meant the loss to the Jews of some of their most prized religious privileges. They were not as a people who had been ' leaders of the blind ' prepared to pay such a price, and so they found in expansive Gentile Christi-anity an ' offence.' Paul, who had so uncompromis-ingly opposed the Judaizing of Christianity, expressed the fond hope that this ' turning away ' to bring in ' the fullness of the nations ' would be only temporary to the end that ' all Israel will be saved.' Nevertheless the future of Christianity was destined to be determined not by the Aramaic mother Church of Jerusalem, but by the Gentile Church of Antioch. In fact, the universalism of Christianity was immensely furthered by the oppor-tune destruction of Jerusalem.

In this evolution from primitive to universal form the Christian movement suffered all the agonizing of the clarifying conflict between the literalists and the en-lightened, between the Judaizers and the Hellenizers, between the puritan and ascetic interpreters and the humanistic and aesthetic, between the ever-present and noisy ' weak brethren ' and the ' strong,' between the institutionalist with his rigid adherence to history and the mystic and philosopher who finds in the events of time and place mere expressions of the eternal ideas. Christianity early took on the character of a *complexus oppositorum,* which it retains.

[1] *What is Christianity?,* lect. I, p. 14.

[2] " It is true that Christianity never would have become a world-religion at all but for the inward experience of Saul of Tarsus, a typi-cally Hellenistic experience of individual soul-redemption. We may say truly that Saul of Tarsus never would have had this experience if he had not been born and bred on Gentile soil " (Bacon, *Christianity Old and New,* p. 95).

The problem of catholicizing a great spiritual religion is always serious, and it cannot be said that any great historical religion has wholly succeeded in bringing its message to the masses without making some concessions [1] to the weakness of average humanity. Many are called but few chosen, though the many may be uplifted by the experiences of the few. Jesus early discovered the colossal task of securing popularity for a religious appeal without contaminating its spirituality, purity, and inwardness, and its high demands for unselfish living, and He consistently turned away from a popularity resting on concessions to lower ideals. In the first days of spiritual fervour the messengers of the Cross had not felt this problem so acutely as their organizing successors, who were forced to recognize the difficulty noted by an observant Greek, that ' for the crowd of women and the uneducated masses ' ' there is need for the instrument of superstition which cannot be aroused without mystery and marvels.' Hence concessions were made at almost every point; for example, in the recognition of a lower and a higher ethical ideal, and of a double Christianity requiring the minimum from the masses or laity, and imposing the maximum upon the few or priestly caste; in finding room within Christianity for the notions and practices to which people were used, as when angels took over the mediatorial functions of demons, or when Christian rites were identified with the magic mystery-rites.

Yet every religious movement, in order to live, must strive to bring its message to the masses. The weakness of Greek philosophy was that it did not feel morally

---

[1] " It is unfortunately by no means true that there is a natural tendency for a higher religion to displace a lower, except at those rare flowering-times of the human spirit which come and pass unaccountably like the wind which bloweth where it listeth. A religion, as believed and practised, cannot be far in advance of the mental and moral capacity of its adherents. A religion succeeds, not because it is true, but because it suits its worshippers. It may be a superstition which has enslaved a philosophy " (Inge, *Platonic Tradition*, p. 14).

compelled,[1] like Hebrew prophetism and the Christian mission, to ' evangelize ' mankind at large. Christianity had qualifications for a catholic destiny and for a religion of humanity beyond its competitors. It was not by any fortuitous concourse of circumstances or by any happy historic accident that it won its way over its competitors, but because it outstripped them in the universality of its appeal, '' the enthusiasm of humanity,'' in its fulfilment of the moral values of Paganism, and in the number and combination of its elements of power and '' the congruity of its teaching with the spiritual nature of mankind.'' '' It was because it was true to the moral sentiments of the age, because it represented faithfully the supreme type of excellence to which men were then tending, because it corresponded with their religious wants, aims, emotions, because the whole spiritual being could thus expand and expatiate under its influence, that it planted its roots so deeply in the hearts of men.'' [2]

The progress of Christianity from a sect of Judaism to a catholic religion is marked within the Graeco-Roman era by various stages and conflicts in the advance from the religion of Jesus to the religion about Jesus, and from the religion about Jesus to a highly contentious metaphysical Christology concerning a pre-existent descending and ascending Lord. The battle of popular and orthodox faith against heretical *gnosis* and Montanist prophecy proved inconclusive, but faith won sufficiently to put an end to the absence of a dogmatic uniformity and to prepare for the days when faith

---

[1] '' Das ist klar, dass die kosmopolitische Tendenz des Christentums eine werbende Kraft besass, mit der die philosophischen und die in einer Gnosis gipfelnden synkretistischen Religionssysteme nicht konkurrieren konnten. . . . Die Liebe, der Paulus seinen Hymnus singt, hat mehr positive Kräfte entfaltet als der philosophische Humanitätsgedanke '' (Wendland, *Hell.-röm. Kultur,* 2nd-3rd ed. p. 233).

[2] Lecky, *Hist. of European Morals,* I, ch. iii. Cf. McGiffert, *Influence of Christianity in the Roman Empire,* p. 43: '' Its victory in the Roman Empire was fairly earned by sheer superiority.''

became practically synonymous with credulity and with submissive obedience to external authority. In another direction this progress was marked also by three stages which might be characterized as the popular, the philosophical, and the political, or as designated by Bishop Westcott [1] " the history of a threefold contest between Christianity and the Powers of the Old World, closed by a threefold victory," which he explains as " the Church and the Empire . . . met in the market and the house; they met in the discussions of the Schools; they met in the institutions of political government; and in each case the Church was triumphant." Thus Christianity asserted " its sovereign power among men by the victory of *common life,* by the victory of *thought,* by the victory of *civil organisation.*"

" The Christian victory of common life was wrought out in silence and patience and nameless agonies. It was the victory of the soldiers and not of the captains of Christ's army. But in due time another conflict had to be sustained, not by the masses, but by great men, the consequence and the completion of that which had gone before."

The religion of Jesus might have secured a spiritual, rather than a political, victory in the ancient world, but for the so-called conversion of Constantine and his elevation of Christianity by edict as practically the state religion and royal cult with the baneful alliance of throne and altar. This establishment of the State Church and the reinforcement of Caesarism with religious sanctions, which was later carried out more drastically by Theodosius and Justinian, were accompanied by the consequent full equipment of the Church with the sacerdotalism to which the peoples of the Empire, legislated into Christians, had been accustomed and by the external splendours with which a religion purchases popularity. Henceforth Christianity won its way partially by

[1] *Religious Thought in the West,* p. 195 ff.

persecution and by attempting to exterminate heretics and Pagans. It became easier to be a Christian than to remain a Pagan or a Jew; and safer to be orthodox than to risk being guilty of thinking. Conscientious objectors were henceforth treated as Christians had formerly been treated for their ' sheer obstinacy.' No one could have dreamed that the Christians, who had themselves suffered so much from persecution and protested so vehemently against the injustice and futility of persecution, would so quickly have turned persecutors [1] and surpassed their Pagan predecessors in fanatical savagery and efficiency,[2] utterly oblivious of the Beatitude of the Divine Master (Matt. v. 10, 44, 45). It became ominous for subsequent history that the first General Council of the Church was signalized by bitter excommunications and banishments. Christians, having acquired the art of disposing of hostile criticism by searching out and burning the objectionable books of their Pagan adversaries, learned to apply the same method to the works of such groups of Christians as were not in power or in favour for the time; when this method proved unsatisfactory, they found it expedient to burn their bodies. The chained skeleton [3] found in the Mithraic chapel at Sarrebourg testifies to the drastic means employed by Christians in making the truth conquer otherwise than by the methods taught and exemplified by the Founder. The stripping and torture to death with oyster-shells in a Christian church and the subsequent mangling of limb from limb of Hypatia, the noblest representative of Neo-Platonism of her day, by the violent Nitrian monks and servitors of a Christian

[1] A papyrus of May or June A.D. 335 (?) (1914 in Bell & Crum, *Jews and Christians in Egypt,* pp. 53-71) has preserved a first-hand account by Callistus of the cruelties and indignities inflicted by Athanasius and his orthodox followers upon fellow-Christians of the Meletian schism.

[2] Halliday remarks: " Whereas pagan persecution failed to crush Christianity, Christian persecution of Paganism succeeded " (*Pagan Background,* p. 321).

[3] Cumont, *Textes et M.,* p. 519; *Mysteries of Mithra,* p. 204 f.

bishop, and probably with his connivance, were sympto-
matic and prophetic of that intolerance and fanaticism
which Christianity was to direct throughout the centuries
upon its disobedient members and troublesome minorities
until the day—yet to dawn—when a purer, more convincing because more spiritual, Christianity gains " the
consent of happier generations, the applause of less
superstitious ages."

The empire was partially Christianized and the Church
partially paganized. The imperialism of Rome rather
than the freedom [1] and educational value of the Greek
tradition generally triumphed with and after Constantine.
With this nominal conversion of the empire, the new
Roman power, based on a Semitic religion for which
Greece had so largely won the victory, began that process
whereby the Roman genius for order and organization
in government acquired a vaster and more permanent
dominion through religion than it had lost in the political
and military fields. The bishops of Rome acquired a
more lasting authority than that secured by their imperial
predecessors and by the legions of Rome.

---

[1] " In the late Roman Empire . . . no political freedom was tolerated, no freedom of speech, thought, or conscience was permitted,
especially after the victory of Christianity " (Rostovtzeff, *Social and
Economic History of the Roman Empire*, p. 473).

CHAPTER VII

CHRISTIANITY AND THE ANCIENT CULTURE

THE record of the relations of Christianity to the great rational Graeco-Roman civilization and culture [1] is an unhappy one, but one for which there are ample parallels in every spiritual upheaval and turning-point in history. Christianity appropriated much of permanent interest and moral worth from that ancient civilization. Christianity also acted in much the same way to its old home as Israel did to Egypt, from which it brought the cult of the golden calves but left the doctrine of immortality. So Christianity appropriated much that had better been abandoned and that has proved perilous and a handicap to its subsequent history. But it also repudiated much as Pagan which impoverished its outlook and narrowed its apprehension of its universal mission. Had Christianity accepted the comprehensiveness of the spirit of Christ, this rich Graeco-Roman heritage need not have been repudiated and almost perished; there is no reason why it could not and should not have been baptized into Christianity as so much—in fact too much—of Judaism was, and there is good reason to believe that such an attitude would have delivered present-day Christianity from many of its divisions and perplexities.

The fact remains that that rich Graeco-Roman culture almost perished and that ancient society was disintegrated while Christianity or a type of Christianity prevailed.

[1] Cf. Wendland, *Hell.-röm Kultur*, 2nd-3rd ed. pp. 225-40; E. de Faye's treatment in *Clément d'Alexandrie, Étude sur les rapports du Christianisme et de la phil. grecque au IIe siècle* (Paris, 1898); Dieterich, *Der Untergang der antiken Religion* (*Kl. Schr.* pp. 449-539); A. Causse, *Conflict du Christianisme primitif et de la civilisation* (Paris, 1920).

That there were disintegrating forces in that ancient culture will be too apparent, but that Christianity attempted to save that culture, or to baptize it into Christ or to stay the dissolution [1] of society, cannot be maintained. The Church did not then consider itself called upon to undertake such a mission. That a thousand years of darkness fell upon the Christian world as a result of the passing of Graeco-Roman culture did not trouble the Church, and those ages are still looked upon by the romantics in religion as the ages of faith. When Europe arose from her long slumber, it was the light from Pallas Athene's holy hill that shone upon her and enabled her to read her own Christian philosophy. When the Renaissance schools opened in Italy under the inspiration of Plato and Plotinus, a day had again dawned for the liberation of the human spirit like that epochal day when the first school of philosophy opened in Ionia. As European philosophy came to birth in Ionia and Athens, so Christianity in its demand for freedom and quest of truth for truth's sake was reborn two thousand years later when Greece "rose from the dead with the New Testament in her hand." It was not by accident that Platonism or Neo-Platonism was in the ascendant during the centuries when Christianity waged its sternest conflict and won its victory, and that the system of the keener logician, Aristotle, "the philosopher" and "the master of them that know" (as the best interpreter of the mediaeval spirit names him), reigned supreme during the thousand years between the passing of ancient culture and the beginning of modern civilization at the Renaissance, and Aristotelianism was pressed into the service and the comfortable practice of submitting complacently to the infallible wisdom of a bygone age and to the divine authority of spiritual powers with civil and temporal means of persuasion. Greece thus proved the link between the old

[1] On their neutrality, so objectionable to Pagans like Celsus, cf. De Faye, *Les Difficultés*, etc., p. 13 ff.

and the new worlds, conserving the tradition of continuity of thought.

The early Christians saw so much of evil in their
environment against which they were in revolt [1] that
they were naturally less conscious of the elements of
good. Paganism essayed to meet the religious situation
by a process of selection and assimilation of the best
elements and by toleration; Christianity by intolerance
and repudiation of surrounding culture as the wisdom
of this doomed aeon. Besides, traditions of culture rarely
or never appeal to the leaders of a popular movement.
Because the Pagans employed physicians and physic,
many Christians regarded medicine as the possession
and mark of heathenism and the employment of
physicians as disloyalty to Christ the Physician. As
philosophy was the occupation of Pagan thinkers, the
term took on for many Christians the connotation given
it by Paul as synonymous with false teaching and became
" caviare to the general." ' What has Christ to do with
Socrates? ' a large section of Christians would ask. And
the unfortunate position arose—unfortunate both for the
conservation of the spiritual values of Paganism and
for the comprehensiveness of Christianity—that the
Christian propaganda offered as irreconcilable alternatives Plato or Christ, Greek truth or Christian
revelation. 'What has the Christian to do with the
philosopher? ' asked Tertullian. Thus came to pass the
same realignment as in every crisis, as, for example, at
the Reformation: some preferred to cling to the ancient
and venerable for the charm of antiquity and the appreciation of an established culture; others with avidity
for the new preferred to try ' the Way.' Some, pain-
fully faced with such false alternatives, chose to adhere
to Plato when they might have discovered that ' the
ever-divine Plato ' was both a forerunner and the most
loyal servant of Him in whom Christians were experi-
encing the way and the truth and the life. The *Octavius*

---

[1] Cf. Wendland, *Hell.-röm. Kultur*, 2nd-3rd ed. p. 227.

of Minucius Felix gives us a welcome insight into the warm friendly relations between the Christian Octavius and the Pagan Caecilius; it also gives us some idea of the serious and unnecessary difficulties which prevented a cultured Pagan from embracing Christianity, especially as it took on a more popular form to enlist the masses. To the Hellenic mind the incarnation was an almost impossible doctrine. Deification or apotheosis was as congenial to the Greeks as the incarnation was repellent. A tragic misunderstanding arose here. On the one hand the Christians stated the incarnation in such stark isolation from the life of mankind and in conjunction with such doctrines as the virgin birth and the bodily resurrection that the Greeks failed to find therein their own high doctrine of the essential unity of the human and the divine, and of the kinship of God's spirit and the spirit of man. Consequently the most promising and fruitful Logos doctrine, which was in many aspects the real meeting-place of Greek speculation [1] and Christian theology, and which superseded the Messianic Christology of the Jews and removed the last Jewish limitation from Christianity, was forced into creedal constructions which obscured the very truth that during nine centuries the Greeks had attained in the Logos conception.

In every great crisis which divides the loyalties of men that crisis is yet to be recorded in which the moderates and thinkers of either party win as against the extremists and iconoclasts. Intolerance and popular prejudice too often sway even a liberalizing movement and finally capture its organization. It is easier to shout battle-cries and hurl anathemas than to reason together. And when " the tumult and the shouting dies " the victor has allowed the vanquished to impose upon him some of the very terms of contention, or points of dispute are ignored in the settlement.

The early Christians took up a position of suspicion

[1] Harnack, *What is Christianity?*, XI, p. 206.

towards ' the wisdom of this aeon ' while they awaited their transference into ' that aeon.' But the question of their attitude toward contemporary education and culture was pressed upon them as ' that aeon ' did not break in according to their programme and as they saw themselves obliged to meet argument with argument rather than with an eschatological threat. Christianity could not dwell permanently in the region of exalted emotionalism and the empyrean of mystical fervour ; it was obliged to construct a formulation of its faith in intellectual categories and elaborate a philosophy to meet the rival religious philosophies. It must offer its solution of the moral problems and intellectual needs of its believers and co-ordinate the data of the new Christian experiences, and both by reasoning and by conduct remove the prejudices and misunderstandings against their faith. Like its competitors, it must attempt to penetrate the mysteries of " this ambiguous world." Without abdicating the high claims it made in a truth-seeking world to be the Truth, it dare not evade inquiry or ignore criticism,[1] or fail to realize that faith and knowledge are inseparable in an adequate religion and that each reacts on the other.[2] Just because of the exclusive character of its claims Christianity stood in special need of the services of philosophy.

The first apologists manifested the cleavage that was destined to run through Christianity and became more marked.[3] The greatest apologists recognized the necessity of providing a philosophy or comprehensive theology of their faith intelligible to their day and of claiming an alliance of culture and faith, of a sincere devotion and the scientific spirit. Such were Clement and Origen. Others, e.g. Tatian [4] and Tertullian, furthered the aliena-

---

[1] Cf. Bréhier, on the absence of a Christian philosophy, *Hellénisme et Christianisme*, in *Rev. philosophique*, 1927, 1 and 2.
[2] Cf. Origen's demand for such faith and religion, *Phil.* 18, 23.
[3] Cf. Boissier, *La Fin du Paganisme*, 2nd ed. p. 277 ff.
[4] Thus in *Oratio* 3, ' I laugh at the teaching of Plato, an imitation of that of Pythagoras.'

tion of many from culture and set Christianity and philosophy in antithesis, as when Tertullian [1] properly designated philosophy as the mother of all heresy. Theophilus has neither an understanding of nor any sympathy with philosophy. Even in the graceful *Epistle to Diognetus* those philosophers who call fire divine will be punished by being hurled into that fire. But Justin Martyr claims a place for and a recognition of Socrates and Plato and Greek philosophy. As a Christian convert he saw no inconsistency in wearing the Greek philosopher's cloak, and he repeatedly cites the philosophers as authorities in his arguments for Christianity.

Clement would have enriched Christianity with the deep spirituality of Platonism and enthroned Christ on the highest culture of the age if the *vox populi* and the masters of ecclesiastical organization had permitted. He acclaimed Greek philosophy as inspired of God while critically sifting its propositions, and he begged Christians not to be frightened of it as of ghosts. [2] He protests against those who would attribute the rise of philosophy to the devil ; ' man has been born chiefly for the knowledge of God,' and Clement discovers in Greek philosophy an aid to the attainment of that knowledge, just as he represents Christianity as ' the faith of knowledge ' (gnostic faith). [3] Indeed, philosophy had been to the Greeks the *praeparatio evangelica* which the Law had been to Israel. [4] The loaves and fishes with which Jesus had fed the hungry multitude symbolized respectively the religion of Israel and the wisdom of Hellas. [5] While the work of the thinkers of Greece was to him ' a torn-off fragment of eternal truth,' Christianity was ' the genuinely true philosophy.' [6] He advocated a Christianity resting not on credulity but on frank inquiry : ' it

---

[1] *De Praesc.* 7. Cf. *ib.*, ' What has Athens to do with Jerusalem ? What agreement between the Academy and the Church ? ' His tone is somewhat modified in *De Testimonio Animae*, and *Apol.* 17.

[2] *Strom.* I. 7. [3] *Ib.* VI. 8 (65, -66, 2, 68, 2).

[4] *Ib.* VI, 17; I. 5; I. 16. [5] *Ib.* VI. 93.

[6] *Ib.* I. 13; VIII. 1.

is impossible to find without having sought, or to have sought without examining, or to have examined without analysing and raising questions with a view to lucidity,' and ' one indeed is the way of Truth, but into it, as into an ever-flowing river, streams from everywhere are confluent,' [1] and one of these main tributaries was the Greek wisdom which other apologists set in opposition to Christianity. The acceptance of Clement's Platonic conception of God would have saved Christianity from those persistent types of Christian theology of Oriental despotism resting upon Aristotelianism and common to Romans and Calvinists—though these were not the only or best alternatives.

Origen recognized the value of the thought and culture of his day, and especially Platonism,[2] as an important element not only in preparing the way for Christianity but in the explication of the Christian faith. ' We should follow reason and a rational guide ' was not generally accepted by the mentality of the early Christians. He observed that a ' gentler spirit ' [3] had entered the world preparatory for Christianity. Himself brought to Christianity through Greek philosophy, he was frank to acknowledge the call to conversion in such philosophy.[4] In his letter to his pupil Gregory Thaumaturgus he exhorts him to devote himself to Greek philosophy as a preparatory study for Christian philosophy. At a later date Porphyry tells that many learned men were beginning ' to pry into the secrets of this [Christian] philosophy.' A man of scientific outlook like Galen testifies to the growing interest of Christians in true philosophy and admits that some of them are the equals of their Pagan contemporaries. The correspondence and warm personal respect between Ambrose of Milan and Symmachus, the impassioned advocate of the ancient religion

---

[1] *Ib.* I. 5.
[2] According to Porphyry, he was constantly studying Plato and very familiar with other Greek philosophy, especially Stoicism (Euseb. *H.E.* VI. 19, 8).
[3] *Contra Celsum,* II. 30.
[4] *Ib.* III. 51-4.

and culture, and the correspondence between the Platonic bishop Synesius of Cyrene and the talented daughter of Theon, destined to be martyred in the cause of Greek culture against fanaticism, are pleasing episodes in the long struggle between Christianity and Paganism. Notwithstanding the angelic rebuke in a dream to his protest that he was a Christian—'Nay, thou art a Ciceronian, for where your treasure is, there also is your heart '— and his vow henceforth never to open a Pagan volume, Jerome confesses later to be still ' enraptured by the grace and beauty of profane wisdom.' [1] The historian Socrates, commending the command of Paul to ' prove all things; hold fast to the good,' declares, ' Whatever anywhere is good belongs to the Truth.' [2]

Yet, *triste dictu,* it was not tolerance and eclecticism and the freedom of inquiry that won the day, but intolerance and ignorance.[3] Not the generous spirit of the writer of the Fourth Gospel, Clement, and Origen and Synesius of Cyrene, but the legalism and intolerance of Tertullian and Augustine, of Athanasius and Jerome and Cyprian, an intolerance not indicative of any deeper loyalty to the Christian faith, for none proved his devotion to Jesus more than did Origen, whose life was ' one uninterrupted prayer ' and whose confession was sealed in martyrdom. Not Antioch and Ephesus and Alexandria, with their finer literary traditions and alert Hellenic mentality and Greek confidence in the truth and in the rationality of man's nature, but Carthage and

[1] *Epp.* XXV, LXXIII. Cf. *Ep.* XVIII, ' What is therein common to Horace and the Psalmist; to Virgil and the Gospel; to Cicero and the Apostles? '

[2] Socrates, *H.E.* III. 16.

[3] As a phenomenon of decay of ancient civilization Rostovtzeff includes '' the development of a new mentality among the masses.'' '' It was the mentality of the lower classes, based exclusively on religion and not only indifferent but hostile to the intellectual achievements of the higher classes. . . . It is revealed by the spread among them of the various mystic religions, partly Oriental, partly Greek. The climax was reached in the triumph of Christianity '' (*Social and Economic History of the Roman Empire,* p. 479).

Rome set the mode for Western Christianity. The West turned away from its greatest teacher, Origen, the ' master of the Churches ' in whom ancient culture, Greek philosophy, and a dauntless Christian faith formed a dynamic unity, in whom the Greek [1] and the Christian met in a marvellous equipoise as the Greek and the Hebrew met in Philo and in a lesser degree in Paul, and as the Oriental and the Greek met in Plotinus. During his lifetime he was forbidden to teach, and after his death his bones were exhumed as a penalty for his heresy.

Contrast Origen's participation in the belief of his Pagan contemporaries which made the contemplation of the heavens sacramental and the contemplation of the beauties and mysteries of nature part of the bliss of departed souls with Tertullian's martyr-cry that in the impending bouleversement the redeemed should find at least part of their felicity in gazing upon the exquisite tortures of their erstwhile tormentors,[2] and the same Father boasts that the pragmatic doctrines of heaven and hell originate from Christianity.[3] Contrast the martyr-philosopher's generous faith that those before Christ who had lived with the Logos were Christians, such as Socrates and Heraclitus, with the effrontery of Tertullian's reference [4] to Socrates' guardian demon as ' doubtless distorting his mind from the Good.' Or contrast Arnobius's vehement protest against the doctrine of the native immortality and divine origin of the soul as calculated to precipitate men into vice [5] with Clement's Platonic view of the inherent deathlessness of the soul. The Gnostics were attacked by the orthodox

[1] " Il est encore un vrai fils de la Grèce. Il se sent lui-même une affinité profonde avec la pensée hellénique. Les philosophes lui en transmis ce qui en est le caractère vraiment distinctif. Il a leur curiosité d'esprit. Comme eux, il éprouve un besoin irrésistible de poser des questions " (de Faye, *Origène*, I, p. 220).

[2] *De Spect.* 30.   [3] *Apol.* 47.

[4] *Apol.* 22. But cf. even Origen's similar remark about Celsus, VIII. 63.

[5] *Adv. Gentes,* II. 15, 29, 30.

Fathers [1] for denying the resurrection of the body and
the flesh, so objectionable to a Greek like Celsus. [2] Again,
contrast the advocacy of an inquiring faith by Clement
and Origen with the attitude of the Africans, such as
Tertullian, ' I believe it because it is absurd,' or of
Augustine, ' I would not believe the Gospel if the
authority of the Catholic Church did not compel me.' [3]
When such alternatives were presented to Christianity we
may well lament with Bishop Westcott " the evils of
that Africanism which has been dominant in Europe
since the time of Augustine " and " the shadow of his
(Augustine's) power is perilous to the growth of truth," [4]
and re-echo the affirmation that Greek Christian thought
" has not yet done its work in the West."

Let us, however, mingle appreciation with criticism,
and gratitude with regrets, and remember that it is our
privilege to speak from full perspective of these early
centuries. Christianity could not what it knows now
know at first. We see the greatness as also the weaknesses and false alternatives of our predecessors. The
issues at stake were so vast that we need not be aston-
ished if extreme positions sometimes won, and if, as in
every crisis, the issues were often clouded. The Fathers
generally repudiated all Greek philosophy rather than
run the risk of accepting evil with the good and false-
hood with truth. An infallible Christianity requires an
infallible human nature. We are the heirs not merely
of the obvious errors, but also still more of the virtues
and the heroisms of those before us. Christianity is still
in the making, still confronted with crises, and regularly
compelled to stand at the parting of the ways and choose,
as it was during the first four centuries, and the spirit
of Jesus has yet many things to declare unto us, opening
up new vistas of truth and compelling to new and larger
loyalties. All our history is the unfolding of a divine

[1] E.g. Tert. *De Resur.* 19.
[2] *C. Celsus*, VIII. 49.   [3] *Cont. ep. Man.* V. 6.
[4] *Religious Thought of the West*, pp. 246, 250.

purpose, under which we are active workers together with God. If some things from the past remain to be undone, more remain to be carried to completion and others to be begun in the name of Christ. Christianity was, like man, " made to grow, not stop."

Yet the Church as an institution has been, and remains, the home of sincere souls in whom the Spirit of Christ is expressing itself for the enrichment of personality and for the regeneration of society—an institution the exalted passion of which has been directed both to kindly and to persecuting purposes, in which hatreds and ignorance have been manifested beside self-devotion and spiritual idealism. It has suffered from phases of degeneration, which, however, have been more than compensated for in its phenomena of development. If it remains for modern Christianity to exorcise the hardness and to correct the defective ethical ideals and narrowness of the past, the task also remains of carrying forward the ideal of making all things new and of realizing a redeemed humanity. Early Christianity was a world-renewing movement carried on by the men of the first four centuries sharing the contemporaneous views and outlook and conscious of, or seeking to discern, the highest strivings of their fellows; twentieth-century Christianity is still entrusted with the same programme under similar conditions and similar limitations. They without us cannot be made perfect.

Christianity, cast upon the stream of evolution and becoming a great social and revolutionary movement, was liable to many unexpected checks and encouragements, and exposed to many diversions and even perversions in its development. The mind of the Master and the mind of the disciples were not always at one, though always assumed to be one. A personality like that of Jesus was certain to attract men in a deeply religious world, but their needs, and yearnings, and presuppositions would play their part in presenting His personality and interpreting His message and functions.

A creative genius like Paul would modify the outlook of the new religion. And the adaptation of an Aramaic gospel to a Hellenistic world necessitated a radical recasting. Such a recasting was justified and furthered by the conversion of the Graeco-Roman Pagan world, rather than the Jewish, to Christ and by the unexpectedly brilliant progress of Christianity in the Greek world. Who can say how far the idealizing tendency of Greek thought and Greek art contributed to place Jesus before the world as the central person of history rather than as a Jew who lived under Tiberius?

During these early centuries of missionary expansion and the facing of new situations and developing formulations Christianity was granted no immunity from the varied influences which surged around it. While maintaining its own marked entity and continuity of life, it evolved a strong self-consciousness responsive to the enlarging currents of thought; in its primitive freedom it learned to take over new elements. The application of the Christian message to the complex conditions and deep needs of the Mediterranean world soon revealed the complexity which was implicit in the religion from the beginning. It could not grow up side by side with other evangels without borrowing and remodelling under contrast. Its history then, as always, was one long process of disintegration and reintegration as a living faith meeting the needs of men. It changed its character drastically while conserving its message. Its native vitality qualified it to become the spiritual centre of the religious movement in the ancient world.

Notwithstanding the unfailing inspiration of Jesus, the conviction in the guidance of the Holy Spirit, and the pretensions of following apostolic teaching and precedent, Christianity could not escape the accidents of history and the conflicts of men, conscientious and selfish, concerning truth. As in many spiritual movements, there were difficult contradictions within Christianity which must lead to conflict in order to be resolved or reconciled

Those conflicting tendencies and problems indeed gave rise to movement and progress, but such movement and progress were determined and qualified by the needs and character of the period and by the limitations of the leaders. Ideas were always in gestation as in every living religion. Certain diversions in its development are obvious; all of which qualified historic Christianity at the time to become a popular and catholic religion; some of which have conduced to the unity of Christendom, while others have become means of division. Some changes were necessary in the interests of the self-preservation of the society and the purposes of propaganda; others were unhappy perversions.

Briefly stated, the main developments affecting the character and programme of the new religion were:

(1) The institutionalizing of the new religion and the growth of increasingly elaborate organization and the rise of an ecclesiastical caste. The Church became authoritative, as the Spirit had been during the first age of enthusiasm and spontaneity. The profound intuition of Jesus was institutionalized in a corporation controlled by a professedly divinely appointed apostolic hierarchy. Ecclesiastical officials secured the precedence over prophets and teachers in the interests of the peace and good order of the society and with a view to arrest the partisanship and fissiparous tendencies manifested in the loosely associated fraternities. These officials then assumed the functions of teachers themselves or claimed the right to select or ' ordain ' teachers, and finally constituted themselves the supreme authorities as to what standard of teaching was to be taught and as the guardians of the traditions of the sacred past. Christianity tended to become more ecclesiastic than Christian. The right of appeal to the individual conscience was thrust aside. It became the religion of authority with a canonical book and an authoritative Church speaking peremptorily and pontifically through the episcopate. As such it was qualified to become catholic by its appeal to the masses,

who welcomed an authoritative dogmatic system which
relieved them from the onerous duty of inquiry.[1] With
this ecclesiasticism there came necessarily a certain ex-
ternalism, since no ecclesiastical power on earth can
control or detect or punish thoughts and dispositions of
the heart. In Christianity, as in every religion, the
priest performs the historic functions of carrying on with
painful conscientiousness the externals of the cult and
forms of worship and maintaining the traditional continuity between the periods, long or short, at which the
prophet with his new vision and revolutionary truth
appears.

(2) Consequently belief hardened into fixed dogmas
and faith degenerated into an intellectual accepta-
tion of creedal constructions. Christian experience
was labelled and catalogued to become normative.
Standardization of opinions and morals superseded the
earlier spontaneity. In the arrest of mental growth a
system could now be imposed. Authority succeeded to
the place of argument, as in waning Paganism.

(3) The radiance and expansiveness and rational liberty
of the religion of Jesus gave way to asceticism and repression. Jesus' religion was not a sombre code of morals
but a liberating faith. The spread of monasticism, the
increasing retreat from the world, the practice of having
' virgin wives ' or ' sisters,' the view of marriage [2] a

---

[1] " The more peremptory and exclusive is the claim of faith which
any religion makes, the more trustworthy and secure does that religion
seem to the majority; the more it relieves them of the duty and responsibility of reflecting upon its truth, the more welcome it is. Any
firmly established authority acts as a sedative. And more: the most
welcome articles of faith are just the most paradoxical. . . . ' Blind
faith ' never gains its final haven until its authority is living, until
questions can be put to it, and answers promptly received from it,"
i.e. the episcopate (Harnack, *Expansion,* I, p. 278 f. Cf. *What is
Christianity?,* 3rd ed. p. 212).

[2] Cf. Tertullian's three grades of virginity: the virginity from
birth (as in Rev. xiv. 4); virginity from the second birth by the laver
either by mutual agreement (as in 1 Cor. vii. 5), or by maintaining
purely spiritual marriage (as in 1 Cor. vii. 25 ff.); and the virginity of one
marriage precluding a second marriage (*De Cast.* 1; cf. *Ad Ux.* I. 6)

ittle better than adultery and the attitude to women as
emptations to carnal desires, the hatred of the world
because of the love of heaven,[1] the indifference to claims
of citizenship and patriotism, were ominous signs of an
unhealthy other-worldliness which fostered an interest
in the Church rather than in the Empire, and which
set the *Civitas Dei* and the *Civitas Terrena* in hopeless
opposition. The principles of the Founder could not be
entrusted to errant human nature; they were therefore
codified into rules of conduct, and the simple ethical fact
quietly overlooked that no rules can be of universal
validity or operate irrespective of the individual motive
and the individual occasion and circumstance. The
application of the eternal principles enunciated by Jesus
is the solemnly responsible task of those who have been
made free by the Son.' In the growing barbarization
of Europe on the decay of ancient culture such rules
were perhaps a necessity, or at least the most obvious
method of reducing the rude peoples beyond the Empire
o obedience.

(4) The direct experience of joy in doing the Father's
will and the morally conditioned accessibility of the
vision of God and the apprehension of spiritual things
were replaced by a mediated religion and by the impartation of grace through sacraments [2] and the requisite
operations of holy persons. The Church and the Sacraments became the exclusive vehicles of saving grace,
and in and through them the Spirit, which once
functioned independently for transformation of life, now
operated and magnified them by such restricted operation. Inspiration belonged to a classic past from which
t could be drawn by an ecclesiastical tradition of
physical impartation by laying on of hands.

---

[1] Knopf, *Nachapost. Zeitalter*, p. 437 ff.

[2] '' Certainly in the long light of Christian history sacraments have
proved bitter enemies to these ideals (of Jesus); they have been the
largest and most easily opened door in the Church through which to
admit sub-Christian teaching and practice in the form of pagan superstition '' (Major, *Mod. Churchman*, XVI, p. 257).

(5) Correspondingly the old priestly religion of intercession and mediatorial functions and departmenta
offices with Deity supplanted the immediacy of Jesus
religion of the direct approach of every son, howeve
sin-polluted and conscience-stricken, to a Father whose
love required no pleader and was moved by deepe
motives than merit. The conception of the equality o
men before God and of the ever-open thoroughfares con
ducting from the soul to the eternal things was displace
by that of an approach through the aristocratic cast
of hierarchs or martyrs. Another God was enthroned
with whom the intercessory offices of a clergy, and saint
and confessors and angels, availed much, and befor
whom Jesus was constituted ' through His blood ' as th
mediator and eternal High Priest procuring access fo
those who merited refusal. The philosophical situatio
became worse as Aristotelianism with its Great Absolut
displaced Platonism and became the means of reducin
philosophy to a mere department of organized religion
of assigning to it a merely apologetic function, rathe
than that of inquiry into the facts of an historical religio
and the data of religious experience.

Consonant with the intensive contemporary pes
simism,[2] and with the ideas of the guilt and weaknes
of man and his utter dependence on supernatural ai
and his distrust in his own power of will, the painfu
and stormy personal experiences of two men—th
student of the universities of Tarsus and Jerusalem an
the Bishop of Hippo, whose theologies must ever attrac
study as direct rescripts of their own unique experience
—became ever more and more normative as types c
religious experience for Christians in general and fos
tered that pessimistic estimate of human nature a
' children by nature of wrath ' so alien to Jesus

[1] Cf. Wendland, *Hell.-röm. Kultur*, p. 240 : " Schon im II Jahr. wir
der christliche Gott in die abstrakten Formen des platonischen gekleide
und dadurch in eine solche Ferne versetzt, dass das Schwergewicht de
religiösen Lebens aus der Welt herausgerückt wird."

[2] Cf. Wendland, *ib.*, pp. 234-9.

optimism. It was found easier to give expression to the remorseful agonies of soul and the loathing and reaction of the spirit after dissipation or labyrinthine wanderings than to the quiet power of the peace of God in the obedient soul. It seemed more obvious to pit flesh and spirit, sense and soul, in constant conflict and irreconcilable antithesis, than to regard them as allies and modes of self-realization. Despite the greatness of Augustine as the typical Church Father of our Western Christianity, a debauchee turned ascetic, with the dualism of an ascetic, was an unfortunate choice as the intellectual guide to the rude West which had yet to be tutored in the deep spiritual things while learning " the uses of the flesh " in the discipline of reducing its fresh energies to a unity. Hence the tempestuous experiences of a Paul, an Augustine,[1] a Jerome, became more typical than the Olympian calm of the Divine Master, the quiet power of the writer of the Fourth Gospel, or the less spectacular history of a Pelagius. Hence, too, divine grace and divine law secured their pre-eminence in Christian preaching, to the detriment of such an earlier conception as that the worst sinner

---

[1] In *Manichaeanism and Augustine's Idea of Massa Perditionis* (*Harv. Th. Rev.* XX, 1927, pp. 117-27), Buonaiuti traces the origin of Augustine's pessimistic doctrine of mankind as a contaminated *Massa* to Manichaeanism working with Pauline language and points out how the anti-Pelagian controversy and the controversy with Julianus of Aeclanum called forth " the deep anthropological pessimism with which his soul and his religious experience were saturated." Ambrosiaster first suggested such a connexion, but " it was Augustine who . . . finally identified the Pauline ' Massa ' with the Manichaean conception of βῶλος. At least there is no doubt that the two most remarkable conceptions of Augustine . . . his anthropological doctrine and his interpretation of history expounded in the *De civitate Dei*, are both based on a dualistic view of human nature and human history, according to which the individual as well as the collective life of men is centred in the highly dramatic effort of light and goodness to free themselves from the *Bolos* of universal corruption and misery. Both of these are fundamentally Manichaean conceptions. The use of the term ' Massa ' reveals in the very language of theology the connexion that links the epoch-making Augustinian formulation to the preceding Manichaean thought " (pp. 123, 127).

can arise and come to the Father. Consequently, especially in the West, the Christian soul more readily learned from its *de profundis* to raise its *miserere mei, Domine,* than on the arduous heights of ethical obedience and faith mysticism to participate in the exhilarating experience of ' all that the Father hath is Mine.'

Tracing the course of Western Christianity, we ask what would be its character and message and philosophy to-day if the great conception of the Eastern and Greek Fathers of salvation as being a deification or divinizing of man, so well expressed by the orthodox Athanasius, ' He was made man that we might be made God,' had become dominant or at least a corrective against the exclusive Western cry for grace? What would have happened had Christianity had the courage, even amid the dangers of heresy and the heat of Christological controversies, to stand by the Greek contention of the unity of the Divine and the human in all men, which was also that of Jesus, rather than on the one hand formulate a two-nature theory of Christ's person and on the other limit the union of human and divine, the in-dwelling of God in man, to Christ? What if the Christian belief in the persistence of personality and the account-ability of man had followed the more spiritual Platonic conception of the divine nature and native immortality of the soul rather than have laid hold with avidity on the more materialistic Jewish eschatology of a resurrection of the body or a resurrection of the flesh? What if the Pagan Greek view of the overflowing love and kindness of God, together with His ineluctable justice, had become more prominent than the awful wrath of God? What if Origen's larger hope for all men and for the whole universe in a final restoration had occupied the minds of the West as conspicuously as the " massa perditionis " of Augustine? We cannot reply, but from the modern trend in untrammelled Christian philosophy and from the results of historical study of the message of Jesus and His view of man, we may anticipate much from the recapturing of truths that were dropped or forgotten by the way. The development of theology was in each outstanding period—necessarily perhaps—one-sided to conserve some vital truth which for the time being threw some other important truth out of perspective, a phenomenon of which examples lie to hand in the controversies with Montanism, Gnosticism, and Donatism.

Restoration of the first or the fifth century is impossible or too perilous to the life of a developing faith. Christianity as a living organism can rest neither in the theology of a Paul, nor in the world-view of an Origen or an Augustine or a John of Damascus, an Aquinas or a Calvin. It is destined to suffer from attempted restorations by romanticists, and to come to a clearer self-consciousness through spiritual upheavals and prophetic revivals, through meeting new situations and making new readjustments to the increasing demands made by man of his religion. Christianity is required to do a great deal more for a Christian to-day than in the first centuries, and while the motive power is the inspiration of the Galilean, Christianity can meet the growing demands made by the life of mankind. Christianity to-day is likewise relieved from several functions which it performed in the beginning, such as guarantees against the astral influences and against magical incantations in names lesser than ' the Name ' and against the invasion and annoyances of demons.

As an historic movement Christianity has yet to learn or confess that no ecclesiastical polity or confessional allegiance can standardize either man or the faith which unites him with the infinite. It has yet to learn that loyalty to Christ is more catholic than the most Catholic Church. Hitherto it has failed to reconcile freedom and authority, to cultivate without contradiction the Western genius for law and order and the Greek-Oriental genius for reflexion and intellectual inquiry. If the prophecy of Kipling '' East is East and West is West, And never the twain shall meet '' is ever to be falsified, it must be in the religion of Christ. Organized Christianity has strenuously essayed to suppress subjectivity in the interests of the external unity of objectivity. It has with more specious success treated the recalcitrant brother or unworthy member on the ecclesiastical principle so naïvely imputed to Jesus, ' Let him be to you as an alien,' rather than with the illimitable patience of the love of ' seventy times seven.'

Yet despite the fact that no seed grows so slowly as that planted in human nature, this Christian institution will learn and unlearn through experience, but chiefly through the deep insight or enlarging visions of its prophets and teachers. It will yet make room for the ritualist and the jurist, the mystic and the philosopher, as abiding types in human nature, and enable them to live together without offence. The Sower went forth to sow, and the firstfruits of nineteen centuries are a promise of the rich harvest to be garnered by the sons of God in the coming generations.

THE RELIGION OF MAGIC, SACRAMENT AND SYMBOL

CHAPTER VIII

ANCIENT SACRAMENTARIANISM

In a living and vitalizing religion like Christianity, developments were inevitable and evolution from germinal to riper forms. But that all the developments which have taken place within institutional Christianity were either inevitable or for the best it would be precarious to affirm. No one conversant with Jesus and with the religion of Jesus and forecasting the fortunes of Christianity when cast upon the stream of history could have anticipated the eagerness with which the new religion at an early stage stepped forth on the by-paths of dogmatism and sacramentarianism, or how the rich and suggestive sacramentalism which was of Jesus' own religion should hold dalliance with the ubiquitous contemporary magic and degenerate into a rigid sacramentarianism—dogmatic, exclusive, miraculous. Jesus, in the interests of ethical and personal religion, protested against the monopolies and pretensions of sacerdotalism, but sacerdotalism survived and secured greater prestige in His religion despite His protests and despite His conception of a God whose love needs no mediatorial offices. No one could have forecasted that the things which have proved divisive in Christendom were concerns for which no sure warrant can be discovered in His teaching and which lay wholly outside His interests. The Divine Master recognized among His followers, disciples and teachers, apostles, prophets and cross-bearers, but no priests; and the priest in the course of Christian history has taken an ample revenge for having been so slighted. How tragically significant in the history of the religion called by His name was that unseemly dispute at the Last Supper as to pre-eminence in the Kingdom among the Apostles, a dispute still continued among those who partake of the same spiritual food and as yet no nearer solution when judged by His standard of fruit-bearing.

Dean Inge holds that if Christ had not instituted Baptism and the Eucharist, the Church would have had to invent them, which may be taken to mean that the Christian cult would have evolved a system of Christian symbolism. He also maintains [1] that " a Christianity without sacraments could never have converted Europe," which is probably true for the kind or degree of Christianity to which Europe was converted, but it would be truer to say with Charles Kingsley that, with the conversion of Constantine and the legislation of the Pagans into Christians, Christianity won rather than converted Europe.[2] And to that wholesale influx of Paganism [3] into Christianity and this partial or superficial conversion are largely due the dialectics of sacramentarianism. *Ab initio sic non erat.*

In the religious life of the centuries in which Christianity arose and made its way to the status of the State religion, and the house-churches of the apostolic period developed into the ancient Catholic Church, one cannot fail to be impressed with the extraordinary attention paid to sacral acts, the excessive importance of ceremonial, the scrupulosity as to correct millinery for religious occasions, and the impossibility of saying where magic ends and where religion begins, where Paganism and Christianity meet and part.

Similarly in passing from the religion of the Founder

[1] *Contentio Veritatis*, p. 279.

[2] " The Christianity that triumphed was the Christianity of blind faith, which Celsus has depicted " (Harnack, *Exp. of Christianity*, I, p. 280).

[3] There was another aspect of Paganism from which Christianity borrowed with advantage and could have borrowed more.

of Christianity to the Christianity of the post-apostolic
days we are made acutely conscious at once of a difference in atmosphere between the religion of immediacy
and that of mediacy through holy rites and holy persons,
between the religion in which ' the pure in heart see
God ' and that wherein such privileges are reserved for
those who have been duly admitted into the Society by
certain ritual acts controlled by a sacerdotal succession.
In the first, a man's standing is determined absolutely
by what he thinks in his heart and by his loyalty to the
Lord Jesus; in the second, his present privileges and
future prospects are determined by his proper relations
to an institution claiming divine origin and authority
and dispensing in rite and ritual the promises of the
Founder. In the first, Jesus says without reference to
initiatory rite in retrospect or prospect, ' Suffer the little
children to come unto Me, and forbid them not '; in
the second, no membership is possible in the organized
Society and no salvation thinkable save by the initiatory
rite of baptism, the Church having overlooked ' the
word of the Lord ' that ' John baptized with water,
but you shall be baptized in the Holy Spirit' (Acts xi. 16).
In the first, faith alone is sufficient; in the second, sacramental potencies are requisite in transforming the
psychic or physical man into the *pneumatic* or incorruptible man. In the first, forgiveness of sins is conditioned wholly by the moral attitude of repentance and
obedience to a loving Father; in the second, this solace
of anxious souls has been theologized into conformity
with an ancient,[1] particularly Semitic, blood-ritual which
interpreted the martyr-death of Jesus as a, or rather
the, propitiatory sacrifice, the ground and objective
means of all God's gracious forgiving activities. Or,
in the first, Jesus and His disciples could declare to the
contrite heart ' thy sins are forgiven ' as an immediate
and verifiable experience of the sin-laden soul; in the
second, ' there is no other way [to forgiveness] except

---

[1] Cf. Marrett, *Evolution of Religion,* p. 121 f.

by coming to know the Christ and by taking the bath
for remission of sins.' [1] In the first, men are sons of God
constitutionally, obedient or far away in the land of
self-indulgence and forgetfulness of their birthright but
able to ' arise and go to the Father '; in the second, a
process of ' adoption ' after mediatorial offices with God
is necessary, and this ' adoption ' becomes synonymous
with baptism, as Hesychius defines adoption ' when one
received the adopted son and the holy baptism,' [2] or,
more ambitiously, ' man is made God (rendered Divine)
by water and the Holy Spirit after the rebirth of the
laver.' [3]

In the primitive Christian Society the rites, which
were not of Jesus' appointment, were of a simple and
very obvious symbolic character, though capable of
infinite expansion in elaboration and in dogmatic
elucidation and in adaptation to contemporary practices.
Baptism was washing in running (living) water to the
use of the Name of Jesus. Anon was added the im-
position of hands as the necessary and material channel
of communication of the Spirit and of the " validity "
of the sacrament, and soon a collateral sacrament was
attached to the primitive rite, unction with consecrated oil.

There are in every religion two synchronous processes
in action—the continuous externalization and institutionalizing or the objectifying of the main ideas in outward
form to render the religion catholic in its appeal; and

---

[1] Justin, *Dial.* 44.

[2] υἱοθεσία ὁτάν τις θετὸν υἱὸν λαμβάνῃ καὶ τὸ ἅγιον βάπτισμα, Suicer,
ad verb.; cf. Clement of Alex., who, treating of Jesus as having been
' perfected by the washing of baptism alone ' as synonymous with
the ' descent of the Spirit,' says ' we, whose example Christ was, have
the same experience. Baptized, we are illuminated; illuminated, we
become sons; being made sons, we are rendered perfect; and rendered
perfect, we become immortal ' (*Paed.* I. 6; cf. also Photius, *Ep.* 97,
ad Basil. Mac.).

[3] Hippolytus, *De san. Theophania,* 8; cf. " In my Baptism, wherein
I was made a member of Christ, the child of God, and an inheritor of
the kingdom of heaven " (Catechism in the Book of Common Prayer).

on the other hand, in the more spiritual circles there is
an ascending in heart and mind to the inmost secret of
the religion, an *introrsum ascendere,* a *Verinnerlichung,*
a movement, in the language of the Roman Catholic
scholar and mystic, von Hügel, from the " exteriorisms "
to the " interiorisms." The former process tends to
obscure and sometimes to crystallize the vital idea of
the religion; the latter tends to release the spirit of
the religion to break through even venerable forms and
contemporary manifestations and to seek the timeless
both in experience and in reflexion, while not necessarily
casting aside cult forms and practices which in the experience of many have proved helpful.

In every religion practices are more tenacious than
beliefs, and changes in beliefs—slow as they are—are
ever ahead of alterations in practice. Cult forms are
even more static than dogmas. Hence new dogmas are
often fitted into the framework of old cult forms, so that
there is half a truth in the words of Sir James G. Frazer,
" The history of religion is a long attempt to reconcile
old custom with new reason, and to find a sound theory
for absurd practices."

Every religion is burdened with survivals which have
been dissociated from their original context. Superstition is dead religion, generally picturesque and always
popular, the fossil of what was once a living faith.

The evolution of historic Christianity in the first centuries was marked by a progressive equipment with
rites and sacraments, and with the rationale thereof, and
concurrently by a constant reshaping of the religion
under apologetic necessity into a philosophy with a
theological system based partially on historic facts, the
life and teachings of Jesus, partially on the mythologizing and speculative tendencies of the times, and partially
on philosophic principles common to Greek thought and
the new religion.

There are several reasons why sacramentarianism as
the belief in the salutary and obligatory importance of

rites and the expectancy of *ex opere operato* efficacies obtained in the ancient world in which Christianity arose and spread.

(1) It is a general principle of religious evolution that rites precede deities, and sacraments enter the field before the gods under whom at a later date they are to enter on a new career. In religion it is a deep-seated conviction that everything ancient is venerable, *quoniam antiquitas proxume accedit ad deos*.[1] The rites which men performed in remote days for corporate safety and to secure the outward means of life were too important to discard when personal gods took over the providence of human life. The course of religion may be conceived as generally proceeding from animism to fetichism, or from totemism to personalism. *Numina* or powers become *di,* anthropomorphic deities. But the religious mind, which is tenaciously conservative, could not, on attaining personalism [2] for its unseen powers, easily break with the idea of the animated forces of the first stage, and still less with the idea of the supernatural powers resident in the external object or visible home of the daemonic powers of fetichism. The conception of ' power ' or *Mana,* in objects and natural phenomena, was through anthropomorphism and rationalism assigned to ' Powers.' This *Mana,* which exists prior to and independently of gods, was merely distributed to the good and evil divine persons, for these ' Powers ' both attack and protect. If ideas of taboo acted deterrently with regard to one object, they heightened the importance of another. The action which once took place as an *opus operatum* of itself or automatically is now addressed to beings endowed with will who can repeat the desired action and assure its mysterious efficacy.

[1] Cicero, *De Legg.* II. 11, 27.

[2] For the persistence in the Graeco-Roman period of a deeper interest in the power or ' virtues ' of the god (ἀρετή, δυνάμεις, ἐνέργειαι) rather than in the personality or in the god himself, cf. A. D. Nock, *Studies in the Graeco-Roman Beliefs of the Empire* (*J.H.S.* XLV, pp. 84-101).

It is also well known that many of the loftiest con-ceptions of religion can be traced back to primitive and naturalistic rites which antedate personal deities, but which through their long-established usage and obvious utility were forced into higher service in a higher stage of religion. Age and custom consecrate religious habits without critical inquiry as to whether they are good now. Man is particularly cautious in his religious ex-periments. He will keep one of his old gods if only to hide under the bed. He retains a wistful hankering after the picturesque and tangible gods whom his fathers worshipped on the other side of the flood. The Israelites were prudential to placate the local telluric gods of Canaan until they should be assured by experience whether their war-god, Jahweh, could grow crops and ensure increase in a strange country. Examples need not be multiplied. The earth-ritual of Eleusis for the fertility of the Rarian plain became the ecumenical sacra-ment for immortality, feeding the ' sweet hopes ' of countless pilgrims through long ages. The local Thes-salian earth-daemon, Aesculapius, became the Saviour and Healer for the Graeco-Roman world. Rites of human fertility were slowly subtilized into sacraments of *henosis* or union with deities.

(2) Though religion probably did not arise from magic,[1] as Sir James G. Frazer contends in *The Golden Bough,* its connexion with magic has from the beginning been of the most intimate and generally friendly kind, and this connexion is far from broken in most institu-tional Christianity to-day. Magic came before cult, and cult forms were largely the adaptation of the postulates of magic to a higher department. Man has always wanted *something done* for him in religion, and long before there were gods to do it. '' Before man learns to address prayers to the gods for the success of his undertakings, he uses magic to effect his object; and when he has learned to believe in the gods he does not

[1] Cf. K. Barth, *Religion u. Magie bei d. Naturvölkern* (Leipzig, 1914).

forget his ancient rites. They survive within or alongside of the cult, that is, if it be a cult with old traditions." [1]

Magic rests on a system of correspondences in nature, which is linked together by a chain of grand potencies and vast affinities. Man as a microcosm of this vast unitary macrocosm stood in closest affinity with all the things around him, and by knowledge of their nature could turn them to his own purposes. If only he knew the ' secret,' the ' powers ' immanent in the world could be turned to account. This sympathetic magic was too deeply ingrained in ancient social and religious thought to be ejected, especially by a new religion which almost from the beginning manifested its reliance on the external ceremonies of worship and shared with its Pagan contemporaries the postulate of the necessity of ritual, both for the enjoyment of religious privileges and for the purposes of rendering religion popular or catholic. This sympathetic magic gradually assumed the character of and furthered a mystic sacramentarianism. [2]

Magic was the primitive meeting-place of human fears and hopes, needs and wishes. It sought to strike a bargain with deity or to employ means of compulsion upon spiritual agents. Magic was also the harbinger of natural science [3] and the first crude form of nature-mysticism. By the process of experimentation, happy coincidences, the power of suggestion and auto-suggestion, and the association of ideas, it attained immense vogue, such as is difficult for the modern student to conceive. This quasi-science that could manipulate theurgic apparatus, sway or control demons, secure or retard fertility, influence the issue in love-affairs, [4] cause the death of doomed victims, even of prospective wearers

---

[1] Nilsson, *Hist. of Greek Religion*, p. 89.

[2] Cf. Harrison, *Proleg. to Greek Religion*, p. 487 f.

[3] " Historically, in the broader sense of the word, there is ground for finding in magic an ancestor of science, of political and social morality, and certainly of medicine " (Glover, *Progress*, p. 16).

[4] Which the demons also control (Tatian, *Ad Graecos*, 17).

of the Roman purple, and bind beyond the grave, could
not lightly be put aside, and its power was all the more
terrible as it was also a semi-religion, which corroborated the working of ritual. It was an arrested development at which the many were content to stop.[1] It
satisfied the inveterate demand of each ' adulterous and
sinful generation ' to ' show us a sign,' and it throve
on miracle and thaumaturgic exhibitions.

This " bastard sister of religion " was kept in control
in the West by the inquisitive scientific spirit of Greece.
The rise of European philosophy in the Ionian colonies
stemmed the tide of sacerdotalism and sacramentarianism
from the East, where magic had always held a more
assured place than in the Graeco-Roman world, and
where it had developed in the temples of the Oriental
deities. " Magic first returns when the genuine Greek
spirit vanishes in the great transformation of philosophy
and religion which began during the Hellenistic
period."[2]

In the first centuries of Christianity and especially in
the final conflict of Paganism and Christianity, a conflict
which was not considered irreconcilable with a liberal
assimilation of phases of Paganism, magic secured such
a hold in ecclesiastical Christianity as was not relaxed
for centuries; it lingers still in theological niches, where
its presence is concealed by a refusal to ask questions
or by a disposition to evade difficulties on the principle
that *omnia exeunt in mysteria*. In the ancient period
of Christianity, the power of the priest must not be less
or less manifest than the power of the magician. If the
magician could bind in this life [3] and beyond the grave,[4]

[1] " As the best points in the Mysteries were absorbed by Christianity,
so the worst were absorbed by magic—magic, which always appears
as the dark shadow cast by religion, and which takes the place of
religion in the view of those who have not in them the seed of religious
growth " (P. Gardner, *Rel. Exper. of St. Paul*, p. 67).

[2] Nilsson, *Hist. of Greek Religion*, p. 52.

[3] Cf. Tacitus, *Annales*, II. 69, and Dio Cassius, LVII. 18 (on the
death of Germanicus).

[4] Quintilian, *Decl*. X. 7.

the Christian priest must not operate with less ghostly powers. Such a confession as, ' I was united with thy holy form (*morphé*); I was strengthened by thy holy name,' [1] made to magical incantation, suggested ritual values not to be overlooked. Where the external evidences of religious worth were essential to establish a religion, the miracles of the officials of the Church must not be less impressive than those of the magician or of the Mysteries. An uttered curse was recognized as operative, and this proved suggestive in the evolution of ecclesiastical excommunication, the beginnings of which we notice in the administration of the Corinthian Christian community under Paul's own directions (1 Cor. v. 5).

(3) The difficulty of, or disinclination for, abstract thinking in antiquity and the preference for concrete forms of thought. A pure religion which produces a spiritual philosophy and seeks that highest rationality commended by Jesus, as ' Thou shalt love the Lord thy God with thy whole heart, and with thy whole soul, and with thy whole mind, and with thy whole strength,' was then, as it is to-day, a formidable undertaking for the multitude. When we consider the arduous character of abstract thinking even to-day, we shall be more sympathetic with the ancients. And their task was all the greater as the Greeks had to forge the instruments for exact and conceptual thinking. One must admire the clarity with which Aristotle defines the categories before the establishment of a philosophical terminology. But Christianity appeared on the scene at a time when the process of the Orientalization of the West was proceeding apace. Except for those who still found a refuge and guide in Greek moral philosophy, the general trend was toward Oriental ways and fashions in religion, with Oriental vagueness and fogginess and *sfumato*. The Oriental thought pictorially rather than in Aristotelian categories. Truth came to him in images rather than

---

[1] Wessely, *Griech. Zauberpapyri*, I, p. 48.

in ideas; it was symbolic rather than dialectic. The Oriental cast his deepest intuitions into the mould of a cult or acted religion; the Greek into that of a philosophy or reflective religion, though he was very sensitive to the value of symbolism in religion.

This mental outlook was more accordant to a religion in mimetic action than to an exact theology. Edification would be promoted more by sacral acts than by an appeal to the mind. It inclined to seek for motions of the soul which might find fitting expression in action.

(4) The function of symbolism in antiquity was of immense influence in the evolution of sacramentarianism. But here the ancient mind was different from ours. In the first place, to the ancients the symbol did not denote the thing symbolized; it was in some mysterious way the thing itself without metaphysical distinctions.[1] And, secondly, in the symbol itself was supposed to be resident the dormant power which, when required, could be evoked by due and correct rites owing to deep and invisible correspondences. Hence the Christendom-dividing distinctions between Romans, Zwinglians, Lutherans, and Calvinists on ' hoc *est* corpus meum ' would to them have been almost unintelligible and certainly indifferent. The line of demarcation between symbol and fact was simply not drawn. Symbols were neither vivid mnemonics, nor pale substitutes, nor mere signs: they were something in their own right and they

---

[1] " The symbol is the mystery, and the mystery was not conceivable without a symbol. What we nowadays understand by ' symbol ' is a thing which is not that which it represents; at that time ' symbol ' denoted a thing which in some kind of way really is what it signifies; but, on the other hand, according to the ideas of that period, the really heavenly element lay either in or behind the visible form without being identical with it. Accordingly, the distinction of a symbolic and realistic conception of the Supper is altogether to be rejected " (Harnack, *Hist. of Dogma,* Eng. tr., II, p. 144 f.). Cf. also p. 207: " The symbolical of that time is not to be considered the opposite of the objectively real, but as the mysterious, the God-produced (*musterion*), as contrasted with the natural, the profanely clear "; also pp. 212-26, IV. 288 f.

did something, and though the exact nature of that action and of the effect was not unimportant, it was not too curiously scrutinized.   In this connexion it is noteworthy that *symbolum* was used by the Early Church for *sacramentum,* and as a synonym with *mysterion.*[1] In fact " the ' symbol ' was never a mere type or sign, but always embodied a mystery," [2] and " each symbol has a mysterious but real connexion with the fact which it signifies." [3]   It was a " mysterious *drómenon* (transaction)," as Windisch terms Paul's rite of baptism.

Ancient religion was symbolic to an extent beyond ours, partly because of the disinclination for abstract thinking and the consequent absence of a rigid theology ; partly because of its closer association with art, ritual being the half-way house between art and religion ; and partly from the consciousness that many things defy articulation, and at least for the masses should be represented rather than defined.   Ancient theology was more poetical than prosaic ; it was *mythus* rather than creed ; and the ceremonial was acted myth.   With the ancients, mythology was more in demand than theology : it was the first form of theology.   They, on the whole, preferred to suggest rather than define ; to produce awe and reverence rather than an intellectual satisfaction ; to encourage emotionalism and devotionality rather than critical inquiry.   It is in the perception of this appeal to human nature at large that Protestantism has failed compared with Catholicism [4] ; it is in the perception that other things are needed beside devotionality, and that a satisfactory personal religion insists on submitting

[1] Cf. Robinson, *Epistle to the Ephesians,* p. 234 ff.
[2] Harnack, *Hist. of Dogma,* IV, p. 289.
[3] *Id., Exp. of Christianity,* I, p. 286.
[4] W. Hale White (Mark Rutherford) writes in *Letters to Three Friends*: " The symbolism of Catholicism, as for example at Candlemas, is sometimes expressive of a deeper truth than anything that can be put into words.   Catholicism here shows profounder insight than Protestantism into the nature of truth and of man.   Catholicism knows what words cannot do.   Protestantism struggles to put everything into words.   The vital part of religion is wordless and purely symbolic."

its faith and most holy symbols to inquiry, that Catholicism has failed compared with Protestantism.

No student of ancient religion can put himself *en rapport* with his subject or realize its message and the beauty of its appeal without a sympathetic comprehension of its symbolism. For example, a few leisurely visits to the lovely underground Neo-Pythagorean basilica [1] by the Via Praenestina, where the Pagan pure in heart were realizing God at the time when the house-churches of early Christianity were meeting in or around the same city, will bring home to one the varied and eloquent appeal of a rich religious symbolism: the frescoes seem to proclaim defiantly, ' Where is thy victory, O Death? ' And no religious man could have gazed in the spirit on the delicately beautiful white marble plaque in the recently discovered (in 1922) Capuan [2] Mithraic chapel without some apprehension of " the forms whose kingdom is where time and space are not." There carved in relief is a winged Psyche draped in a pleated robe fastened with straps crossing between the breasts; beside her stands Eros, holding a lighted torch, grasping her left hand and wistfully looking at her with confident entreaty. " Love faileth not," seems to be the message.

(5) Closely associated with this symbolism was ancient realism, which makes ancient axioms modern enigmas, and which throve in an atmosphere of mysticality and supernaturalism in the absence of a scientific spirit of inquiry. Realism, it should be remembered, is not necessarily to be identified with materialism, though it may conduce to it; it may go hand in hand with credulity or with mysticism. Under the religious syncretism—during which Christianity spread—magic and theurgy, spiritism and occultism, grew apace and fostered a kind

[1] Cf. Lietzmann, *Vorträge d. Bib. Warburg*, 1922, I. 60 ff.; Paribeni, *Culti et Religioni in Roma*, etc., in *Atena e Roma*, 1920, p. 169 ff.; Carcopino, *La Basilique pythagoricienne*, 1926.

[2] *Notizie d. Scavi* (1924), XXI. 1924, pp. 353-75, by A. Minto, with reproductions of the frescoes.

of realism. The bright light of Hellenic philosophy was a less favourable milieu for realism than the crepuscular Hellenistic light. As the symbol was in some real way the thing itself, so the thought and the object bore to each other more than an epistemological relation. The question of differentiating between the symbol and the transaction was not seriously pressed. One fruitful cause of regnant realism was that in the ancient mind the identity of subject and object was scarcely questioned. " It is indisputable that the Greek people never completely outstepped the confines of their pre-logical mentality and that they attained only at a late stage, after Plato, a truly rational and genuine mentality. In Greek philosophy we must come down to the Stoics to find the distinction, so obvious for us, of the subjective and the objective." [1] Later the tides of realism swept over the Pauline churches, carrying with them magical sacramentarianism.

In that ancient world spirit was only the most attenuated matter; it was corporeity near but never at the vanishing point. In fact the immateriality of the spirit or *Nous* was first clearly established by Plotinus. Popular as well as theological conceptions never refined the Christian Spirit to the high transcendentalism of the Platonic *Idea,* but retained its nearer kinship with the quasi-material Stoic penetrating Spirit and the Hebraic *Ruach*. Hence the bestowal of the Spirit was not through the rich and overflowing personality of Jesus, but by His breathing on His disciples. This conception of the Spirit was soon heightened when Jesus' followers could transmit the Holy Spirit by the touch of the hand or by the act of water-baptism. The ' power ' of Jesus could be invoked together with the spirit of an apostle at a distance to cause the death of an unworthy Church member. Images were possessed of demonic powers, and inanimate objects could through a proper ritual handling be changed in nature for weal or woe. A

[1] Macchioro, *Zagreus,* p. 165; cf. *id., Orfismo e Paolinismo,* p. 59 ff.

material instrument might even be tried and found guilty. One should abstain from meat offered to idols, since through such offering the demons secured entry into the food, and thereafter, as Pagans and ecclesiasts knew,[1] they would find lodgement in the stomach and cause physical disturbances. Certain foods seem to have offered easier lodgement than others to evil spirits.[2] By a solemn act of *consecratio* a material object could be endowed with mysterious efficacies and produce sacramental grace or exercise a sacramental curse. The latter is familiar in the *devotiones* and *dirae* of magic which devoted the victim to the lower powers, and in Christian excommunication. Through a misuse of the elements of the Lord's Supper in the first generation in the Corinthian Church an epidemic of serious illness broke out resulting in several deaths.

Papias's account of the miraculous change in the composition and appearance of Judas Iscariot's body presented no difficulty as a solution of divine justice in a world of magical postulates.[3] Only by means of this realism does Clement of Alexandria [4] struggle through his argument on milk as transmuted blood. An able apologist of our religion in critical days believed not only in the existence of demons as really as in that of God and the angels, but asserted that these beings became visible to advanced or spiritual Christians.[5]

In the apocryphal *Acts of John,* John's body is at one time quite impalpable, so that the hand could pass through it like air; at another, normally tangible—a view which was merely a further elaboration of the late orthodox realistic corporeity of the resurrection-narratives of the Gospels. Hermas's speculations [6] were readily comprehensible to his readers when he boldly

---

[1] Angus, *The Mystery-Religions,* p. 256.
[2] Eusebius, *Praep, Evang.* IV. 22, from Porphyry.
[3] *Patr. Apost.,* Gebhardt's ed. minor, p. 73; *Greek Catena on Matt.* xvii. 5.
[4] *Paed.* I. 6, 39 f. [5] Tatian, *Ad Graecos,* 15.
[6] *Sim.* IX. 16, 2 f., opposed by Clement, 1 *Ep. to Cor.* 49, 1; 50, 3.

cut a Gordian knot in soteriology by averring that the unbaptized Old Testament saints were baptized with water in Hades after they had heard the proclamation of the evangel in that quarter by Christ and His apostles, thereby conserving the theory of the necessity of baptism with water and of Church membership to eternal salvation. For this purpose these saints naturally retained their physical human shape and the ministrants their hands. So unquestioned was this realism that one who endeavoured, while maintaining the necessity of the sacramental practices of his day, to correct or moderate the regnant magical views, could write by the end of the first century, ' Unless one is begotten of water and spirit he cannot enter into the kingdom of God,' and ' Unless you eat the *flesh* of the Son of Man and drink His blood, you have no life in you.'

Clement of Alexandria [1] quotes Artapanus as relating how Moses, miraculously released from prison, overwhelmed Pharaoh Chenephres by speaking in his ear the name of the Hebrew God, and later revived the speechless king. This supernatural and magical realism was easily and as a matter of course, in a world devoid of natural science and hungry for miracle, transferred into the sacramental department of Christianity, where it retains its place. Jesus by His own baptism conveyed sacramental power to the water: ' Our God Jesus the Christ . . . was born and baptized that by His suffering (or experience) He might purify the water.' [2] In an even more realistic fashion the great Church Father of the West could write: ' For He took from the earth earth, because flesh is from the earth, and He received flesh from the flesh of Mary. And because in that very flesh He walked here and gave that very flesh to be eaten by us for salvation, no one eats of that flesh unless he has first adored . . . and not only do we not sin by adoring, but we sin if we do not adore.' [3]

---

[1] *Str.* I. 23 (154, 1).   [2] Ignatius, *Eph.* XVIII. 2.
[3] Augustine, *Enar. in Ps.* xcviii. 9, cited *Modern Churchman*, XVI. p. 386.

As a further and—for the history of the sacraments—instructive example of this realism may be cited Irenaeus's bald doctrine of the corporeal presence of Christ in the Eucharist. Attacking those who ' deny the salvation of the flesh and despise its regeneration as being incapable of incorruptibility ' he asserts:

' If this [the flesh] is not saved, then of course the Lord did not redeem us with His blood, nor can the cup of the Eucharist be the participation in His blood, nor the bread which we break a participation in His body. For there is no blood except that from veins and flesh and other human substance. . . . Since we are His members and nourished by the material creation . . . He acknowledged the cup of material creation to be His own blood from which He moistens our blood; and the material bread He affirmed to be His own body from which He causes our bodies to grow. . . . When the Eucharist becomes Christ's body, from these the substance of our flesh grows and consists. How can they deny that the flesh is incapable of receiving the gift of God which is eternal life—the flesh being nourished from the body and the blood of the Lord? . . . We are members of His body, of His flesh and His bones.' [The blessed Paul] ' does not say this of some spiritual and invisible man, for the spirit has neither bones nor flesh, but about the genuinely human condition consisting of flesh and nerves and bones, such as is nourished by His cup which is His blood and grows from the bread which is His body. . . . So also shall our bodies, fed by the Eucharist and after being deposited and dissolved in the earth, rise at their appropriate time.' [1]

This extract conveys some idea of how and where sacramentarian doctrine began and of the extremes to which it was certain to be carried. It also reveals the tendency of controversy to overpress logic and isolate truth. Irenaeus, contending for the orthodox view of the resurrection of the flesh as against the Hellenic

[1] *Adv. Haer.* V. 2-3; cf. IV. 6.

doctrine of the immortality of the soul adopted by Gnostic Docetists, discovered an ingenious argument for his cruder doctrine in a magical doctrine of the Eucharist.

(6) " What's in a name? " was an attitude utterly unknown to ancient mentality, Jewish, Pagan and Christian alike. Names were never to the ancients mere appellatives or convenient designations. The name was an essential part of the person, indeed the power of the person ; it partook of the essence and was pregnant with the *Mana* of the owner. Hence the mystic-magical use of the name was axiomatic. " The modern logical view of names as merely indifferent speech-symbols, which can be changed without affecting the essence of things, was by no means the old-world view. The formula *nomina sunt numina* was valid in all the old religions of the Mediterranean area, including earlier and even later Christianity ; the divine name was felt to be part of the divine essence and itself of supernatural potency." [1] The daemonic power of the name was accepted both in magic [2] and in religion. There was a secret name of Rome, hidden from its most learned and patriotic citizens, but revealed to and kept secret by the priests, lest enemies should take away the protection if the mystic name were divulged.[3] A scholar like Origen sees the main difference between Pagan and Christian exorcisms to lie chiefly in the greater potency of Jesus' Name, in addition to the superior magical effect of the repetition of Christian scriptures.[4] So potent is the Name of Jesus that it will prove effectual even when pronounced by wicked men.

---

[1] Farnell, *Evolution of Religion*, p. 32.   " Name and thing tend to be one in essence. The name is not a mere convention; in some deep mysterious bond of nature it *is* the thing; and if anyone knows the name he is master in some measure of the thing " (Glover, *Christian Tradition*, p. 114). Cf. Jevons, *Intr. to History of Religion*, p. 245.

[2] E.g. δῶρόν μοι ἐδωρήσω τὴν τοῦ μεγίστου σοῦ ὀνόματος γνῶσιν, in *Pap. Paris.* ed. Parthey, II. 127.

[3] Macrobius, *Sat.* III. 9, 5.   [4] *C. Celsum*, I. 6.   Cf. also 24, 25.

The psychological effect of this attitude of mind could not fail to prize the material channels and visible elements of sacramentarianism and to stress the ritual appeal of the Name. The nominalism of contemporary magic was transferred into religion. Symbols secured an importance in their own awful and exclusive right. Grace by unction, which smacks of the magical, was more in demand because more obvious than Plotinus' union with God in contemplation. Association of religious experiences and hopes with cult acts became causal. The ethical association of baptism and spiritual renewal was transcendentalized into baptismal regeneration.

Such being the religious outlook of the world of early Christianity, it is only natural that sacramentarianism should be regarded as the prevailing mode of religion,[1] and that grace should be sought especially in cult acts and salvation be dependent on sacrament. And it was historically almost inevitable that Christianity should be swept into the mighty current of refined magic, despite Jesus' own religion and the deep spirituality which accompanied the launching of the new movement into a world of religious ferment. It was the whole mentality [2] of the ancient world, which Christians shared with Pagans, which forced this missionary faith to equip itself with what were regarded as the essentials or tokens of a religion in that age: miracle, secrecy and sacrament.

[1] Cf. Harnack, *Exp. of Christianity*, I, p. 288.

[2] " We may admit that the triumph of a new and great creed may imply a potent revelation, perhaps a sudden mental transformation in the catechumens difficult to equate with any formulated law of evolution. Still, we cannot gainsay the experience that as the religion establishes and organizes itself, it draws nourishment from the old soil which is full of living germs of past organisms " (Farnell, *Evolution*, p. 23).

CHAPTER IX

ENTRY OF SACRAMENTARIANISM INTO CHRISTIANITY

OPERATING on and through the contemporary mentality and the same realistic supernaturalism, a combination of causes tended to make the new religion conform as far as possible to its sacramentarian competitors.

The Old Testament and Judaistic heritage had a two-fold tendency: on the one hand, toward the personal and spontaneous and immediate religion of prophetism, independent of ritual and liturgy; and on the other, the religion of rule and ritual and intercession, dependent on a class of religious specialists. Unless we are justified in interpreting the account of the relations between believers and the Jewish Church in the opening chapters of Acts as part of the author's re-working of history in favour of the view that the Christians were the true Israel and their religion of the requisite antiquity, the early preachers never for a moment contemplated withdrawal from the ancestral cult. They were not the heralds of a new religion, but of a new era. The pomp of the Temple seems to have been intriguing to the Galilean provincials, who inaugurated what was merely to be a Messianic movement within the pale of Judaism. The ' New Way ' took over wholesale the Jewish Scriptures and ceremonial. In spite of the religious reaction of Philo and the Alexandrines in favour of a religion of faith, the general trend in Judaism was back to Ezekiel and Ezra and away from Jeremiah and the *Wisdom of Solomon*; it was toward a punctilious ritualism, and this was hastened by the silence of prophetism. Religious men accustomed to the meticulous observance of externals did not become less meticulous, but inclined to be rather more.

As Christianity became officially organized the Old Testament priest appeared more to the front than the prophet and the laity were pushed steadily into the background. As soon as the early Gentile Church won in its anti-Judaistic conflict it proceeded to appropriate the spoils. The Jewish Scriptures suggested lines of advance for Christian theology and administration. Such tenets as the necessity of bloody sacrifice, the prescriptions as to externals of cult, and the intercessory functions of priests, were too venerable and too deep-rooted to be discarded. The splendour of the ritual of the great Day of Atonement, bearing upon a human need, appealed to the Church which found in Christ's blood the last and final sacrifice for sin; likewise the necessity of priestly office was a postulate which was not to be antiquated but was taken over in two ways: first, by making Christ the Great High Priest mediating between man and God, as the priest did in all contemporary religions; and secondly, by establishing a Christian order of priests with functions and powers analogous to those of the Old Testament priesthood and of the Mysteries.

It is also remarkable how readily Jerusalem lent itself to the appeal of Hellenism under Antiochus until his mad attempt to hasten the process provoked the inevitable reaction of the Maccabean revolt. Apparently the Jews were growing more responsive to aestheticism in religion. Pseudo-Aristeas (99) speaks of the marvellously transporting effects of the sight of the public processions and the ceremonies in Jerusalem. And Judaism, in its attempt to make its creed attractive, inclined to bring its cult, so far as its exclusivism permitted, into line with the competing Mystery-Religions, which magnified the priestly office. Even two centuries before Philo's day Judaism had been presented as a Mystery in conformity with prevalent esotericism.[1]

[1] Cf. Cerfaux, *Influence des mystères sur le Judaïsme alexandrin avant Philon* (in *Muséon*, 1924, vol. XXXVII, p. 87).

The long-continued and penetrative influence of the
leader of that *prophetic* revival out of which Christianity
arose enhanced the importance of *ritual*.   It was a
strange fate indeed which attended this ascetic's revolt
against the priestly type of religion and his protest
against reliance on conformity with the externals of cult,
but no more strange than that which attended the prophetic ministry of the greater ' Coming One.'   It was
as if the Cynics and the Cyrenaics had laid claim to
be the real successors of Socrates by putting in the
foreground what had been secondary or adventitious
elements in Socrates' teaching.   The Baptist's influence
was greatest in the very centre of Pauline-Johannine
Christianity, Ephesus, and the sect within the Christian
Church which adhered to ' the baptism of John ' died
out only in the nineteenth century.

There is considerable uncertainty as to the nature and
object of the baptism of John due to the scanty references of the Gospels with their differences and the
probability of the influence of later Christian theology,
and to the wholly different account given by Josephus.[1]
According to the Synoptists, the baptism was an eschatological rite, a symbol of repentance as preparation for
the expected Kingdom and ' for remission of sins.'
According to Josephus, John's rite was originally for
' body purification ' for the few ascetics who had renounced the world ' after the soul had been previously
thoroughly cleansed by righteousness,' marking an
advance in virtue rather than a sign of repentance for
remission of sins.   Then, according to Josephus, came
' the others ' (' the multitudes ' of the Synoptic story),
whose arrival as penitents may have modified the rite
somewhat along the lines of the Synoptic account.   The
brief references and the later tendency to accentuate the
sacramental and magical point rather to a symbolic [2]

---

[1] Cf. Jackson & Lake, *Beginnings of Christianity*, I, pp. 101-9.
[2] As by Schürer, *Gesch. d. jüd. Volkes*, 3rd-4th ed. III, p. 185
(n. 90).

interpretation than a sacrament.[1] It was a lustral bath
whereby John received and sealed penitents for the
Kingdom without any indication that thereby or *ipso
facto* their sins were purged away, but with no ambiguity
that they were thereby pledged to ' bring forth the fruits
meet for repentance.' Further, John came as a prophet,
in the succession of those who saw in the cult-worship
symbols rather than efficacious means of cleansing. And
his emphatic contrast of water-rite with the spiritual
baptism of the new era decidedly points to the immersion in the Jordan as a symbol and seal rather than as
a sacrament.[2] The adoption by Peter and the first
Apostles of this rite of the prophetic forerunner casts
welcome light on the primitive usage of the Christian
baptism.

Early Christianity could not forget, even to its em-
barrassment, its connexion with the Baptist's personality
and mission, which offered to its opponents an obvious
means of depreciation and called forth such an apologetic
motif as Matt. iii. 14, 15, and such a protest as that of
the Fourth Gospel, in which the Baptist is reduced from
the great prophet with an original and independent
mission of the Synoptists to the lesser figure of a personal witness to point out the Messiah. If John the
Baptist as ' the greatest of mortals ' exercised such an
influence over Jesus Himself, it is not surprising that
he exercised a still greater and lasting influence on Jesus'

---

[1] In a recent review of the problem a Jewish scholar interprets the
Johannine rite as the baptism of repentance in conjunction with the
Levitical purification: " Le baptême de Jean n'a donc été ni le baptême des prosélytes, ni le baptême juridique au sens de la future com-
munauté chrétienne, ni la lustration lévitique ou le baptême de
pénitence seul, mais le baptême de pénitence joint à la purification
lévitique " (Rubinstein, *Le Baptême de Jean* in *Rev. d. études juives,*
LXXXIV, p. 70).

[2] " Since what he emphasizes is not the efficacy of the rite but the
obligation to bring forth fruits worthy of repentance, and since, further,
he contrasts it with an efficacious Spirit-baptism of the future, there
can hardly be a doubt that he views it as no more than an outward
seal of the inner reformation " (Morgan, *Religion and Theology of Paul,*
p. 209).

followers. But Jesus' originality, compared with that
of John, and His independence in important elements
of His Gospel, as in His personal habits and methods,
are equally striking. It was not without some weighty
reason that Jesus discarded the rite so characteristic of
His predecessor's mission—a rite to which He Himself
had submitted and at the performance of which He had
received His call—the ' baptism of repentance for remission of sins.' The origins of Christian baptism are
notoriously obscure, but it appears that with the found-
ing of the Church the Johannine rite was revived as
the token of admission into the new Messianic Society
which looked for the speedy consummation of the
Advent. The connexion of repentance and the forgiveness of sins was inherent in the rite from its adoption
by the Apostles, and this connexion, at first indeterminate and symbolical as in a Jewish rite and not a Pagan
sacrament, became increasingly causal and transcendental until it issued in ' the laver of regeneration and
of spiritual renewal ' (Titus iii. 5).

As Christianity was carried into the wider world in
which baptism was an initiatory and immortality-
bestowing rite in the ubiquitous Mysteries, the Christian
rite became the equivalent and was embellished with the
ideas and the postulates of such rites. While the rite
was the complete immersion of an adult moral agent
confessing his sins and signifying his desire to secure
the life of the coming aeon, its symbolism as marking
the need of cleansing and his complete change of moral
attitude to his past was obvious and necessitated no
subtle question-begging explanations, but the last trace
of this symbolical and moral significance was lost when
immersion gave way to the sprinkling of a few drops
of water on a morally unconscious infant. Already
before the close of the first century (as in the Fourth
Gospel) this process of the interpretation of the rite had
set in which was to receive its full sacramentarian-
magical expression in the syncretism of the third to

fifth centuries, which dominate the thinking of the present in the Christian Churches.

The rise of officialdom and formalism must be regarded as a contributory cause to the evolution of sacramentarianism. In the Christian Church as elsewhere " Genius does what it must and Talent what it can." When creativeness gives way to imitation, punctiliousness in such imitation becomes a prime virtue. The imitator also probes into the theories and rules of the creator, forgetting that the latter was guided by inspiration and not by an elaborated theory. The original prophetic or apostolic ministry began at an early stage to be displaced by the official or administrative ministry, which naturally stressed order, uniformity and tradition, and magnified its authority, first, by assuming control of the administration of the religious rites of the Society, and secondly, by attributing enhanced, even eschatological, importance thereto, on the supposed authority of Jesus. The men who thus assumed control of the Society did so out of conscientious motives and from a sincere desire to maintain the faith unimpaired, even if reduced to a reproduction of the character of an assumed classic past and in the interest of a fictitious original uniformity. They were largely unconscious of the extent or the direction of the process of consolidation which they were conducting. Such a development was inevitable in a Church which was obliged to subsist longer than it had expected among ordinary earthly conditions; and such an administrative ministry was necessary to counter the aberrations arising out of the tense apocalyptic chiliasm [1] under which the earliest converts were secured and still more necessary to counter the greater aberrations of the psychological reactions of the second and subsequent generations due

[1] " The dying down of the fervid inspiration of the first Christians, and the formation of a hard skeleton of creed and a crust of mystery and ritual, cannot be a pleasant thing to observe " (Gardner, *Growth of Christianity*, p. 185).

to the disappointments in regard to the so surely promised Parousia of the Lord. This delay necessitated giving more attention to matters of organization, discipline and ritual. In these conditions, and with the increasing authority assigned to tradition, it was inevitable that greater importance should be attached to the rites, and from such importance to the magical-mystic theory of them the step was easy and natural in the ancient world. The *episcopos* or overseer was at first mainly concerned with financial matters, but soon took over the office of the ' teacher ' and became the authority for doctrine, and thereafter assumed the office of priest as the dispenser of grace-conferring rituals and as the custodian of the kingdom of Heaven entrusted with the dread ' power of the Keys.'

The so-called conversion of Constantine formed an epoch in the transition of Christianity into the form of a Mystery equipped with the requisite sacerdotal sacramental apparatus. Constantine turned the servants of the Church into priests and pontiffs in political succession to the imperial pontiffs, whose chief function was public ceremonial with its impressive external effects. Constantine gave the priest the supremacy in the new faith, and the politics of the Empire became a formative factor in the creed and practices of the Church. Not only were the religions which were competing with Christianity for Graeco-Roman civilization intensely sacerdotal and scrupulously sacramentarian [1] and insistent on a *disciplina arcani,* but through Constantine's edict and the persecuting enactments of his successors

---

[1] " The day is far distant when the mass of men will be capable of the austere mystic vision, which relies little on external ceremonies of worship. Certainly the last ages of paganism in the West were not ripe for any such reserved spirituality. And the religions which captivated the ages that preceded the triumph of the Catholic Church, while they strove to satisfy the deeper needs of the spirit, were more intensely sacerdotal, and more highly organized than the old religions of Greece and Rome " (Dill, *Roman Society from Nero,* p. 610).

the whole sacerdotal system of the previous State religion of Rome and of the most successful of the Mysteries was taken over *en bloc* into the new State religion. The increasing love of pomp and ritual under the Empire had now to be catered for by the established Christian Church. And that religion—Mithraism—which was specially in the ascendant politically near the time of Constantine's conversion, and which had been declared the State religion less than twenty years before Christianity succeeded to the same perilous status, was a sacerdotal-sacramentarian Mystery with its ' high Pontiff of Mithra,' its *ordo sacerdotum,* its holy virgins, and its stern ascetics.

The exclusiveness of the early Christian society as that of the spiritually elect out of a sinful world was now necessarily modified by the forcible opening of the doors of the Church by legislation and by the ' compelling ' of Jews, Pagans and heretics ' to come in ' ; but such modification only accentuated its exclusiveness by magnifying the sacerdotal powers of those set apart to keep or to impart the ' secrets,' and by stressing the magical-sacramentarian character of the rites of initiation, and the cult acts of communion. Its catholicity was co-extensive with its exclusiveness, whereby it became the great secret religious society of the Empire, persecuting and exterminating competing religious secret societies.

The new principle of exclusiveness which had been introduced into the West by Orphism in the sixth century B.C., namely, that without initiation there can be no salvation or immortality, culminated in the Cyprianic ' outside the Church no salvation,' and admission into the Church in a world where God only knows the secret conditions of the heart was effected by baptismal rites according to the religious traditions of Paganism and Christianity. The original adult baptism gave place to the sprinkling of infants as soon after birth as possible lest the ' little ones ' should by dying without the water-

rite face a dread destiny in the next world.[1] And the
baptism of the blood-stained and utterly unscrupulous
Christian emperor *in extremis mortis* was the forerunner
of numerous other similar theurgical acts and magical
expedients of escape from penalties hereafter. But as
in the best ages of the Church, and even in the worst
ages through spiritually-minded members, the moral
earnestness of Christianity is never wholly silenced, so
the conviction that purity is an inward disposition of
soul restrained the Church from fully naturalizing the
sacramentarian magic of its milieu during the first centuries and ever recalled it to the moral appeal of Jesus.[2]

Esotericism.—While historic Christianity in some
respects uncompromisingly set itself in opposition to the
contemporary outlook and customs (e.g. on tolerance,
sexual morality), in others it hastened to adapt itself to
the religious fashions in vogue, and in thus becoming
popular it lost something of the creative spirit of its
Lord. One of these fashions which early intrigued it
was the principle of esotericism in religion. To the
ancient mind secrecy was an essential in a respectable
religion—secrecy as to the correct name of the Deity,
of the proper ritual of approach, of the method of
initiation into membership, of the nature and the mode
of working of the symbols, and so on. And this principle

---

[1] Cf. Loofs, *Symbolik*, p. 269. According to the Tridentine Catechism children dying unbaptized " are born to eternal misery and
perdition." This awful injustice is somewhat ameliorated by the Jesuit
scholar Bellarmine by locating such children in a higher part of Hell
than Purgatory, so that the fire cannot reach them : " est tamen com-
munis opinio scholasticorum limbum puerorum esse in loco inferni
altiore, quam sit Purgatorium, ita ut ad eum ignis non perveniat " (*De
Purgatorio*, II. 6; ref. in F. J. Paul, *Doctrinal Decrees of the Council
of Trent*, p. 21).

[2] " Auch wäre es leicht zu zeigen, wie bald die Kirche in ihrer
Sakramentspraxis dem heidnischen Mysterienwesen verfallen ist. Aber
so stark war das einmal eingepflanzte Element der sittlichen Forderung,
der Reinheit der Seele, dass es sich in der katholischen Kirche auch
neben der schlechten Sakramentspraxis behauptete " (Harnack, *Texte
u. Unters.* VIII. 4, p. 134).

of secrecy not only necessitated the existence of a select person or persons, charged with the observance and the impartation of the secret, but it aggrandized sacerdotal pretensions and gave added value to rites of initiation and rites of advance in degrees of membership. A hierophant was a person clothed with unique authority, on whom the present and future salvation of the non-initiated depended. The uninitiated might not have much to learn, and might have a limited understanding of their motives and actions, but however few or trite or traditional were the solemn words, they were fraught with significance as passwords to bliss. The mimetic or interpretative ritual might be difficult for a thoughtful person to explain, except by a liberal allegorism such as Plutarch applies to the offensive items of the Osiris-Isis cult, but it was by agelong theory the gate to salvation. A certain religious habit of mind was engendered which affected Christians in the formulation of a new religion in an esoteric milieu, and disposed them toward a strange romanticism under the charm of the antique in religion.

It is one of the many striking phenomena in the evolution of historic Christianity that a religion which was at first preached by Jesus ' with authority ' to the understanding of the common people, and brought within their apprehension, ' for without a parable spake He not unto them,' which proclaimed its secrets to the unchurched classes and outcasts, and offered its Beatitudes to peasants and fisher-folk and day-labourers, and of which an early apologist declared ' brief and concise were His discourses, for He was no sophist, but His word was the power of God,' [1] should so rapidly [2] accept the

---

[1] Justin, *Apol.* I. 14, 11.

[2] " Just as the Gospel courts publicity, so its scope is universal. . . . There is nothing esoteric in the teachings of Jesus from first to last. It is one of the great and comforting features in His character that love of mystery and aristocratic self-sufficiency are alike alien to Him. Hence Christianity and the Mysteries are mutually exclusive " (Wernle, *Beginnings of Christianity*, II. 124).

prevailing mode of a *disciplina arcani*—so rapidly, for in
the earliest Gospel the writer, without being conscious
of any incongruity and without reference to other corrective statements of his own, represents Jesus as justify-
ing Himself in one of the most lucid of the parables
thus : ' To you is given the mystery of the kingdom of
God, but to outsiders everything is imparted in parables
that they may see and not perceive, that they may hear
and not understand, lest they should be converted and
be forgiven ' (Mark iv. 11). Christianity began with
Mystery as something not concealed, but as something
once concealed and now revealed to all or revealed as
far as possible.[1] At first Christians were not pledged
to secrecy even concerning their *mysteria*—a noted difference from the adherents of the Mysteries. The first
Apologies intended for the public, such as those of
Justin, not only speak without reserve of the Christian
doctrines and sacraments, but challenge their opponents
to ' study our religion ; you will be convinced how little
reason we have for avoiding light.' Indeed, Justin's
frank and welcome description[2] of the Christian
Eucharist about the middle of the second century should
not have been penned by an apologist of the succeeding
century.

By the second century the existence of an esoteric and
an exoteric type of Christianity was beginning to be
recognized[3] and is distinctly evident in Origen and
Tertullian. The evolution was probably inevitable—due
to the natural differences manifested by catechumens in
their training, the rise of the official ministry over the
prophetic, the organization of Christianity as an exclusive
society, the contemporary postulate of the value of the
secret, the differentiation between catechumens and
initiated, the effect of persecutions and the refusal of
the State to recognize Christianity as *religio licita* (which
forced Christians to hold secret meetings and live as it

---

[1] Cf. Chrysostom, ad 1 Cor. vii. 2.   [2] *Apol.* I, ch. 65 f.
[3] Cf. Hatch, *Influence of Greek Ideas*, p. 293.

were underground and to guard their scriptures and rites), together with certain scriptural references, such as that cited above from Mark's Gospel and Paul's reference to the distinction of spiritual nourishment as milk for babes and food for the maturer, and such a logion as ' cast not your pearls before swine.' But Paganism was the chief tutor of Christianity in the mysterious values of esoterics.[1] Stobaeus [2] lays down the principle: ' the mystical secrecy of the rites renders the divine more awesome by imitating this nature which eludes our comprehension.' Hence the value of the ' secret ' was highly prized and the obligation to secrecy was strictly observed.[3]

Celsus's first objection against Christianity was as a system of ' secret societies,' which Origen does not deny but proceeds to justify the co-existence of esoteric and exoteric Christianity after the example of philosophies and the customs of the Mysteries.[4] The same advocate of esotericism elsewhere [5] dilates on the purport of scripture with its ' mysterious economies,' which explain such tales as the intercourse of Lot with his daughters, and the two wives of Jacob and his two slave-girls who became mothers of patriarchs. Because of the ineffable mysteries, individual readers make serious mistakes without the ' key of knowledge,' which is mainly deftness with allegory. Of a threefold character are scriptural ideas; the common man is edified by the ' flesh ' of scripture, the more advanced or psychic by the ' soul ' of scripture, and the ' perfect ' by the spiritual things. As God has compounded man of body, soul and spirit, so He has ordered the scripture according to the same

---

[1] Ammonius, Origen's teacher in philosophy, refused to commit his doctrines to writing and imposed a promise on his students not to divulge his secret teachings.

[2] X. 3, 9, p. 467.

[3] Cf. Angus, *Mystery-Religions*, p. 77; Graillot, *Culte de Cybèle*, p. 175; and ' tu pius mystes sacris teletis reperta mentis arcano premis,' *C.I.L.* VI. 1779 d.

[4] Origen, *C. Celsum*, I. 1, I. 7.   [5] *De Prin.* IV. 9-20 (IV, 2, 4).

arrangement for the salvation of man.   Certain passages
are fraught with a ' corporeal,' others with a 'soul ' or
psychic sense, and others contain the very spirit.   The
possession of the Spirit enables one to sit loose to history
and to historical interpretation.   Origen carried his
principle of esoteric explanation so far as to affirm that
certain Christian secrets should not lightly be committed
to writing for fear of being divulged : thus ' it is not
without danger to commit to writing the elucidation of
such things, inasmuch as the masses do not need
more teaching than that concerning the punishment of
sinners.' [1]

Clement, Origen's teacher and predecessor, accepts
the same cleavage of a common and a secret Christianity.   He quotes a logion [2] of Jesus from an apocryphal
gospel, ' My mystery is for Me and for the sons of My
house.'   He describes,[3] for example, the two kinds of
knowledge corresponding to milk diet and flesh diet,
blood ' being as it were liquid flesh.'   He adopts the
Greek analogy of the Lesser and Greater Mysteries to
the Christian discipline.

The Gnostics vied with the orthodox Church in maintaining the principle of secrecy.   The first charge brought
by Epiphanius against his opponents is their ' hiding
in silence their unspeakable mysteries.' [4]   Tertullian [5]
brings a like charge against the Valentinians.   The
Gnostics differed from their orthodox brethren only in
bringing their cult earlier and more thoroughly into
alignment with the Mysteries and in the success with
which they established secret, aristocratic, sacramental
societies, the entrance into which was zealously guarded.
To a greater extent than they were conscious of, the
Christian officials were influenced by the Mysteries,
especially in their ideas as to the character and efficacy

[1] VI. 26.   [2] *Str*. V. 10, 63; cf. *Clem. Homilies*, XIX, 20.
[3] *Paed*. I. 6, 39.
[4] *Phil*. I *pro* (Cruice, pp. 2-3).   " Yet this very secrecy was natur-
alized in the Church " (Hatch, *ib*. 293).
[5] *C. Valent*. I.

of sacraments, and in the ordinary ranks of the laity this influence was all the more subtle because of the facility with which converts from Pagan mystery-societies would carry over their magic-sacramental ideas and esoterics into the service of the Lord Jesus.

One cannot overlook historically the propagandist value for the early Christian mission of the possession of such occult holy lore guarded by Christian hierophants, ' the mystagogues of the secret Mysteries,' endued with more terrible prerogatives over their fellow-men here and hereafter than their Pagan predecessors and contemporaries and operating in connexion with sacraments ensuring salvation and delivering from devils.[1]

Moreover, Christianity spread in a world of Paganism with deep-rooted artistic-religious cravings, and not in the mother-soil of Judaism, which was indifferent to plastic and pictorial art. The Mediterranean world, tutored by the Greeks in aestheticism, sought the satisfaction of sensuous impulses in worship. The aestheticism of Graeco-Roman Paganism lived on in Christianity, the love of a well-ordered impressive ceremonial and a liturgy appealing to the imagination through the senses. It was a world which pressed art, plastic and pictorial and choregic, into the service of religion. Ritual was the bridge between art and religion, and as the taste for art was too innate to be exorcised by early Christian puritanism, ritual was greatly esteemed. The importance of this factor is borne out by the observation that the old lands of Graeco-Roman culture are those which cherish the rich and elaborate ceremonial of the Greek

[1] " It is beyond question that this aspect of Christianity, which went on developing almost from the very hour of its birth, proved of the highest moment to the propaganda of the religion. Christianity acquired a special weight from the fact that in the first place it had mysterious secrets of its own, which it sought to fathom only to adore them once again in silence, and secondly, that it preached to the perfect in another and a deeper sense than it did to simple folk " (Harnack, *Expansion,* I, p. 289).

Church and of Rome, while the northern lands are satisfied with a simpler form of worship.

If the religion of Greece was one in which Beauty was consecrated in worship and the sensuous represented in rich symbolism, that of Rome was concrete and materialistic. It consisted largely in things done, cult acts performed to a crowded, sacred calendar and to the most meticulous ritual. Because of the more solid qualities of Roman character, Roman religion was more strongly institutionalized in static forms which survived tenaciously; the Romans never turned criticism so relentlessly on their religion as did the Greeks. Roman cult and ritual were never supplemented in Roman life with anything corresponding to Greek philosophy or the richness of Greek mythology. Hence Roman religion, intellectually barren, tended to become and remained statuesque and external, unimaginative and materialistic, dignified, while overburdened by ceremonialism and picturesque formalism, and never hospitable to change like that of the Greeks. Roman religion bequeathed to its imperial successor the deep interest in a cult, the importance of accuracy in the routine of ritual, the conception of religion as a mode of political power, the appeal of rich vestments and stately processions, and the value of organization against centrifugal forces of thought and questioning of authority. "As materialism crept into the sacraments through the influence of Asia, so materialism crept into ritual through Roman influence." [1]

Art was perhaps more certain to be accompanied by devotion than by morality. The gorgeous processions that wound their way to sacred shrines or through the streets of the Graeco-Roman cities did not cease; they merely changed their banners and some of their symbols, but generally retained their costumes and their festive moods. Greece, which made such a strong impression on the creeds of the new faith, was still vital enough,

[1] Gardner, *Growth of Christianity*, p. 150.

even amid the loss of nerve and the tyranny of asceticism, to impart somewhat of its message of Beauty and a sensuous response thereto, and its characteristic alliance of art and religion. More particularly was this so when after the conversion of Constantine the Christian Church was augmented by hosts of Pagans, because it was the State religion and because of its repressive measures towards other faiths, and the confiscation of Pagan ecclesiastical endowments. The long-established habits of seeking a religion interpreting itself in action and mimetic rite and symbol and in *mythos* rather than in creed and philosophy persisted, and the thirst for satisfaction of the aesthetic tastes abetted picturesque ritual,[1] which necessitated a clerical succession to the venerable priesthoods that had so long and so excellently catered to aestheticism. In Greek lands, and especially in country districts, to this day, one can at special seasons of the Church calendar easily transport himself back over the centuries and witness the genius of ancient Greece for supplementing her metaphysical interpretation of religion by an interpretation in festive ceremonial and mimetic aestheticism.[2] And Greek aestheticism had long been acclimatized or at least imitated in Roman ritual, and was supplemented by Roman love of display. The penchant of the Roman mind for pageantry, festive religion, and processions,[3] the poverty of Roman mythology, and the ingrained desire of Rome for an imposing State religion as a mode of political power, disposed the Romans towards borrowed ceremonial. The thirst for pageantry and processions grew apace

---

[1] Cf. Hatch, *Influence of Greek Ideas*, p. 309.

[2] For the Epiphany as the Christian development or adaptation of the Parousia festival of Dionysos, cf. Usener, *Das Weihnachtsfest*, VII.

[3] "Meaningless as they were, the stately processions remained, and could be watched with pride by the patriotic Roman all through the period of the Empire until the Roman Church adapted them to its own ritual and gave them . . . a new meaning. As the cloud-shadows move slowly over the hollows of the Apennines, so does the procession of the patron saint pass still through the streets of many an Italian city " (Fowler, *Religious Experience of the Roman People*, p. 218).

under the Empire, to meet which religious and other spectacles were multiplied.

Another cause decidedly favourable to the elaboration of a supernatural machinery of rite and the materialization of the Christian sacraments into what they became toward the end of the Pagan supremacy and through the Dark Ages and what they are to the majority of the Christians to-day was the passing of Platonism and the coming of the long reign of Aristotelianism in the Christian Church. The impetus given to dialectics, the advances in biology, and the original and fruitful metaphysical work of Aristotle were gains dearly bought at the price of the arrest of the brilliant and promising career of Greek science, for which the authority of Aristotle may rightly be held responsible.[1] Had Aristotle retained Plato's predilection for mathematics and interest in astronomical studies, the whole course of Christian theology, especially of the sacraments, would have been far other than it has been. Had Aristotle understood more intimately his master's mystical craving, which sought something deeper than intellectual satisfaction and security, the history of Christian mysticism would have been different—and saner. Platonism in alliance with Stoicism was supreme during the centuries of the heroic struggle and victory of Christianity, but Aristotelian realism [2] came in from the end of the fifth century onwards, and for a thousand years " the Master of them that know " dominated Christian thought. He was the master of the keen scholastic intellects with their brilliant dialectic. To this

[1] Prof. A. E. Taylor in his last book on Plato (*Comm. on Plato's Timaeus*) has much to say on this topic in commending the Pythagorean and Platonic combination of ' mathematics ' with philosophy: " Pythagorean and Academic science was moving as directly in the *direction* of Galileo and Newton as in that of Copernicus and Kepler, and it is a tragedy of the human intellect that Aristotle and the Stoics with their crude Ionian prepossessions were able to arrest the tendency as thoroughly as they did " (p. 441).

[2] Westcott, *Religious Thought in the West*, p. 222.

day Aristotle remains the master philosopher in the
theology of the Roman Church, especially through
Aquinas, in whom one can detect the constant conflict
for authority between these rival philosophies of Plato
and Aristotle, in which, however, the logic of Aristotle
wins. Had Aquinas, the last great representative theologian of united Western Christianity, sought to Christi-
anize Plato, as he so successfully Christianized Aristotle,
the division between Western Christianity to-day would
not be so acute.   Under Aristotelian categories only
could the typically Western doctrine of Transubstantiation have evolved.   Outside the Roman Church his
supremacy has been and is increasingly disputed by
Platonism.

In the early centuries even the idealism of Plato could
not prevent the Christian rites from being assimilated
to their Pagan analogues, but it did prevent the literaliz-
ing and materializing [1] of them by ever keeping open
a door of escape from the accidental, individual and
corporeal to the *Form* or *Idea*. But when Aristotle inaugurated on its long history the distinction between
substance and accident, a new weapon had been forged
for miraculous realism.

And as Latin Christianity parted company with Greek
Christianity and lost touch with the humanism and more
comprehensive breadth of view of the Greek Fathers,
the domination of Aristotle was strengthened by the
character of the Western mind, which, not being philo-
sophically inclined, formulated its doctrine with a crude
concreteness. The transcendental ideas and sublime
abstractions of Greek thought took on under the Latin
genius the character of magical realism and supernaturalism resting upon an ultimate mysterious divine
fiat and a palpable theurgy. Greek science was dead
and modern science not yet born: neither philosophy
nor theology had yet parted company with mythology.
Mystagogic theology held the field and fostered sacra-

[1] Cf. Inge, *Contentio Veritatis,* pp. 292-9.

mental magic in ever coarser and more extravagant forms of theurgy. The sacraments have not yet recovered from their implication in the barbarization of Europe on the passing of classical culture. When Christianity adopted the Pagan basilica, it took over much of its furniture and practices.

CHAPTER X

THE EVOLUTION OF MAGICAL-SACRAMENTAL IDEAS
AND USAGES

THE progressive materialization of the Christian sacraments cannot be assigned directly to any of the above-
mentioned causes or to the conjunction of them all, or
perhaps even to the direct influence of the Mysteries,
but rather to the whole ancient mentality;[1] to the retreat
of the Jewish influence and the preponderant influence
of Pagans who from the *damnosa haereditas* of Constantine were transferred by legislation from Pagan
conventicles into the Christian ecclesia with their Pagan
ideas and practices; and to the difficulty of maintaining
the spirituality of large and mixed masses at the high
fervour of the first missionary preaching.

At the cost of millennia of experimentation it was
brought home to man that ' God is not to be worshipped
with bulls but with a devout and righteous will,' [2] and it
will require millennia yet adequately to realize that
' neither in this mountain nor in Jerusalem shall ye
worship the Father,' or that God has no decided
preferences for one mode or tradition of cult-acts above
another.

There were among the ancients, as among ourselves,
two main ways of approach to the Deity, though not
necessarily exclusive: the path of intuition and reflexion,
in which spirit to spirit speaks and reason unites with

[1] " For the materialization of the sacraments we need seek no origin
but the constitution of human nature. The mass of mankind tends to
be materialistic, dominated by that which is seen and felt, unable to
recognize spiritual truth unless it is incorporated in some material
vehicle " (Gardner, *Growth of Christianity*, p. 178).

[2] ' Colitur Deus non tauris sed pia et recta voluntate ' (Seneca, *Ep*.
95). Cf. Iamblichus, *Protr*. II, p. 10, ed. Pistelli.

its source, and the path offered by institutional religion
in cult forms and outward acts which symbolize or typify
or convey inward benefits. The former path is taken by
the mystic and the philosopher ; the latter by the masses
of men who find fasting easier than concentration or
contemplation and prefer visibility even in spiritual
experiences and crave for something material in religion.

One fact should never be allowed to drop out of sight
in considering the history of Christian sacramentarianism.
While the sacraments took their rise within Jewish
traditions and from Jewish cult rites, it was on Pagan
soil and under Hellenistic traditions and mysticism that
they acquired their premier place in the life of the
Church. This is of course but one aspect of the rupture
of early Christianity with Judaism, the failure of Christianity to gain a secure footing on its native soil, and its
amazing success on Gentile soil. But the bearing of
this epochal transition or change of fulcrum upon the
evolution of sacramentarianism is not always adequately
recognized.

It should not therefore be overlooked that the early
house-churches of Christianity developed into the
Catholic Church under the dominance of Gentile (Greek-
Oriental) Christianity,[1] and that the end of the second
century and the third century was the era of consolidation of Christian doctrine under Clement and Origen
under whom Christianity was taken into the category
of Mystery-Religions, and that the organization of the
Catholic Church was largely the creation of the genius
of Cyprian, who was a firm believer in magic. Cyprian
cites four examples [2] of the elements of the sacrament

---

[1] " It was inevitable that Hellenic religion should leave a deep
impression upon earlier and later Christianity; partly because the religious temper of the Greek world, throughout the centuries immediately
preceding the adoption of Christianity, was more powerful and fervid
than it had been in the days of Homer or Pericles, and mainly because
Hellenic converts became the pillars of the Church " (Farnell, *Evolution of Religion*, p. 23).

[2] *De Lapsis*, 25, 26.

partaken unworthily; one on the inability of a little girl
to consume the elements of the sacrament after she had
eaten the demon-charged food offered to idols. In
another instance a woman, surreptitiously partaking of
the elements, 'received not food but a sword' and suffered from internal convulsions. Another woman sought
'with unclean hands to open the box in which was the
holy thing [body] of the Lord, and was prevented by
fire breaking forth from it, so that she dare not touch
it.' Again, a man unworthily participating received
from the priest the elements, which turned to cinders
in his hand.

Such language presented no difficulties to Pagans. In
several of the Mystery-Religions baptism was the means
to the remission [1] of the penalties of sin, and of regeneration. The baptism of the *taurobolium* was valid for
twenty years, only the idea of baptism in certain
Christian circles being able to surpass this as conferring
an indelible character. Initiation in the Orphic brotherhoods delivered from 'the wearisome painful wheel' of
reincarnation, and resulted in deification. The sacramental meal of the Mysteries had almost the vogue in
popular religion which the Eucharist enjoys to-day in
Christian circles, and it offered the same wide field of
speculation as to its blessings and modes of operation.

It is but a slight transition from this world of
sacramental efficacies to Christian sacramental grace.
Ignatius [2] views the Eucharist as 'the medicine of immortality' and 'the antidote against death' and the
guarantee to Christians of their resurrection. Irenaeus [3]
proves the incorruptibility of Christian flesh by appealing
to participation in the Eucharistic meal, in the elements
of which Christ is present far other than symbolically or
spiritually, in a way which conserves material bodies.
Similarly, but with less realism, Gregory of Nyssa [4] holds

[1] Cf. Tertullian, *De Bapt.* 5; *Adv. Haer.* 40.   [2] *Eph.* 20.
[3] *Adv. Haer.* IV. 18, 4 f.
[4] *Cat. Or.* 37 (ed. J. H. Srawley).

' God the Word ' ' blending Himself with the bodies of believers, to secure that by this union with the immortal, man too may be a sharer in incorruption.'

The magical power or physical efficacy of baptism is startlingly prominent in Tertullian. For example, it seems to him a perverse and amazing thing that one should regard the ' attainment of immortality ' through immersion in water and the repetition of a few words as incredible. ' Surely we cannot wonder that death is abolished by the laver.' He essays to treat ' regeneration by water ' and the supernatural powers infused into the ' water of the sacrament,' and tells how the waters after the invocation acquire the sacrament of sanctification by the Spirit immediately descending from heaven and sanctifying them for Himself and thereby imparting to them the power of sanctification. Through the supernatural medicinal qualities of the consecrated waters and angelic agency the spirit is corporeally cleansed and the flesh spiritually cleansed.[1] He prudentially recommends the postponement of baptism because of the mortal danger attendant on post-baptismal sins, previous sins being left behind in the laver. Clement [2] of Alexandria sees in baptism ' healing medicine,' παιώνιον φάρμακον. Gregory of Nyssa [3] says categorically, ' I affirm that it is impossible apart from the laver-regeneration for a man to have part in the Resurrection,' and he attributes immortality-bestowing qualities to the baptismal waters. He also describes baptism as *muesis* (initiation). Hippolytus [4] assigns to the Christian rite the mortality-removing powers familiar in the contemporary Mysteries : man by becoming ' immortal becomes also God,' and he is ' rendered God [divine] by water and the Holy Spirit.' And Cyril [5] of Jerusalem declares ' partaking of the body and blood of Christ, that you

---

[1] *De Bapt.* 2-6.   [2] *Paed.* I. 6, 29.
[3] *Or. Cat. Mag.* 35, δίχα τῆς κατὰ τὸ λουτρὸν ἀναγενήσεως.
[4] *On Holy Theophany*, 8.   Cf. Gregory of Nyssa, *Cat. Or.* 37 above.
[5] *Catech.* 3.

may become *concorporate* and *consanguineous* with Him; for thus we become Christophori by His body and blood entering into our members.' Origen [1] affirms that the invocation of the name of Jesus even by worthless men may be potent for exorcism. He shares with his contemporaries their unquestioning belief in magic and admits the efficacy of incantations according to secret formulae. Methodius remarks on the repetition of the passion by the indwelling Christ, ' for not otherwise could the Church continually conceive believers and bear them anew through the bath of regeneration, unless Christ were repeatedly to die, emptying Himself for the sake of each individual.' [2]

This sacramental religion was not confined to the orthodox. The apostle John [3] by prayer and breaking of bread accomplished the death of the impenitent Fortunatus after he had been restored from the dead to his wife Drusiana, so that John could say, ' Thou hast thy child, O Devil '; whereupon follows: ' John therefore was with the brethren rejoicing in the Lord.' Another instance: ' Now they brought to Paul [in Rome] bread and water for the sacrifice,' when Rufina, an adulteress, appeared ' to receive the Eucharist of God,' and at Paul's rebuke she collapsed. [4]

The magical character of sacral rites is better revealed in their vicarious potencies in the beliefs of Jews, Pagans and Christians. The noble Judas, when his soldiers died so heroically but, alas ! in such mortal sin—symbols and tokens of the idols of Jamnia being found on their bodies —took up a collection and sent it to Jerusalem to make a sin-offering on behalf of their resurrection; ' wherefore he made a thorough atonement on behalf of the dead that their sins might be discharged.' [5] Plato [6] tells of Orphic

---

[1] *C. Celsum*, I. 6, I. 22-4.
[2] Cited Inge, *Christian Mysticism*, p. 100.
[3] *Acts of John*, 73 (James, *Apoc. N.T.* p. 246).
[4] *Acts of Peter* (*Vercelli*), 2 (James, p. 304 f.).
[5] 2 Macc. xii. 38 ff.   [6] *Rep.* II. 364.

rites extending to the dead, and we read of Dionysiac
rites performed for those who died unhouseled: ' They
will perform rites aiming at the deliverance of godless
ancestors.' [1] Even in the imposing ritual of the *taurobolium,* bath in bull's blood, substitutes were possible as
surrogates for non-initiates.[2]

Examples among Christians are more striking. Paul,
so far from rebuking, founds an argument upon the
vicarious baptisms for the dead at Corinth. As these
rites had a tremendous eschatological value, it is not
surprising that the custom spread. Thus Chrysostom [3]
tells us of the Marcionites: ' Whenever any of the
catechumens among them dies, they conceal the living
under the bed of the dead and then approach the dead
and talk with him and inquire if he wishes to receive
baptism. Then when he makes no reply, the one concealed replies for him that he wishes to be baptized,
and so they baptize him in the stead of the dead.' The
Cerinthian Gnostics had the same rite which they
practised as ' tradition,' [4] and Tertullian knows of the
same practice. In his treatise *On the Resurrection of
the Flesh* he comments with approval on ' vicarious
baptism ' as being ' beneficial to the flesh of another
with a view to the resurrection ' and as being meaningless ' unless bodies thus baptized rise again.' [5]
Epiphanius bitterly attacks Aerius for disparaging rites
and prayers for the dead, the heretic's objection being
on the moral ground that such practices would encourage
the living to adopt the easier method of securing good
friends, even by payment of a fee, to attend to their

---

[1] Abel, *Orph.*, *fr.* 208, ὄργια τ' ἐκτελέσουσι λύσιν προγόνων ἀθεμίστων
μαιόμενοι.

[2] Cf. Anrich, *Das Antike Mysterienwesen*, p. 120. For an interesting
vicarious blood-baptism (*taurobolium*) of one priest on behalf of another,
vide Réville, *Religion à Rome*, p. 96.

[3] *Cat.* 310.

[4] Epiph. *Haer.* 28, 6.

[5] 48. Cf. *De Corona* 3, ' oblationes pro defunctis, pro natalitiis, annua
die facimus.'

eternal safety after death.[1]   In Africa the Montanists administered both baptism and the Eucharist to the dead.[2]
That the practice was far from confined to heretics is
attested by the regulation of the Council of Carthage
in 397: ' item placuit, ut corporibus defunctorum
eucharistia non detur . . . deinde cavendum est, ne
mortuos etiam baptizari posse fratrum infirmitas credat.'
In Hermas baptism is not merely an absolute condition
of salvation for the living, but for the saints under the
Old Covenant because it blotted out all prior sins.[3]

It should be noted that Pagan protests were registered
against *ex opere operato* virtues from at least four centuries before Christ.   The Orphics had a proverb based
on bitter experience of human frailty, ' Many are the
thyrsus-bearers, but few the mystae.'   Plato [4] protests
vehemently against the religious charlatans who, appealing to scriptures of Musaeus and Orpheus, profess by
means of sacrifices, incantations and Mysteries, to
procure absolution both for living and dead, and, for
a monetary consideration, to make due amends for the
misdeeds of a man's ancestors, and even, ' at a trifling
cost,' to sell indulgences to those who intend to inflict
an injury upon a detested victim, whether good or
wicked.   His protest rests on the fact that these things
cannot affect character and they give wrong impressions
to serious-minded young men.   After such sacraments
men live lives contemptible here and after death enjoy
' an eternity of carouse.'   Like a true Greek, he calls on
man to ' adorn the soul in her own jewels—self-restraint,
justice, courage, nobility and truth.   Arrayed in these,
the soul is prepared for her journey to the Underworld
when her time comes.'   And again, the man who ' fixes
his gaze upon truth ' lives honourably, virtuously, and
can suffer no evil.[5]

---

[1] *Panarion*, III. *Haer.* 75; Oehler, *Corpus Haeresiologicum*, II, pt. I,
p. 180; p. 907, Petav.
[2] Philastrius, *Haer.* 49.   [3] *Sim.* IX. 16.
[4] *Rep.* II. 364a-365a.   [5] *Gorgias*, 527d.

Plutarch [1] represents Diogenes, on hearing of Sophocles' threefold beatitude of the initiated, as trenchantly asking: ' Shall Pataikion, the brigand, have a fairer lot in death because he received the sacrament than Epaminondas? ' and Diogenes Laertius [2] represents the same Cynic, when invited by the Athenians to accept initiation at Eleusis, as replying, ' It would be absurd that Aegesilaus and Epaminondas should lie in mud [in the lower world] while some vile wretches, because of initiation, should enjoy the Islands of the Blessed.' [3]

A Pythian oracle [4] declared ' the temples of the gods stand open for all good men: there is no need of purification, for no stain can cleave to goodness. But avaunt, whosoever is baneful of heart, for thy soul will never be cleansed by the cleansing of the body.' And the Saviour of Epidauros maintained, ' within the incense-filled shrine one must be pure, and purity is to have righteous thoughts.' [5]

Even Ovid [6] protests against the externality of sacraments:

> ' Omne nefas omnemque mali purgamina causam
> Credebant nostri tollere posse senes.
> Graecia principium moris fuit; illa nocentes
> Impia lustratos ponere facta putat
> O nimium faciles, qui tristia crimina caedis
> Fluminea tolli posse putetis aqua.'

Epictetus [7] emphasizes the preparation of sacrifice and prayer, of bodily and inward purification before approaching the Eleusinian Mysteries, and scoffs at the idea that ' the words have a holy power within themselves.' Philo testifies: ' If often happens that good

---

[1] *De Audiendis Poetis*, 4 (21 F).   [2] VI. 39.

[3] Julian (*Orat.* VII, 239 B.C.) adds: ' Because he observed that the one who recommended initiation neglected uprightness in his life while setting great store by his initiation '; and ' Initiation is for those who have lived worthily of it,' and ' No advantage comes to the wicked, though they gain access into the inner shrine.'

[4] *Anth. Pal.* XIV. 74 (Farnell's tr. *Evolution*, p. 138).

[5] Wilamowitz-Möllendorf, *Isyllos*, 6.

[6] *Fasti*, II. 35 ff.   [7] *Diss.* III. 21.

men are not initiated, but that robbers and murderers
and base women are, if they pay cash to the initiators
and hierophants.' The ancients were confronted with
the same practical enigma about sacral operations as
moderns when they observed that some who had participated in the sacraments (Pagan or Christian) led
lives of questionable worth, while others who took no
sacraments or sat loose to them, lived irreproachable
lives. Origen [1] regretted that ' not all those who are
bathed [baptized] in water are forthwith bathed in the
Holy Spirit.'

So great is the gulf between the mentality [2] of the
Graeco-Roman world and ours that the early Christians
would hardly recognize any of our sacraments (not even
the Roman Mass nor the mysterious rites of the modern
religious romantics). Even the Roman Church may be
said to have maintained the early realism and thoroughgoing *opus operatum* credence more in theory than in
practice: the lessons of its mystics have not been lost
upon it. And now, lest magic should perish from
Christianity, the romantics born out of due season are
coming in ever-increasing numbers to its rescue. Historically the early Christians who first practised our
sacraments and later elaborated them would repudiate
our ideas of sacraments as symbols, even if we omit
the word " *mere* " before symbols. Such modern
" symbolism " would have to ancient minds annihilated

[1] *Hom. in Num*. III. 1.

[2] Loofs, in art. *Abendmahl in Realencyk.*, 3rd ed. I, p. 41, quotes
the striking paragraph from Strauss's *Leben Jesu*: " For the writers
of our Gospels the Bread in the Supper was the Body of Christ; but if
one had asked them whether the Bread was changed, they would have
denied it; if one had spoken to them of a partaking of the Body with
and under the Bread, they would not have understood it: if one had
inferred that the Bread means or represents the Body, they would not
have been satisfied with that." Loofs's comment on this is: " So
far as concerns the writers of our Gospels, these words are scarcely
quite true: but they apply *mutatis mutandis* to the Fathers of the old
Catholic Church " (from F. J. Paul, *Doctrinal Decrees of the Council
of Trent*, p. 24).

13

the ' mystery ' or prevented it from imparting its blessings.[1] They would likewise unanimously repudiate all ideas of the Eucharist as merely a memorial of redemption. They would likewise probably disagree with all of us in making the Eucharist the major sacrament. Neither could they conceive fellowship here or elsewhere with those many Christians who do not accept Church sacraments, nor with those still more numerous Christians who accept them because of tradition and ancestral sentiment, but with the minimum of belief in or the maximum of doubt about their efficacies. And in no Church would they easily discover the thoroughgoing supernaturalism [2] in which Christianity took its rise.

There was a continuity in the historic and psychological reactions between the Paganism and the Christianity which was recruited out of it. The Gnostics, who once represented half the Christian Church, differed from what became the orthodox Catholic Church in the greater zeal with which they laboured to combine Pagan and Christian practices and metaphysics. It was, generally speaking, religious-minded Pagans who became Christians, and they could not leave behind them their habits of thought. Dominant ideas or deeply-rooted primitive conceptions in one religion do not vanish in its successor, particularly on the same soil geographically. Such ideas either take a new life and enter upon a more extensive career or, if lopped off by the new religion, while their roots are deep in the same soil they produce a plentiful growth of saplings. For example, the Mediterranean Maid-Mother,[3] by imparting her prestige and garments to the Virgin-Mother, has exercised a colossal influence in historical Christianity. The lineage of the ancient ' holy butcher ' with his concrete

---

[1] Cf. *Sakramente* in *Rel. in Gesch. u. Geg.* V. p. 210.

[2] Cf. Holtzmann, *Neutest. Theologie,* 1, p. 114.

[3] Vide Usener, *Religionsgesch. Unters.* p. 27 f.; Farnell, *Evolution,* p. 34 f.

mentality has not become extinct. Or the dogma of apostolic succession, mostly physical and material in Graeco-Roman lands, has been refined in Christianity into semi-material; one may say quasi-spiritual notwithstanding its questionably spiritual working. Yet Christian sacramentarianism, though of the same genus as Pagan sacramentarianism, was widely different, above all in two phases: (1) the historical reality in the *myth* of its most frequent sacrament, and (2) the emphasis on concomitant morality due to the heritage of Judaism and the native spirit of Christianity. The early mystical-ethical connexion established by Paul was never quite lost in the process of either transcendentalizing or of materializing. There was a continuity in permutation in Christian sacramentarianism from the simple rites of the common meal and breaking of bread of the first Jerusalem Churches to the sacraments and their doctrinal position in Paul and to the quasi-magical rites of the third century and the magical *opera operata* of mediaevalism.

A similar continuity of life may be noted between the sacrament and sacramental theology of the first Christians and ourselves—the identity of life and not that of imitation. As the sacraments were conceived under the regnant philosophies of antiquity, first Neo-Platonism and then Aristotelianism, they must to-day be conceived under the regnant forms of present-day thought. Further, all the theologies of sacramentarianism accepted by the Church were fashioned under a belief in magic, and since the almost complete disappearance of this malign influence no Aquinas or Calvin has arisen, a simple fact but worth bearing in mind in disputations about sacraments.

CHAPTER XI

ANCIENT sacramentarianism persists and defends itself in divers ways:

(1) By the unquestioning acceptance of tradition, and the dogmatic asseveration of a definite establishment of sacramental rites by Jesus and His command to continue such rites 'in remembrance of Me.' The sacraments, therefore (with all their accrued theories of ' working ' and overworked logic), must be continued in obedience to the command of Jesus Himself. Their observance is based on an explicit authority and is obligatory. Being divinely instituted, they must *ex hypothesi* be regarded " as generally necessary to salvation." Thus the Council of Trent (1547) pronounced anathema against anyone holding that " all the sacraments of the new law were not instituted by Jesus Christ our Lord, or that they were more or fewer than seven." [1] The Reformers as definitely asserted " there be only two sacraments ordained by Christ our Lord in the Gospel, that is to say, Baptism and the Supper of the Lord."

It is amazing to find so much dogmatism where there is so much obscurity. One of the most perplexing problems confronting historical research [2] is just to discover what happened ' on the night in which He was betrayed,' and only less baffling is it to find the Ariadne thread guiding us from the common meal (apparently memorial and eschatological) of the Jerusalem community to the sacramentalism as observed in Corinth,

---

[1] Sess. VII, Can. 1.

[2] Cf. Völker, *Mysterium und Agape*, 1927, p. 14 ff.

and then further to the magic-sacramentarian realism of Ignatius and Irenaeus. Similarly strewn with difficulties is the path from ' the baptism of John ' to that of the Petrine preaching and thence to the symbolic-mystical baptism of Rom. vi and 1 Cor. x, and further to the full-blown magic-sacramentarianism of the second century.

Fortunately when, if ever, the theologians of sacramentarian doctrine, which base the worth and validity of sacraments wholly or partially on the express command and institution of Jesus, recognize how precarious their position is, and when, if ever, they accept the verdict of an ever-increasing number of independent investigators of at least a *non liquet*, the sacraments need not disappear [1] with the disappearance of this, now important, support from early Christian history, any more than they need disappear with a recognition of much superstition, magic and exclusiveness from other ages which have gathered round them.

Some recent and valuable treatises on the sacraments rest on the assumption of their historical institution by Jesus and on His command to memorialize Him. Thus Bishop Gore has no doubt whatever on the question of Dominical institution, on which he bases the objective operation of the sacraments and their right to the premier place in the corporate life of the Church. [2] Though Dean Inge considers that the point whether Jesus instituted baptism " cannot be proved either way," [3] he will not

[1] Cf. *Modern Churchman*, XVI, p. 262.

[2] Dominical institution is of course a postulate in Father Dalgairns's *Holy Communion* and in all Roman theology. Cf. from a Presbyterian writer, Wotherspoon, *Religious Values in the Sacraments*: " The symbol can become sacrament—that is to say, a means by which God takes action in the soul—only in the hands of Christ; and we can recognize it as sacrament only by tracing it to the appointment of Christ which guarantees to us its content " (p. 23 f.; cf. p. 145). For an authoritative statement of the Roman attitude to this historical question, cf. de la Taille, *Mysterium Fidei*, ch. vi; *Eucharistie* in Vacant & Mangenot, *Dict. de Théologie catholique*, col. 1024 ff.; *Messe, ib.* 797 ff.

[3] *Contentio Veritatis*, p. 282; cf. *Christian Mysticism*, p. 258.

dispute the tradition. Fortunately, though he argues on the assumption of Dominical institution, he writes with such sanity and comprehensiveness on the sacraments that their place would remain if this assumption were invalidated. It is otherwise in such a presentation as that of N. P. Williams, who bases the value and validity of the sacraments on their institution by Jesus: " there would seem to be in logic, as there has always been in Catholic belief, a tenacious mutual connexion and cohesion between the ideas of Dominical institution," " general necessity for salvation," and " objectivity of operation," [1] and then proceeds to an examination of the historical evidence in the New Testament which is largely question-begging and wholly overlooks the cavalier fashion in which the early Christians, who were interested in dogma and aetiological concerns, treated the historic events of their tradition.[2]

But the observance of sacraments may rest on surer than historical grounds. If Christian sacraments do not derive from the institution by Jesus, they may still be accepted as of divine origin and rest on the sacramentalism which is as old as our human nature or which makes the whole order of nature instinct with meaning for spiritual beings.[3] This sacramentalism Jesus Himself practised in observing the lilies of the field, or in the acted parable of foot-washing, or in finding spiritual analogies in the natural world.

Students of the New Testament and of primitive Christianity fail to find such a warrant of the direct

[1] *Essays Catholic and Critical,* pp. 373, 377 ff.

[2] " Veracity in matters of fact suffers as readily as righteousness in every religion. This is writ clear upon the pages of Church history from the earliest period right onward " (Harnack, *Exp. of Christianity,* I, p. 272).

[3] Sacramentalism " is no excrescence of primitive superstition, but corresponds to a permanent demand of the human consciousness, the demand that the visible and tangible should be a seal to faith of that which is unseen and eternal " (Kennedy, *St. Paul and the Mystery-Religions,* p. 263).

authority or the practice of Jesus. Dr. Clow [1] admits
" it is doubtful whether Christ Himself ordained the
sacrament of baptism "; and Glover remarks: [2] " There
is a growing consensus of opinion among independent
scholars that Jesus instituted no sacraments." The
history of the first generation of apostolic propaganda
is very obscure, and at the end of the first generation
rites appear in the practice of the Church which bear a
strange resemblance to the rites of surrounding cults,
such a resemblance that Christian apologists attribute
the latter to diabolic plagiarisms from Christianity.
Thus ' the wicked demons have imitated [the Eucharist]
in the mysteries of Mithra, commanding that the same
thing be done,' [3] and ' the Devil has his Christians.' [4]

An examination of our earliest documents reveals that
(a) it cannot with any degree of assurance be affirmed
that Jesus established any sacraments or ritual acts;
(b) the Church from practically the beginning adopted
and practised two rites, baptism, the Lord's Supper,
and from a very early stage the laying-on of hands and
unction; (c) interesting vestigial evidence of a primitive
period when Christian baptism was conceived as
' baptism in Spirit ' as contrasted with Johannine
' baptism in water,' though this tradition is overlaid by
or interwoven with another which adds the Spirit to
the water-rite. Thus the promise put on the lips of
Jesus in Acts i. 5, ' John baptized with water, but you
shall be baptized in the Holy Spirit,' could not arise
out of the later Catholic practice of the ritual act, and
so must represent an authentic early source. Similarly
the Pentecostal phenomena are interpreted in the Petrine
preaching as the fulfilment of Joel's prophecy, ' I will
pour out My Spirit upon all people ' (Acts ii. 17), with
which the subsequent editorial modification ' repent,

[1] *The Church and the Sacraments*, p. 26.
[2] *Conflict of Religions*, p. 158.
[3] Justin, *Apol.* I. 66.
[4] Firm. Mat. *De Err.* 22. For the ' devices of the devil ' vide Tert.
De Corona, 15.

and let each of you be baptized in the Name of Jesus Christ for remission of your sins ; and ye shall receive the gift of the Holy Spirit ' ill accords. A like striking incongruity appears in the duplicate account of the incident of Cornelius, in which after the reception of the Holy Spirit by his hearers, Peter says, ' I remembered the word of the Lord, that He said John baptized with water, but ye shall be baptized in the Holy Spirit,' without reference to a preliminary or subsequent ritual act of water-baptism as in the first account of the same incident (Acts x. 47). All this is corroborated by the well-attested logion of the Second Source (Q), in which the contrast between the Baptist's mission and the Messianic epoch is stated as ' I baptized in water, but He shall baptize you in the Holy Spirit and in fire ' ; (d) the rites practised from a very early date by the Church in its native Jewish environment were not sacral acts, but symbolic acts, to which the Jewish mind and its synagogue proselytes were accustomed. Baptism was immersion, a dramatized religion, in which the subject broke with his past and received the token of ' remission of sins,' and the Eucharist was an eschato-logical meal of memorial ' until He come ' to preside at the banquet of the Messianic Kingdom. These symbolic rites rapidly and inevitably in the larger Hellenistic environment developed into sacraments and were equipped with the efficacies of Hellenistic mysticism.[1]

(2) By refusing to permit the question to be raised or discussed of the nexus between the visible and the spiritual, i.e. the *modus operandi* of the symbol, the relation of cause and effect. Thus Inge:[2]

---

[1] Prof. E. F. Scott, speaking of Paul's relations to the Mystery-cults and Hellenistic influences, says: " The two peculiar rites which the Church had practised from the first were now construed as *sacra-ments*. . . . From the time of Paul onward a like virtue was attributed to the Christian ordinances. They ceased to be merely symbolic rites and became in the full sense sacraments " (*First Age of Christianity*, p. 199 f.).

[2] *Christian Mysticism*, p. 258 (italics not in original).

" Most of the errors which have so grievously obscured the true nature of this sacrament [Supper] have proceeded from attempts to answer the question ' How does the reception of the consecrated elements affect the inner state of the receiver? ' To those who hold the symbolic view, as I understand it, it seems clear that the question of cause and effect *must be resolutely set aside*. . . . We should abstain, I think, from speculating on the effects of the sacraments and train ourselves instead to consider them as *divinely-ordered* symbols."

We shall see later why Inge recommends this asylum. It would deprive sacramentarians of their second line of defence and it would abolish the difference in *kind* between Pagan and Christian sacraments, and between " divinely-ordered " symbols and divine symbols apparently not ordered but in Christian experience indubitably effective.

One should have grave suspicion of any theory resting on a refusal to raise [1] or attempt to answer a question, not because we can ever comprehend everything,[2] which would require omniscience, but because our business in this world is to raise questions wherever we suspect them, to attack problems and pursue their solution to the utmost horizon. Besides, as a matter of fact, " man's meddling intellect " was made in the same divine workshop as the centre of his emotions and refuses to accept any notice of trespassing until it has

---

[1] Dr. Major (*Modern Churchman*, October 1926, p. 264) enumerates the " sacramental dangers " as (1) " being dominated in our conception of them by the authority of the past " and (2) " intellectualization of the sacraments. This was the temptation which beset Patristic, Scholastic, and even Protestant theologians. Sacraments are essentially mystical, dramatic, poetic, creative, but not dogmatic. They exist that we may duly use them, not dispute about them." But in using them we cannot arrest the faculties of our nature: we must *seek* to understand our sacred emotions, whether we can give a full answer or not, and we can do so without turning " poetry into prose " or " symbolic action into a metaphysically definable process " (*ib.*).

[2] On the " irrational " in religion cf. R. Otto, *West-östliche Mystik*, p. 191 ff.; *The Idea of the Holy*, *passim*; K. Edward, *Religious Experience*, ch. III.

convinced itself of the sin of trespassing. Further, we are Westerners, the ever-grateful sons of Ionia, and we recognize, with one [1] who accepts mysticism as the way of life and sacramentarianism even beyond Inge, that the three chief forces of our Western civilization are Hellenism (" the thirst for Richness and Harmony "), Christianity (" the revelation of Personality and Depth "), and Science (" the apprehension and conception of brute fact and iron law ").

Now, Inge's faith rests on the lawful appeal to the emotions and sentiment while denying the equally lawful appeal to the mind. As a matter of fact, psychology is on the track already, though sane psychology will never deny the seemingly impenetrable mystery surrounding our life or the mysterious relations of the material and the spiritual. Moreover, psychology makes it no longer necessary to fall back with Thomas Aquinas on miracle as the only or chief explanation of the spiritual efficacy of sacraments.

(3) The psychological effect of every dignified worship is necessarily quickened enthusiasm and an access of or intensification of feelings. Moral danger and spiritual power are found in close proximity. The refinement and exaltation of feeling is of practical moment for moral aims. And the recognition of the *Numinous* with its ineffability and of the *mysterium tremendum* which prompts worship is essential to the fullness and vigour of personality. But the danger of stressing the non-rational elements in religion is perhaps greater even than the ruthless ratiocination of intellectualizing religion. The feelings even at Communion are morally indifferent or even neutral. Modern Christians need a *charisma* to test sacramental feelings as the early Christians sorely needed one to test the spirits in pathological outbursts (1 Cor. xii. 10). The *Numinous* expresses itself not only in feelings but in rational and ethical terms.

[1] Von Hügel, *The Mystical Element of Religion*, I, pp. 10-39.

The emotions experienced or enjoyed in receiving a sacrament cannot be adduced as proof either of the supernatural or miraculous character of the ritual transaction, or as corroborative evidence of its validity, or as intrinsically of spiritual import. The value of ecstasy or feeling depends entirely on the methods by which they are caused and the state of moral health of the subject. It cannot therefore be too emphatically maintained that he who in faith and love receives a sacrament will acquire an access of grace whether or not he feels this grace in emotions which rest on a biological basis. The operations of psychological states of suggestion, concentration, or the contagion of mass psychology are not in abeyance at the altar, and the aesthetic effects of dim religious light and of appropriate symbolism act, but act at the altar by the same modes as elsewhere. The Spirit may be imparted in a physical process such as laying on of hands or eating consecrated elements. But again it may not; it may be, and in religious experience is known to be, imparted also and perhaps more potently and immediately in some solemn intimacy of the soul or in the call of a great duty, or in some high resolve " to grapple danger whereby souls grow strong." The emotions at the Communion may denote the physical significance of the sacrament, but may not always assure its spiritual significance or prove that through the physical processes the Spirit has operated: " Certain persons habitually receive the sacraments of the Church, and habitually are conscious that they derive benefit after so doing. On this is based the theory that they derive this benefit because they receive the sacraments. It is held that this is *propter hoc* as well as *post hoc*. This theory of course is open to argument." [1] The physical may conduce to the spiritual and the psychical to the ethical, but not by any law of psychological necessity. The emotional condition neither proves that

---

[1] Kirsopp Lake, *Earlier Epistles of St. Paul*, p. 495.

the spiritual process has taken place nor justifies the contention that it does not take place except synchronous with or dependent on the physical and intrinsically operative action of the sacrament.

There are vast differences in sacramental experiences due to philosophical presuppositions, credal allegiances, culture, and the poise, or lack of poise, which obtains among the various faculties of our being, particularly the emotional and the aesthetic. For example, a man who believes in a special miracle taking place in the use of consecrated physical objects will have one class of emotion based on and accordant to his expectancies; another who believes that the Divine Love is doing in the same way—but in a special degree or fashion—in the ecclesiastic sacramental cult what it is doing in the whole revelation of the external world will have another kind of emotion. Yet another who approaches in the spirit of reverent obedience to a supposed dominically instituted observance as a means of conveyance of grace and act of fellowship will have another set of emotions. It would be a marvellous argument for sacramentarianism if it could be shown that such high emotions as are experienced by these three different worshippers were denied to those who would join with them in the sacramental cult, but without the belief that these sacraments were dominically instituted and that their observance rests on authority and the promises of Christ, rather than on the nature of the symbolism itself and its relation to the historical person of Jesus and His spiritual presence with them.

Nor dare any theologian of sacramentarianism assert that the similar high and uplifting emotions, which mean so much to the sacramentarian, do not visit the hearts of those who, while holding aloof from ecclesiastical sacramentarian practice, consecrate themselves to the Highest; nor dare he deny that in the great spiritual states, especially of love and sorrow, the soul undergoes experiences that are very immediate and morally com-

pelling, and also inexpressible save in poetry or symbol
or music.

The claim made for sacraments by Bishop Temple—
" that they are something more than efficient instruments for producing a psychological state: it is claimed
that in them God Himself takes action upon the soul "
—may be admitted, provided that one does not overpress the claim to mean that these are the chief or exclusive methods or occasions in which " God takes action
upon the soul." On such sacramental occasions many
have been visited by new and life-transforming visions,
as was Jesus Himself on His reception of the Johannine
baptism. Saint Teresa, for example, was visited by her
visions at the reception of the Eucharist.

But some of the greatest experiences which have
proved epoch-making for Christian history came quite
apart from and unmediated by sacrament. It was while
' breathing threatening and slaughter ' on the road to
Damascus that the greatest of all Jesus' followers was
' apprehended by Christ ' in a direct experience which
rendered the sacraments secondary to faith-mysticism.
It was not by sacrament but by the preaching of Ambrose
that Augustine was won from debauchery to Christianity. Similarly, God took action upon the souls of
Francis of Assisi, Martin Luther, George Fox, and John
Wesley apart from sacramental mediation—whatever
their attitude to sacraments may have been after the
crisis. And in the convent chapel, without special
reference to sacramental operations, Catherine of Genoa
passed through her crisis of conversion into the " transports of pure and all-purifying love." Pagan and
Christian mystics alike have discovered that the *scala
perfectionis* is not the monopoly of the votaries of sacramentarianism. There are powers inalienable from the
soul which enable it to make its ascent in its own divine
right through the three stages of exaltation recognized
by Augustine, self-abasement, illumination, identification; or the three similar stages distinguished by

Iamblichus:[1] (1) μετουσία, presence; (2) κοινωνία, fellowship; (3) ἕνωσις, identification.

On the other hand, it cannot be asserted that those who are most susceptible to ecclesiastical sacramental experiences and influences are most susceptible to the finer issues of the spirit. Not the most devout sacrament-practising Christians are the most catholic in their love, or conspicuous by the ethical quality of their self-effacing service. When such sacrament-practising Christians put to shame by the beauty of their lives and the winsomeness of their service those who accept sacramentalism as an all-pervading divine principle, an irrefragable argument shall have been discovered for sacramentarianism.

(4) By isolation of certain sacral acts, two or seven, from the operation of the general psychological principles of sacramentarianism and from the indisputable effect of symbolism, whether ecclesiastical or Pagan or that of daily life. Inge[2] may say truly " the reciprocal action of spirit and matter is the one great mystery which, to all appearances, must remain impenetrable to finite intelligence," but this same mystery obtains in extra-ecclesiastical symbolism. If we could tell *why* and *how* a primrose lifts us into the world of Beauty, or why and how music transports its chosen into worlds unknown to others, we should have solved the sacramental nexus.

And the Dean proceeds that we should consider the sacraments as " divinely-ordered symbols, by which the Church, as an organic whole, and we as members of it, realize the highest and deepest of our spiritual privileges." But if the earth is the Lord's and the fullness thereof, " if Nature the body is, and God the soul," and if man is surrounded by symbols which lift him to that plane of life where man meets his God, and

---

[1] *De Mysteriis*, III. 5. Cf. Adam, *Religious Teachers of Greece*, p. 393.

[2] *Christian Mysticism*, p. 258.

if to a thinking man his whole environment is sacramental and infused with an unseen power, are not all symbols both divine and divinely-ordered? And is it *only* or *especially* through the two alleged " divinely-ordered symbols " that we realize our deepest privileges? Do the pure in heart not see God at any time and immediately? Does the love of heaven not make us heavenly whether at the Lord's Supper or in the office or field?

" The Catholic sacramental system is in part an imperfect attempt to realize that side of life (relation of happenings of life to the real world). The mistake which so many Protestants make is in thinking that, because they can see the mythical element in the Mass, or the sacramental system in general, they can achieve truth within merely by cutting those things out; whereas the error in the Catholic system is not in claiming a sacramental value for the Mass, but in denying the possibility of that same value to all the events of life. The Protestant who rejects the Catholic Mass and puts nothing in its place has lost rather than gained. The Protestant who rejects the Catholic Mass . . . but finds in all life true sacraments has learned the lesson of Catholicism: and such a man is not eager to speak unmixed evil of the Catholic Mass, . . . because he realizes that it is not so much wrong as an imperfect and limited appreciation of a truth which he has come to find on a larger scale throughout life." [1]

In the earlier stages of a religion men are willing to assume or assert *belief* in what they cannot *understand,* and to accept and operate with postulates which are only examined later when equivocation becomes distasteful.

(5) By accepting as authoritative or final statements made by Church Fathers on one particular phase of religion which was so sensitive to contemporary thought, while in other—once important—matters rejecting

---

[1] Lake, *Religion of Yesterday and To-morrow,* p. 37 f.

wholesale the considerate views of the same Fathers, e.g. on demonology, physiology, the nature of the soul, the resurrection of the flesh, physical fire of eternal punishment, and their fanciful etymologies and allegorical biblical interpretations. For example, transubstantivists, consubstantivists, receptivists, and memorialists all seek to buttress their sacramental doctrines in such an account as the following from Justin Martyr, and all perhaps rightly, inasmuch as their discriminations were not present to Justin's mind:

' For not as common bread and common drink do we receive these, but in like manner as Jesus Christ our Saviour, having been made flesh by the Word of God, had both flesh and blood for our salvation, so likewise have we been taught that the food which is blessed by the prayer of His Word, and from which our blood and flesh by transmutation are nourished, is the flesh and blood of that Jesus who was made flesh.' [1]

The Patristic writers should be studied, as all ancient sources, not to verify private predilections, but first to understand them in the context of their age. It is another matter to inquire whether in light of the increasing revelation since their day we can hold their opinions, and not only hold their opinions but hold them for the reasons given by the Fathers. What divine right of authority have the Fathers over the living Church of the present which claims the same sources of inspiration open to the Fathers? Christian theology followed Origen on such a central doctrine as the Atonement by paying tribute to Satan for a thousand years for man's release until the *Cur Deus Homo* of an Archbishop of Canterbury by his satisfaction theory put God's justice in the place of Satan. On the sacraments the Fathers are neither unanimous nor explicit in their statements. Origen differs from the mystical-realism of his age by interpreting the Bread Discourse in Capernaum—the Johannine doctrine of the Eucharist—allegorically. The

[1] *Apol.* I. 66.

first theologian of the Latin Church, Tertullian, may be plausibly cited for both the symbolic and the mystic-magical view. The difficulty of deducing a consistent doctrine of the Eucharist from the various statements even of one Father, Augustine, is confessed. And by what canon are we commanded to acceptance of such a doctrine when formulated and relegate to the department of antiquities his statement of the bearing of the literal raising of Lazarus' already putrefying body upon the future physical resurrection of believers [1]; or that Christ ascended into heaven with His flesh in which He arose [2]; or how discriminate between the faith-healings and fancies in the list of miracles [3] recorded in the *City of God*, XXII. 8, *ut crederet mundus*? Or are we to-day committed to acceptance of the corporeity of the soul because attested in a Father like Tertullian?

The Fathers must be understood in the light of the cosmology, the mystic-realism, and the thriving Mystery-cults and the controversies of their day, and be allowed to diverge in opinions and in emphasis as earnest and sincere men do to-day. We shall recognize that the life-and-death struggle of the Church with Gnostic Docetism in favour of the reality of Jesus' humanity has left its trace as deeply upon the conception of the Eucharistic ' body of Christ ' as upon the apocalyptic doctrine of Resurrection. But the appeal to Patristic authority proves both too much and too little, for we are not living in the Patristic age, and it is impossible to label any one confessional sacramental system as Patristic. The language of the Fathers tends to prove

---

[1] *Tractate* XLIX. 1.   [2] *De Civ. Dei*, XXII. 8.

[3] ' Miracles wrought in the name of Christ, whether by sacraments, prayer, or relics,' including the restoration of a dead boy in the shrine of a martyr; an Innocentia cured of cancer of the breast by the signing of the cross over the affected spot by the first woman coming from the baptistery at Easter; a doctor delivered from both gout and the visits of black demons ' by the laver of regeneration '; an Hesperius freed from malign influence of evil spirits by the sacrifice of the Eucharist.

that the Church held to the doctrine of transubstantiation long before this doctrine was ecclesiastically formulated.[1] To Justin and Ignatius, for example, the consecrated elements were the flesh and blood of Jesus, though the method of ' conversion ' is not stated, but the realism of their language and the absence of any qualification agree best with what was later formulated as transubstantiation. Augustine, who held to the magical working of sacraments in such a way that the sacraments administered by heretics were valid, maintains that such heretics, even of unblemished lives and with valid sacraments, cannot be saved; their valid sacraments, being outside the Church, are deprived of efficacy. Thus ' let us suppose someone, therefore, chaste, continent, free from covetousness, no idolater, hospitable, ministering to the needy, no man's enemy, not contentious, patient, quiet, jealous of none, envying none, sober, frugal, but a heretic; it is, of course, clear to all that for this one fault only, that he is a heretic, he will fail to inherit the Kingdom of God ' [2]; to which some Christian Diogenes with a sense of spiritual proportion might have replied, like his Pagan predecessor, ' Shall Pataikion the highwayman have a fairer lot in death because he was initiated than Epaminondas? ' who died unhouseled. To see how far Patristic authority would carry us we may cite the doctrine of Gregory of Nyssa, who held that man is a composite of soul and body, the former of which can be saved by faith, but not the latter, which can only be saved by the antitoxin of another body (that of Christ), which was ' the receptacle of the Deity ' and ' received the grace of immortality.' [3]

[1] Cf. Baumgarten, *Relig. in Gesch. u. Geg.* V, p. 212.

[2] *De Bapt.* IV. 25; cited *Modern Churchman*, XVI, p. 385.

[3] *Cat. Orat.* 37, in which he also says: ' We believe that now also the bread which is consecrated by the Word of God is changed into the body of God,' who ' disseminates Himself in every believer through that flesh whose substance comes from bread and wine, blending Himself with the bodies of believers, to secure that by this union with the immortal, man too may become a sharer in incorruption ' (cited *ib.* p. 380).

(6) By the failure to recognize that the steady movement in religious history is from rites to deities, from protoplasmic magic to institutional cult, from spell to prayer, and from cult-acts to a deepening of man's consciousness of his native divinity and of his kinship with the Father of his spirit. The movement is inward, toward a deepening of man's self-consciousness, and of the world of eternal verities immediately within his grasp. The security which he once sought by *doing* for himself or through ghostly representatives certain acts he seeks later by *being*. He has also discovered by experience that he can elevate himself better by the exertions of his will and the agonizing of moral decisions about the things primary and secondary to life than he can by any ceremonial. He may not lose faith in ceremonial as a help, but he has learned to find the springs of action within his own God-endowed nature. A recognition of the immoral and unscientific character of magic has induced him to eject magic from his religion. He is coming to realize that the true line of religious advance is by the apostolic succession of Jeremiahs and Amoses and not by that of Ezekiels, Ezras and Malachis. And history seems to corroborate that " the strongest moral impulses have not been given to mankind by the guardians of ritual and sacrament; they have come from without." [1]

Yet the practical value of sacraments (not their theological validity) in religion and perhaps their necessity for the masses of religious adherents may be granted. The day of immediacy and of pure spirituality is yet far distant, except for the few,[2] though Jesus

---

[1] Glover, *Progress in Religion,* p. 84.

[2] " It is true the day will probably never come when the religion of many will not begin and end in solemn, stately rite, consecrated to the imagination by ancient use, and captivating the sense by scrupulously ordered ceremonial. The ritualist and the puritan conception of worship will probably always exist side by side, for they represent two opposite conceptions of religion which can never entirely blend " (Dill, *Roman Society from Nero,* p. 603).

assumed that ordinary men and women could rise to an immediate vision of God and could enter with Him into the secret of the Father. But usage in religion is more tyrannical than elsewhere, and the weakness of human nature so obvious that Dean Inge asserts:[1] "The need of sacraments is one of the deepest convictions of the religious consciousness. It rests ultimately on the instinctive reluctance to allow any spiritual fact to remain without an external expression. . . . Nearly all the states or motions of the soul can find their appropriate expression in action." But what of the states or motions of the soul for which an external expression cannot be found? And would Dean Inge affirm that to the contemplative Mystics sacraments are either necessary to evoke their intuitions or to confirm them? Do the pure in heart anywhere and always not see God immediately? Further, Dr. Inge very persuasively represents sacraments as " symbols of mystical union " ; yet individuals have repeatedly experienced that that mystical union is independent of and prior to sacramental acts. Would he affirm that the heart of Paul's religion, the Christ-mysticism, was induced by or dependent on sacraments rather than on justification by faith? He says again: " That deepest sense of communion with God, which is the very heart of religion, is in danger of being shut up in *thought* and *word,* which are inadequate expressions of any spiritual state." Does the Dean mean that symbols even in his ecclesiastical sense are adequate expressions of either the soul's unutterable intuitions or its enlarging uprisings? Does he not himself warn of the danger?—" The maintenance of a real correspondence between sign and significance seems to be essential to the idea of a sacrament, but then the danger of degrading it into magic lies close at hand."

Professor Kirsopp Lake admits " sacraments have, I believe, their own great value in religion. Myths based on sacraments, or sacraments based on myths, have

[1] *Christian Mysticism,* p. 253 f.

been the door which has opened the way to Reality,"
with which we agree, with the caveat that these are
neither the exclusive nor the necessary door to Reality
for many souls, and also with the reminder that holy
seasons of the soul are dependent not on seasons of sun
and moon or on hours of day, or on an ecclesiastical
calendar, but on the tides that sway the spirit—tides
which have their ebb as also their flood.

Sacraments have their place and use. They belong
to the first of the three modalities or forms of appeal and
outlook of religion as classified by von Hügel as Insti-
tutionalism,[1] Intellectualism and Mysticism, or feeling
and volitional requirements, the co-existence and succession of which in history he describes. The first is
historic or static or traditional, and makes its appeal to
sense and memory; the second is analytic, and works by
question and argument; the third is synthetic, and makes
its appeal to unifying experiences. The first expresses
itself in cult; the second in a philosophy of religion;
the third in experimental-ethical life. The first takes
shape under the regnant social, legal and political
thought-forms and habits; the second is influenced by
the critical and speculative ideas of its day; the third
is dominated by individual and racial habitudes and
gifts. The priest dominates the first, the philosopher
or theologian the second, and the prophet the third.

Hügel has also drawn attention to how each of these
three modalities tends to isolation and excess: the first
tends to excess in superstition, formalism and legalism;
the second in rationalism; the third in fanaticism.
" And whole races have tended and will tend, upon the
whole, to one or other of these three excesses: for
example, the Latin races to Exteriorism and Superstition;
the Teutonic races to the two Interiorisms—Rationalism
and Fanaticism." [2] This tendency of the Latin races
to Exteriorism and Superstition is not to be overlooked,

---

[1] *The Mystical Element of Religion,* I, pp. 59-75.
[2] *Ib.* I, p. 59.

inasmuch as the genius of the Latin races has contributed most to the formulation of our Western theology (Augustine, Aquinas, Calvin). Hügel has also remarked that each of these elements is liable to encroach upon or even suppress the others, and of these the first has been most successful in this narrowing process.

Yet the overworking of a helpful principle does not abolish its use. There are in experience and practice two opposite tendencies in regard to sacraments—the sacramentarian and the sacramental. The one, giving to sacral actions efficacies in their own awful right, tends to magnify sacramentarianism and multiply the occasions and the material channels and tangible *sacra* of sacramental communications; the other passes through and beyond the propaedeutic symbol to the inward truth and spiritual experience. The one tends to rely upon the external means; the other tends to outgrow them. The one furthers a devotional mysticality; the other a moral enthusiasm. The one justifies itself in a reverential mysteriosophy which evades the main difficulties and through an unwholesome deference to antiquity and tradition pays its tribute to magic; the other seeks to attain the " faith that inquires " and attempts a reverent philosophy of Christian life and experience, for which it claims no infallibility. When sacraments become *opera operata,* magic has again claimed its own; when ritual becomes more than a vehicle of religious expression, the moral appeal is weakened rather than strengthened. " Certes," says Chaucer, in " The Persone's Tale," " a shadwe hath the lyknesse of the thing of which it is shadwe, but shadwe is not the same thing of which it is shadwe," which may be supplemented by Isaac Penington's words: " All truth is shadow except the last. But all truth is substance in its own place, though it be but a shadow in another place. And the shadow is a true shadow, as the substance is a true substance."

CHAPTER XII

RELATION OF ST. PAUL AND THE FOURTH GOSPEL
TO SACRAMENTARIANISM

So strongly was the tide moving towards sacramentarianism that Paul and the Fourth Gospel writer were claimed as sponsors for the heightened importance of cult-acts as vehicles of grace and necessary to salvation. Certain phrases of Paul provoked explanations which in their apprehension by Hellenistic modes of thought could not result otherwise than in the accommodation of Christian rites to the rites of the Mystery-cults.[1]

Many scholars — Loisy,[2] Heitmüller,[3] Hoffmann,[4] Lietzmann,[5] Wernle,[6] J. Weiss,[7] Weinel,[8] Wrede,[9] Lake [10]—maintain that Paul is the first Christian sacramentarian, the first to transform Christianity from its

---

[1] Cf. Wetter, *Das chr. Mysterium: Stud. z. Gesch. d. Abendmahles* (1921), p. 122 ff.

[2] *Les Mystères païens et le Mystère chrétien* (*Hibbert Journal*, October 1911).

[3] *Taufe u. Abendmahl bei Paulus.*

[4] *Das Abendmahl im Urchristentum*, p. 156 ff.

[5] *Handb. z. N.T.*, ad Rom. vi, p. 29; *Messe u. Herrenmahl.*

[6] *Beginnings of Christianity*, I, p. 273: "It was Paul who first created the conception of a sacrament"; II, p. 128.

[7] *Urchristentum*, p. 496 ff.

[8] *Bib. Theologie d. N.T.*, p. 330 ff.; *St. Paul*, p. 119 f.

[9] *Paul*, p. 120.

[10] *Earlier Epp. of St. Paul*, pp. 200 ff., 231 ff., 385 ff. "Baptism is for Paul and his readers universally and unquestionably accepted as a 'mystery' or sacrament which works *ex opere operato*, and from the unhesitating manner in which Paul uses this fact as a basis of argument, as if it were a point on which Christian opinion did not vary, it would seem as though this sacramental teaching is central in the primitive Christianity to which the Roman Empire began to be converted. Three factors were regarded as essential—Water, Name, and Spirit."

more primitive form into a Mystery-Religion, or that
Paul operates with two conceptions of sacrament—the
primitive and the Hellenistic,[1] or that he begins with
the conception of a memorial and ends with a Sacrament,[2] after mystery precedents.

Other scholars — Anrich,[3]   Harnack,[4]   Dobschütz,[5]
Feine,[6] Deissmann,[7] Kennedy,[8] Morgan,[9] Glover[10]—as
emphatically exonerate Paul from having introduced
sacramentarianism into Christianity.

There is no dispute that Christianity became pro-
nouncedly sacramentarian at an early date.   The
question is whether this departure began with Paul.   At
first sight there is much to lend support to the view of
Paul as the first sacramentarian, due largely to
" Pauline germs of unpauline thought." [11]   Paul as a
son of the Diaspora was thrown into intimate contact
with Hellenistic mysticism, which would make him
familiar with the main doctrines and practices of the
Mysteries with their communion meals and raptures of
initiation.   And in Paul's world there is evidence of a
deepening spiritual conception of the Mystery-rites from
the magical to the sacramental, from the physical to the
spiritual, which would facilitate the employment of their
usages and analogies in a new religion.   His native

---

[1] As J. Weiss, *Urchr.* p. 502: " Die ältere, aus der Urgemeinde
stammende wonach die Mahlzeit vor allem ein Akt der Gemeinschaft der
Jünger ist . . . und die jüngere, die hellenistische, wonach der Herr selber
nicht nur der Mittelpunkt, sondern irgendwie auch der Gegenstand der
Feier ist."

[2] J. Hoffmann, *Das Abendmahl im Urchristentum,* p. 150: " Begnügt
sich Paulus nicht damit, die Wirkung des Herrenmahls zu verobjek-
tivieren, sondern er materialisiert sie auch geradezu."

[3] *Das antike Mysterienwesen in seinem Einfluss auf das Christentum,*
p. 111 f.

[4] E.g. *Expansion of Christianity,* I, p. 289.

[5] *Sakrament u. Symbol im Urchristentum* (in *Theol. St. u. Kritiken,*
1905, p. 1 ff.); *Christian Life in the Prim. Church,* p. 19.

[6] *Theologie d. N.T.* 2nd ed. p. 490 ff.

[7] *St. Paul.*   [8] *St. Paul and the Mystery-Religions.*

[9] *Religion and Theology of Paul,* p. 203 ff.

[10] *St. Paul.*   [11] J. R. Ropes, *Apostolic Age,* p. 257.

Tarsus was a centre not only of Stoicism, which in his day had manifested decidedly mystical tendencies, enabling its adherents to become one with the all-pervasive Spirit, but also of Oriental mysticism. His missionary journeys led him through the great centres of the Mediterranean world where the Mystery-cults were predominant.

It is clear that Paul's gospel underwent some drastic modification after his acquaintance with the Alexandrian Apollos, who, to an apostle familiar with the cosmic Sophia and eager to adapt the new religion to Hellenism, could point the way to a more universalistic and mystic interpretation. It is noteworthy that Paul, who would resist to the death Judaizing opponents or any who would assail his apostolic authority, not only had no jealousy of this Apollos with his ' wisdom,' but accepted him as a fellow-worker. Paul's long residence in Ephesus must have brought him through his converts into close touch with the ideas of the Mysteries, and his literary activity from that centre in defending his gospel must have revealed to him the advantages accruing to Christianity from the adaptation of suggestive religious ideas in a Pagan world familiar with sacramentalism. Thus in the Mysteries the conception of regeneration was associated with baptismal rites.[1] In these too regeneration is compared with dying.[2] But Paul never conceives baptism strictly as rebirth or regeneration, but as a mystic death.

Initiation, which guarantees regeneration, is also conceived as a dying,[3] or as participation in the death

---

[1] Cf. Tertullian, *De Bapt.* 5.

[2] *Liturgy of Mithras* (Dieterich, 3rd ed. p. 15).

[3] Cf. Themistios (or Plutarch?) in Stob. *Flor.* IV, 128; Maas, *Orpheus*, p. 303 ff. Apuleius records that Lucius at initiation underwent the ' symbol of a voluntary death ' (*ad instar voluntariae mortis*, XL. 21). The candidate for initiation into the mysteries of Attis is admitted as *moriturus,* ' about to die ' (*De Err. Prof. Rel.* 18) In the Dionysiac-Orphic, ' most secret of all initiations,' symbolic burial was practised. Cf. Angus, *Mystery-Religions*, p. 96 ff.

and resurrection of a Mystery-Saviour. That Paul
should use such conceptions in connexion with baptism
does not, however, prove that baptism was viewed by
him as identical with initiation rites in Paganism. It
should also be noted that in Paul's day the Church was
as yet not alarmed at the arresting similarities between
Pagan and Christian sacraments; there would not be
the same suspicion of Pagan sacraments as when the
charge of plagiarism was raised by Christian Apologists
against the religious fraternities and the initiations
assigned to the wicked demons.[1]

The use of the terminology of the Mysteries such as
*soteria, mysterion, psychikos, pneumatikos, pneuma,
Nous,* τελείος ('initiated' and 'perfect'), μυεῖσθαι, ἐμβατεύειν
certainly implies a considerable knowledge of their
current use, though no conclusive proof of Paul's slavish
borrowing without modification.[2] He "presupposed
his hearers' acquaintance with these terms through the
medium of the Mystery-Religions, and at least to some
extent adopted the current usage."[3]

It is also true that baptism and the Lord's Supper
are represented as acts or occasions of fellowship
in the death and sufferings of Christ as the Mystery-
sacraments were the means of union with the
periodically dying and again living Deity. Also
Paul speaks not only of fellowship with Christ, but
of fellowship in 'the body' and 'the blood of
Christ.' He also speaks of 'the cup of the Lord'
and 'the table of the Lord' in contrast to 'the cup of
the demons' and 'the table of the demons.' Further,
the cosmic sweep of Pauline redemption, the use of
Kyrios as the favourite designation of Christ, and the
personal mysticism 'in the Lord' of the Christian cult,

---

[1] Justin Martyr, *Apology,* I. 66; Tert., *De Praesc.* 40.
[2] Reitzenstein (*Zeitsch. f. d. neutest. Wiss.* XIII, p. 17) argues that
the employment of mystery terms implies the use of mystery
ideas.
[3] Kennedy, p. 171.

point towards the usages of the Mysteries. The possibility of unworthy partakers ' eating and drinking judgment ' also suggests the magical associations of the Mysteries. As a wise missionary, eager to bring the Gentiles to Christianity, Paul was not the man to refuse to avail himself of the propaedeutic value of the current sacramental ideas [1] of his converts from the Pagan guilds, for whom the Mysteries had proved a ' paedagogue to Christ ' as the Law to Israel.

But all this is inconclusive, and there appears in dubitable evidence that Paul must be acquitted of sacramentarianism which finds the physical cult-act the means of or necessary medium of the spiritual condition. Of the physical significance or objective operation of either sacrament, not one sure word can be cited from Paul. In his scanty references we find no elaborate sacramental doctrine. The very scantiness of the references to the sacraments is unfavourable to the view of the writer as a sacramentarian, and this difficulty cannot be evaded by asserting that Paul took for granted the acceptance of sacramentarian doctrines.[2] Sacramentarians accept as a postulate the necessity of a priest and of due priestly succession as essential to a valid sacrament. Yet never once does Paul mention priests as among the ' gifts ' given by Christ to the Church; never once does he appropriate the title or claim its exclusive prerogatives in his impassioned defence of the originality and independence of his apostleship. While Paul strove for a seemly and orderly worship, he laid no stress on the externals of cult-acts and physical ritual and holy days. ' Christ sent me not to baptize, but to evangelize ' is at least a surprising assertion from one who saw in sacramental acts the chief means of union. It is indeed striking that the apostle nowhere argues for or even suggests the uniqueness or superiority of a

[1] Cf. Kennedy, p. 280 f.
[2] As by Lake, *Earlier Epp.* p. 233.

formal ordinance like baptism as an initiation rite in contrast to circumcision.[1]

In Pauline thought *Gnosis* overshadows Sacrament. Though Paul is familiar with the term ' Mystery,' he sedulously avoids applying it to either sacrament. The mysteries of the Christian faith were not for him the sacraments.

Paul was a mystic, and mystics may be either sacramentarians or sacramentalists. Paul's theology is essentially experiential theology, a rescript of his own experiences. Never once does he appeal to his own baptism as a verification of his experiences or revelation of the mind of Christ. He does appeal to the fact that ' I saw the Lord,' and that ' God revealed His Son in me ' and ' the dawning of the Light of the Glory of the Gospel of Christ,' which were divine transactions on the road to Damascus, rather than to a subsequent water-rite. His statements concerning the sacraments must be interpreted in the light of his undoubted mystic experiences, such as ' I have been crucified with Christ. I no longer live. Christ lives in me,' or in accordance with his recognized allegorical exegesis, as in 1 Cor. x. 1.

In fact, this disputed chapter in 1 Cor. is most intelligible as a protest by the apostle against the physical quasi-magical ideas from the sacraments of the Mystery-Religions which his converts were already attaching to Christian baptism as bestowing an indelible character or ensuring salvation. So thoroughly had his converts been tutored by Greek symbolism and the Mysteries in the miraculous and soteriological qualities of initiation rites, that they naturally heightened the supernatural values of corresponding rites in the name of the superior

[1] " The apostle constantly lays emphasis on faith and the Spirit of God as the characteristic factors of the Christian experience. It would seem that if, denying all spiritual value to such a physical rite as circumcision, he ascribed effective force to baptism, his arguments should have turned, as they nowhere do, on the superiority of baptism to circumcision " (Burton, *Galatians* in *I.C.C.* p. 205).

' Lord Jesus.' The experiences which he found in the sacraments were those of his ordinary or daily mystic apprehension of Christ; they were ethical-mystic, not physical-magical.

In his doctrine of regeneration it is striking that the sacraments do not even come in for mention; surely this was the proper place for a sacramentarian to treat of sacraments, or at least to relate them to the teaching of the ' new creation ' and the life in the Spirit.

Closely bound with the faith-mysticism is Paul's original and fruitful conception of Spirit, and neither explicitly nor implicitly is the Spirit once mentioned as conferred by baptism. " In the vast majority of cases in which Paul speaks of the giving of the Spirit there is no reference to any material medium; in definite terms he makes its communication contingent on faith." [1] Only in two passages—1 Cor. xii. 13, vi. 11—is the Spirit associated with baptism. " But it is not asserted and not necessarily implied that the former is mediated by the latter." [2] No causal connexion is established binding the Spirit to the ritual act. That Paul should bring into association baptism and the reception of the Spirit was natural because of their primitive association, and also because baptism with personal confession would generally follow immediately upon conversion, and in the psychopathic conditions in the early community would generally or often be accompanied by visible ' spiritual ' manifestation.[3] The symbolism of primitive baptism was also too obvious and too instructive to fail to find a place in Paul's mystic-ethical apprehension of the Gospel.

[1] Morgan, *Religion and Theology of Paul*, p. 206.   [2] Morgan, *ib.*
[3] Cf. Morgan, p. 207: " That the apostle speaks of renewal as washing rather gives the impression that the rite is no more than the symbol of a spiritual change spiritually wrought. In view of the fact that in general he speaks of the Spirit as given directly by God and explicitly establishes faith as the condition of its reception, nothing short of an unambiguous statement would justify us in attributing to him the idea that it is communicated through a material agency. But such is nowhere to be found."

The chief obstacle to interpreting Paul as the first Christian sacramentarian lies in the confessedly central place of faith-mysticism in Paul's own life and teaching; this was neither induced by nor dependent on sacramental operations. In his gospel, which is ' the power of God to salvation *to every believer,'* salvation comes only and always through faith and accompanied by the Spirit. This faith-mysticism stands in irreconcilable antithesis to a union vouchsafed through physico-spiritual acts. The antithesis is so apparent, the religious attitude of faith so basal, and the ethical conditions so stressed that some interpreters like Heitmüller,[1] Weinel,[2] Holtzmann,[3] Hoffmann,[4] who find a warrant for sacramentarianism in Paul, accept the antithesis and leave the riddle unsolved. Sacramentarianism they detect present in certain forms, but only as a foreign ingredient in Paul's thought and quite incongruous with his conception of the union of the Christian with the life-giving Spirit and the unrestricted activities of the Spirit. In Paul's thought the Christian life begins in a mystic act of justification by faith, and it remains throughout a ' life hid with Christ in God ' in this same unbroken fellowship, whether at the Lord's table or at work or in prison. The Christian is always ' in the Lord,' whether he eats or drinks or whatever he does.

Paul accepted the rites which he found in existence in the Church at his conversion, but he left nothing in Christianity the same as he found it. In these rites he saw not a renewal of fellowship or a supernatural act of union—for the Pneuma-Christ was always in the

[1] *Taufe u. Abendmahl bei Paulus,* p. 35 ff.
[2] *Bib. Theol. d. N.T.* p. 330 ff.
[3] *Neutest. Theol.* II, pp. 198, 207.
[4] Hoffmann, p. 152, speaks of " a clear contradiction " between the conception of the body and blood of Christ as symbols of His sacrificial death and again as the means of participation in the life of the Spirit which is Christ. This contradiction is assigned to a fusion of the Jewish conception of a memorial meal and the Hellenistic conception of a mystical relation with God through sacraments.

Christian—but rather the cult-expression or venerable symbol of what was the daily and hourly privilege of the Christian. It is thus that there are scores of references to this initial and sustained communion through faith-mysticism in which Paul never mentions the sacraments as the antecedent causes or media or material vehicle; and this unquestionable usage of the apostle deprives the one solitary reference, 1 Cor. x. 14 ff., to fellowship in connexion with the Supper of any exclusive potency or *ex opere operato* significance: " The truth is that the Supper did not lend itself in the way baptism did to body forth the mystical union as Paul conceived it. While it might express the idea of union with Christ in His death, it could not express the complementary idea of union with Him in His resurrection." [1] This suggests that Paul's expressions regarding the sacraments should be treated as mystic experiences. If this explanation fails, recourse may be had to the physical-sacramentarian. But starting with the faith-mysticism, there is not a single expression which eludes the mystical explanation, and indeed on this explanation his statements are not so remote from modern thinking as are words like ' I have been crucified with Christ.'

Such statements as Rom. vi. 3–5, and 1 Cor. x. 16–17, might be forced into an *ex opere operato* significance if Paul's ever-present faith-mysticism did not stand in the way. Or they might be given this construction if we had any hint elsewhere in Paul to support this view, but they demand no more and permit no less a meaning than the mystic experience. [2]

There is no reference to the Supper outside the passages 1 Cor. x, xi, and in them there is not a word to indicate without dubiety that the Lord's Supper is either the medium or the objective cause of union with Christ, or even a bond of union with one another, or that the

[1] Morgan, *ib*. p. 226.
[2] Cf. Kennedy, *St. Paul and the Mystery-Religions*, p. 296.

elements are spiritual nourishment.[1] Neither is there a trace of evidence of an infusion of supernatural or mysterious powers into the bread and wine. Never is the water ' consecrated ' or supernaturally charged, nor are the elements spirit-infused and ' converted ' as they appear by the end of the first century. Nor in Paul does the official position of the ministrant (who is never designated as priest) lend any validity to the sacrament: as yet sacerdotal control of the machinery of the sacraments with its inevitable magical implications is absent, though such control is to the modern sacramentarian of prime importance. As yet, however, any Christian, especially a presbyter or overseer or teacher or prophet, could administer a sacrament long before Ignatius forbade baptism ' without the bishop.' [2] What constitutes the whole value of the sacraments is the moral condition of the participant and a life of faith.

Whenever Paul mentions the means of union with Christ or the ground of forgiveness, it is never once a cult-act or rite that he indicates, but faith or grace or the love or power of God: the absence of one such unambiguous declaration assigning to either sacrament an effective and causal value in its own divine right is surely noteworthy. Forgiveness which gives peace with God and righteousness never appears in association with baptism. And it is by way of exception [3] that references to death with Christ or union with Christ in death appear in sacramental association, the only two clear references being Rom. vi. 3–4, Col. ii. 12.

Paul's relation to the magical-physical sacraments and mystic [4] ritual was similar to his relation to contemporary

---

[1] " Even the conception of the rite as binding believers into a fellowship with one another never emerges. . . . A memorial of Christ's sacrificial death, a means of proclaiming it—that and that alone is what the Supper signifies to Paul " (Morgan, *ib.* pp. 221, 224).

[2] *Ad Smyr.* VIII. 2.   [3] Cf. Kennedy, p. 225 ff.

[4] The differences between Paul's mysticism, as determined by its character of Christ-mysticism, and Hellenistic mysticism, are exaggerated by Deissner into a repudiation of mysticism by Paul, but quite

religious ideas. He was not averse to using Pagan ideas and fostering mystic yearnings which made his gospel intelligible to his hearers, nor to employing the analogies and suggestions of rival cults, in which he could discover, as in the Law, a *praeparatio evangelica*. The prevalent Hellenistic conception of mystic union with the Divine had much affinity with his own personal experience, though never to the point of either identification or absorption. His attitude to the Mysteries has been instructively compared by Wendland [1] to Plato's toward Orphism. The origin of a religious idea did not trouble Paul, nor did the idea itself compel him to sheer imitation. He seems to have had no fear that his terminology through its kinship with Pagan ideas would mislead his converts. In Paul's efforts to formulate for himself the content and scope of Christianity and to commend it to others, he eagerly laid hold of every idea and suggestion that could do Christ service. The aspirations fostered in his converts by the mystic rituals of Paganism, their emotional experiences of communion, and their hopes of incorruptibility attained in prior worships would not be rudely thrust aside. [2] But Paul's emphasis upon the moral aspects [3] of the Christian message was of infinitely greater and more lasting worth to Christianity than his application of Hellenistic mysticism in the interpretation of the new faith.

That Christianity became soon after Paul's day a

unconvincingly (*Paulus u. die Mystik seiner Zeit*, 2nd ed. p. 80 ff.). Schweitzer designates Paul's mysticism as " eschatological mysticism " explicable from Jewish and primitive Christian ingredients (*Gesch. d. paul. Forschung*, pp. 176-89).

[1] *Hell.-röm. Kultur*, 2nd ed. p. 185.

[2] " We believe that he found the practices of the Mysteries suggestive as a practical method of mysticism, and that he indeed reinterpreted the old practices of baptism and the Church meal in the light of this experience, and opened the way to further developments in the sacramental direction. But with Paul the sacraments are mystical rather than magical, symbolical rather than miracle-working, and secondary to the spiritual and ethical elements of faith " (Bulcock, *The Passing and the Permanent in St. Paul*, p. 34).

[3] Cf. Dobschütz, *Der Apostel Paulus*, I, p. 42 f.

15

Mystery-Religion, and that even Paul's presentation of this missionary faith tended in this direction cannot be denied, but evidence is wholly lacking that Paul changed Christianity into a Mystery-Religion and transformed the primitive rites into the magical *ex opere operato* sacraments in vogue in the Church from at least the end of the first century and prominent in Ignatius and Irenaeus. Where rites of initiation were deemed requisite and of mysterious efficacy, it was inevitable that Christian baptism should be brought into line with parallel practices. Out of sympathetic magic it was natural that a sympathetic rite should be evolved.

Indirectly, however, sacramentarianism traced its ancestry to Paul. His mystic significance of the sacraments easily declined into magical or semi-physical operations. His symbolic and mystic connexion of baptism and the Supper with union with Christ prepared the way for a causal connexion.[1] His ethical idea of the sacrament retreated before transcendental ideas. Regeneration by the Spirit and the association of baptism with the Spirit without mention of the laver lent themselves readily, in magic religious associations, to the Paulinist evolution of the ' laver of regeneration and of spiritual renewal ' (Titus iii. 5).

Further, it was inevitable that some of Paul's expressions, such as ' baptism into Christ's death,' ' fellowship in the body and blood of Christ,' ' buried with Him in baptism,' ' eating and drinking judgment,' in the circle of his Pagan converts, many of whom had come from mystery-guilds, should be interpreted along lines familiar in the Pagan worships. As in the cult of the Great Mother the primitive sacrifice of the *taurobolium* evolved [2] into a grand act of initiation and the supreme sacrament of ' rebirth for eternity,' so in an age subsequent to Paul when rites were multiplied and rituals elaborated, when " every hand that was stretched out

---

[1] Cf. Holtzmann, *Neutest. Theol.* II, p. 197.

[2] Cf. Hepding, *Attis*, p. 199 f.; Graillot, *Culte de Cybèle*, ch. iv.

for religion tried to grasp it in a sacramental form; the eye saw sacraments where sacraments there were none and the senses gave them body," [1] certain germs latent in Pauline thought rapidly put forth a new growth, and secondary elements kept in the background in Paul's own experience and in his sane reflexion thereon came to the front consonant with the materializing of religious conceptions.

Though a positive magical working of rites is not to be discovered in Paul, it could with plausibility be asserted that he recognized at least the negative or destructive effects. The epidemic of illness and deaths attributed by Paul to the abuse of the *Agape* in the Corinthian Church would most naturally be interpreted as parallel to the destructive agencies of magic through the infusion of supernatural power in objects rather than, as Paul may possibly have wished to indicate, as a result of divine judgment. [2] How even a learned ecclesiastic like Cyprian would read the account is not a matter of conjecture. [3]

An excommunication ' in the Name of our Lord Jesus ' to effect the physical death of an immoral Church member in order that his spirit might be saved at the Parousia could not fail to suggest to the ancient mind the powers of the invocation of a Name rather than a special punitive act of Providence. Such punishments would not sound so strange when death [4] was the penalty awaiting those who proceeded prematurely to initiation without the express permission of the Deity mediated through a spiritual Father.

Similarly Paul's enployment of the custom in the

---

[1] Harnack, *Expansion,* II, p. 288.   [2] As in Morgan, *ib.* p. 223.

[3] Cf. Angus, *Mystery-Religions,* p. 256; Bigg, *Church's Task,* p. 83 f.

[4] Cf. the threat of death by the high-priest Mithras to Lucius in Apuleius, XI. 21. Also the words in a letter of Apollonius, a neophyte of Serapis in the temple of Memphis, to his spiritual father, Ptolemaeus: ' And if we cannot die and if you see that we are to be saved, let us be baptized,' so interpreted of a baptism in obedience to a divine vision by Reitzenstein, *Hell. Mysterienreligionen,* 2nd ed. p. 85, but modified, 3rd ed. p. 297. For a different interpretation vide U. Wilcken, *Urkunden d. Ptolemäerzeit,* I, p. 330 f.

Corinthian community of vicarious baptism on behalf of dead friends as an *argumentum ad hominem* in his proof of the resurrection, would suggest intrinsic efficacies in the rite and encourage this magical practice until it assumed such proportions that it was prohibited as an abuse by an ecclesiastical Council in A.D. 397.

As Gentile Christianity came into more familiar contact with Paganism and its theological formulation proceeded, as Pagan and semi-Pagan doctrines secured full right of citizenship in Christian theology, the questions which Paul either did not raise or at least did not attempt to answer were raised and answered according to contemporary conceptions: causal and transcendental connexions were evolved out of his symbolic or suggestive associations.

As the ecstatic condition normally experienced at adult baptism ceased, as ' the spiritual gifts ' became unfamiliar, baptism became the recognized mode of the reception of the Spirit conceived as akin to the impartation of the supernatural substance in the Mystery-sacraments.

The moral emphasis [1] of Paul on the sacrament as a pledge of loyalty became less popular than the ritual guarantee of a fresh access of grace or infusion of power or a supernatural assurance of resurrection or immortality.

Passing from Paul to the Fourth Gospel, a distinct advance towards sacramentarianism has been made, though the author of this ' spiritual Gospel ' halts far short of the ecclesiastical sacramentarianism regnant in his day and becoming ever more marked as organization

---

[1] " Paul was the first and almost the last theologian of the early Church in whom sacramental theology was really held in check by clear ideas and strictly spiritual considerations. After him all the floodgates were opened, and in poured the Mysteries with their lore " (Harnack, *Exp.* I, p. 289).

displaced spontaneity and liberty. Nowhere does the writer advance the position of any *per se* validity of an ordinance, nor does he intimate that consecration brings down supernatural power into material objects of cult, nor does he venture to assert that Spirit is always the concomitant of correct ritual. The enhanced importance of ritual since Paul's day, the inevitable interpretations given to Paul's expressions in closer contact with Pagan mysticism, the current inability to differentiate between symbol and effect, the penetrative influence of the Mysteries with the increasing preponderance of Gentile Christianity, all tended to externalize and magnify the earlier rites.

Though the Fourth Gospel writer disparages all magical-physical operation of rites, he advances considerably beyond the Pauline standpoint. While holding the Pauline mystic-symbolic doctrine, he attempted to graft thereon a refined sacramentarianism. He claims a greater place for the sacraments in the corporate life of the Society than does Paul, or he attaches a greater importance to them, though always to the accompaniment of a warning or a corrective statement. Hence this Gospel, more than any New Testament writing, has promoted the cause of sacramentarianism.

The attitude of the Fourth Gospel to sacraments is determined, first, by the marked paradoxical character or duality of Johannine thought,[1] whereby the higher spiritual conception does not drive the lower and more material entirely off the field. Thus the free activities of the Spirit appear in co-ordination with the material acts, but in such wise that it was easier for the spiritual man duly to evaluate the physical channel of grace, than for the orthodox member of the Church of his day to correct the seemingly extravagant claims for the sacraments by the qualifications and warnings ; and, secondly,

---

[1] " Nearly every sentence in the Gospel might be paralleled with another which appears to indicate a view of different tenor " (Scott, *Fourth Gospel*, p. 12). Cf. Holtzmann, *Neutest. Theol.* II, p. 551).

by the author's twofold conception of Life [1] which is
conceived spiritually and metaphysically, so that the
Logos-Christ imparts life directly by knowledge or faith
and again mediates it through the sacraments.

In the discourse on Baptism the Synoptic assertion
that John's baptism was a water-rite and that of the
Coming One a baptism in Spirit is modified into a
baptism of water and Spirit as co-efficients of rebirth.
The being ' begotten from above ' is absolutely essential
for entrance into the Kingdom, but such rebirth is both
a spiritual and a ritual transaction : a man must be ' born
of water and of spirit.'

Regeneration is associated with baptism, certainly not
yet causally but in a more intimate fashion than in Paul.
Statements like those in xix. 34 and 1 John v. 6 could
only be interpreted in accordance with the sacramentarianism which gripped the Church before the
beginning of the second century. A step has already
been taken in the direction of Tertullian's statement [2]
that ' we little fishes after the example of our Fish,
$IX\Theta Y\Sigma$, Jesus Christ, are born in water, nor have we
salvation in any other way than by permanently remaining in water.'

The Bread Discourse in Capernaum particularly
reveals the author's point of view and his problem of
adjusting his own personal and fundamental conception
of salvation through faith and knowledge and that of
the Church through sacramental mediation. He seems
at times perplexingly conscious of the superfluity of
material mediation of that Life which is imparted directly
to faith and enjoyed in the mystic experience of abiding
in Him who is the Life. Throughout this discourse

---

[1] " His conception of Christ as Logos involves him in a view of
Life which can only be described as semi-physical, and which runs
parallel throughout with the purely religious view. Life as so regarded
cannot be communicated except by a magical agency, and John discovered this agency in the Lord's Supper " (Scott, *Fourth Gospel*,
p. 128; cf. also p. 260 ff. and Holtzmann, *Neut. Theol.* II, p. 508).

[2] *De Bapt.* 1.

Christ is the Bread of Life, the Nourisher of Souls, but in the first part, vi. 26–50, Christ is the life-giver through faith to the believer (47). The language is clearly symbolic: ' I am the Bread ' is parallel to ' I am the Life,' as in Philo [1] the manna is symbolically ' the heavenly Logos.' But with 52*b* there is a startling transition. ' Body ' with its mystical possibilities is replaced by ' flesh ' with its realism; ' eating,' φαγεῖν, is reinforced by ' manducation,' ὁ τρώγων. Such expressions as ' unless you eat the flesh of the Son of Man and drink His blood, you have no life in you '; ' he that eats My flesh and drinks My blood has eternal life '; or ' abides in Me and I in him,' seem strange or superfluous to us after the assertion of 47, ' truly I tell you that he that believes has eternal life,' but they represent the orthodox sacramentarian view of the writer's day which he cannot see his way rudely to cast aside. His estimation of the Church and his loyalty to its traditions induce him to reassert the Church's point of view of the sacraments even in the immediate context of the more spiritual mode of reception of eternal life, though he takes pains in the immediate subsequent context to supply the corrective that ' the Spirit is the life-giver.'

In the discourses on both sacraments the writer treats the established sacraments as problems, as paradoxical experiences defying definition in a way unknown in Paul. In the one case Nicodemus, the type of the cultured man of his age, appears as being initiated into the mystery of rebirth in sacramentarianism. In the other case a twofold problem is enunciated: how can ' Jesus son of Joseph ' be the bread which descends from Heaven and by faith gives Life to the world? and how can the Son of Man give His flesh to be eaten and His blood to drink?

In the discourse on baptism the writer unambiguously quotes the current ecclesiastical view of regeneration

[1] *Quis Rerum Div. Haer.* 15.

through the co-operation of water and Spirit. But he immediately takes steps to correct or supplement the ecclesiastical physical-magical ideas which had gathered as accretions around the rite. The words must be read in the light of i. 33, ' this is he who baptizes in the Holy Spirit.' Water is mentioned, but only with Spirit in the first instance ; in the subsequent three references Spirit is mentioned independently and as sole agent.[1] Again, three corrective truths are thrown into promin- ence, first that baptism by itself cannot effect the transmutation of substance from material or psychic to pneumatic or spiritual, as the sacraments of the Mysteries effected. Only spirit can produce spirit. Thus the Pauline ethical-mystical doctrine of baptism into Christ as Spirit and the indwelling of the Spirit in the ' new creature ' guides the writer in his speculations in perilous proximity with the magic already baptized into Christ. Secondly, the water-rite may effect or guarantee re- generation, but then it may not, for ' the spirit bloweth where it pleases ' and its operations are inscrutable. As was known in the writer's day, the manifestations of possession by the Spirit may precede baptism or arrive independently of it. Thus while not denying, or even conceding, the current doctrine of the co-ordination of Spirit with water-ritual, he asserted that the Spirit cannot be restricted to the baptismal operation.[2] Thirdly, the Pauline doctrine of the Spirit-Christ appears in the form of the ascent of the Son of Man with the soteriological purpose that ' everyone who believes may have in Him eternal life,' to which there is found a corresponding conception after vi. 53, ' The words that I have spoken to you are spirit and life.' It is noteworthy that in the Farewell Discourse the central theme of the doctrine of

[1] " Aber die letzte Meinung des Evangelisten ist diese Konzession an die kirchliche Praxis doch nicht. . . . Auf keinen Fall aber tritt die Taufe als ein selbständig wirkendes Prinzip neben den Geist hin, son- dern beide wirken in und mit einander, trotz begrifflicher Unterschei- dung " (Holtzmann, *ib.* II, pp. 555-7).

[2] Cf. Pfleiderer, *Primitive Christianity,* IV, p. 232.

the Spirit is treated quite independently of ritual transactions.

In his conception of the Eucharist the writer so esteems
the Church sacrament that he cannot and will not set
it aside. But he would purify it of all magical *ex opere
operato* significance as if to deprive it of any intrinsic
office: (1) By connecting the Eucharist not with the
sacrificial death of Jesus on the last night, but with the
miraculous feeding in Galilee in such a way that the
language of the first part could not fail to be understood symbolically or allegorically. He practically
separates the Agape of the new commandment from the
Synoptic Eucharist of the new covenant. (2) He leaves
no dubiety that faith-union with the Logos-Christ is
eternal life now and assures it eschatologically, thus
logically as well as in religious experience rendering the
mediation through material channels superfluous. The
life of Christ is imparted immediately to and by faith,
whatever the sacrament may effect or fail to effect.
(3) After the declarations of eating the flesh and drinking
the blood, he as emphatically asserts, following Paul,
2 Cor. iii. 6, ' it is the Spirit that gives life,' whereby
he does not intend to stultify himself by retracting what
he has just said about the Eucharistic rite: he does not
disparage the rite, but he disparages all popular ideas
as to its working. It has an importance which he apparently cannot explain to himself or reconcile with his conception of life in Christ, an importance probably due to
his own experiences at participation ; it is to him perhaps
also a substitute for the apocalyptic presence, *Parousia,*
which he sets aside. (4) Immediately after the ' hard
discourse ' which offended many, Peter is represented
as, out of profounder insight, making the assertion
' Thou hast the words of eternal life,' which brings the
mind back to the first part of the discourse, in which
Christ as the heavenly manna and the bread of life is
immediately the life-bestower. (5) The ' offence ' lies
in the hearers' failure to understand that the reference

is to the flesh and blood of ' the Son of Man ascended
to His former estate ' (62), and so the flesh and blood
are not realistically by ' conversion ' of the elements
the body and blood of Jesus son of Joseph (42) or even
of Christ from Heaven, but mystically and spiritually
of one who by exaltation became spirit for spiritual
fellowship (vii. 39). Only spirit can produce life and
impart spirit (iii. 6 ; vi. 63).

The doctrine of the sacraments in the Fourth Gospel,
with its blend of what Réville calls " materialistic
mysticism " [1] with spiritual immediacy, admits most
readily of interpretation as a double apologetic [2] against
what appears to this writer two extreme views, that of
the popular magical offices of material things of the
Christian cult, and that of the Gnostics [3] who denied
that the elements were the very flesh and blood of Christ.
Others besides the Gnostics objected to the idea of eating
flesh and drinking blood in the Lord's Supper. At a
later date Porphyry on John vi. 53 asks, ' Is it not then
bestial and absurd, surpassing all absurdity and bestial
coarseness, for a man to eat human flesh and drink the

---

[1] *Quatrième Évangile*, 2nd ed. p. 182. " Déjà l'incarnation du
Logos était une infidélité à l'idéalisme strict; cependant il était encore
possible de l'expliquer au point de vue philonien tout au moins. Mais
la manducation de la chair et du sang dans lesquels ce Logos s'était
incarné, pour assurer la vie éternelle à ceux qu'il sauve parce qu'ils
ont foi en Lui! En vérité, cette parole était dure à entendre "
(pp. 182-3).

[2] Professor Scott includes an apologetic against Judaism, with which
Christianity came into conflict through the sacrament of the Supper
(p. 71). In the Eucharistic address (Bread Discourse) the Evangelist
had also probably in view the heathen and Jewish calumnies against
the Christian communion meal as ' Thyestean banquets ' (Holtzmann,
Neutest. Theol. II. p. 560).

[3] " Weil er der kirkliche Gnostiker ist, der gar wohl die Berechti-
gung des Anstosses erkannte, den die Gnostiker in doppelter Hinsicht
an der üblichen Abendmahlsauffassung nahmen, dass nämlich (1) der
Genuss der Symbole des Sühnetodes Christi, d. h. seines irdischer
Leibes und Blutes, in der Tat absurd sei, und dass (2) die starke
Betonung des realen Genusses leicht zu der Vorstellung von einer
magischen Wirkung des Sakraments hinführe " (Hoffmann, p. 201).
Cf. Holtzmann, II, p. 572, Pfleiderer, *Primitive Christianity*, IV, p. 232.

blood of his fellow-tribesman or relative and thereby win life eternal?'[1]

The writer is conscious of the value both of sacraments and of *Gnosis,* and he goes as far as possible with the sacramentarians and Gnostics [2] of his day while opposing both. He could not advocate the magical and materialistic views of Ignatius, to whom the Eucharist was ' the medicine of immortality and antidote against death,' and who in opposition to the Gnostics asserted the factual identity of the elements with the body and blood of Christ. Nor could the writer commit himself to such statements as appeared in Irenaeus,[3] to the effect that participation in the Eucharist guarantees incorruptibility of the flesh for purposes of a resurrection of the flesh.

It is not by accident that the writer introduces the Eucharistic discourse by two ' signs ' conveying the idea that Jesus' body is free from earthly limitations and unconditioned by time and space, which is of course possible only through his Logos-Christology and from the Pauline conception of the incompatibility of flesh and blood in Christ with the offices of Spirit.

The evangelist's deft apologetic method [4] causes him to cite the baldest and most extreme sacramentarian statements of the Church, which he seeks to correct [5] and supplement by putting his own personal view of the reception of life by faith or knowledge or mystic union in the foreground. That the transition from death unto life is an act of faith (v. 24) remains fundamental, and

---

[1] In Macarius Magnes, III. 15, cited Harnack, *Exp.* I, p. 287.

[2] Cf. Heitmüller in *Rel. in Gesch. u. Geg.* I, p. 150; Holtzmann, II, p. 568.

[3] *Adv. Haer.* IV. 18, 4.

[4] " He does not discard the common beliefs, even when they clash with his own, but accepts them formally in order to interpret and spiritualize them . . . he takes the popular conception of the religious value of the Supper, and sets it in the light of a higher and more reasonable conception " (Scott, *Fourth Gospel,* p. 124 f.).

[5] " It is his usual plan, when he has said anything which may tend to confirm ritualism, thus to supplement it with an antidote " (Gardner, *Ephesian Gospel,* p. 206).

cleansing can be effected through the word (xv. 3). He
would retain the outward ordinance because of his conception of the Church, while subordinating it to the
essential spirit: " With his profound insight into the
spiritual meaning of Christianity, John saw a danger
in the increasing reverence attached to the outward rite
of the Supper. The natural craving for something
visible and material in religion had seized on the simple
ordinance bequeathed by Jesus and invested it with a
superstitious value." [1]

But in the writer's attempt to blend popular and
philosophical Christianity, the baptismal doctrine of the
reception of the Spirit and of regeneration by baptism
with the more inward view of rebirth by faith, and to
accommodate the conception of the Mysteries of the impartation of immortal substance by sacrament, to his
own conceptions consonant with his guiding Logos-
speculation of Christ as being life and imparting it, there
results directly a strange contradiction which is left un-
resolved.[2] Hence his teaching, which was intended to
evaluate the sacramental principle while subordinating
it to the Spirit and to serve as an antidote to the
paganizing of Christian worship, has, contrary to the
writer's intention, conduced to the evolution of sacramentarianism in Christianity.[3] The parallelism which
he left unexplained between the transformation accomplished by faith in and knowledge of the Life-giving
Logos and regeneration by semi-physical miraculous
ritual acts hastened the evolution of the very magical
conception and miraculous working of ordinance which
he endeavoured to stay. He operated with two conceptions of Life and of its impartation, and of these
credulity chose its own.

The instructive and timeless Hellenistic idealism,

[1] Scott, p. 122.

[2] " Ganz ähnlich also, wie wir es beim Herrenmahl finden werden,
ist das sakramentale Moment der Taufe gleichzeitig gesetzt und ver-
leugnet, anerkannt und verfluchtigt " (Holtzmann, II, p. 557 f.).

[3] Cf. Gardner, *ib*. pp. 195-210.

mysticism and symbolism [1] were not able in lesser minds to maintain their high place over or beside the puzzling contemporary supernatural realism. Even expressions of his deep spirituality have been wrested from their contextual settings and forced to support [2] the heightened value of outward ordinances and to confuse the distinction, so clear to his mind, between the symbol of the cult transaction and the spiritual reality of religious facts. Sacramentarian ideas were indirectly deduced from his statements isolated from their correctives.

According to his mind, the whole validity of the sacrament was spiritual and inward, not physical and intrinsic. There is as yet not a trace of the magical working to appear so clearly from Ignatius and Irenaeus onward, not a hint that God or Christ can be drawn down from Heaven through or in ritual act, nor that ' consecration ' can infuse elements so as to charge them with supersensual potencies. And as yet the only baptized are adult moral agents on their own confession, and not non-moral infants.

The evangelist's healthful sacramental doctrine, the perception that the Spirit may work through material things, could not thrive save in the lofty mysticism suffused with ethical qualities, and could not but suffer declension into the magical fashion of the days when, on the cessation of the primitive spiritual manifestations, the outward rite was correspondingly highly esteemed, and when the idea from the Mysteries had taken permanent root in Christianity that no member of the brotherhood could be saved or benefit by the grace or blessings of the religion except through participation in its rituals of initiation and rebirth.

It is of course another matter that by making concessions to contemporary sacramentarianism, and by adapting even its extreme expressions in his own

---

[1] The amalgamation of which Inge finds characteristic of Johannine thought (Swete, *Essays*, p. 258).

[2] Cf. Scott, pp. 128, 132.

elucidating contexts, the Johannine writer commended the religion of Truth both to the cultured classes familiar with Oriental-Hellenistic mysticism and to the masses [1] expectant of physical-magical preparation for immortality by transmutation of their natures into the divine substance. To both classes Christianity early appeared to offer the best means [2] of satisfying their yearnings for union with the divine and their hopes of divinization (becoming *pneumatikoi*) into the deathless nature.[3]

[1] Cf. Harnack, *Expansion*, I, pp. 287, 292.

[2] '' Gerade der transzendente Hintergrund des hellenistischen Christus dazu diente, das Christentum als die wahre Erfüllung der heidnischen Mysterienweisheit, als die Befriedigung ihres ungestillten Verlangens nach Erschliessung der geheimnisvollen jenseitigen und göttlichen Welt erscheinen zu lassen '' (Pfleiderer, cited Holtzmann, II, p. 423, n. 5).

[3] In a writer of a Jewish cast of mind like Hermas, ' ascent through water ' is necessary to the dead for life and entrance into the Kingdom of God, because the only means of ' putting off the mortality of their prior existence ' (*Sim.* IX, 16, 2).

CHAPTER XIII

THE PLACE AND FUNCTION OF SACRAMENT

THE need and utility of sacraments rest primarily on the obstinate fact of man being a creature of two worlds, the successive and the Eternal: ' that is not first which is spiritual, but that which is natural.' Man is neither body alone nor spirit alone, but a body informed by spirit and receiving all the impacts of the outer sense-world. Spiritual experiences are often inextricably woven with natural or physical experiences. Body and spirit may in unhealthful asceticism or in dualistic philosophy be set in antithesis and opposition, and the futile attempt made here in our time-space existence to separate what God has joined together. This is fraught with serious perils to both body and spirit: properly speaking, they are in our present constitution allies. The body informed by spirit connects [1] through sensory nerve channels and emotions with the outer world from which it brings much useful information to the spirit; while the spirit, not disdainful of such information, converts it to the purposes of a clearer self-consciousness, and through sense learns to transcend sense. Through sense and the sensuous man can rise to the spiritual. Deep correspondences link him with the material order which reflexion proves to be instinct with vast significances. [2]

[1] " It is not magic, but a sheer fact traceable throughout our many-sided life, that we often grow, mentally and spiritually, almost solely by the stimulation of our senses or almost solely by the activity of other minds. Magic begins only when and where things physical are taken to effect spiritual results apart altogether from minds transmitting and receiving " (von Hügel, *Essays and Addresses*, p. 251).

[2] " The physical echoes and repeats the spiritual. ' Things made ' are figures of reality. The external is the outward sign of the inward

The problem of sacramentalism is therefore only one aspect of that agelong problem of the meeting in our mysterious being of the material and the spiritual, the finite and infinite, which, since the days of Heraclitus and particularly since the intuition of Plato, has engaged the mind of our Western thinkers. It is and will continue to be a philosophic problem to resolve the seemingly oppressive antithesis of time and eternity within us. But it is also a problem for every man who has a serious purpose to discover the meaning and end of his life. As denizens of—

> " two worlds immense,
> Of spirit and of sense,"

we experience strange pressures from a mysterious Beyond; we catch momentary glimpses of an intriguing Otherness than ourselves which, though they pass, leave us not as we were; again and again in some definite place we are compelled to say, ' Surely the Lord is in this place, and I knew it not,' or to cry with the Psalmist, ' Whither shall I flee from Thy Spirit? '

Various indeed has been the expression given to this consciousness of our compound nature, and various the solutions offered. It is almost as futile to attempt to flee the body as to escape the spirit. The body has been tortured and maligned by some of the greatest of the saints for the sake of the health of the spirit, and the spirit has been cramped and mutilated in the vain attempt to comport itself as if discarnate. Yet the alliance of sense and spirit persists after all our protests. Our consciousness of the finite is the measure of the consciousness of the infinite. We may be cribbed,

and imponderable. The concrete and the abstract in some inexplicable fashion correspond, and in our consciousness answer to one another. We who are in God's image understand both forms of utterance, the voice of God in creation and the voice of the Spirit who bears witness with our spirit: both are intelligible to us, and both carry to us the same messages. Light and truth, darkness and evil—they have something more than analogy: they connote each other " (Wotherspoon, *Religious Values in the Sacraments*, p. 10).

cabined, and confined in this " too too solid flesh," but
at least we know it, and we know also by experience
that we can and may take a holiday ' in the heavenly
places.' We know, with Plato, that the spirit of man
does not beat its wings in futility against the barriers of
time.

> " There's not a man
> That lives who hath not known his godlike hours,"

and in such hours we have transcended time and space
sufficiently to return in triumphant confidence to walk
the firm earth. Even if we are imprisoned in the dark
cave of the world, it has an ' entrance exposed to the
Light ' and even the moving shadows evoke disturbing
thoughts of another order: we can cast off our chains
and make the ' transition from the shadows to the
images and from the images to the Light.' [1]
The recognition of this twofold existence of ours is the
first step in our education. Discounting the Neo-
Platonic disparagement of matter, Plotinus' recognition
of this twofold order may be taken as representative:

' Since there exists a twofold nature, Intelligible and
Sensible, it is indeed better for the soul to dwell in the
Intelligible, but being what she is she must needs participate the Sensible also; and she has no occasion to
be vexed with herself if she is not everywhere her noblest
self, seeing that in the universe she fills an intermediate
station. She is of the divine estate, but her dwelling is
upon the last confines of the Intelligible, so that she has
the Sensible for neighbour and gives to it a part of what
is hers. From that Sensible she must in turn receive,
if in guiding it she stay not by the unfaltering part of
herself, but through overmuch zeal sink into the deeps
of Matter, no longer resting in entireness with the All-
Soul.' [2]

[1] Plato, *Repub*. VII. 514, 532*b*.
[2] *Enn*. IV. 8, 7; tr. in Dodds, *Select Passages illustrating Neo-
Platonism*, p. 79 f.

In a beautiful passage [1] from Dio Chrysostom's *On the First Notion of God,* Pheidias is made the spokesman for the use of images for those who cannot form a mental image of the Divine:

' Pure spirit and thought by itself no sculptor or painter can portray. . . . We attribute a human body to God, seeing in it the vessel of thought and reason. Unable to show the unimaginable and the unpresentable by an example of it, we try to do so by means of the visible and the representable. We so use this that it has the virtue of a symbol. . . . No one surely will maintain that it would be better if no statue or image of the gods at all had been appointed among men and that we ought simply to look up to the heavenly bodies. Certainly every reasonable man offers adoration to the heavenly bodies, believing that he is looking at blessed Divine Beings from afar. But something in man drives him towards God. There is in all men an urgent craving to come to close quarters with the Divine Beings whom they honour and serve, approaching them and handling them with confident faith, sacrificing to them and crowning them.' Surely ' the symbols of heaven and earth have been placed side by side.' [2]

The use of sacramentalism rests also on the sensitiveness of our human nature, both physical and spiritual, to impressions of the external world. The appreciation of the existence of a successive and an eternal world, and of the former as the temporal reflexion of the ideal world, does not rudely set aside or depreciate the material world by means of which we have been awakened to another sphere.[3] If ' Time is the moving image of

---

[1] Tr. by Bevan, *Later Greek Religion,* p. 114 f.

[2] οὐρανοῦ δὲ καὶ γῆς παρίδρυται τὰ σύμβολα (Philo, *De Vita Mosis,* II (III), 10, C.-W. 105.

[3] " They [the Sacraments] are the harmonious incidents of an economic system within a concatenated universe, in which the material is uninterruptedly expressive of the spiritual and is the peculiar instrument of God for spiritual ends. The symbol (and sacraments are in the first place symbols) is the spirituality of matter emerging into service " (Wotherspoon, *Religious Values in the Sacraments,* p. 20).

Eternity,' surely Time is of an immense worth to us other than the problems it prescribes us. We have more than an awareness of the external world: in this awareness there are possible all degrees of response and interpretation—the whole diapason of emotional and spiritual sensitiveness, from a Peter Bell's uncomprehending attitude to the primrose by the river's brim, to the comprehensive sympathy of a St. Francis with all nature; or the lofty sacramental use of Nature as in Wordsworth and the Lake School of poets, to whom on the going out of the light of sense " a flash that has revealed the invisible world " imparts " a faith that fails not." [1]

It is at this meeting-place of the finite and the infinite within us that sacraments play their chief rôle. In some circumstances of the soul and for many people—

" Sacramental religion does open a door, through which the Infinite comes with its gifts right down into the common life of our half-animal race ; and we again can go out towards it, so far as our love, purity, and courage permit us—for this path between the soul and God is utterly misconceived by us, if we allow ourselves to think of it as a one-way street. So apparently hedged in by our most humiliating and least spiritual limitations, so full of distressing reminiscences of a racial past that we should like to ignore, it does give in human ways and under human conditions a veritable access to Ultimates." [2]

The symbol or external thing may be either natural or artificial or even conventional. For a Wordsworth the beauty of Nature may induce the spirit of worship and lift to God as the sacraments may do for another, because in both cases the symbol mediates the universal and because the sacramental power of Nature comes from God: in the words of Sir Thomas Browne, " In

---

[1] *Prelude*, Book II.
[2] Underhill, *Man and the Supernatural*, p. 183.

brief all things are artificial, for Nature is the Art of God." If the mystery and grandeur of Nature expand our capacity for God ; if there lie in this external world such aids and stimulation for the spirit, it is altogether fitting that proper use should be made of the sensible appeal in religion and in cult. If our outward world with its sensibly conveyed appeals can bring—

> " A presence that disturbs me with the joy
> Of elevated thoughts, a sense sublime
> Of something far more deeply interfused,"

it is rational to suppose that in worship, God will come to the soul along sense-channels as He does in the unity of Nature, provided in each case we have the power to see and to feel and the receptiveness of love, in a word, " the Vision and the Faculty Divine."

A rude wooden cross [1] gathering for us an intensity of meaning by concentrating thoughts on the Passion of Jesus in both His life and death and summoning us to acknowledge that for us, as for Him, we must lose life to find it ; a war-worn flag on a hard-fought field ; a Gothic cathedral ; the mutilated Parthenon—all operate by the same laws of our being, though they affect different people in different degrees. The spirit of man is ever rising through the " sensible signs " of his world to grasp the immensities, through the sensuous to be transported to the eternal: " in these weaker glories " it spies " some shadows of Eternity." The sensuous ravishment may give an awareness of immaterial things. According to the mysticism of Dante, the love of a woman becomes the most fitting medium of communion with the Divine. Every Uranian lover finds his Beatrice both on earth and in heaven.

Religion may usefully avail itself of this economy of

---

[1] " Thus the crude image, the simplest suggestion, may do just as well for religion as the aesthetic masterpiece: often indeed better, because it offers a freer passage, a wider range of interpretation to the many grades of soul using this great human highway towards God " (Underhill, *Man and the Supernatural*, p. 171).

all nature [1] by which external things suggest invisible things and evoke a sense of the Infinite in its proximity to us: " To eliminate the sensible as aids to spiritual life has against it all analogy. The appeal to psychology and history, so decisive in favour of cultus, carries logically with it the admission of some sensible signs as contributing, when used by souls in and with the cultus, to the spiritual awakening and sanctification of such souls." [2]

Another reason for the use of sacraments is the recognition of the immense stretches of the inarticulate in religion and in all human life. There is something transcendental and ineffable in all the deepest experiences of life, especially of love and sorrow and rapturous joy. The most eloquent and carefully chosen words can convey but a most inadequate idea of these estates. Words are " under-agents " and represent while they also perforce misrepresent. There is always something more than can be said; much so mysteriously elusive that " it lies far hidden from the reach of words." But our nature has within it an unresting urge towards self-expression: hence art, music, poetry, and sacraments. In the rationality of our being we often feel more than we see or can express. Often, like the herdsman in " The Excursion," a man may—

> " feel his faith,
> Nor did he believe—he saw."

Philosophy, which in the nature of its office strives most to make all things articulate and to label them each in its place, suffers from the limitations of logical verbal expression and, despite itself, must fall back on concrete terms and use spatial symbols. And as religion has for its special sphere the emotions, it is compelled to avail

---

[1] Cf. Alice Gardner, *History of Sacraments in Relation to Thought and Progress*, p. 46 ff.

[2] Von Hügel, *Essays*. Cf. similar words in *Eternal Life*, p. 328, on " the elimination of sensible impressions and of sensible things as joint-awakeners and joint-vehicles of spiritual life " (cf. *op. cit.* p. 389).

itself of symbolism to suggest and for purposes of worship. Although God cannot be attained by the faculty of sense, yet through sensibly perceived signs the mind may be prompted in its striving towards God. It was not without reason that an artist-philosopher like Plato passed at the high and enthusiastic pitch of his argument from dialectic to myth. Absolutes can be comprehended only by an Absolute Being, but may be brought near to us in symbols.

Another use of sacraments arises from the supreme difficulty of maintaining the high levels of spirituality equally at all times, and the consequent need of trysting-places where the spirit meets its better and diviner self and renews its sense of communion with the Divine or Infinite. Sacraments may contribute to the renewal of spirituality to those who have been apprehended or seek to be apprehended by the spiritual: they may in certain moods of the soul supply the requisite ' evidence of things not seen '; they may not only *express* religious desire and faith, but in some measure awaken such desire and faith. Thus writes Baron von Hügel:[1] " I kiss my child not only because I love it: I kiss it in order to love it. A religious picture not only *expresses my awakened faith*; it is a help to my faith's awakening."

" There is a difference between one and another hour of life in their authority and subsequent effect. Our faith comes in moments; our vice is habitual. Yet is there a depth in those brief moments which constrains us to ascribe more reality to them than to all other experiences."[2] We wish to multiply these brief constraining moments of vision; we wish to recapture the transporting emotion; we wish in drab days to renew the strength of which we once were so conscious. A special effort is demanded, a concentration of awareness, a determined resolve to retrace the stream of our life to its source.

---

[1] *Essays and Addresses*, p. 251.
[2] Emerson, *Essays*, " The Over Soul."

Every normal life knows these experiences of ebb and flow. Every one knows that the Spirit, like the wind, ' bloweth where it wills,' betimes without our knowing its whence and whither, and that—

> " We cannot kindle when we will
> The fire that in the heart resides."

The renewal of power and the recapturing of the vision come to individuals very differently; to some in contemplation and intuition; to some in the general sacramentalism of the outer world; to some in confronting a crisis and making a fateful decision; and to multitudes of others in sacraments.

" Human instinct in its vague reaching-out towards the supernatural has always tended to make special places traps as it were for the celestial sunshine. It has always set apart and held precious, certain suggestive objects, actions, and ideas; which carry a weight of meaning, a halo of significance stretching far beyond appearance, and are able to release from succession the mind that surrenders to their appeal." [1]

In this recognition of the general use of the outer world to the interpreting spirit it is impossible to restrain the inrush of the Infinite or the access of God to the soul to one channel of sense more than to another. All depends on the spiritual health and training and tradition and temperament of the individual and of the mixture of the emotional, aesthetic, and intellectual elements in his essential selfhood. Some symbols may contain a more catholic appeal than others, or from their aura of reverence and hallowed association of history may prove more generally effective than others. A sacrament like the Eucharist has a wider appeal through the simplicity of its elements and its historical associations with the life of Jesus and the traditions of Christian worship than Nature-mysticism or art. The Church sacraments may represent the theology of the masses and present to their

[1] Underhill, *Man and the Supernatural*, p. 163.

eyes and ears what others can formulate in dogma.
They are acted dogma, dramatized ritual. No other
sacrament can compete with the Eucharist in the combination of simplicity with profundity; nor can any
other sacrament present in such a vivid and dramatic
way the essence of Jesus' self-sacrificing life and so unite
us in ' the fellowship of His sufferings.'

In a world where God only can register all the
movements of the soul and respect the distinguishing
individuality of selfhood, it is precarious to differentiate
between sacrament and symbol or to delimit the sacraments, as the Seven Mysteries of the Greek Church, or
the Seven Sacraments of the Latin Church, or the two
Sacraments of the Evangelical Churches. God may
have as little respect for numbers as for persons. Nor
does it necessarily follow that the ecclesiastical sacraments—two or seven—are more effective because of the
Evangelical belief that there be only two sacraments,
or the Roman anathema against those who either dispute
their number or deny their Dominical institution. In
the practice of sacraments, man's eager demand for aid
and for at least occasional escape from self will recognize
differences of values where such exist, and he will exalt
that sacrament which most exalts him by enabling him
to transcend himself.

The value of the sacrament depends neither on its
Dominical institution, nor on the sacerdotal qualities of
the ministrants, nor on the correct posture or impeccable
ritual or vesture of the clergy, but on the receptivity and
faith of the participant. The claims of Ethics are more
compelling in the long run than the powers of magic.
We must take up towards ecclesiastical sacraments the
position taken by Philo [1] towards the sacrifices of his
religion and ' the intention of the one who offers ':

---

[1] *De Vita Mosis*, III, 10, C.-W. 106-8. Cf. also the strong protest
against the outward things of cult unaccompanied by purity of soul
in *De Cherub*. 28, C.-W. 94 ff. Cf. Porphyry's remarks, *De Abs*. II.
15, 34, 60.

' For if he is witless and unrighteous, the sacrifices are
no sacrifices, his acts of worship unhallowed, and his
prayers unacceptable, bringing only sheer destruction.
For when they appear acceptable, they effect not remission but remembrance of sins. But if the worshipper is
holy and righteous, the sacrifice remains valid even if
the flesh be consumed, nay, even if no victims at all be
offered. For what is the true worship save the piety of
a God-loving soul? '

The protagonists of sacraments consider it part of their
duty to aggrandize sacraments by strictly delimiting
sacraments from symbols, and " divinely ordained
sacraments " from other rites of a quasi-sacramental
value.[1] " Symbols suggest and represent; but sacraments work. They always have a dramatic and dynamic
quality. They are special deeds, in which the action
proceeds at two levels. Something genuinely done
within the natural sphere by and to the body—a real
washing, eating, touching, or anointing—involves something genuinely done within the supernatural sphere by
and to the soul." [2] A symbol may be fortuitous or
universal, but " a rite outside the ordained use has not
the nature of a sacrament," according to Melancthon.[3]
Or according to the Roman view, a sacrament surpasses
symbol in that " the sacraments confer the grace which
they contain."

Symbols are occasional and representative, but the
sacraments are also causal; symbols merely symbolize or
convey a message, but sacraments effect. Thus " sacraments are not merely dramatic but effectual signs."

---

[1] Miss Underhill protests thus: " The Christian theist does or should
reserve the term ' sacramental ' for this real self-giving of Spirit along
the channels of sense; and ' symbol ' for that object or image which
evokes in us an intuition of the Transcendent, or creates for religious
emotion a suitable path of discharge. We ought therefore to resist
the diffuse application of ' sacrament ' to any and every natural act
and thing which seems to carry a religious reference " (*op. cit.*
p. 176).

[2] Underhill, *op. cit.* p. 176 f.

[3] In *Saxon Confession*, cited *Modern Churchman*, XVI, p. 415.

and " when we say that sacraments are effectual signs we mean that certain actions or objects are invested by divine authority with certain spiritual or supernatural properties." [1]

According to N. P. Williams, sacraments differ from symbols in that they are invested not merely with the powers of auto-suggestion and congregational hetero-suggestion of symbols, but by the presence of " an element of divine invasion and hetero-suggestion—a power which comes entirely from without and which transforms and quickens the emotional forces evoked by the mere symbolism of the rite from within," and " sacraments are in some sense *causal*; they are *verae causae*, and not merely symptoms, of the reception of grace." [2]

The strength of this dogmatic position lies in the fact that those who approach with such sacramental faith accompanied by moral receptivity will by all the laws of psychology receive an access of grace. The weakness of this dogmatism lies in the fact that the highest offices of the Holy Spirit and the profoundest and most ethical experiences granted to such sacramentalists are not inaccessible or denied to those who approach the sacrament with a wholly different mentality and with a faith poles apart from the above, though such undeniable spiritual results are forsooth among the " uncovenanted mercies " graciously permitted by Bishop Gore to fall like crumbs from the divine table at which he and his traditional sacramentarians have the privilege of occupying the chief seats. Nor are these experiences denied to those who do not observe ecclesiastical sacraments at all. Truly God's thoughts are not as man's, and God's *ecclesia* must be—to some confessionalists—disturbingly catholic and comprehensive, even as wide as envisaged by the philosopher-martyr who claimed as Christ's all those in whom from the beginning of time the Logos dwelt, including the ' obscure ' mystic Heraclitus and

[1] W. Spens, *Essays Catholic and Critical*, pp. 428-9.   [2] *Ib.* p. 371.

the ethical mystic Socrates.[1] The world will be nearer a decision on this divisive question of symbol and sacrament, and the operating and validity of sacraments, when, e.g. within the Church of England the Anglo-Catholics shall have manifested a superior type of manhood and " soul-making " to their Modernist brethren; we shall then have a conclusive argument in favour of the greater preponderance of the objective efficacy of sacraments. Or when the Greek Church members prove their pre-eminence in character over the Quakers, or when members of the imperial Roman Communion are known beyond the Presbyterians for their greater success in obeying ' the greatest and first commandment ' of the Divine Master, we shall have surer guidance as to one sacramental usage above another. To assess the worth of a Church or a religion by the often-used test of the number of its adherents is a crude and unsatisfactory method: it may be in every religion that the seven thousand who have not bowed the knee to dominant religious fashions or been carried away by crowd-psychology count for more ultimately than the obvious majority. Fortunately the salvation armies of the Kingdom are otherwise known than by their banners and their war-cries.

Since—

> " men from men
> Do, in the constitution of their souls,
> Differ, by mystery not to be explained,"

there is and must be a vast difference in the sacramental experiences of Christians, as diverse as our human nature [2] and as incalculable as our inviolable individualities: we are both solitary and social beings.

But there is also a vast difference among sincere Christians in their attitude towards the Church sacraments. To some the sacraments, magnified by an aura

---

[1] Justin, *Apol.* I. 46.

[2] ' Mille hominum species et rerum discolor usus;
Velle suum cuique est, nec voto utitur uno '
(Persius, V. 52 f.).

of reverence acquired through centuries of their use, are the very breath of their spiritual life; to others they are " optional appendages " of worship. To some sacraments are obligatory and rest on the supposed Dominical institution and command to memorialize; to others they are blessed privileges to be exercised in the religion of the Spirit. To some sacraments are, genetically and by objective efficacy, Mysteries of a unique order; to others they belong to and hold a supreme place in the general sacramental order with which the universe is informed. To some they are endowed with virtue in themselves because of the sacerdotal consecration and miraculous response to produce beneficent effects; to others they are the means by which God provides effects commensurate solely with the sacramental experience of the adorant. To some they are the core or the *sine qua non* of mystical religion; to others mystical religion is the whole of life and consists in the fellowship of our spirit with the Father of our spirits in the consciousness that at all times ' I am not alone; the Father is with Me.'

Or on the presence of Christ in the sacraments: all who accept sacraments believe in the Real Presence, but to some this Presence is localized [1] in ' converted ' elements; to others it is an intensification of ' I am with you always ' in obedient hearts. By some this Presence cannot be conceived as localized objectively save through the correct invocation of an officiant; by others this Presence is felt independently of such sacerdotal mediation. By some the Gift is identified with the Elements; by others the Elements are esteemed as the material channel of the sacrament, while the sacrament as a whole is the means of the conveyance of grace.[2]

[1] On localized presence cf. Dalgairns, *Holy Communion,* 8th ed. I, p. 119: " In the little round of the consecrated Host is He contained. Here is my Lord and not there."

[2] " The real is not that which occupies a limited area of space, but that which is present to the healthy consciousness of a personal being " (Inge, *Contentio Veritatis,* p. 307). Cf. Temple, *Christus Veritas,* p. 239, and his doctrine of " convaluation."

If such is the case, it is tragic that confessional and theological differences over the sacraments should have produced so much bitterness and evoked so much uncharitableness. It seems a travesty of Christianity that the Eucharist of Love and Communion has been and remains the storm-centre in the religions of authority. But despite divisive rites and attempts to explain Christian experiences yet in the hearts of the faithful, ' Faith, Hope, and Love abide,' and still ' the greatest of these is Love.' Facing a similar divergence over externals, cherished by some and neglected by others, the great apostle with his comprehensive charitableness and toleration proclaimed, ' Let not him that eateth set at naught him that eateth not; and let not him that eateth not judge him that eateth, for God hath received him. . . . Let each man be fully assured in his own mind. . . . He that eateth, eateth unto the Lord, for he giveth God thanks ; and he that eateth not, unto the Lord he eateth not, and giveth God thanks ' (Rom. xiv. 3 f.). Love remains the most catholic and most potent sacrament.

It is acknowledged even by sacramentarians that the practice of sacraments is liable to gross abuse [1] and to unethical exaggerations, but abuse and exaggerations are no valid argument against the legitimate use of sacraments. In no department of our religion do the crudities of bygone superstition threaten re-emergence more persistently than in the practice of sacraments. Atavism to primitive and absurd rites is all too easy, and magic is ever ready to renew its old and seductive alliances. Fetichism in regard to the elements entered Christianity with the inrush of Pagan converts, and from at least the time of Cyprian it has been persistent in the theology of the sacraments and promises to remain persistent. When the light within burns low, compensation is sought in an over-emphasis on the objective element in worship.

[1] " The use of sacraments has always a tendency to degenerate into superstition " (Dr. Gore, *Can We then Believe?* p. 119).

a special department, of divine communications or mysterious messages in "things."

"The acknowledgement of symbols and sacraments as true bridges to Reality, especially calculated to meet and satisfy the needs of the whole man, weaving together his double nature and double capacities—this must never mean for us the equation of sacraments and grace, a binding down of the soul to this one means of access to the Transcendental. Still less must it mean any arbitrary limitation of the Transcendent to this one mode of self-giving to the human soul." [1]

The overworking of sacraments [2] is more perilous to their proper operation and to their practical benefits in experience than the underestimation of them. Historical symbols, especially religious symbols such as the Eucharist, which have acquired an aura of spiritual meaning and suggestiveness, have a place—a larger place, perhaps—in deepening and strengthening personality than natural symbols. The religious life, which is the most unstable portion of our being, must strive to maintain the same balance and harmony and control as we recognize essentials of that ideal of "man complete as man."

It is also misuse of the sacraments to make them obligatory, either as being "generally necessary to salvation" or as the hall-marks of Christian faith. However the ecclesiastically minded may judge of sacramental allegiances, the world in general will apply the simpler and more obvious test of ' by their fruits ye

----

[1] Underhill, *Man and the Supernatural*, p. 186.

[2] "Let the faithful soul take care that, whilst contemplating an image, the senses be not absorbed in it, whether it be material or in the imagination, and whether the devotion it excites be spiritual or sensible. Let him . . . venerate the image as the Church commands and lift up his mind at once from the material image to those whom it represents. He who shall do this will never be deluded" (St. John of the Cross, *Ascent*, cited by von Hügel, *The Mystical Element of Religion*, II, p. 344).

shall know them.' Despite institutional Christianity, Christians cannot be standardized in creed or in their estimation and use of sacraments. The man whose main interests are ethical values may find less in sacraments and feel less need of sacraments. Mystics of the intuitive type, like the master-mystic Plotinus [1] and George Fox, are not so dependent [2] on external symbols for their realization of the Eternal world within themselves and as the background of this world. And St. Paul's Christ-mysticism did not originate in the use of sacraments, but in the deeps of his own sensitively mystic nature in touch with the exalted Christ as Spirit. The ineffable experience enjoyed by Monica and her son at the window in the garden of Ostia [3] was one in which the senses were completely transcended. Both the experience and the description of it owe more to the insight of Diotima in Plato's *Banquet* and to the personal experience and intuition of Plotinus than to the author's theology of sacraments.

To one man there comes an inrush of a larger consciousness of the Unseen in the meteor-flash of intuition ; to another in concentrative contemplation ; to another in a transporting joy or a purifying sorrow ; to another in the sacrament at the altar. But the sacramentarian

[1] A pupil of Plotinus who understood and loved his master informs us that ' to this inspired man, lifting himself often to the first and transcendent God by meditation and by the path explained by Plato in the *Banquet* [i.e. by Eros or Divine Love], that transcendent God appeared,' and this without sacramental mediation (Porphyry, *Vita Plotini*), 23.

[2] J. C. Hardwick, writing on " Sacramental Tolerance " in *Modern Churchman*, XVI, p. 479, suggests that " the unique role of sacramental religion " is to supply the " tertium quid " alongside " the religion of miracle and mystical religion." " Sacramentalism may stand between the cruder forms of miracle religion and the more exalted forms of mysticism. A sacrament may be defined as the concentration of an idea in tangible and visible form, as the temporary embodiment of a permanent and universal principle. It enables us to find in a particular instance what the mystic finds everywhere, and thus may help us to do for ourselves what the mystic can do even without a sacrament to help him."

[3] Augustine, *Conf*. IX. 10.

17

has no right to deny the worth of the experiences of the others, or to assert his mode of contact with transcendental things as obligatory upon or essential to the others. *Deus non alligatur mediis,* and neither is the spirit of man at all times.

CHAPTER XIV

SACRAMENTS TO-DAY AND THEIR FUTURE

WHAT is a sacrament to-day? There are three essentials:

(1) The requisite psychological attitude disposing the adorant to find what he seeks and to see what he expects —an attitude valid alike in religion, in psychology, and in some phases of medicine. You have the expectancy, the first thrill caused thereby, and then through association of ideas that first thrill tends to induce the next more easily. The initiand of the Mysteries knew by faith-knowledge that he would witness a theophany because he was convinced of it. The Australian aborigine *knows* he will die as a result of the lethal rites which he witnesses in operation against his life, and he dies. However acrimonious the dispute about the objectivity of sacraments, there is complete consensus as to the indispensability of the subjective preparedness. The saying of Heraclitus that ' eyes and ears are poor witnesses to men if their souls lack wit ' [1] is no argument against the use of eyes and ears, but an assertion that only the soul can interpret sense.

This correspondence of expectation and emotion is the secret, or one secret, of the Mass in which Protestants see so much superstition and too close an affinity with the magic of the ages during which it was developed. But the Mass is not merely the superstition seen in it by Protestants, nor is it effective only for the more ignorant Roman Catholics, though it is naturally more effective to credulity. Educated and enlightened Catholics as well as some Protestants experience the uplift of that

[1] Bywater, fr. 4.

sacrament. It brings by visible means and a perverted theology before the eyes of the mind the reality of the great Passion which is the central principle of all spiritual life. ' Be it unto you according to your faith ' is the ever-valid principle of the use of sacrament, and the Mass affords to many Roman Catholics the *locum refrigerii, lucis et pacis.*[1] A symbol can mean anything a man wishes when he uses it. There are as wide divergences in the sacramental experiences of Christians as in their opinions.

(2) The objective means or material channels. It is easier for all to realize the tangible existences than the immaterialities, and it is easier, perhaps necessary, for the many, to realize the spiritual through the material, the invisible through the visible. Even Philo, whose deep intuitions gave him immediate access to the eternal verities, admits that only the perfect, the saints ' born of God,' can dispense with symbols. And Suso, with some exaggeration, contended: " It is better to learn the inward from the outward than the inward from the inward." Spiritual results can be attained only and always through spiritual causes, but spiritual causes may be uprisings from the soul itself, or deep haunting intuitions of truth, or mental anguish and moral self-loathing; or, on the other hand, these causes may arise from or accompany physical events—the death of a loved one, the revisiting of a scene of moral conflict, the decision which thrusts us face to face with the great authenticities of life, the discovery of a Bethel, the sight of something that links us with the *alter ego* of an esteemed friend, or the sudden discovery of that higher life within us which wings the soul into the Infinite—in fact a " sunset-touch, a fancy from a flower-bell." The things visible may be fading and fade, but before fading they may have made lasting impressions of spiritual values on the soul. Life has many ways of teaching with Francis Thompson's *The Mirage*:

[1] Words from Commemoration of the Dead in the Canon of the Mass.

> " Even so
>   Its lovely gleamings,
> Seemings show
>   Of things not seemings." [1]

These " lovely gleamings " may project the mind " far in the Unapparent."

(3) The spiritual background in which the subject of the first condition and the object of the second condition unite, i.e. a belief in a world of unseen powers which impinges on this world of ours and the faith which unites, which draws the infinite as it were within the finite. It is not the sunset in itself nor the act of the gazer that makes the sunset far more than a sunset: it is an intuition of a world of Light which ever overcomes darkness both physical and spiritual.

Where these three conditions obtain we have unfailingly effects produced, deepened intuitions, purified emotions, thirst for goodness, the fountain of the great devotional deep within broken up, which is far from an assertion either that such effects are produced apart from the subjective precondition mentioned or that they are effected *only* through such helpful visible means, or even that these external media are the highest means of lifting the soul into the high levels of Love where man walks with his God. In the words of a Pagan contemporary of St. Paul, ' only the pure and holy soul can receive God,' whether through rite or independent of it.

Living in a tangible and visible world, we may profitably use these things to reach the interpenetrating and interpretative Spirit. The long-continued practice of sacraments in Paganism and Christianity witnesses to their utility, though this argument by itself would be dangerous. The use and even necessity of symbolism are deep-rooted in human nature, but the working of

---

[1] Or, in prose form, " Earthly Beauty is but heavenly Beauty taking to itself flesh " (*Works*, III, p. 87). " The roots of the Seen remain unseen " (George MacDonald).

this great principle is rather hindered than helped by exclusive theories of the " two symbols divinely instituted."

The intrepid Maid of Domremy faced the flames in the market-place of Rouen with firmer faith when an English soldier acceded to her request for a cross by making an impromptu one from the end of a stick. " Joan received it reverently and kissed it with tenderness, making prayers to our Lord who had suffered on the Cross for redemption, of which this was the sign and the representative. She placed it in her breast, between the flesh and her garment. She then asked me humbly to have the cross brought from the church, in order that she might be able to see it continually until her death," says Massieu.[1]

Mary of Scots found a similar comfort in the crucifix which she grasped upon the scaffold.[2]

In R. L. Stevenson's poignant *Olalla* the Protestant lover looks upon the wayside crucifix to which the Catholic girl directed his attention and says:

" I looked at the face of the crucifix, and though I was no friend of images, and despised that imitative and grimacing art of which it was a rude example, some sense of what the thing implied was carried home to my intelligence. The face looked down upon me with a painful and deadly contraction; but the rays of a glory encircled it and reminded me that the sacrifice was voluntary. It stood there, crowning the rock, as it still stands on so many highway sides, vainly preaching to passers-by, an emblem of sad and noble truth; that pleasure is not an end, but an accident, that pain is the choice of the magnanimous, and that it is best to suffer all things and do well."

Keats negotiated the lonely passage into the silence holding constantly in his hand through the closing days

[1] A. B. Paine, *Joan of Arc*, II, p. 304.
[2] Sir Walter Raleigh confessed that his familiar long carved silver pipe aided him to face the ordeal on the scaffold.

the little white cornelian given him by Fanny Brawne and her last letter unopened.

Even a great general and consummate strategist— inured to the shock of battle—was not indifferent. Robert E. Lee not long before he died referred to the oak in the yard of the Fitzhugh mansion at Chatham overlooking Fredericksburg: " It was under that oak that I courted my wife ; and standing yonder on Marye's Height, at the fiercest moment of the battle of Fredericksburg, I yearned to get a sight of that tree. When the smoke cleared a bit, I caught a glimpse of its upper branches—and it strengthened me for the day's work." [1]

Were the selfishness of the disciples and their shameful conduct at the Last Supper with their Lord not brought home to them better by Jesus' use of the towel and basin than by a direct denunciation? It was a wonderful psychological appeal, an acted parable.

If through sacraments the spirit has in any real measure—

> " From the top of sense looked over sense
> To the significance and heart of things
> Rather than things themselves,"

they have profited. But this does not imply that this is exclusively the way, or deny that many souls, in antiquity and in the present, have without rite and sacrament seen the things that are invisible. If sacraments in any way assist during an eclipse of faith ; if they vouchsafe to men an uplift into the ideal world of their striving ; if they give even inadequate expression to the uprisings of the soul ; if they purify the emotions ; if they rend the veil of our earthliness to envisage the encompassing eternities of human life ; if the use of visible objects suggests invisible aids to human effort, they justify themselves, however false or unhistorical or unpsychological our theories of their working may be. They prove aids to devotion, though devotion is far from being all of religion. They also foster the social

[1] *Scribner's Magazine*, November 1925, p. 471.

aspects of religion and so promote the communion of the saints. A company of men and women meeting together, taking part in the same devotional act, with approximately similar expectancies, will be fused into a unity and entranced with a spirit of worship better than solitaries.[1] This congregational or fellowship value of sacramental acts is important. This is one valuable function of sacraments. They are more social and democratic than poetry and art; they body forth beyond poetry and art our membership one of another and one with Christ; they help to correct the asperities of creedal barriers in declaring more impressively than by dialectics that we all partake of the same spiritual food.

Sacraments as symbols retain their value for religion, and so far as we can see of human nature are likely to continue in some measure to do so because of hallowed associations, the power of sentiment to move masses untouched by logic, the conservatism of religious people, and the natural correspondences in things and the deep-seated desire of the majority for visualization of truth rather than verbal or logical enunciations. Verily *nihil enim animo videre poterant, ad oculos omnia referebant.*[2] Thus Bishop Stephen Gardiner, the conservative of Tudor days, advocating images for the commonalty: " If the Cross be a truth, why may we not have a writing thereof such as all can read, that is to say, an image? " A Platonist of the second century in a sermon on the use of images or external objects in worship remarked:[3]

' It is not that the Divine Being stands in any need of images or statues. It is poor humanity, because of its weakness and the distance dividing it from God, " as

[1] " Ritual is more impressive and emotion more active when a whole society is concerned in the same ritual and the same emotion " (Whitehead, *Religion in the Making,* p. 23).

[2] Cicero, *Tusc. Disp.* I. 16, 37.

[3] Maximus Tyrius, *Diss.* II, 2 (tr. by Bevan, *Later Greek Religion,* p. 147).

the heaven is high above the earth,'' which has contrived these things as symbols. People who have an exceptionally strong power of mental realization, who can lift their soul straight away to heaven and come into contact with God—such people, it may be, do not stand in any need of images. But such people are few amongst men. You never find men in the mass with a realization of God and able to dispense with aids of this kind. It is as with the teaching of letters to children.'

Philo,[1] exegeting the words ' all the people saw the voice ' of lightning, comments, ' It happens that the voice of men is to be heard, but the voice of God is in reality to be seen. Why? Because what God speaks is not words but deeds, such as the eyes appreciate before the ears ! '

But while accepting these external means of grace and aids to devotion and expressions of communion, we may do so only if remembering:

(I) That to hold sacraments as *opera operata* or as the means of salvation or the pre-condition for highest spiritual privileges is to strengthen the ancient alliance between magic and religion without strengthening religion. Neither the performance of sacraments nor their non-performance avails, but only faith working through love. To make the performance of Church sacraments or the acceptance of the Church's theology of the sacraments the mode of Church membership [2] or the bond of Christian communion is to fail to appreciate Jesus' religion of immediacy.

Sacraments may be a means of grace, even a means of salvation, but then they may not. The correct sacramental system went with Daphnic morals during more than one age of the Church and can be maintained even when periodically a deep sleep falls on the Church.

---

[1] *De Decalogo*, II, C.-W. 47.
[2] The dying Jacob Boehme of the *Mysterium Magnum* was permitted to receive the sacrament only on condition of accepting the Lutheran Confession.

Even Augustine admits ' the sacrament is one thing, the virtue of the sacrament another. How many receive it at the altar and die, even die because of receiving it ? ' [1] As a man thinketh in his heart, so is he. To the pure in heart all things are pure, and to the man spiritually prepared to find grace in sacraments grace will flow. But this man will probably not be the man to excommunicate his Christ-like brother because of his failure to accept sacraments or *his* sacraments. Neither will he be the man to affirm that Plotinus' communion with the Divine through direct contemplation was inferior to the method of the quasi-magic Mystery-sacraments and those of fifth-century Christianity.

(2) We admit that sacraments are to their predisposed participators the means of grace and the gateway to reality. This does not affirm that they are the only or even chief gateway to reality, though to many they may be so.

The " sacramental system," by which is " meant the regular use of *sensible objects, agents,* and *acts* as being the means or instruments of Divine energies, ' the vehicles of saving and sanctifying power,' " [2] need not be repudiated or slighted, but in the interests of spiritual religion and on the sure evidence of human experience as valid as that under the sacramental system, " sensible objects, agents, and acts " must be repudiated as the exclusive, or necessarily highest, " vehicles of saving and sanctifying power " ; and in the interest, too, of a great truth for which Neo-Platonism stood, that, in the words of Proclus, ' the soul has its sense ' independent of external media, that ' it is not the sense of the body but the sense of the soul by which alone truth and false-hood are recognized,' [3] that ' there is access in one Spirit to the Father.' The priest of God is not necessarily

---

[1] *In Joh. Tract.* XXVI. 11.

[2] Paget, in *Lux Mundi,* 8th ed. p. 406.

[3] Philo, *De Vita Cont.* 2, M. 473, C.-W. 10. Cf. *De Conf. Ling.* I. 418, C.-W. 92, ' the eye of the soul, the most penetrating and purest and keenest of vision of all, by which alone it is possible to see God.'

or only he who is duly and canonically "ordained," but every man whose presence is an incentive to men in the pursuit of goodness and truth and a sanctuary to those who are discouraged in this pursuit. And the sacrifice of God is not necessarily that material thing "consecrated" by prayer formulas, but that described by Persius,[1] ' a heart rightly attuned towards God and man ; a mind pure in its inner depths, and a soul steeped in nobleness and honour.' It is no derogation to specific Church sacraments to assert that God has a thousand doors by which He enters the soul and that the apprehension of truth comes in manifold ways. What may find entrance to one experience through sacral acts may find entrance to another in a parable or in an allegory, or in the rhythm and fantasy of poetry, or in the appeal of music or in the world of colour. Symbols are visible or acted parables, but neither symbol nor parable is the only or necessarily the best way to the heart of man. Augustine's testimony to the deep influence of the reading of the Pagan book *Hortensius* is instructive: it implanted in him a thirst for God. Could sacraments do more? Brother Lawrence could realize the presence of God when buying wine in Burgundy or engaged in the prosaic work of the monastic kitchen just as when he knelt at the sacrament.

(3) We must, both in the interests of religion and the interests of man's nature, remove the difference *in kind* between the ecclesiastic or canonical sacraments and other Christian rites and the general symbolism of human life, thus abolishing Inge's category of the "other religious forms *for which no divine institution* is claimed, but which have a *quasi-sacramental* value." The sacramental principle, having to a degree discarded its primitive magic and fetishism, must be released from the prison-bars of sacerdotalism. Again, this does not impair the grandeur of the regular or historical sacraments, but it does enlarge life by finding the same

[1] II. 71 (G. G. Ramsay's tr.).

principle of symbolism everywhere around us.[1] The difference in degree of appeal and also in the catholicity of its appeal may be considerable. The Lord's Supper as a symbol of self-sacrificing love is certain to maintain its place. We would carry the sacramental principle all through life, and hear God speaking in every portion of His universe, until we overcome the falsity of the distinction between the secular and the sacred. Though unrecognized as a Church sacrament, surely there never was a more impressive one than Jesus' use of the towel at the last meal with His disciples—an act so in keeping with the whole of His life.

If men had been taught to find the sacramental principle in the sincerity of little children, in the sanctities of human love, in the glory of the sunset, and in everything fitted to purify our affections or increase our reverence, life would be larger and richer to-day. The three essentials of a sacrament may be satisfied, in varying degrees according to the depth of insight and richness of personality, and the accumulated wealth of association, in connexion with a photograph of a loved one, or with an image, or with a ring, or with a special scene of former conflict or uplift, and if so, these and other such objects prove sacramental.

(4) We must likewise remove the difference *in kind* between Christian and Pagan sacraments. The Christian sacraments can stand in their own grand right, and the Name of Jesus is still above every name. Wherever, within or without Christianity, we meet the operation of the three essentials given, we have sacramental influence. That the sacraments of the Mystery-Religions were real sacraments to man cannot be disputed on the testimony of the initiates. That the reverent use of symbols with the due psychic preparation produced religious effects is what we should expect. The baptismal waters not only signified purification, but in some way effected it: the resultant faith was in remission of sins. The average

[1] Cf. Inge, *Contentio Veritatis*, p. 289.

peasant woman and the cultured woman of the Graeco-
Roman world gazed upon the Egyptian Madonna with
similar inward emotions to those felt to-day by the
average peasant Catholic woman and the educated lady
in devotional contemplation of the Virgin. Even in the
Hermetic religion, which discarded sacraments, a plea
was made for the use of images. And a reformer like
Maximus of Tyre, who held a high view of prayer,
recommended the use of images as means of devotion.
It might be said that Christianity naturally took over
more readily and easily the external forms and uses of
tangible *sacra* than the spiritual heritage of Paganism.
It was only natural that those who were moved by the
intriguing beauty of Pheidias' Olympian Zeus should
demand similar visualizations in Christianity.

For the future what shall we prophesy? Here we
must note the cleavage between popular religion, whether
Christianity or other religions, and the religion of those
who have reflected upon their faith in the effort to secure
a unity of the emotional, intellectual, and intuitional.
The former will always incline to superstition, the latter
to experimentation. The former will manifest the conservatism which has strangely accompanied religion in
all its history; the latter will try to bring history and
experience, the past and the present, into harmony. The
adherents of the former accept religion, Christian or
other, as a heritage of holy rites, ancestral customs, a
book-religion, or a group of invariable opinions handed
down by an idealized classical past, as ' the faith once
delivered to the saints ': those of the latter regard
religion as an emprise of the soul and the mind, as an
ever-increasing comprehension of God, antiquating and
confirming. As in all ages of history, it appears as if
the former will prevail quantitatively and the latter
qualitatively. As in antiquity the masses chose the way
of ritual and sacrament in preference to that of intuition and reason aided by divine grace, so it is likely
to be. The philosopher held that immortality is a native

quality of the soul or the health of the soul; the Oriental cults insisted that it was attained by initiation and sacrament, and the multitudes took the easier path and accepted the sacerdotal authority. The Neo-Platonists preferred intensive contemplation and ecstasy as a surer gateway to truth than ritual observances, which however some of them admitted as predisposing to ecstasy. Porphyry admitted that sacraments might operate advantageously on the lower or ' pneumatic ' part of the soul, but were powerless in the highest or ' intellectual ' part; they could elevate the soul to the stars,[1] but could not unite it with the Supreme Being. The philosopher is his own priest. But the greatest of Neo-Platonists, Plotinus, repudiated sacraments in favour of ecstasy or more commonly of silent contemplation: revelation or gnosis is morally conditioned rather than vouchsafed in liturgy.

Historically the lower and the higher elements have co-existed on friendly terms in the highest religions. Remote primeval conceptions can thrive beside their maturer counterparts, and ancestral instincts may not seriously upset individual reactions. Religious logic is not always of the same order as workaday logic or the relentless logic of the classroom. Yet revolt in religion against its ancestry is not infrequent. And religion is often compelled to quicken its stride to keep pace with secular advancement. If, however, we are to judge a religion by its prophets rather than by its priests, by its audacious explorers rather than by its fearful saints, by its ideals, alluring and unachieved, rather than by its deposit of dogma and programme of cult, then we may venture to say that the religion of the future will advance and expand along two lines:

(a) The sacramental principle will be carried all through life and the difference between the secular and the sacred [2] will disappear in a recognition of our total

---

[1] Cf. Cumont, *After-life in Roman Paganism*, p. 125.
[2] Cf. Alice Gardner, *History of Sacraments*, p. 96.

environment as a means of grace and spiritual growth. Since " earth's crammed with heaven " the sacraments of Nature are also the sacraments of God. Like Meister Eckhart, we shall " not dally with the symbols but penetrate to the actuality," and everything will be a sacrament which brings man into union with God, or clarifies his vision of life. Such a commonplace act as ' considering the lilies ' quickened the faith of Jesus in the care of a loving Father on whom He could cast Himself utterly. And Paul taught that in ordinary eating or drinking or whatever we do we may do it to the glory of God and so make the daily acts of life sacraments. " He does not bind the working of God to material agencies. Of the sacraments he might have said what he said of circumcision, that neither their observance nor their non-observance avails anything, but faith working through love." [1] If the long-established usage of specific Church sacraments tends to widen the spiritual perception of men, they have historically been part of the revelation ' in many pieces,' and the employment of tangible things and visible signs dear to Christendom may be justified by educating men to rise from the things that perish to the things that endure and to look out on God's whole world in the faith that ' the invisible things of Him . . . are clearly seen, being perceived through the things that are made.'

> " What if Earth
> Be but the shadow of heaven, and things therein
> Each to other like, more than on earth is thought? "

This will lessen the bitterness of theological controversy and register ecclesiastical pride as the first or unpardonable sin. This will enable the children of the Kingdom to say, " I love to feel the oneness of feeling which pervades the sons of God amidst vitally opposed communions." [2]

(b) The other and, I believe, surer and more important

---

[1] Morgan, *Religion and Theology of Paul*, p. 227.
[2] Letter of Robertson of Brighton, of date May 22, 1841.

line of advance will be toward a healthy mysticism of
the Platonic order. Herein I agree with Professor Lake
that one of the two functions of the religion of the future
" is to afford a centre towards which mystics may turn.
. . . The religious society of to-morrow will have room
for mystics." [1] Religion will be inspired more by vision
carrying us into the unknown future than by ceremonial
which links us with those to whom we owe such a debt
in the past and with whom we maintain unbroken fellowship even with difference of ritual.

The present revival of mysticism, despite much morbid
mysticality and mysteriosophy and sentimental anti-
quarianism accompanying it, is a wholesome and
prophetic sign. It is an index that the general trend of
religion is from external to internal concerns, from what
Hügel calls the " exteriorisms " to the " interiorisms."
Of course with mystics, as with prophets, the Spirit is
like the wind, and it would be embarrassing to give them
the front seats in institutional Christianity or on ecclesiastical councils.

The symbolic mystics will always be able, without
inconsistency, to avail themselves of sacraments and
ceremonial, but only consistently in the acknowledgement of the sacramental idea in general as just mentioned. Indeed sacraments will mean more to them than
to the uncompromising institutionalist.

The intuitive or contemplative mystic may avail himself of sacraments, but will be independent of them.
This is the mysticism of the pure in heart, and this
apprehension of spiritual things is within the grasp of
each. Religion as worship or devotion will not cease,
but religion as experience of self-attesting truth will
increase with an increasing impatience with sensuous
media. The Church has taken her orders largely from
the institutionalist and to a lesser degree from the
philosopher and theologian with uneasy awakenings
from the mystic. But when the Church shall have in-

[1] *Religion of Yesterday and To-morrow*, pp. 177-9.

culcated and fostered the mysticism of Jesus for nineteen
centuries as she has for nineteen centuries sacramentarianism and sacerdotalism, we shall find a new
earth on which the long-delayed Jeremiac oracle shall
be fulfilled in each knowing the Lord. It will be confessed with one of the greatest and sanest of ancient
mystics that ' the man who is a lover of God and loved
by God, though not of priestly lineage and standing
outside the lustral shrine, is in reality in its inmost
recesses,' [1] and it will be experienced with his greater
contemporary that Christ-Mysticism is neither induced
by nor necessarily maintained by cult-acts. Lactantius'
protest [2] is not yet out of date, and he knows not God
who imagines that God esteems vestments and jewels
and such precious things which even a man would be
rightly commended for despising.

Worship need not be stripped of symbols, ancient or
recent, but worship with symbols is not the exclusive
worship or the only worship which produces reverence
or provokes in the spirit a receptivity of the eternal.
Spiritual idealism cannot be forced to cling to one symbol
more than to another. Christianity, without ceasing to
have its institutional and sacramental aspects, will place
God's altar in the obedient heart; it will insist that not
that which enters into a man consecrates him, but
elevated thoughts which arise within. Having so long
emphasized objectivity in religion and failed to escape
its excesses, it will no longer dread or denounce the
corrective subjectivity that ' the spirit of man is the
candle of the Lord.' Early Christianity did not secure
its victory through or because of its sacraments; neither
shall modern Christianity win the world to spiritual
obedience and to all that the Name of Jesus stands for
through its sacramental system, which divides Christians
on the externals of cult and polity rather than unites
them in the spiritual unity of ' one, even as we are one.'

[1] Philo, *Quis Rer. Div. Haer.* 16, C.-W. 82.
[2] *Div. Inst.* VI. 25.

18

ASTRALISM, OR THE RELIGION OF ASTROLOGY

CHAPTER XV

ASTRAL RELIGION AND ITS CATHOLIC APPEAL

As we hear St. Paul's triumphant asseveration, ' I am persuaded that neither the ascension of the stars nor their declinations shall be able to separate us from the love of God,' or read his reference to the previous condition of Christian converts as ' we were enslaved to the elements of the world,' [1] we are reminded that his Gospel was preached to first-century Christians and to an age " servile to all the skyey influences " when astrology was the queen of the sciences. It is not without some effort that we can put ourselves *en rapport* with the ancients in the cosmic sweep of their religion without losing their religious ardour, or wallowing in the slough of arid speculation, or sinking into the abyss of occultism. And perhaps we are deterred and handicapped somewhat by the tenuity of modern survivals of this once venerable faith. It may sound strange to us, but it seemed necessary to the greatest philosophers of early Christianity, that Jesus should die for all creation, including the stars: ' He did not die on behalf of men only but on behalf of all other rational beings. . . . It would be absurd to affirm that it was only for human sins He tasted Death, and not also on behalf of every other creature beyond man who has been involved in sins such as the stars.' [2] Or when Jesus says,[3] ' Many times

[1] Cf. K. Dieterich, ΑΓΓΕΛΟΣ, I, p. 1 ff.; Bousset, *Hauptprobleme* p. 223 ff.

[2] Origen, *In Joh.* I. 35 (Brooke's ed. I, p. 48).

[3] *Texts and Studies*, IV. 2, 130.

now I have told you that I must needs be crucified and taste death for the universe,' the term universe has in this connexion the comprehensive connotation familiar to minds acquainted with astralism.

To the early Christians, whose wrestling was not with flesh and blood but with the Principalities and the Powers, there was a vital content in the cosmic declarations of the Gospel message which it is somewhat difficult for us with our modern conceptions of the universe to recapture. An instructive example may be taken from Eusebius:[1] ' Is not the Gospel of our Saviour, Jesus Christ of God, great and marvellous which teaches every race of men to worship with becoming thoughts the Lord of the sun and moon and Maker of the whole universe as being far above and beyond all? And to praise not the Elements of the heavenly bodies but the Nourisher of life itself and the Dispenser of all blessings ; nor to be affrighted at the visible parts of the world or by anything apprehensible by the outward senses, which is of a perishable character, but to stand in awe of him who is invisible in all these, the only creative Mind both in the part and in the whole.'

We must remember that if Astralism in one respect had a depressing effect[2] because of its determinism, in other respects it proved a joyous and even enthusiastic religion. Moreover, the gulf now yawning between science and religion in the weird survivals of astrology[3] had not opened. Astrology and astronomy had not yet parted company. There was therefore no conflict between science and religion to the believers in astral salvation. Their religious system could claim on the one hand to rest on the most respectable philosophical

---

[1] *Praep. Evang.* III. 6. Cf. Cicero, *Som. Scipionis*, 8, 18.

[2] Cf. Wendland, *Hell.-röm. Kultur*, 3rd ed. p. 156 ff. Dobschütz designates astrology " the chief tendency of the time, the most impious and most immoral of all religions " (*Christian Life in Primitive Church*, p. 367).

[3] Cf. W. S. Urquhart, *Theosophy and Christian Thought.*

basis, no less than Plato [1] and Posidonius and far behind
them, on Sumerian, Chaldean, and Persian science [2];
and on the other to have much in common with earnest
and progressive circles such as the Orphics, Neo-
Pythagoreans, Neo-Platonists, Hermeticists, the leading
Stoics, and the Judaeo-Alexandrines like Philo. Aristotle, as against Plato, had represented the earth as
fixed and the world as geocentric, set in a system of
rolling concentric spheres. His mistaken physical
theories, adopted and furthered by the Stoics, prevented
any advance in astrology until Copernicus. Of course
there were hefty opponents of astrology, especially the
later Academicians and Sceptics like Sextus Empiricus,[3]
and Stoics like Panaetius. Plotinus [4] severely repri-
mands the astrologers and denounces their astral
fatalism, against which he sets reason as more potent
than external phenomena. Macrobius [5] approves of
Plotinus' contention and holds that portents are the
most that can be expected.

This ancient religion commands our attention because
of its long persistence and because of the lasting influence
it exerted on leading systems of thought for centuries
before and for a millennium and a half after the Christian
era, and on Pagan, Jewish, and the Christian religions.
Students of religion cannot dismiss without serious
attention " a learned superstition, which up to modern
times has exercised over Asia and Europe a wider
dominion than any religion has ever achieved," [6] nor
can it be without profit to review " that desperate error
on which the intellectual powers of countless generations
were spent." [7] And for the environment of early
Christianity astralism is important, inasmuch as " after
having reigned supreme in Babylon, it subdued the cults

---

[1] Cf. Bouché-Leclercq, *Astrologie*, I, p. 247; K. Kerényi, *Astrologia
Platonica* in *Archiv f. Religionsw.* XXII, pp. 245-56.

[2] Bouché-Leclercq, *ib.* 206.   [3] E.g. *Adv. Math.* V. 2.

[4] *Enn.* II. 3.   [5] *Com. in Som. Scip.* I. 19, 27.

[6] Cumont, *Astrology and Religion*, p. xv.

[7] *Ib.* p. xxv.

of Syria and of Egypt, and under the Empire—to mention only the West—transformed even the ancient Paganism of Greece and Rome." [1] Astralism guided even the Great Alexander, swayed the shrewdest of Roman emperors, Augustus, and brought terror or comfort to his successors; it formed an element in the connotation of salvation for the early Christians, and it forced its way—with deplorable results—into our New Testament, in the Apocalypse.

Astrology stood high in esteem throughout the Graeco-Roman centuries [2] as at once a religion and a science, [3] a speculative system and a mystical experience. It was " the scientific theology of waning heathenism." [4] It offered its answer to man's Whence, Why, and Whither. It offered man support in the present world [5] from the thraldom of Fate and beyond death a home in or beyond the stars, as Titus assured his soldiers at the siege of Jerusalem that the souls of the fallen warriors would enter the ether and be seated in the stars. It was of sacerdotal origin and bore the charm of venerable antiquity, to which the Graeco-Roman age was so sensitive. From the days of Alexander the Great, whose campaigns disestablished the priestly colleges of the Euphrates, the influence of Babylonian stellar religion grew apace in the Greek world, the soil of which had been prepared by the philosophies of Plato and Aristotle, who assigned high honour to the heavenly bodies. From

[1] Cumont, *Astrology and Religion*, p. xvi.

[2] Cf. H. Gressmann, *Die Hellenistische Gestirnreligion* (Beiheft z. " Alt. Orient," 5, Leipzig, 1926), pp. 28-31.

[3] Cf. Boll, Bezold, (3rd ed. by) Gundel, *Sternglaube u. Sterndeutung*, ch. VI.

[4] Boll, *Erforschung der antiken Astrologie* (in *N. Jahrb. f. d. klass. Alt.* XXX, p. 111).

[5] " So bot die Gestirnreligion ihren Gläubigen nicht nur einen festen Halt im Diesseits durch eine wissenschaftliche Weltanschauung und nicht nur eine hohe Gottesvorstellung in theologischer Beziehung . . . sondern sie stillte zugleich auch das religiöse Sehnen, indem sie die sichere Hoffnung auf ein jenseitiges Leben in Aussicht stellte und Verwandschaft des Menschen mit den Göttern ihn in den Schauern der Mysterien schon im voraus erleben liess " (Gressmann, *ib.* p. 31).

the beginning of our era it made rapid progress in the Roman world to become predominant in the third century.[1] It is not by accident that it was in the most virile competitor of Christianity—Mithraism—that astralism played the largest part.

Wide, therefore, was the appeal of this religion, despite the fact that it was essentially a learned religion [2] and a cult for the elect, for indeed *paucissimi pura mente praediti sortiti sunt caeli suspiciendi venerabilem curam*.[3] Because of its scientific interest and speculative acumen it appealed to the intellect. Because of its Nature-mysticism it awakened exalted sentiments. Because of its cosmic unity it promoted that pantheism which drew the Greek mind like a magnet and fostered the cosmic emotion to which the ancients were so susceptible. Because of its evident centre in the shining Sun it promoted monotheism.[4] Because of its demonstrated harmony and mathematical regularity it confirmed faith in a Providence and adumbrated order within man as without, in the microcosm as in the macrocosm. Because of its silent contemplation it proved congenial to the mystic tendencies of the age. Because it required special knowledge or instruction it appealed to the ancient spirit that considered that there must be something secret in a true religion to be divulged only to the esoterics.

This imposing faith rests on four basal ideas without which it would be unintelligible:

First, that Element-mysticism which took its rise from Greek, particularly Stoic, pantheism, astrological lore, and sympathetic magic. Its text is that of Posidonius, ' Light is apprehended by the light-like power of vision; sound by air-like hearing; and similarly the nature of the universe must be apprehended by the Reason which is akin to it.' [5] That is, the elements of which we are

---

[1] Cf. Cumont, in Daremberg-Saglio, *Dictionnaire*, V. 1056a.
[2] Cumont, *Mysticisme astral*, p. 257.
[3] *Asclepius*, 9.   [4] Cumont, *ib*. 2, 256.
[5] Sext. Emp. *Adv. Math*. VII. 93.

compounded are of the same order as the cosmic
elements which adhere in the one cosmos. '' Element-
mysticism teaches that men reach the vision of God
which deifies by means of the elements in them of which
the first principles exist in the deity.'' [1]

We have in us the very nature of the planets: [2] ' these
star-gods were assigned the race of mortals, and we
have within us Moon, Zeus, Ares, the Paphian Lady
(Venus), Kronos, Helios (Sun), Hermes: wherefore it
is our lot to draw from the ethereal spirit (breath) tears,
laughter, anger, birth, speech, sleep, and desire,' [3] so that
' the powers and passions ' ($\delta \upsilon \nu \acute{\alpha} \mu \epsilon \iota \varsigma \kappa \alpha \grave{\iota} \pi \acute{\alpha} \theta \eta$) are common
to us with the planets.[4] The soul took on the qualities
of the planets on its earthward passage,[5] which it will
render back to each on its upward flight.[6] This doctrine
of community of elements was essential to astral
religion. ' In the first place,' says Firmicus Maternus—[7]

' You must know that God, that artificer of man, has
produced under the directions of Nature the form of
man and his whole stature and substance after the
pattern and fashion of the world. He has compounded
man's frame, as that of the world, out of the four
elements, fire and water, air and earth, so that out of
the mixture of these He might equip a living being after
the divine fashion. He compounded man by divine

---

[1] Kennedy, *St. Paul and the Mystery-Religions*, p. 204.
[2] Cf. *Tusc. Disp.* I. 19, 43.
[3] Stobaeus, I, p. 77, Wach; Scott, *Hermetica*, I, p. 532.
[4] *Cat. Cod. Astr. Graec.* III. 100.
[5] Cf. Servius, *Aen.* VI, 714: ' Docent autem philosophi, anima ad
ima descendens quid per singulos circulos perdat. Unde etiam mathe-
matici fingunt, quod singulorum numinum potestatibus corpus et anima
nostra conexa sunt ea ratione quia, cum descendunt animae, trahunt
secum torporem Saturni, Martis iracundiam, libidinem Veneris, Mercurii
lucri cupiditatem, Iovis regni desiderium; quae res faciunt pertur-
bationem animabus, ne possint uti vigore suo et viribus propriis.'
[6] Cf. *Poimandres*. Also Servius, *Aen.* XI. 52: ' Dicunt physici, cum
nasci coeperimus, sortimur a Sole spiritum, a Luna corpus, a Venere
cupiditatem, a Saturno humorem, quae omnia singulis reddere videntur
exstincti.'
[7] *Math.* III, *prooem.* 2.

handiwork, that within the small compass of his body He might bestow under the requirements of Nature the whole energy and substance of the elements, thus preparing an abode, frail if you please but similar to that of the world, for that Divine Spirit which descended from the celestial mind to sustain the mortal body. Wherefore man, as a microcosm, is sustained by the five planets and the Sun and the Moon by their fiery and eternal motion, so that as a being endowed with life after the fashion of the world he should be controlled by the same divine substance.'

The astrologists were unanimous: ' since all material substances are composed of the four elements or bodies, man too because of community of nature must participate in these four elements.' [1]

This participation in the elements was put to practical purposes in the two religious-philosophical doctrines: (1) that like is apprehended by like, a doctrine which Aristotle refers to Empedocles [2] and which Sextus Empiricus [3] characterizes as a venerable opinion among the physicists; and (2) that we are endowed with ' sunlike eyes.'

The Orphic verse, [4] ' It is by brightness we see; with the eyes we see nothing,' would be accepted by the greatest physicists, philosophers, and mystics such as Plotinus and Philo. ' That which sees must be akin to and made like unto that which is seen to be adapted for vision. Never would the eye have seen the sun unless it were constituted sunlike, nor could the soul ever have seen the Good unless it had first become good.' [5] The same view meets us in Proclus [6] and in a devotee of astrology like Manilius, who asks, in the

---

[1] Cat. Cod. Astr. Graec. I, cod. Flor., p. 146.

[2] On Aristotle's view of vision cf. De Anima, I. 2; II. 7; De Sensu, II f.; and for the difference from the Platonic cf. Archer-Hind, Timaeus, pp. 156-7.

[3] Adv. Math. VII. 116. Cf. Proclus, In Remp. I, p. 255, 22 (Kroll).

[4] Kern, Orphicorum Fragmenta, p. 337 f.

[5] Plotinus, Enn. I. 6, 9.

[6] In Remp. II, p. 164, 12; p. 52, 10 (Kroll).

famous lines: 'Who could know heaven save by the
gift of heaven or find God unless himself were part of
the Divine?'[1]

This possession of a vision-faculty akin to and corresponding to the object of vision was a favourite
thought.[2] Gifted with 'sidereal eyes' we can contemplate the stars; gifted with sunlike eyes we can
contemplate the sun. So Sextus Empiricus,[3] supporting
this postulate, cites Empedocles: 'By earth we have
perceived earth; by water water; and by air the celestial
air; but destroying fire by fire, and love by love, and
strife by baneful strife.' It is man's unique privilege—

> 'stetit unus in arcem
> Erectus capitis victorque ad sidera mittit
> Sidereos oculos,'

just as the mystic Blake says:

> "The sun's light, when he unfolds it,
> Depends on the organ that beholds it."

This doctrine of the 'light-like vision' was not
orginated by Posidonius, but popularized through the
combination of science and religion in his cosmic
mysticism. It furnished at least a scientific hypothesis
and it supplied a new religious epistemology; for the
astrologists, natural law prevailed in the spiritual world
and spiritual law in the natural world. And this religious
epistemology was capable of immense development in
later Neo-Platonic and Christian mysticism. Plotinus is
emphatic that the soul only by becoming good may
attain the vision of the Good.[4] His whole system rests
on this epistemology, e.g. stated in *Ennead* VI. 5, 9.
Philo too could speak of 'knowledge the most sun-like
light of the soul'[5] and Ps.-Aristotle asserts[6] that 'the
soul readily recognizes its kinship and by the divine

[1] II. 115.
[2] Cf. L. Weniger, *Wär nicht das Auge sonnenhaft* in *N. Jahrb. f. d. klass. Alt.* XXXIX. 1917, p. 238 ff.; Boll, *Studien z. Ptol.* p. 238.
[3] VII. 92.
[4] *Enn.* I. 6. 9.
[5] *De Congr. Erud. Gratia*, 9; C.-W. 47.
[6] *De Mundo*, c. 1.

eye of the soul apprehends divine things.' This ancient mysticism of an all-penetrating kinship finds many echoes in that familiar Nature-mysticism of the Wordsworth type with its poetic beauty, philosophic truth, and religious appeal.

Secondly, a corollary of this element-mysticism was the doctrine of cosmic unity, the prevalence of a system of deep affinities and endless correspondences.[1] The astrologists saw the universe as Dante saw it in the story of creation in the *Divine Comedy* as " legato con amore in un volume." Never until modern times did such a unitary conception of the universe dominate thought. The cosmos is one, and the cosmos is in God and God in the cosmos. Never did religion and philosophy hold more unhesitatingly to what Emerson calls " the linked purpose of the whole." " Never was there an age which heard so distinctly and responded so willingly to the call of the *cosmos* to its inhabitants. The unity of all life, the mysterious harmony of the least and nearest with the greatest and most remote, the conviction that the life of the universe pulsated in all its parts, were as familiar to that ancient cosmic consciousness as to modern biology and psychology." [2] A subtle and deeply mystical pantheism had altered the whole Hellenistic-Oriental theology.[3] Γνῶσις Θεοῦ (' knowledge of God ') was identical with *rerum cognoscere causas* and with γνῶθι σεαυτὸν (' know thyself '), for, as the oracle declared, ' know thyself, and thou shalt know God and the universe.'

None were more emphatic on this unity than the Stoics,[4] who in this respect did not permit their materialistic monism to interfere with their pantheistic penetrating spirit. Marcus Aurelius is a representative

---

[1] Cf. the latest and excellent study of cosmic *sympathy* in K. Reinhardt's *Kosmos u. Sympathie: Neue Unters. üb. Poseidonios* (Munich, 1926).

[2] Angus, *Mystery-Religions*, p. x.

[3] Cf. Mead, *Quests*, p. 191.

[4] Denied by Panaetius, Schmekel, p. 191.

Stoic spokesman that the universe is a ' web spun of
one texture,' and ' all things have been interwoven and
holy is the bond. Nothing can really be said to be alien
to anything else. Things have been marshalled and
combine to make an ordered universe. There is one
universe consisting of all, and one God through all, and
one substance, and one law, and one reason common
to all intelligible beings, and one truth.' [1] ' Don't you
think,' says another Stoic, ' that all things have been
reduced to a unity? . . . that the things of earth are
in sympathy with the things of heaven? ' [2] The
harmony and providence of the universe are emphatically taught in the early second-century *De Mundo,* which
presents a God through whom and from whom all things
have their source. A Platonist like Plutarch asserts ' the
soul [of the world] participating in mind, reason, and
harmony, is not merely the work of God, nor was it
made by Him, but it has come from Him and out of
Him,' [3] with which we may compare the cosmic theology
of Paul in 1 Cor. viii. 6; Col. i. 16; Eph. iv. 5.

To the same end worked the Stoic doctrine of the
Spermatic Logos or Logoi (Seminal Reason) common to
all and that of a quasi-material interpenetrating Spirit.
' Chrysippus lays it down that all existence is brought
into a unity by the penetration as it were of spirit through
it all, whereby it is both drawn together and remains
compact and the whole is harmonious [sympathy] with
itself.' [4]

Because one spirit pulsated in the whole life of the
universe there obtained a mysterious ' *sympatheia* of the
whole,' [5] by means of which man could enter into fellowship with the cosmic process. The soul was a fragment
of the celestial fires with which it maintained its kinship

[1] *Comm.* IV. 40; VII. 9; cf. V. 21; VI. 38.
[2] Epict. *Dis.* I. 14, 1.
[3] *Q. Plat.* II. 2.   [4] Alex. Aphr. *De Mixt.* 142.
[5] ' Estque in ea (natura) iste quasi consensus quam συμπάθειαν Graeci
vocant ' (Cic. *N.D.* III. 28; cf. *De Div.* 2, 34).

and to which it would return. Men are not merely
members one of another, but of the whole cosmic order.[1]
The world is the image of God and man the image of
the world. Man as part of the cosmos is sympathetic
with it as a whole. The salvation of the part is to
recognize its place and fulfil its function in the whole.
There is nothing alien to man because there is nothing
alien in the whole. ' The things of earth are in
sympathy with the things of heaven.' [2] ' Earthly things
depend on the heavenly things by a kind of natural
sympathy.' [3]

This cosmic harmony and universal sympathy were
dear to the adherents of astral religion. Manilius dwells
eloquently upon the harmony and immanent divinity in
Nature, until he asks (II. 105), ' Quis dubitet post haec
hominem conjungere caelo ? ' for into the soul of man
alone God descends and dwells and seeks Himself (II.
107 f.). It lifted man above himself to experience that
" the love of heaven makes us heavenly."

Thirdly, this cosmic unity implied for the ancients
an ensouled cosmos.[4] ' Just as we ourselves are controlled by a soul, so the world possesses a soul holding
it together, and the soul is designated God, primordially
and ever-living and the source of all life.' [5] ' The world
is one living organism (ζῶον) with one substance and
one soul.' [6] As a living being, *animal*, the world is
possessed of a World-Soul, a doctrine which Plato's
Timaeus and Posidonius' commentary thereon popularized. Even though the Stoics identified God and the
World-Soul, they held to the Platonic idea.[7] Cleanthes [8]
maintains ' there is one soul interpenetrating the whole
cosmos, by participation in which we too become

[1] Cf. Sext. Emp. IX. 78 f.   [2] Epict. I. 14, 2.
[3] Philo, *De Op. Mundi*, C.-W. I. 41.
[4] Cf. J. B. Mayor, on Cicero, *N.D.* II. 19; Arnim, *St. Vet. Frag.* II,
p. 191 ff.
[5] Cornutus, *Comp. Theol. graecas* 2; cf. Cic. *N.D.* I. 14, 37.
[6] M. Aurelius, IV. 40.
[7] Arnold, *Rom. Stoicism*, p. 184 f.   [8] *Doxogr. Gr.* 654, 30.

endowed with soul.' Man was made ' *animal quod ad imitationem mundi factum est, simili divinitatis substantia gubernetur.*' [1] According to Pliny,[2] ' Hipparchus can never be sufficiently praised for having better than anyone else proved the kinship of the stars with man and that our souls are part of the heavens.'

The stars and planets [3] are ' the heavenly race of gods,' ' gods visible and created.' [4] Plotinus [5] bitterly attacks the Gnostics for denying the divinity of the stars, necessitated by their dualism. This doctrine was familiar from the days of Anaximander [6] and goes back ultimately to Berossus. Even plants have soul.[7]

We must keep this conviction of a working soul-permeated unity before our minds to do justice to astral religion and to understand the ardours of its adherents and the apparent extravagance of their cosmic emotion. It will bring them near to many mystics of the objective type to whom Nature-worship is a religion and the world of order and beauty calls forth ready responses from the human spirit. The Platonic Bishop Synesius [8] exclaims, ' Wise is he who knows the kinship of the parts of the universe.' The modern Platonist Taylor [9] quaintly says:

" I confess that I am wholly at a loss to conceive what could induce the moderns to controvert the dogma that the stars and the whole world are animated, as it is an opinion of infinite antiquity, and is friendly to the most unperverted, spontaneous, and accurate conceptions of the human mind. Indeed the rejection of it appears to me to be just as absurd as it would be in a maggot, if it were capable of syllogizing, to infer that

[1] Firm. Mat. *Math.* III, *prooem.* 3.
[2] *H.N.* 11. 26, 24; cf. Cic. *N.D.* II. 37.
[3] Cf. Maas, *Tagesgötter*, p. 24 ff.
[4] Plato, *Tim.* 40 A.D. Cf. Ps.-Apul. *De Deo Socratis*, 2.
[5] *Enn.* II. 9.   [6] Cic. *N.D.* I. 25.
[7] Porphyry, *De Abst.* I. 18.
[8] *De Insomniis*, 2 (Migne, LXVI. 1285a).   [9] I, p. xviii f.

man is a machine impelled by some external force when
he walks, because it never saw any animated reptile so
large."

Fourthly, another doctrine familiar to Hellenistic
Oriental theology was basal to astral religion,[1] namely
man is a microcosm of the macrocosm, an epitome of
the universe, who holds the secrets of the universe
within himself and who knows and is known by his
infinite affinities. It is only for such a microcosm that
astral salvation is possible, and only in such can deep
cosmic emotion be evoked. ' Is it astonishing that men
should be able to know the world, since the world is
in themselves and each man is a copy of God in a small
image ? ' [2] Firmicus Maternus shows how man, compounded out of the same elements as the universe, is
sustained by the sun, moon, and five stars ' as it were
a smaller world ' and ' as a living being made after copy
of the world.' He is possessed of body, soul, and spirit
like the larger cosmos ; he is, in his present body embracing all the elements, the product of divine workmanship ' in order that God might prepare an abode
frail but like the world, for that Divine Spirit which
descended from the heavenly mind to sustain the mortal
body.' [3]

It was Posidonius who popularized in religious interests the microcosm-macrocosm doctrine originating
in Chaldean speculations. He held that ' the world is
administered according to Mind, since Mind permeates
each part of it as Soul does in us.' [4] Of Posidonian
origin is the statement of Macrobius [5]—' the physicists
had declared that the world is a great man and man a
little world.' Posidonian influence in Philo [6] has caused

---

[1] Cf. Boll, *Stud. z. Ptol.* p. 288 ff.; Bouché-Leclercq, *Astrologie
grecque,* p. 76 ff.; Dieterich, *Mithraslit.* 3rd ed. p. 55 f.

[2] Manilius, IV. 893.   [3] *Math.* III *prooemium.*

[4] Diog. Laert. VII. 138.   [5] *Comm. in Somn. Sc.* II. 12, 11.

[6] Cf. Apelt. *De Rationibus quibusdam quae Philoni Alex. cum Posi-
donio Intercedunt.*

the same thought to appear frequently, e.g. ' traverse the greatest and most perfect man, this world ' [1]; and ' thus some have been bold enough to declare that the smallest animal in the world, man, is equal to the world on the ground that each man is composed of body and rational soul: hence analogically they make man a little world and the world a great man, and in this they are not far wrong.' [2]

I. In the practical working of this eminently practical religion which envisaged both the daily affairs of earth and the high things of the celestial world, we discover what might be termed a Calvinistic combination of determinism and freedom, fatalism and joy, which is another illustration that men's theories and their practices are not always brought into alignment. If the adherents shuddered at the dread mysterious powers of the world-rulers (Kosmokratores) and especially ' the Seven,' they also experienced the thrills of cosmic emotion and the elevating joys of sidereal mysticism.

Astrology contributed to ease the bewildering complexity of the world. The faith *certa stant omnia lege* [3] rested on the double basis of an order and harmony which established a Providence and a fixity of order which issued in fatalism. Inexorable Fate became at least intelligible, being explained by the order of the astral divinities. If on the astralists' theology the course of human life was predetermined apart from man's voluntary exertions and independent of his moral antecedents, they at least pursued virtue as if happiness depended on their own efforts. Man through self-knowledge is a Son of God and not a Slave of Fate, as Poimandres revealed.

This religion was grounded on an all-embracing series of correspondences which magic and divination [4] sought

---

[1] *De Migr. Abr.* 39, C.-W. 220. Cf. *De Plant.* 7, C.-W. 28; *De Providentia,* I. 40.
[2] *Quis Rer. Div. Haeres,* 31, C.-W. 155.   [3] Manilius, IV. 14.
[4] Cf. Kroll, *Erforschungen der antiken Astrologie,* p. 107.

to turn to practical use. Astrology held to both fatalism and freedom and encountered no serious difficulty in reconciling them. If astrology laid on the ancient world the heavy burden of a necessity arising out of cosmic mechanism, it also balanced its credit ledger by so treating Fate as to make it an incentive to effort rather than a cause of despairing pessimism. This " belief in Fate not only became a source of moral inspiration to noble minds, but also proved a justification of the necessity of positive worship." [1]

The burden of this fatalistic creed [2] was also lightened very considerably by the fact that the laws and order and beauty of the celestial mechanism established a Providence, even the existence and working of a controlling Deity, and also the mighty stellar Powers were conceived as personal deities [3] who might be known and therefore propitiated. There was further a way of escape for those astrologists who were sufficiently catholic in their tastes or prudential in their motives to seek identification with the potent Lords of the Mystery-Religions, the proud boast of the adherents of which was that their gods were cosmic deities who, like Isis, could awaken the victorious faith: ' Thou unravellest even the inextricably tangled web of Fate. Thou dost alleviate the tempests of Fortune and restrainest the harmful courses of the stars.' There was also another method of escape or release from the cosmic powers which was open to anxious or fearful adherents of astralism in common with the adherents of every ancient form of religion—magic. The magician was the expert in astral lore who by possession of esoteric knowledge and correct formulae could sway or compel the dreaded powers to the will of man.

II. Another expression of astral religion was sidereal mysticism with its accompanying cosmic emotion, a form

---

[1] Cumont, *Astrology and Religion,* p. 161.
[2] ' Voluit hoc astrum meum ' (Bücheler, *Carm. Lat. Epigr.* 1536).
[3] Wendland, *Hell.-röm. Kultur,* 3rd ed. p. 132 ff.

of religion which was popularized largely through the genius of Posidonius, who united scientific knowledge with religious enthusiasm.

We have abundant testimony [1] to the impression made upon the ancients by sidereal mysticism and their sensitiveness to the cosmic emotion which in all ages arises from Nature-mysticism. It was a sentiment which united the Epicurean Lucretius and the mystical Plotinus.[2] The ancients were no strangers to such an experience as that of J. Russell Lowell: " I never before so clearly felt the spirit of God in me and around me. The whole room seemed to me full of God. The air seemed to hover to and fro with the presence of Something, I knew not what."

No one is more sensitive to this astral mysticism than Philo, who was so deeply indebted to Posidonius: thus, commenting on the necessity of distinguishing between the spiritual and the sensible, he adds: ' But the vision sent upward by Light and beholding the nature of the stars and their harmonious movement, and the well-ordered revolutions both of the fixed stars and the planets . . . and the harmonious dances of all arranged by the laws of perfect music, imparts to the soul an ineffable joy and pleasure.' [3]

This sidereal mysticism [4] was a contribution of no mean character to the religious life of the Graeco-Roman world. About 1000 B.C. the mystic strain had been introduced into Greek religion by Dionysiac enthusiasm, and a re-enforcement of mysticism came again in the sixth century in the Orphic identification with Deity, and these were enlarged by Pythagorean symbolism. But astral mysticism differed from these in that the religious sentiments were stirred to their depths not by

---

[1] See references collected in Badstübner, *Beiträge z. Erkl. d. phil. Schriften Senecas*, p. 11 ff.; Cumont, *Acad. royale de Belgique*, Cl. des Lettres, 1909, p. 260 ff.

[2] Cf. Lucr. V. 1214-40; Plot. *En.* V. 8, 9.

[3] *De Op. Mundi*, 17, C.-W. 54.

[4] Cf. F. Boll, *Jahresb. des philolog. Vereins zu Berlin*, 1921, p. 1 ff.

19

quasi-magical sacraments nor by external stimuli, but by the quiet contemplation of the beauty and harmony of the world, especially the firmament of stars. " The source of mysticism is transferred from earth to heaven." [1]

III. Astral religion did not merely appeal to the intellect and stir the emotions, but it affected purity of soul and was shot through and through with ethical issues. It takes an effort of the imagination fully to realize how this science-religion evoked such exalted feeling [2] and moulded to virtue and beauty the lives of its adherents and caused them to record their enthusiastic testimony to its salutary effect. Cosmic emotion was not a torrent picturesquely rolling over precipices of ecstasy and exaltation: it was harnessed to moral life. " The love of heaven makes us heavenly," was its *credo*. In Manilius' phrase the knowledge of heaven calls us ' *in caelum sacra ad commercia,*' ' into holy fellowship with heaven ' (II. 125). Man, who to Plato was ' the spectator of all time and all existence,' becomes to his disciple, Posidonius, ' the contemplator and exegete of the universe.' Physical beauty became the symbol of and incentive to moral beauty. The first effect of this contemplation of the visible things of the universe is the conviction of an artificer and an orderly Providence. Thus Cicero, after a survey of the earth and heavens and man himself as ' contemplator of heaven and earth,' concludes:

' Therefore when we see these and other innumerable objects, can we possibly doubt there is some one as their Author, if, according to Plato, they came into

[1] Cumont, *Astrology*, p. 147.

[2] Dill, *Roman Society from Nero*, p. 598 f. : " It is well to remember that there was a time when the mystery of the stellar spaces, and the grandeur and beneficence of the sun, were the most awful and impressive things in human experience."

[3] Cf. Wendland, *Philos Schrift üb. Vorsehung*, and Capelle, *Schrift von der Welt*, p. 534. ' The beauty of the world manifests it as the *poema* of God ' (Diog. Laert. I. 35).

being, or if they have always existed, as according to Aristotle, that there is a Director of such a work and function? So the mind of man, although you do not see it as divine, you recognize as divine from its works.' [1]

In a memorable passage of the *De Natura Deorum*, II. 95, he translates Aristotle with strong commendation of this argument which a later writer than Cicero likewise uses: ' The invisible things of Him since the creation of the world are clearly seen, being understood through the things that are made, even His everlasting power and divinity.' Aristotle likewise assigned a unique value to the moral significance of the celestial phenomena.

' Aristotle held ' (says Sextus Empiricus) [2] ' that the knowledge (*ennoia*) of God has come to men from two sources, from the experience of the soul and from the celestial phenomena. . . . For having observed the sun by day making its circuit, and by night the well-ordered movement of the other stars, they concluded that there must be a God as author of such motion and order,'

as Plato had affirmed that earth and sun and stars and seasons proclaim a Deity. [3]

The contemplation of the heavens became a means of grace as a communion with the Divine, because ' there is a fellowship common to the soul with heaven and the stars.' [4] The wonder of heaven evokes wonder in man's soul: ' The mind which has observed their rotations and movements has proved that his own mind is like to Him who had made these in the sky.' [5] The astrologist Vettius Valens testifies that ' men tracing out the circle of heaven and the movements of the stars and the course of the sun and moon . . . from such foretaste of immortality would seem to have partaken before the time in communion with the gods ' [6]; and again he adds in

[1] *Tusc. Disp*. I. 28, 70. [2] *Adv. Math*. IX. 20 and fr. 12.
[3] *De Legg*. X. 11. [4] Macrobius, *Comm*. I. 14, 16.
[5] *Tusc. Disp*. I. 25, 62.
[6] *Anth*. p. 346, l. 16 ff., and p. 242, l. 29.

a parenthesis: ' The writer enjoys enthusiasm, especially
on these things, and seems to hold converse with God.'
And this communion rests on ' the kinship of the stars
with man and the fact that our souls are part of
heaven,' [1] so that the poet [2] asks, ' Who could know
heaven save by grace of heaven, or find God unless he
were part of God? '

The testimonies of the ancients to the practical moral
effects and religious uplift of this cosmic communion
are too emphatic and sincere and too firmly grounded
in their personal experience to permit us to discredit
them. They believed, and therefore they spoke. In
the midst of his great scientific work Vettius Valens
pauses to give his testimony: ' I desired to obtain a
divine and reverential contemplation and thoroughly to
cleanse my way of all wickedness and of all defilement
and to render my soul immortal beforehand.' He
' regrets that he did not live in the classic days of the
great astrologers,' who ' manifested such zeal and virtue
that they abandoned earthly interests to walk in heaven
with immortal souls and in full concord with divine and
holy thoughts.' [3]

Marcus Aurelius [4] supports these testimonies: ' The
impressions of these [stars] cleanse the defilement of
earth-life.'   Julian [5] prays to the King Sun to grant
him ' a good life and more perfect understanding and
a divine mind.' In the Pseudo-Platonic *Epinomis*—
" the first gospel preached to Hellenes of the stellar
religion of Asia "—the study of the celestial phenomena is recommended as the means to the beautiful
life.

In this connexion Philo cannot be overlooked, both
because of Posidonian influence and because he is one
of the world's master mystics. In his *De Opificio
Mundi* [6] he tells how the Mind—

---

1 Pliny, *H.N.* II. 26, 95.   2 Manilius, II. 115.
3 *Anth.* p. 242, 16; p. 241, 13. Cf. *Tusc. Disp.* I. 19, 45.
4 VII. 47.   5 *Or.* IV. 158b.   6 23, C.-W. 70.

' Raised aloft on wings to the air and having surveyed
conditions therein is carried still higher into the ether
and to the circuit of the heavens. There it is carried
round in the dances of the planets and fixed stars according to the laws of perfect music, and following the Love
that leads to Wisdom and surmounting everything of
the sensible world, it strives to attain the spiritual. And
on contemplating in yonder world the patterns and ideas
of surpassing beauty which it saw in the world of sense,
it is overcome with a sober intoxication and enjoys
enthusiasm like the Corybantic, but it is filled with a
different desire and a loftier yearning by which it is
inspired to the very height of the spiritual things and
seems to enter the very presence of the great King
himself.'

And again [1] God provided generously for man ' both
to live and to live nobly,' the former by supplying the
things requisite for his enjoyment, and the latter by
' the contemplation of the heavenly things, by which the
Mind is smitten to conceive Love and Desire for these
things, whence arose philosophy, whereby man, a mortal
though he is, is rendered immortal.'

Commenting on the command,[2] ' Look up to heaven
and count the stars,' he finds the real meaning to be
that the soul of the wise man is ' a copy of heaven,'
or hyperbolically ' a heaven upon earth within itself,'
manifesting ' most starlike and radiant rays of virtues.'

IV. Another result of astralism of far-reaching
importance was the culmination of the sidereal cult in
Sun-worship,[3] the purest and most elevating form of
Nature-worship. This was partly a natural evolution
of sidereal devotion, since among the planets the Sun
was the most conspicuous as the source of life and light,
' the heart of the world ' or ' the eye [4] of the world '

---

[1] *Op. cit.* 25, C.-W. 77.   [2] *Quis Haeres,* 17; C.-W. 87.
[3] Cf. Fr. Boll, *Die Sonne im Glauben u. in der Weltanschauung der
alten Völker.* (No. 3 of *Astr. Schriften des Bundes der Sternfreunde.*)
[4] Cf. Ovid's address to the Sun (*Met.* IV. 227):
   ' Omnia, qui vides, per quem videt omnia tellus,
   Mundi oculus.'

or ' the mind of the world,' and the mover of the planets. Of course, all the constellations were objects of reverence, the seven planets, and the twelve signs of the Zodiac, and the thirty-six Decans. In the hot plains of Mesopotamia the Moon had the premier place, but as Babylonian celestial lore moved westwards and north-wards to colder climates where the Sun was not so overpowering, it was inevitable that the Sun should secure its place of primacy. But other factors were working towards the practice of adoration of the Sun. The scientific influence of Greek astronomy working on Oriental astrology was bound to recognize the natural superiority of the Sun. Further, Stoic hylozoism, with its deification of the world, and its theory of a universally penetrating principle, easily lent itself to the advance of astral pantheism, which also recognized a ' heart of the world.' As the Stoics regarded fire as the highest and purest of the elements and as divine and creative, they were tending in the same direction as astralism. Leading Stoics had from the beginning recognized the principate of the Sun: ' It was the opinion of Cleanthes that the Sun is the ruling power of the world ' [1] and also that ' the Sun is the potent ruler and master of the universe.' [2] Though the whole heavenly bodies are divine, the Sun is as it were the concentration of Divinity.[3] The principate of the Sun became increas-ingly a religious and scientific dogma. The Sun is ' leader and ruler and regulator of the other lights, the mind of the world which tempers it,' [4] which Macrobius [5] re-echoes as *Sol mundi mens est*. To the astrological writer Julian of Laodicea,[6] ' the Sun has been appointed King and ruler of the universe, leading and originating

---

[1] Arnim, *Frag.* I. 499.   [2] Cic. *Acad.* II. 41, 126.

[3] Cf. Seneca, *Benef.* VII. 31, 3.

[4] Cic. *Som. Scip.* IV. 9, cf. *Tusc. D.* I. 28, 68. Cf. Thiele, *Antike Himmelsbilder*, p. 136 f.

[5] *Sat.* I. 19, 9.

[6] *Cat. Astrol. Gr.* I. 136; Cumont, *Rel. Orient.* (Eng. tr.), p. 259, n. 87, and Pliny, *H.N.* II, 6, 12, cited *ib.*

all.' And to " the Hegel of Neo-Platonism," [1] the Sun
is ' King of the Universe ' whom ' the Demiurge set
over the Universe and established as guardian ordered
to rule over all.'

As men looked upon the external world as divine and
replete with symbols of divinity, it was inevitable that
the Sun should be accepted as the supreme symbol of
the divine unity. It might—with that ancient disregard
of the distinction between symbol and that beyond the
symbol common to Pagans and Christians—be regarded
indifferently as the symbol of the Supreme God or the
Supreme God Himself. But thinking men recognized a
distinction between the Sun of the sensible world and the
Intelligible Sun, or the light of the Spirit, which was the
creator or source of human reason.

Naturally astrological pantheism with a Sun-centralized
cosmos and a deified world came into conflict [2] with
another religious and philosophical conception, chiefly
Platonic and Neo-Platonic, which placed God beyond
and above the universe and out of contact with matter.
Thus astrological immanence and philosophical transcendence joined that issue on which the last word is
not yet said either in science or in philosophy. Neither
conception—of astrological immanence or philosophical
transcendence—drove the other off the field. To the
former the Sun was the supreme power [3] and deity; to
the latter the Sun was a subordinate power but the
supreme symbol and highest sensible expression of the
spiritual Sun. Thus there arose two Suns, corresponding to the two worlds, the Visible Sun and the Spiritual
Sun. And finally, in later Neo-Platonism of Iamblichus
and Julian, a third Sun, ' the Intelligent Sun,' appeared
as the intermediary between the ' intelligible ' and the
' sensible ' worlds.

---

[1] Proclus, Bury, *Later Rom. Empire*, I. p. 13.
[2] Cf. Cumont, *After-life*, p. 134 f.
[3] Cf. the hymn *In laudem Solis*, in Baehrens, *Poetae Latini Minores*,
IV, pp. 433-7.

But solar monotheism was also due to the philosophical and religious quest for unity: it was the working toward a spiritual synthesis and the result of syncretism. So alluring was the solar adoration that the most aggressive deities of the Mystery-cults were identified with the Sun or brought into a working agreement with him.

Julian's view of solar theology in his *Hymn to the Sun* is of great interest. He contemplates the Sun in three aspects, or rather three Suns corresponding to his triad of worlds, the Sun of the Intelligible World, and that of the intermediate world of Intellectualism, and that of the Sensible world, in which the Sun is identified with Mithra. The ardent and sincere language [1] of Julian at the opening and close of his *Hymn* gives some idea of the emotional warmth and moral power of this religion.

This solar faith was the culmination of Hellenistic-Oriental and Roman Paganism. It was the vitalizing [2] power in pagan theology and afforded the most convincing symbol of that light which was the aim of philosophy and religion. It was the source of a mystical devotion in which peasant and philosopher could participate.

" Heliolatry, the last refuge of monotheism in heathenism, which refused to accept the religion of Galilee, swept all the great worships of strong vitality into its system, softened their differences, accentuated their similarities, by every effort of fancy, false science, or reckless etymology, and in the end, ' Sol Invictus ' and Mithra were left masters of the field." [3]

Solar adoration occupied a prominent place in ancient hymnology, if we may judge by what has survived. In Proclus' *Hymn to the Sun* we read:

[1] Cf. especially 130c, 131ab, 158b.

[2] Cf. the " plus important des cultes populaires, celui du Soleil, qui avait peu à peu effacé les autres et dans lequel semblaient se concentrer en ce moment toutes les forces vives du paganisme " (Boissier, *La Fin du paganisme,* 2nd ed. vol. I, p. 113).

[3] Dill, *Rom. Society from Nero,* p. 556.

' Hear, thou King of the intellectual fire, Titan of the golden-reins; O thou Prince who hast the key of the life-sustaining Fountain. From the world above thou dost direct a rich stream of harmony to the worlds of sense. . . . Grant me, O Lord, if thou please, the secure wealth of gladsome piety, for thou art able to accomplish all things willingly; thou possessest mighty and boundless strength. But if any mischief befalls us from the spindles of Fate as they make their revolutions to the star-driven threads, do thou restrain this for us by thy potent sway.'

Of the same tenor is the *Hymn to the Sun* found in the Orphic Hymnbook (VIII), of which the following are excerpts from Taylor's translation:

> ' Agile and vig'rous, venerable Sun,
> Fiery and bright around the heav'ns you run,
> Foe to the wicked, but the good man's guide,
> O'er all his steps propitious you preside.
> With various-sounding golden lyre 'tis thine
> To fill the world with harmony divine.
>
>   .   .   .   .   .   .
>
> Propitious on these mystic labours shine,
> And bless thy suppliants with a life divine.'

Truly in a world in which religious thought was deeply exercised with the themes of Life and Light, this solar symbolism was suggestive. The φῶς νοερὸν, ' intelligent light,' of the physical luminary suggested the φῶς νοητὸν or ' intelligible (spiritual) light ' of truth. The Sun is in the macrocosm what the Reason is in the microcosm.[1] Sun-worship was also the justification of ancient cosmic religion. It confirmed the unity of the universe and was another phase of the doctrine of συμπάθεια τῶν ὅλων, ' universal sympathy.' [2]

Against astralism Christian preachers naturally inveighed, as did also the Jewish sects. Arnobius, without specifically designating the astrologists, speaks of adherents of ' presumptuous schools ' who, ' born of

[1] Cf. Diog. L. VII. 139.
[2] Cf. Proclus, *In Remp.* II, pp. 258 f., 372 (Kroll); Bouché-Leclercq, *Astrologie,* I, p. 28 ff.

God ' and ' superior to Fate,' can after a life of self-control return ' without let as to their Father's house.' [1]

Tatian, though agreeing with the astrologists that the ' spirit ' in stars and angels, plants and waters, men and animals, is ' one and the same,' boldly attributes astralism, ' the placing of living beings in the heavens,' to demons, but Christians are ' above Fate. Instead of wandering demons we have come to the knowledge of one Lord who wanders not.' ' The Sun and Moon were made for us; how am I to worship what are my servitors? ' and ' I refuse to render worship to the planets.' [2]

Clement has preserved an ancient testimony to the release of the Christians from no merely imaginary ' Powers ':

' From this strife and conflict of the Powers the Lord rescues us and grants us peace from the combats of the Powers and the Angels '; and ' Up to Baptism Fate is valid, but after this the astrologers no longer assert truly. It is not the laver only that releases us, but the *gnosis* of what we are, why we are, where we are, whither we were cast, whither we tend, and whence we are ransomed; what is birth and rebirth.' [3]   Origen, who held more in common with the astrologists than any other Christian philosopher, declared that the sun and moon and constellations pray to God.

[1] *Adv. Gentes,* II. 62.
[2] *Ad Graecos,* 4, 9, 10, 12.   Cf. *Sapientia,* XIII. 1-10.
[3] *Exc. ex Theodoto,* 72, 78.

CHAPTER XVI

ASTRAL IMMORTALITY

IF after nineteen centuries of institutional Christianity and insistence on uniformity and standardization of dogma there obtain such diverse conceptions on the hope of man as the realistic and spectacular chiliasm of popular Christianity, the intellectual conceptions of spirit of philosophic reflexion, and the anticipatory experimental faith of mystics, it will not surprise us to discover the absence of dogmatic uniformity among the adherents of astralism. The yearning for felicity and the aspiration for perfection express themselves with as marked uses of imagery as is natural for transcendental experiences and hopes beyond bounds of time and space. Out of this fluidity of conceptions arise personal or quasi-personal and impersonal eschatologies, the eschatology of absorption and that of blissful consciousness, an eternal and a limited immortality. The rendezvous of the blessed was left alluringly indefinite—the moon in lunar immortality, the sun in solar immortality, the highest heaven of the fixed stars in stellar immortality, or that supramundane world of immediate vision of the true and beautiful, which was suggested by the astrological conception of the ascent of the Soul ever up and onward.

The astrologist might be indifferent to the logic of early Stoicism and make way for an astral mysticism and personal immortality, or he might cleave to Stoicism with the logical conclusions of its physics and its ethical view of the life here as the scene of man's self-realization and reward; or he might—as became increasingly the case—veer from Stoicism to Platonism with its more spiritual and other-worldly conceptions;

or again his dominant outlook might be that of Neo-Pythagoreanism with its re-incarnations; or he might find a spiritual home in Hermeticism with its essentially cosmic salvation; or his chief faith might be in the sacramental system of the Mysteries. His view of astral immortality would be determined by the amalgam of beliefs produced by syncretism and by his relative interest in science or in religion, and by the relative importance attached to logic or to intuition. In fact religious and philosophic syncretism neither demanded nor permitted strictly logical consistency: its result was variations of belief, e.g. as in Seneca and Cicero. The ancients were also permitted to give expressions to varying religious moods of faith and unfaith.

The bliss of the blessed spirits [1] in heavenly abodes is variously conceived as necessary with such ineffable experiences. The estate of the ascended provoked thought, and the ancients, like ourselves, were obliged to argue from the known to the unknown and to seek there the fruition of the highest hopes cherished here. Generally speaking there were, among many suggestions, three main ideas as to the occupation or condition of the blessed.

(1) The astral salvation was a complete release [2] from the body which was a hindrance to the soaring soul. It was an elevation above the crassness of earth existence and above the mists and gloom of the sublunar atmosphere into the pure empyrean of endless light. It was a translation from darkness to light; ' restoration to the light of perennial life,' [3] elevation from the earthly things which cannot delight the soul to the supernal things which impart lasting joy.[4] As the Persian and

---

[1] Clement (*Str.* IV. 26; 167. 2) quotes with approval Epicharmus, that ' if you have become pious in mind you will in death suffer no evil, but the spirit dwells above in heaven '; and Pindar, that ' the souls of the pious dwell in heaven ' engaged in praise.

[2] Cf. Badstübner, *Beiträge*, p. 2 ff.

[3] Macrobius, *Comm. in. Som. Scip.*, I. 12, 17.

[4] Cf. Seneca, *Ad Helv.* IX. 2.

the Hebrew thought Glory or Light-existence the form of the presence of the Divine and the accompaniment of immortality, so astrologists dreamed of unbroken splendour. ' Having traversed all the lower planes the soul makes its way through to the supreme height and enjoys the most beautiful spectacle of the divine ones, and, mindful of its eternity, it inquires into all that was and shall be for ever.' [1] The newly arrived soul *inter felices currit animas* [2] and knows no longer in part, *ex conjectura,* but *ex vero peritus in arcana naturae.* In that region ' we see not like you on earth enveloped in deep night.' [3] Again, in his *Consolation to Polybius* [4] Seneca affirms: ' the soul of my brother, released as it were from its long prison, exults at length in its freedom and enjoys the spectacle of nature and looks down from its higher reaches on human things beneath, but it contemplates the divine things with immediacy, the understanding of which it had so long sought in vain.'

This conception of blissful observation above ultimately derives from Heracleides [5] of Pontus in his story of the vision of Empedotimus, whence it was popularized by Posidonius and Varro.

(2) Another occupation of the blessed was to be enraptured by the harmony of the spheres and to be carried around in the chorus of the stars.[6] If the music of earth could so intoxicate the soul and awake it to Corybantic enthusiasm, how ravishing must be the sweet harmony produced by the rhythmic rotation of the spheres. Ancient religion had more than a poetic connexion with the—

" Mystical dance, which yonder starry sphere
    Of Planets and of fixed, in all her wheels
    Resembles nearest; mazes intricate,
    Eccentric, intervolved yet regular

---

[1] Seneca, XX. 2.   [2] *Ad Marciam*, XXV.
[3] *Ib.* XXVI. 3.   [4] IX. 3.
[5] Rohde, *Psyche*, pp. 330, n. 111; 517, n. 54.
[6] Cf. Macrobius, *Com. to the Dream of Scipio*, II. 1-7.

Then most, when most irregular they seem;
And, in their motions, harmony divine
So smooths her charming tones, that God's own ear
Listens delighted." [1]

It was the fruition of their religious ' uniting ' with the
Soul of the World, of which foretastes were granted in
exalted or ecstatic experiences now. The enraptured
dreamer in the *Somnium Scipionis* [2] asks ' what is the
sound so impressive and so sweet, which fills my ears? '
and is informed that it is this marvellous harmony
produced by the stars, to which *oppletae aures hominium
obsurduerunt.*

(3) Another oft-repeated beatitude will be the contemplation of the earth from the celestial heights and
that of the stellar spaces in their brilliance. The
Somnium Scipionis dwells eloquently upon this esteemed
privilege of the elect. The same author expatiates on
the same theme in his *Tusculan Disputations: quum
totam terram contueri licebit.* [3] The *domesticus interpres*
on high ' commands to cast your gaze upon the deeps
of earth, for it is pleasant to look back from on high
on the things left behind.' [4]

The attitude of two men, both Stoics, one of whom,
Posidonius, made astrology a warm and mystic faith,
and the other, Seneca, who was very susceptible to
astral mysticism, is of interest to us.

Posidonius reacted against his teacher Panaetius'
scepticism [5] on the question of survival, and taking
advantage of the great freedom on eschatological
speculation permitted by Zeno, the founder, and combining oriental mysticism and emotion with his physics,
he held to both the pre-existence [6] and post-existence
of the soul. ' The whole air is full of immortal souls ' [7]

---

[1] *Paradise Lost*, V. 620 ff. Cf. Cumont, *After-life in Rom. Paganism*,
p. 212.
[2] V. 10.   [3] I. 19, 44-7.   [4] Seneca, *Ad Marciam*, XXV.
[5] Arnold, *Rom. Stoicism*, p. 267.
[6] Schmekel, *Phil. d. mit. Stoa*, p. 250.
[7] Cicero, *De Div*. I. 30, 64, citing Posidonius.

which have ascended from the murk of earth to find
their equilibrium in the sphere of the moon,[1] where they,
like the stars, are fed by the exhalations from the earth-
region and form a choral company round the moon.[2]
This lunar immortality, advocated with the learning,
enthusiasm, and religious earnestness of an inspired
teacher like Posidonius, not only proved attractive in
itself, but it opened the way to further evolution of
celestial immortality in solar and stellar forms.

Seneca's ideas about immortality fluctuate considerably, from a philosophical questioning [3] or an intriguing
possibility of ' a beautiful dream ' [4] or an assent to
the position of Cleanthes [5] ' that only the souls of the
wise outlast the conflagration,' [6] or the practical denial
in ' death as non-existence,' [7] to the faith in a real and
personal future existence.[8] But apparently to Seneca's
mind, after entry upon the *aeterna requies,* and the life
in the higher ether, and the converse with blessed souls,
the final consummation will be to " suffer a sea-change "
back to the original elements at the conflagration and
begin the cycle again: ' when the time has arrived that
the world should be extinguished for renovation . . .
we blessed souls who have obtained our eternal lot . . .
shall revert to the former elements.' [9]

Other Stoics who were in sympathy with astral
religion availed themselves likewise of the liberty of
speculation permitted by Zeno. ' Cleanthes held that
all souls endure till the conflagration; Chrysippus only
those of the wise.' [10] A limited immortality till the final
conflagration was the most general doctrine, and then
the individual souls mingle with the world soul or are
re-absorbed into the elements.

---

[1] Cf. Norden, *Komm. zu Aen,* VI, p. 23.
[2] Arnold, *ib.* p. 263; Cumont, *ib.* p. 98.
[3] *Ad Polyb.* IX. 1-3; *Ad Mar.* XXV.   [4] *Ep.* 102, 2.
[5] *Ad Mar.* XXVI. 7; *Ad Helv.* VIII. 4; *Ep.* 57, 9.
[6] Arnim, *Frag. St.* II. 811, p. 223.   [7] *Ep.* 54, 4.
[8] *Ep.* 102.   [9] *Ad Mar.* XXVI. 6-7.
[10] Diog. L. VII. 157.

" On certain points all Stoic teachers seem to be agreed ; first that the soul is, as regards its substance, imperishable ; secondly, that the individual soul cannot survive the general conflagration ; lastly, that it does not of necessity perish with the body. . . . We find it generally held that the souls of the good survive till the conflagration, whilst those of the wicked have but a short separate existence." [1]

Marcus Aurelius is a typical representative of this immortality of absorption along with the ethical effects of astral religion. Assuming the survival of souls he says—

' How can the air hold them from all eternity ? How, we reply, does earth hold the bodies of generation after generation committed to the grave ? . . . so too the souls transmuted into air, after a period of survival, change by processes of diffusion and ignition, and are resumed into the seminal principle of the universe, and in this way make room for others to take up their habitation in their stead,'

and again, ' You exist but as a part inherent in a greater whole. You will vanish into that which gave you being, or rather, you will be re-transmuted into the seminal and universal Reason.' [2]

It would seem as if the attitude of Stoic faith to celestial immortality was determined by the ascendancy of physics or ethics or religious sentiment.

The astrologers proper cannot be said to be insistent upon individual immortality [3] or upon that high mysticism of Plotinus in ' the flight of the Alone to the Alone.' It is a great testimony to the power and fascination of astral religion that in competition with the

---

[1] Arnold, *Rom. Stoicism*, p. 263.

[2] IV. 21; IV. 14; quotations from Arnold, pp. 270, 126.

[3] Cumont (*Le Mysticisme astral*, p. 276): " D'une façon générale, les espérances eschatologiques n'occupent aucune place chez les astrologues."

Mysteries and Christianity which offered more definite
and individual immortality, it exercised such a sway and
forced recognition from these competitors. Instead of
the apparently more satisfying immortality of these,
astrology offered the exaltation and refinement of the
emotions here by heavenly contemplation, the converse
in ecstasy with the divine now and a foretaste of
immortality, and a soul purified in this world by its
self-consciousness of heavenly kinship; and after death?
some, like Posidonius, might offer a limited personal
immortality, but the majority would, while denying
individual survival, maintain a continued existence in
the larger whole, by conceiving the soul as a spark of
the divine fire returning to its origin in the cosmic fires,
or a release from the pitiless laws of mechanical necessity
which was somewhat to be discounted through loss of
personal consciousness. Release from fate was also the
release from the bonds of individuality. Others anticipated a celestial existence in the bliss of the knowledge
of the secrets of nature and the music of the heavenly
choirs until *in antiqua elementa vertemur*. The great
astrologist Ptolemaeus seems to have no need for a
future existence, his deepest desires being satisfied in
the profound occupation here with the heavenly
bodies. Another astrologist, Vettius Valens, is quite
inconsistent, expressing a doubt as to whether there is
' requital for good and evil after death ' while again
holding that ' the godless and evil-doers have not only
missed their share in immortality, but also that of
humanity.' [1]

The influence of philosophy upon astral religion led
to further developments and refinement in conceptions
of the supreme bliss. The aspiration of the soul *sublime
ferri* [2] could not rest satisfied with a seat of bliss in the
Moon, or in the Sun as the centre of the seven planetary
spheres, or even in the Hebdomas or seventh sphere of

---

[1] Refs. in Cumont, *Le Mysticisme astral*, p. 275, n. 1.
[2] *Tusc. Disp.* I. 17, 40.

Saturn: the soul still continued its ascent into the Ogdoad, or eighth sphere of the Fixed Stars, the ὑπερουρανιὸς τόπος where Fate lost its sceptre and which for a time satisfied as the abode of God.[1]   But thought discovered a higher God than the *summus ipse deus, arcens et continens ceteros* [2] of the eighth sphere, the Most High,[3] ὕψιστος, the Ultra-mundane and *Exsuperantissimus* enthroned above the Eight in the purest Light beyond the spherical world.   This God is ' seated on the most high place, his power inter-penetrating the whole Universe, giving motion to sun and moon and causing the rotation of the whole heaven, and the source of safety to all upon earth.' [4]

The change in religious outlook was due to the in-creasing influence of Platonism and Neo-Platonism over Stoicism; it was a movement from the immanence of Stoicism with its highest God *within* the cosmos to Platonic transcendence with its God *beyond* the cosmos.

Hence the highest bliss, both in experience now and the hope beyond, was the complete escape from the Sensible world of the astrologist to the Intelligible or Spiritual world of the Idealist, from the world of the visible gods—the stars—to that of the incorporeal in-visible Deity.   Man was privileged to outsoar the height of heavens to the rapturous heights of the *unio mystica* in the world of pure Ideas and to the beatific vision of ineffable Beauty and of intuitive immediate Truth.

The highest phase of astral religion—the solar cult —was likewise spiritualized by philosophic reflection and religious experience.   The great visible orb became but the symbol of another Sun which shines in the soul of man and in the infinite ultramundane Light, the

---

[1] Cf. Cicero, *N.D.* I. 34.   [2] *Som. Scip.* 4, 9.

[3] Cf. Cumont, *Juppiter summus exsuperantissimus (Arch. f. Reli-gionsw.* IX. 1906, p. 329 ff.).

[4] Ps.-Aristotle, *De Mundo,* 398*b*, 6.

loftiest symbol of that eternal light " that never was on
sea or land." A Platonist like Philo [1] knows that the
contemplative who sees ' not with the eye of the body
but with the eye of the soul, by which good and evil
are distinguished,' ' in desire for the vision of reality,'
must ' overpass the material Sun ' to God who is ' the
Sun's Sun,' the νοητὸς αἰσθητοῦ, who from his invisible sources ' causes the visible rays to shine upon
him who sees.' ' For as the rising sun dissipates the
darkness and floods all things with light, so when God,
the Intelligible (*noetos*) Sun, arises and shines in the
soul, the darkness of passion and evil is dissipated,
and the purest and spotless character of most radiant
virtue is manifested.' This is an experience here
and now which makes men ' ravished with divine
Love ' leave earth life behind, while it is also the
foretaste of immortality of a severe and pure
spirituality.

Plato's suggestive symbolism of ' the wings of the
soul ' was gladly laid hold of for religious purposes,
and in the lofty spirituality of Platonism the soul so
equipped by nature could not rest anywhere, even in
the purest ether, in the material and planetary system.
It must outsoar even ' the hyper-celestial place ' to the
transcendental world.

Another thought of Plato's was also destined to bear
much fruit both in Pagan and Christian mysticism, the
Eros or Divine Love by which the ravished soul is
carried into unity with the object of its longing. It was
not enough for the Soul to gaze upon the ennobling
beauty of the earth and firmament: strengthened by
Eros the Soul may make a sacramental use of sensuous
beauty to rise to the supersensuous.

Religious, mythical, and psychological motives run
concurrently in the evolution of the high doctrine of

---

[1] *De V.C.* C.-W. 10-11, M. 473; *De Hum.* 22, M. 403; C.-W. 164.
See passages collected in Conybeare's note in Philo, *About the Contemplative Life*, p. 41.

Eros. The myth of Psyche and Cupid (the unfortunate Latin translation of Eros) is an expression of this religious eroticism. It is recognized by psychologists how closely the religious emotions run to the erotic, so close that the mystics have found it too congenial to express their ineffable experiences in erotic language which is harmless or perhaps even helpful to themselves but dangerous to second-rate or imitative mystics. But the members of the Graeco-Roman world in their profound desire for love, could, no more than we, draw definitely the line of partition between the heavenly and the earthly love. And when they faced the problem of the relation of sex love to the celestial love they were no more successful than many individuals and sects to-day. They saw in the process of generation a demonic or divine quality which closely allied it with the unity of deep religious emotion. Or again, they viewed it as on the one hand a matter of indifference as a material act which could not touch the spirit separated by the impassable gulf of dualism from the body, and hence antinomianism, or on the other hand a diabolic bodily function which soiled the soul and must be shunned— hence asceticism.

The sensuous, and even sensual, and the religious could in ancient thought lie contiguous. This need not surprise us in whose Hebrew canon an ancient ritual of a fertility-cult [1] has taken a permanent place as a devotional book, and for whom the language from that suspicious quarter has, especially through the sermons of Bernard of Clairvaux, become the expression of the soul with its bridal deity and the classic religious erotic. Bernard's use of the language of marriage and fecundity has had a disastrous effect on Christian devotion, especially in the substitution of Eros for Agape, in the elaborate use of sexual imagery for the union of the soul, and in directing the later mediaeval mysticism to

[1] Cf. Th. J. Meek, *The Song of Songs: a Symposium* (Philadelphia, 1924), pp. 48-79.

the Old Testament rather than to the New Testament.[1]

Greek aestheticism was sensitive to the sensuous beauty, in which it saw the reflection of a higher beauty.[2] Hence it need not surprise us that Plato sees a progression in love from that of beautiful forms to that of the unchangeable beauty, or that he treats his doctrine of Eros in connexion not with the love of the sexes but in connexion with that perilously moral Greek form of friendship, *paiderastia,* though forbidding its excesses.[3] A new world was dawning with a passion for love and liberation of the soul. And it is this new thing to which Augustine has given expression in ' I did not yet love and I was loving to love and I sought something to love, being in love with Love,' [4] and which was prefigured by the beautiful myth of Cupid and Psyche. Correctly has Whittaker remarked—[5]

" A thought arrived at by Graeco-Roman civilization only at the end was thus present to the new civilization of the West from the beginning. Among other things there appeared in the world, after a long and complex transition, the elements of a new kind of love; something not without sex, yet directed in a new way to the inward essence of the individual. In this kind of love there is a metaphysical element."

And the erotic poetry of paganism was transmuted into an erotic of the spirit, to which the unwholesome, because excessive, asceticism of early Christianity, the disparagement of sex love as represented by Jerome,

---

[1] Cf. Dom C. Butler, *Western Mysticism.* " With surprising spirituality Bernard uses the texts of Canticles to set forth the love of the soul to Christ, of man to God. The texts are what they are, burning, sensuous, fleshly, intense, and beautiful—everyone knows them; but in Bernard's sermons, flesh fades before the spirit's whiter glow " (Taylor, *Mediaeval Mind,* I. 428).

[2] Cf. Zeller, *Plato,* p. 194 f.   [3] Zeller, *ib.* p. 455.

[4] ' Nondum amabam; et amare amabam; quarebam quid amarem, amans amare ' (*Conf.* III. 1).

[5] *Macrobius,* p. 2 f.

the practice of living with virgin-wives, and the indifference to the future of society in an exclusive other-worldliness, all conduced.[1] The passion for love which is a passion of normal selfhood was diverted into other channels, and the repression obliged an excessive concentration which produced tense psychopathic conditions.

From the days of Plato onwards Eros and Psyche, originally synonyms, appear side by side. And Psyche represents both the present incarnate soul in its apprehension of truth and the discarnate soul in its future immortality. Eros is also that subtle quality of the soul by which it rises to its true home in ecstasy or purification from evil; it also appears as the psychopomp which leads the soul over the waters of death into bliss, and ushers it into the eternal existence. Both the conception and the experience of the eternal within the present order were known to philosophic Judaism as represented by Philo, to Neo-Platonic Paganism as represented by Plotinus, and to Pauline and especially Johannine Christianity.

In truth Plotinus' ' Yonder World ' is not so much the discarnate existence as the elevation of the soul from the ' things here ' which are perishable to the Spiritual (Intelligible) World of present-eternal realities. His Yonder is the state entered into at any time by ' the Spirit (*Nous*) in Love,' which can in Goethe's phrase '' dem Augenblick Dauer verleihen.'' A later philosopher of another race and school expresses this in *mens aeterna est quatenus res sub aeternitatis specie concipit* (Spinoza).

Truly the ' ever divine Plato ' builded better than he

[1] A recent writer in *The Times Literary Supplement* (July 1, 1926, p. 442) calls attention to '' one of the most extraordinary and triumphant metamorphoses in the history of civilization: the fusion in the work of Dante and his contemporaries, of Ovid with Christianity, of the Art of Love with the Worship of the Virgin; the formation consequently of the most complete and most exalted *erotic* . . . that the world has ever known . . . European *erotic*, by which we mean not ' eroticism,' but the conscious refinement and intensification of the sex impulse, which is one of the great achievements of Europe.''

knew in the *Phaedrus* and *Symposium* when, in one of those symbolic myths so congenial to this mystic-philosopher, he gave expression to the yearning of the soul. Love is the remembrance of the archetypes, the quickening of the *anamnesis*. It produces in the soul enthusiasm akin to frenzy (*mania*) and to Bacchic conditions. It is aroused by Beauty which is inseparable from the Good. ' All beauty is the object of Love ' says Diotima in the *Symposium*. But this love, awakened by external and sensuous beauty, evolves through gradations of different forms to ever higher forms.[1] The goal of Eros is immortality or the fruition of self-realization.[2]

As a result partly of Plato's antitheses which are often interpreted as dualism and partly of his Greek aestheticism, there emerges an apparent dualism in his great doctrine of Love, that of the Earthly Love and the Heavenly Love, but only an apparent dualism. Whatever the source from which Love may rise it flows steadily toward and empties itself in the ocean of Reality, which is both a present experience and a condition beyond death.

This phase of Platonic idealism and recognition of the deep intuition of humanity has had a long and unbroken history. Perhaps no one has more faithfully presented it than Edmund Spenser in the *Hymn of Heavenly Beauty*.

---

[1] " Love is, generally speaking, the endeavour of the finite to expand itself to infinity, to fill itself with what is eternal and imperishable, to generate something enduring. The external condition of Love's existence is the presence of Beauty. . . . Love is as various as Beauty in kind and in degree . . . He (Love) is realized in a graduated series of different forms. The first is the love of beautiful shapes—of one and then of all; a higher step is the love of beautiful souls, which operates in moral words and efforts, in works of education, art and legislation; a third is the love of beautiful sciences—the seeking out of Beauty wherever it may be found; the highest of all is the love which rises up to the pure, shapeless, eternal, and unchangeable Beauty, unmixed with aught finite or material—to the Idea " (Zeller, *Plato*, p. 193 f.).

[2] *Symp.* 208e-212a.

But Plato found an earlier disciple [1] in another mystic, Philo, who remembered that Eros was in Platonic symbol the son of Want (*Penia*) and of Plenty (*Poros*) the son of *Metis* (Counsel). Philo, like Plotinus and Plato, spoke because he believed and believed because of having the personal experience of practising mystics and inquiring philosophers. They were ' men who were lovers of wisdom both in their characters and in their discourses.' [2] ' Those also aim at attention to the Divine (θεραπείαν) not from convention nor from the encouragement and promptings of other people, but because ravished by the Heavenly Love, they enter into the condition of enthusiasm, like Bacchic and Corybantic worshippers, until they behold the objects of their longing.' Then, such is their yearning for the deathless and blessed life, they consider that they have already died to their mortal life and leave their goods to their sons and daughters and kinsfolk.[3] Philo is sensitive to the difference between ' the Eros and heavenly Aphrodite ' and ' the common and vulgar Eros.' [4]

In a famous passage [5] answering the question ' who is the heir of divine things? ' after averring ' only he who is inspired from above is deemed worthy (to inherit the incorporeal and divine things), having obtained his heavenly and divine portion, that is the *Nous* in its greatest purity . . . for only incorporeal natures can inherit the things of the Spirit,' he apostrophizes thus:

---

[1] Philo criticizes his master while acknowledging his greatness in his remarks on the *Symposium* (*De Vita Contemplativa*, 7, C.-W. 57), though his criticism is lacking in insight through his Jewish misunderstanding of Greek aestheticism and his failure to observe that, as Walter Pater remarks, Plato is " a seer who has a sort of sensuous love of the Unseen " (*Plato and Platonism*, ch. VI). And " Philo, like St. Paul, was insensible to, if not unconscious of, those higher and more ideal aspects of Greek chivalry, which had in a measure once redeemed it, but had not survived the decay of the old Greek city life " (Conybeare, *Philo about the Contemplative Life*, p. 235).

[2] *De Vita Cont.* M. 480, C.-W. 57.

[3] *Ib.* 2, C.-W. 12-13.   [4] *Ib.* C.-W. 59-60.

[5] *Quis Rer. Div. Haer.* M. 482; C.-W. 64-70.

' If therefore any yearning comes upon thee, O Soul, to inherit the divine blessings, abandon not only ' thy country ' (the body), and ' thy kinship ' (the senses), and ' thy father's house ' (ratiocination), but flee from thyself and leave thyself, like the god-possessed Corybantes, and in ecstasy be divinely inspired to some prophetic exaltation. For while thy thought is in condition of enthusiasm and no longer self-centred, but vehemently agitated by Divine Love and guided by Reality and drawn to Reality, Truth leads the way and clears the obstacles that it may advance by an easy path.'

The next to be captivated by this fruitful conception of Divine Love was Plotinus, whose memorable words in *Ennead,* III. 5,[1] on Love are spoken under the inspiration of his master and from his own profound experience of soaring on the wings of the soul. The function of Love is ' the motive power of the soul to the Beauty of Yonder World or to augment the already conceived aim for such,' ' love is the energy of the soul in its striving for the good.' And ' Yonder World ' is not after death but an experience of the present.

This myth of Eros and Psyche became a favourite symbol of the aspiration of the soul for the divine. And Platonic philosophy, working in and with astral religion, modified it by aggrandizing the native powers of the soul for flight upward, by the intense moral appeal against evil as depriving the soul of its wings,[2] by the necessity of Beauty, Wisdom, and Goodness as the means of strengthening the wings of the soul, and above all by bringing the deepest realities from beyond the grave into the present experience of ' the soul in Love.' The supramundane world lay not in or beyond the highest heaven, but in the soul of man; it was indeed emphatically a world beyond the senses, but a world apprehensible by Nous, or highest part of man's life. If

---

[1] Cf. also VI. 9, 4.   [2] *Phaedrus,* 246d.

astral religion elevated the conception of the heavenly world philosophic reflection spiritualized astralism.[1]

Eros also became a common symbol of the soul beyond death on sarcophagi and in religious Pagan art. In the Capuan [2] Chapel of Mithra, recently discovered, a Psyche is represented as gently encouraged by an Eros. In the basilica at the Porta Maggiore Erotes are prominent in the stuccoes. In the rich symbolism of the apse stucco [3] there is presented an apotheosis of the soul by water in which an Eros gently assists a veiled lady bearing a lyre—the soul or the dead initiate —into the stormy waters of death, while on an opposite promontory Apollo, god of Light, is graciously beckoning the soul to the last ordeal while a Victory is ready to crown her.

[1] Cf. Cumont, *After-life in Rom. Paganism*, p. 212 f.

[2] *Notizie degli Scavi*, XVI. 1924, p. 353 ff. For the Mithraeum at Ostia vide *ib*. XVI, p. 68 ff.

[3] Cf. D. Curtis, *Il rilievo nell' abside del monumento sott. fuori Porta Maggiore* (*Diss. dell' Accad. pont. di Arch.* XV, p. 311 f.); E. Strong and N. Jolliffe in *J.H.S.* XLIV, p. 103 f.

CHAPTER XVII

THE ASCENT OF THE SOUL

AMONG the doctrines of Astralism none was of greater power than the Ascent of the Soul [1] (ἄνοδος ψυχῆς), or the Soul Drama, a tenet held in common with variations by the Stoics, Platonists, Pythagoreans, the Hermeticists, Gnostics, and the adherents of the Mystery-Religions, particularly the Mithraists.

It is futile to seek to designate the ultimate source of this widely spread idea. Anz [2] traces it back to a Babylonian source influenced by Iranian soteriology; Bousset [3] claims an Iranian origin with Babylon as a secondary origin; Reitzenstein discovers its source in popular Iranian beliefs as a replica of the destiny of the World-Soul. [4] Cumont [5] views it as Chaldaean-Persian; Dieterich, [6] rejecting all Oriental influences, claims it as an ancient popular Greek idea. Kroll [7] more guardedly affirms that the idea is essentially Greek but transformed under Oriental influences.

The belief in the Ascent of the Soul is of too remote antiquity definitely to date, and too universal to assign to the religious thinking and mythical symbolism of one

[1] Cf. K. Hönn, *Studien z. Gesch. d. Himmelfahrt*; Bousset, *Himmelreise d. Seele* (*Arch. f. Religionsw.* IV, pp. 136-69, 229-73), Kroll, *Lehren d. Hermes Tris.* pp. 294-316, 363-72; Dieterich, *Mithraslit.* 3rd ed. pp. 179-212; Diels, *Himmels u. Höllenfahrten* (*N. Jahrb. f. d. kl. Alt.* 1922, p. 239 ff.); Cumont, *After-life*, ch. VI; Strong, *Apotheosis*.

[2] *Z. Frage nach d. Ursprung d. Gnostizismus*, pp. 71-8.

[3] *Ib.* pp. 136 ff., 229 f., 250.

[4] *Das iran. Erlösungsmysterium*, and *Die Göttin Psyche* (in *Sitzb. d. Heid. Akad.* 1917, no. 10).

[5] *After-life*, pp. 95, 107.

[6] *Ib.* pp. 196-203.

[7] *Ib.* pp. 302, 358.

race. It is well known that early speculations as to man's soul and its destiny, being of a fluid character, readily blended in man's search for some comforting and rational faith as to his future. Ancient eschatologies rejected nothing that could nourish hope. Illogicality has never been a serious obstacle to combining alien elements in a theological system, hardly excepting that of an Aquinas and a Calvin. So the idea of the Ascent of the Soul was welcomed as one of the early solutions of the perennial problem, and fitted into, or naïvely placed in juxtaposition with, other cognate and with disparate ideas. It was also an attractive faith, which later reflexion would modify and corroborate. Popular imagination, poetical symbolism, and mythical theologoumena would work eagerly upon such material.

The abode of souls and the means of transport thither engaged serious reflexion. The future might be located in the graveyard, or in the lower region in the heart of the earth, or beyond the West separated by the water of Ocean from here, or in the Blessed Isles, or in the world of light in the heavens, or beyond the region of the planets in the Ogdoad, or highest heaven, or in the transcendental ultramundane region.

Mythologies, ancient and modern, are familiar with the idea of a journey of the dead to the next world. Such a journey might be conceived as a pilgrimage on foot; or a voyage by water in a boat [1] to a far land; or transit by ferry across a river; or a descent of the demonic self into the lower world; or a leap from the rock of the dead; or an ascent by a ladder [2] or translation by a chariot into the heavens, like Parmenides; or a journey on horseback, as in the myth of Bellerophon, or by the winged steed Pegasus; or a conveyance upward

[1] The ship for the dead is well illustrated in the discovery at Oseberg in Scandinavia, dating from ninth century.

[2] For the seven-stepped ladder in Mithraism cf. Origen, *C. Celsum*, VI. 22; Cumont, *Textes et Mon.* II, p. 525; Kroll, *Oracula chald.* p. 63.

on wings,[1] of which there are many classical myths, such as the rape of Ganymede.[2]

The Ascent of the Soul, though an early, is a relatively mature form of eschatological faith, which has been influenced and transformed by other solutions. It is, e.g., obviously more recent than the belief in Elysian Fields on earth or the descent into Hades. For a variety of reasons, which we can detect, the ascent became the most catholic of eschatological doctrines in serious religious and philosophical circles. And like every other victorious idea it laid its rivals and auxiliaries under heavy tribute.

The religious dualism of Iran, which in the physical conflict of Light and Darkness saw the symbol of a moral cosmic conflict into which men were pressed as combatants, made participation in the Light the main element in its soteriology. The region of Light was the scene of ultimate victory and there the blessed *milites* (soldiers) will find their abode. If ' the Mediator ' Mithra secured enthronement with the victorious Sun, the follower of Mithra saw in this the symbol of his ultimate victory and eternal hope. In the religious literature of Paganism the idea of Light as the symbol or synonym of life and truth and salvation is frequent. The prevalence of such symbolism could not allow the descent of the soul into the murky darkness of Hades to retain a vital place in faith.

Again, the way was specially prepared in the Greek world by Orphism, Pythagoreanism, and by Plato's adoption of Orphic-Pythagorean ideas, as in the *Phaedo*, which depicts the descent of base souls and their entanglement in bodies. The Orphics were the first to bring into the West the solemn doctrine of souls fallen from their native high place and handicapped by original

---

[1] Cf. G. Weicker, *Der Seelenvogel in der antiken Lit. u. Kunst* (1902). On a relief in the Palazzo dei Conservatori in Rome, Antoninus Pius and Faustina are represented as being carried to heaven by a winged figure.

[2] Cumont, *Études syriennes*, p. 86.

sin,[1] their punishment or purification during the ' cycle of births,' their deliverance through sacraments of identification with a saviour-deity, by means of which, after submitting to a judgment in Hades, they could say, ' Child of Earth and starry Heaven, my race is divine.'

The Orphics were also the first in the West to insist that ethical discrimination must extend to all souls after death, not merely to egregious sinners or eminent saints, and that souls must find abodes fitting their merits. They were therefore the first to moralize Hades, separating it into the regions of penal Tartarus and blissful Elysium. Hades was for the Orphic believer not a home, but merely an intermediate region [2] from which the soul was released into the larger freedom of the next incarnation. Later Orphics, like other religious sectaries of later antiquity, yielded to the tendency to remove the kingdom of souls from the earth or from the lower world, Hades, to the upper world of light, an eschatological transition to which the Syrian cults and Mithraism contributed much.[3] Hades became more an episodic experience of judgment or purgation, and later Orphics co-operated with philosophic speculation in making the air or the higher ether the abode of souls, and in transferring Hades thither.[4]

The Orphics, having first segregated in the underworld the region of the blessed, Elysium, from that of the damned, Tartarus, the next step was taken by their followers, the Pythagoreans, in removing Elysium from the underworld to the region of the moon and in identifying the Blessed Islands with the Sun and Moon.[5] The Pythagoreans were therefore the first to preach celestial immortality to Greece and Southern Italy,[6] and were

[1] Farnell, *Higher Aspects of Greek Religion*, p. 134.
[2] Cf. Rohde, *Psyche*, p. 343.
[3] Cf. Cumont, *Religions orientales*, pp. 186, 235; *Études syriennes*, p. 80 ff.
[4] Cf. Rohde, *Psyche*, p. 356, n. 45; p. 359, n. 75.
[5] Cumont, *After-life*, p. 97.   [6] *Ib.* 194.

dogmatic on the stars and planets, especially Sun and Moon, as the abodes of the elect souls.[1] Their profounder scientific interests and mathematical speculations promoted an immortality in alignment with astrology by bringing their system under the influence of Babylonia and Egypt. The renaissance of Pythagoreanism in the syncretistic capital of the Ptolemies and the rise of Neo-Pythagoreanism in the Roman Empire under senator Nigidius Figulus, astrologer and mystic, removed Pythagoreanism still farther from the parent faith, or, rather, the influence of the astral religions of the Empire became as marked as the severe ethics of Orphism. The Pythagoreans, confronted with the rival eschatologies of an underworld and the upper regions, adopted the latter,[2] declaring ' the whole air is full of souls.'[3] The Orphic purgatory was removed into an aerial position. The soul was conceived as a particle of the eternal ethereal fires, which at birth condescended to enter the body with the charter of its reascension at death to its source above. This sublunar world is the dark cave of imprisoned souls yearning for the upper light.[4] The Neo-Pythagorean Numenius in the second century elaborated the doctrine of the descent of the soul from the summit of heaven through the seven planetary spheres, each of which contributed its peculiar qualities to the soul in transit, and to which the soul in toilsome purificatory ascent would render back those qualities to attain its primal purity in the Ogdoad, or the eighth heaven.[5]

Plato's adoption of the doctrine of the ascent into light gave immense impetus to the belief.[6] The beautiful and

---

[1] Cf. Rohde, *Psyche*, p. 357, n. 76.
[2] Cumont, *ib*. pp. 81, 96. [3] Diog. Laert. VIII. 32.
[4] Cf. Plato. *Repub.* VII. 514. [5] Cumont, *ib.* p. 107.
[6] " (Spätere Himmelfahrtslehren) bekommen durch Platons Hand den markanten Zug, der sie, bis in späteste Zeit in all dem Gewirr mystischer Gedankenstriche hell hervorscheinen lässt. Seit Platon hat in der greich. Welt jedes tiefere religiöse Denken u. jede philosophische Lehre, wenn sie nicht eine Unsterblichkeit der Seele ausdrücklich ablehnte, den Aufstieg der Seele zum göttlichen Licht als festen Vorstellungsbesitz weitergeführt " (Dieterich, *Mithrasliturgie,* p. 199).

impressive imagery of the *Phaedrus* in the description of the upward-tending charioteer of the soul could not be forgotten with the penetration of Platonism into subsequent systems.[1] In the *Timaeus* (42 B) he asserts, ' He who has lived well during his allotted span should depart again to his abode in his kindred star and there enjoy a blessed and congenial life.'

As a result of Orphic mysticism and philosophic speculation on the nature of invisible beings, *pneumata,* Greece transposed the future of her dead from the orthodox dark underworld to the regions of light:[2] ' It is impossible to suppose that souls should be carried downwards; they are composed of the subtle particles, and being of the nature of fire or spirit they tend upward by their lightness.'[3] Among the first evidence of the change is the inscription erected by Athens over her soldiers who fell at Potidaea: ' The earth received their bodies; the ether their souls.'[4] Henceforth immortality was prevailingly conceived as the ascent to the ether or to the highest regions, and finally to the supramundane region.[5]

In the Roman world the doctrine was popularized by Stoic ideas operating in the atmosphere of mysticism. The Stoic conception of the soul as refined fire, part of and akin to the celestial fires, and their doctrine of a quasi-material *pneuma* (fiery breath), the *divinus spiritus per omnia,*[6] readily lent itself to such mysticism. The soul is composed of two parts, one *ignea* and one

[1] The Naassene Hymn in Hippolytus, *Phil.* V. 10, represents the aspiration of the soul in Gnosticism.

[2] " The establishment in later Orphic poetry of the theory that the ψυχαὶ dwelt in the air may have been assisted by the philosophic theory of the soaring-up of the πνεύματα into their element, the aether " (Rohde, p. 356, n. 45).

[3] Sextus Emp. IX. 71. Cf. Badstübner, *Beitr. z. Erkl. d. phil. Schriften d. Senecas,* p. 2 f.

[4] *C.I.A.* 442; Kaibel, *Epig. gr.* 21.

[5] Cf. Rohde, cited Dieterich, *ib.* p. 200.

[6] Seneca, *Ad Helv.* VIII. 3; cf. Arnim, *St. Vet. frag.* II. 1027, p. 306.

animalis, i.e. fire and air, and therefore ' it is clear that
souls on leaving the body, whether they are *animales,
id est spirabiles, sive ignei,* must be borne aloft.' [1] Also,
according to Stoic conceptions, souls inhabit the air, and
Chrysippus held that ' after death souls take on the
character of spheres ' (σφαιροειδεῖς) [2]; ' to remove
into the air ' became a euphemism for death. As
Pauline speculation provided the early Christians with a
' pneumatic ' body for purposes of participation in the
Parousia and the enjoyment of immortality above
' where Christ is,' so philosophic thought conceived an
ethereal or light substance for Pagan souls. The Stoics
even held that the soul itself is ' an ethereal body ' or
' light-character ' or even *lumen.*[3]

But it was above all the Platonizing Stoic, Posidonius,
and the Stoicism [4] remodelled by him through the
accession of mystical emotionalism and the adaptation
of Babylonian cosmography and astral immortality,
that popularized the upper air or highest ether as the
place of souls. Pythagorean suggestions [5] and theories
of Heracleides Ponticus regarding the Milky Way as
the dwelling of souls [6] contributed to the establishment
of the dogma of the Descent and Ascent of the Soul
through the planetary spheres with the accompanying
cosmological conception of a finite universe with a
geocentric centre as an integral part of the religious,
magical, and philosophical systems of the age. The
starting-point was the Platonic view [7] that the soul after
death departs to the upper regions or to heaven. This
idea is recurrent in all the literature influenced by
Posidonian mysticism, as, e.g., in Cicero's *Dream of*

---

[1] Cic., *Tusc. Disp.* I. 17, 40.   [2] Arnim, 222.
[3] Rohde, *Psyche,* p. 517, n. 53.
[4] Cf. Halliday, *Pagan Background,* pp. 174, 209, 224 f. Bevan,
Stoics and Epicureans, p. 98 f.
[5] Cf. Rohde, p. 395, n. 35; p. 517, n. 53.
[6] Rohde, pp. 330, 517. Cf. Thiele, *Antike Himmelsbilder,* p. 148,
for the Milky Way as one of the stations in the ascent.
[7] *Phaedo,* 81b.

Scipio. In the *Tusculan Disputations* Cicero tells how the soul, the most swift of all things, escaping from the air—

' must enter and pass through all this region in which clouds, storms, and winds gather, and which is damp and misty by the exhalations from the earth. When the soul has risen above this region and attained to a nature resembling its own and recognizes it, it takes its place with the fires composed of the most rarefied air and of the tempered heat of the sun; the soul then ceases to ascend. For it has thus secured a lightness and warmth like its own and has been as it were brought to equilibrium and remains motionless. That is its natural abode, where it has reached that which is akin to itself, in which it will be in need of nothing and will be nourished and sustained by the same qualities by which the stars are sustained and nourished.' [1]

Elsewhere he could ask, ' Is not almost the whole heaven peopled with the human race? ' [2] by the dead becoming stars or taking up stellar abodes.

The same idea is enthusiastically expressed by Seneca. In his *Consolation to Marcia* (25) he reminds her that the grave does not contain the personality of her son, but only bones and dust and garments, for—

' He himself is untouched, leaving on earth nothing that was his: he has escaped and departed in his entirety. Hovering for a little while over us, until he undergoes purification, puts off his faults, and doffs the whole manner of mortal existence, he is carried on high and takes his place among the blessed souls. The holy assembly has received him. . . . Although in that world everything is akin to everything, your progenitor attaches himself to his grandson as he rejoices in the new light and teaches him the movements of the neighbourly stars; he gladly initiates him into the mysteries of nature, not from guess-work but from real experience; . . . he is to him an intimate interpreter as he wishes to pry into the causes of heavenly things.'

[1] I. 19, 43.   [2] I. 12, 28.

This astral doctrine is composed of several ingredients. First, it implies a descent of the soul from its primitive abode into man who is at least a double being, of soul and body, or a tripartite being, of body, soul, and mind (*nous*) or spirit (*pneuma*). According to Orphic theology we are duplex, composed of Titanic, or evil, and Dionysiac, or divine, elements,[1] yet ' we are part of him (Dionysus) ' [2] and ' the Mind in us is Dionysiac and a veritable image of Dionysus.' [3] The soul cannot rise higher than its original source. It could not rise to heaven unless it had come from heaven and unless, despite its fall and weakness and wanderings, it had retained some vague entrancing memories of its prior existence in bliss. It is because we are ' of the race of heaven ' that the contemplation of the heavens is a divine communion and a means of purifying the soul from the tarnishing touch of earth. The *Poimandres* gives an elaborate myth of the incarnation of the soul through ignorance and deception with the burden of qualities which it took on in its descent through the spheres to the bosom of Nature (*Phusis*). From the same Hermetic circles the *Kore Kosmou* describes the fall of man and the descent of the soul into the sensible world and the sad plaint of the soul on discovering the stern actualities of earth-life. But the fall is not beyond repair, the promise of restoration being held out on certain terms.

Another constituent of this astral doctrine is the kinship of the soul with the sidereal world. Assuredly ' every soul by its nature tends upward as if aspiring to its natural abode.' [4] Souls are of astral stuff,[5] of the intelligible fire ($\nu o\epsilon\rho\grave{o}\nu$ $\pi\hat{u}\rho$), and of the same consistency as the celestial bodies: ' Composed of the finest particles, and indeed being of the character of fire or

---

[1] Cf. Eisler, *Weltenmantel*, I, p. 448 f.; II, p. 664.
[2] Olympiodorus, in Rohde, p. 355, n. 42.
[3] Proclus, *In Crat.* p. 82 (Bois).
[4] Proclus, *In Remp.* II, p. 126 (Kroll).
[5] Cf. Kroll, *Lehren des Hermes Trismegistos*, p. 241.

spirit (breath), they are carried upward by their own lightness into the more elevated regions . . . there (in the sublunar region) on account of the greater purity of the atmosphere they tarry longer and enjoy their proper nourishment in exhalations from the earth like the stars.' [1] Again: ' The soul is always striving to view on high the things akin to itself.' [2] The revolutions of the planets teach the contemplative soul that ' his soul is like that of Him who created these in the heaven.' [3] It is after ascending *omne caelum hoc* that the soul recognizes *naturam sui similem.*[4]

Thirdly, this kinship cannot be realized without purification of the soul from the contacts of earth and of vice, and many are the dangers of the transit of the soul on its upward way. Cicero, speaking under the inspiration of the *Phaedo*, makes Socrates declare that—

' There are two ways and two courses open to souls departing from the body. Those who have polluted themselves with the vices of humanity and surrendered themselves wholly to passion . . . take a certain devious way far from the assembly of the gods, but those who have maintained their moral integrity and purity, to whom there was the least possible contagion with body and who always held themselves aloof from bodies and in their bodies imitated the life of the divine beings, find open an easy path of return to those from whom they had taken their departure.' [5]

The soul is here in a state of agitation because its home is elsewhere, and it attains psychic equilibrium only in a region of the same rarity and purity of atmosphere as itself.[6] This can be effected only after release from the body and from earthly cares.

Elevated above the confusing mists by which we are

[1] Sextus Emp. IX. 71, 73.
[2] Cf. Seneca, *Ad Helv*. VI. 8: ' i nunc et humanum animum ex isdem quibus divina constant seminibus compositum moleste ferre transitum ac migrationem puta.'
[3] Cicero, *Tusc. D.* I. 25, 62.
[4] *Ib.* I. 19, 43.
[5] *Ib.* I. 30, 72.
[6] *Ib.* I. 19, 43.

now surrounded (*circumfusi caligine*), we shall see clearly
with the perception of the mind (*acie mentis*). On the
necessity of virtue and the difficulty of the upward
transit we may cite the beautiful passage of Seneca:[1]
man, ' mindful of his origin, strives ' for equality
with God.

' Our soul is endowed with capacities; it is carried
thither if vices do not keep it down. . . . If the soul
uses its native powers and stretches up into its own
region, it is by no alien faith that it struggles to the
heights. Great would be the task to journey to heaven,
but the soul is making its return. And when once it
has discovered the way, it marches boldly and despises
all things.'
' It is ordained for every soul, whether or not it possess
Mind (*Nous*) on leaving the body, to spend a period, not
the same for all, in the space between earth and the
moon, . . . but the virtuous must spend an appointed
time, long enough to purify and exhale the pollution
from the body, as of a poisonous atmosphere, in the
mildest portion of the atmosphere which is called the
Meadows of Hades. There, as if returning from banish-
ment and exile to their homeland, they taste joy such
as the initiates know, mingled with tumult and dread
but with a peculiar hope '—

is Plutarch's statement.[2]

Both the righteous and the wicked die ' the first death '
in the region of Demeter (earth), by which the tripartite
man becomes bipartite (soul and mind) by losing the
body, and of which the earthly Hermes is patron; but
only the righteous die ' the second death ' admitting
' to the blissful life of the gods,' and this ' second death '
takes place ' in the moon of Persephone,' and by it man
progresses to be one, or *Nous,* the *Psyche* (soul) being
returned to the Moon which gave it, whereas the *Nous*
was furnished by the Sun.[3]

[1] *Ep.* 92, 30-32. Cf. *Ad Marciam,* 24, 5.
[2] *De Facie in Luna,* 28, 943d.   [3] *Ib.*

As the soul had fallen from high estate, so it must rise again laboriously. By descent into the sublunar region it had taken on a thick misty substance which must be sloughed off before it may pass the limit between the atmosphere and the fluid ether of the celestial spheres. By realizing the littleness of earthly things (and ' angustus animus est quem terrena delectant ' [1]) and by the ethical effects of the contemplation of heaven and its splendours it may purify itself for entrance upon the upward way. All the terrors and toils of the Descent to Hades were carried over into the later conception of the Ascent to Heaven. The process of purgation continues through the entire ascent. Through air to ether, and through winds, clouds, rain, snow, hail, and scorching air, it must struggle until the lucid ether envelops it. Even to attain to the Moon—on the humblest eschatological ambition—was toil considerable ; but to attain to the Sun —in the fourth and central circle of the spheres—or to attain to the eighth region of the Fixed Stars was sore labour and of age-long duration.[2] So essential was purification that the traditional Purgatory was removed from the Underworld to the air between the Earth and the Moon. And in this interspace souls effect their atonement:

> ' aliae panduntur inanes
> Suspensae ad ventos, aliis sub gurgite vasto
> Infectum eluitur scelus, aut exuritur igni.' [3]

Ancient myths were—as usual in ancient religion— pressed into service to teach the difficulties and perils of the way and the bliss of the final ascent. The Pythagoreans chose the letter Upsilon as a symbol of the moral life of man. At the junction of the arms each stands on reaching the years of responsibility or a moral crisis. At these cross-roads he is bound to choose between a life of ease and vice and that of arduous

---

[1] Seneca, *Ad Helv*. 9, 2; cf. *Ep*. 92, 31.
[2] Cf. Cumont, *After-life*, pp. 185 f., 196.
[3] Virgil, *Aen*. VI. 740 ff.

endeavour, with the promise of final rest to be enjoyed
in the celestial light.

In a common conception the soul was obliged to pass
through all the elements represented by the planets, each
of which was conceived as a tightly-barred sphere, the
entrance of which was guarded by a Ruler who exacted
the correct password and suitable credentials. The soul
had descended through these same spheres, and in
making its ascent must give back to each the qualities
acquired in downward transit. To Saturn, the seventh
and last, it surrendered its slothfulness and finally
emerged into the luminous bliss of the eighth sphere.
This doctrine was popularized by the Neo-Pythagorean
Numenius [1] and by the most morally strenuous of the
Mysteries, Mithraism, in which the seven-stepped ladder,
composed of seven different metals, symbolized the
seven labours of the soul to identification with the
victorious Mithra. But the Mithraist must on earth
have submitted to his cult-discipline and taken advantage
of the holy sacraments, and then even after death
undergo an ordeal of judgement in the presence of
Mithra ere the soul might dare the ascent and be accepted
by Mithra in the eternal light. Having descended from
the presence of Ormuzd by the low gate of Cancer, the
much-tried soul finally emerges through the distant and
lofty gate of Capricorn to the presence whence it came. [2]

No impious soul may hope to escape purgation or elude
the heavenly watchers, for ' no wicked or unpurified
person ' ascends to the region beyond the limit of earth ;
' the wicked and unchaste pay the penalty for their
wrong-doing,' while the righteous behold some wicked
souls failing to reach the Moon, and others on reaching
it ' being hurled headlong back into the abyss.' [3] An
interesting sepulchral Pythagorean bas-relief [4] tells the

---

[1] Cf. Cumont, *ib.* p. 107.
[2] Cf. Dill, *Roman Soc. from Nero*, p. 600.
[3] Plutarch, *De Facie*, 27-8, 943*b* f.
[4] Brinkmann, *Rhein. Museum* 1911; LXVI, p. 622; described Cumont,
After-life, p. 151.

same moral. The symbolic Pythagorean letter Upsilon divides the scene into sections: on the right Virtue as a woman is seated with a little child, while above her the arduous life of virtue is depicted under the symbol of a ploughman driving his plough, and above this another scene depicts him seated at the celestial banquet as a reward. On the other (left) side there comes to view another woman, symbolizing wantonness, also with a child, and above her an indolent figure reclining in bed; while the third scene presents the recumbent figure being hurled head-foremost into a great gulf.

A confirmed believer in stellar religion, Macrobius, knows, beside the blissful condition of the soul which has passed through its probation, an endless exile of the wicked soul from the presence of God.[1]

As to the means of the Ascent, there were various religious and cosmographical theories working concurrently. Naturally with the removal of the place of the dead from the Lower World to the Upper Regions the means of transit must be altered so far as religious conservatism would permit. Religion still used the suggestive and symbolic myth where definiteness of expression was impossible.

The soul made its ascent partly in virtue of its physical constitution,[2] partly in virtue of its moral character, and partly because of the grace of the deity. The soul was not conceived as quite immaterial or ' essential,' but as the most attenuated matter.

(1) Souls ascended into the air because they were of airy-fiery [3] composition, or as igneous breath, *pneuma*. This physical *ex inflammata anima* nature of the soul and its upward-tending character is elaborated by Cicero, under Posidonian inspiration,[4] in *Tusculan Disputations*

---

[1] *Som. Scip.* I. 13 .

[2] ' Nititur illo unde demissus est ' (Seneca, *Ad Marciam,* 24, 5); ' Sursum illum vocant initia sua ' (*Ep.* 79, 12).

[3] Cf. Rohde, *Psyche,* p. 516, 53.

[4] Cf. for Posidonian mysticism, Holl. in *N. Jahrb. f. d. klass. Alt.* XXIX, p. 416 f.

(I. 18, 42–44), but that the soul naturally strives upward was a tenet common to Platonists, Pythagoreans, Stoics, and Astrologists. ' It is impossible to conceive of souls bearing downwards,' says Sextus Empiricus [1]; and ' every soul by its very nature strives upwards,' says Proclus. Souls were of *demonic* character, and demons were creatures of the upper world.

(2) Another view of the means of ascent was solar attraction,[2] a doctrine popularized by the Pythagoreans,[3] according to whom the motes dancing in the sunbeams were souls emitted on the rays of light by the King-star to be incarnated on earth, and on discarnation to return on ' his upward-bearing rays '[4] to their home above. As the Sun attracts and repels the other heavenly bodies, so he sends down and brings up souls. His action on earth is thus both physical and psychical. According to Porphyry,[5] the Sun has two gates, the gate of descent, Cancer, and the gate of ascent, Capricorn. Julian is explicit on ' the uplifting rays of the Sun ':

' The Sun, by his vivifying and marvellous heat, draws up all things from the earth and calls them forth and makes them grow. . . . We ought then to make these things proofs of his unseen powers. For if among corporeal things he can bring this about through his corporeal heat, how should he not draw and lead upwards the souls of the blessed by the agency of the invisible, wholly immaterial, divine and pure substance that resides in his rays ? . . . It has been demonstrated that the god's rays are by nature uplifting ; and this is due to his energy both visible and invisible, by which very many souls have been lifted up out of the region of the senses, because they were guided by that sense which is clearest of all and most like the sun.'[6]

This form of ascent appears in the sepulchral inscription *Sol me rapuit incautum* (' the sun has caught me up ').[7]

[1] IX. 71.
[2] Cf. Cumont, *After-life*, pp. 101, 160.
[3] Rohde, p. 395, n. 35, 40.   [4] Julian, V. 172a.
[5] *De Antro Nym.* 22.   [6] V. 172b f. (Wright's tr.).
[7] *C.I.L.* VI. 3250a.

The ancient belief in a bird-soul was accommodated to solar attraction by the popularity of the eagle [1] as the symbol of ascent. This belief was largely of Syrian origin, the eagle being in Syria the bird of the sun.[2] A popular belief in the Roman Empire was that the eagle carried the blessed aloft not with his talons, as in the myth of Ganymede, but comfortably on his back. Hence the eagle became the token of apotheosis for Roman emperors, an eagle always being fastened to the funeral pyre of the deceased emperor for this purpose, but " this kind of aviation was not peculiar to monarchs. The eagle has often this meaning in funeral art." [3]

(3) These semi-physical theories yielded to increasing moralization so that they remained symbols of an ascent which was conditioned wholly by the soul's health and purity. A ' Pythagorean life ' of discipline and virtue was essential in such circles to attain the celestial felicity. The Mithraic aspirant could ascend only after a life of strenuous endeavour demanded by his cult. Only blessed souls might be lifted by the rays of the Sun.[4] In the instructive scenes of apotheosis in the underground basilica of a mystery-cult near the Porta Maggiore in Rome there is an elaborate symbolism of the *palaestra* of life and of purifications before the reception of the crown of victory. The way to heaven was unambiguously the steep and rugged path of the Hesiodean parable and of the Pythagorean Υ. The more spiritual the aspirant the more arduous became the ascent. Thus Porphyry:[5]

' It is impossible that those who desire to be mindful of their return should accomplish their journey home from this terrestrial exile pleasantly and easily, as through some smooth plain. For no two things can be more entirely opposed to one another than a life of

---

[1] Cumont, *Études syr.* p. 57 ff.
[2] *Ib. After-life*, p. 158 ff.; *Études syr.* p. 85 f.
[3] *Ib.* p. 159.   [4] Julian, V. 172a-c.
[5] *To Marcella*, 6 (tr. Alice Zimmern).

pleasure and ease, and the ascent to the gods. . . . Ease
is most dangerous for souls which have sunk to this
earthly life, making them forgetful in the pursuit of alien
things, and bringing on a state of slumber if we fall
asleep beguiled by alluring visions.'

(4) Corresponding to the increasing sensibility to a
doctrine of divine grace, we find that the soul, though
endowed with the upward-tending nature and purified,
welcomes for the ascent the personal assistance of a
divine escort. In the passage of Plutarch, cited above,
' the heavenly Hermes ' is the patron (σύνοικος, con-
tubernalis) at ' the second death ' of the purified one
whereby he attains to the unity of spiritual existence
(Nous). As a psychopomp, notably Hermes, had formerly conducted souls on the downward journey to
Hades, so now he performed like functions on the
upward transit. The tombstone of a sailor who died
at Marseilles witnesses : ' Among the dead there are two
companies ; one moves upon the earth, the other in the
ether among the choruses of the stars. I belong to the
latter, for I have obtained a God for my guide,' [1] and
his popular conception appears again in an epigram
of the first century : ' Hermes of the winged feet, taking
hee by the hand, has conducted thee to Olympus and
made thee to shine among the stars.' [2]
There were other developments of the idea of the
Leader (ἀναγωγεύς) of the soul so beautifully described
by Plato [3] in the Phaedo. As in Egypt, the dead em-
barked in the boat of Ra (Sun-deity) for a personally
conducted voyage to Amenti, the dead of the Graeco-
Roman period found in him a favourite psychopomp [4]
or ἀναγωγεύς. To Julian this was a comforting

---

[1] Kaibel, Epigr. gr. 650, cited Cumont, After-life, p. 163.
[2] Haussoullier, Rev. de phil. XXIII, p. 6; cited Cumont, ib. In the
Mithraic Catacomb on the Appian Way Mercury or Hermes conducts
he initiated before Pluto and Proserpine : Réville, Religion à Rome
ous les Sévères, p. 94.
[3] 107d ff.   [4] Cf. Cumont, After-life, p. 160.

thought. His Mithra-Sun's rays were 'uplifting':
towards the end of his satire on the *Caesars*,[1] where the
company is invited to select each his 'guardian and
leader,' Hermes addresses Julian: ' Do thou keep his
commandments, and thus procure for thyself a cable
and sure anchorage in life, and when it is necessary to
depart from this world thou shalt with fair hope find
him a Leader-God propitious to thyself.'

The doctrine of the ascent of the soul to heaven and
of the attainment of communion with the celestial bodies
being a composite of philosophical, scientific, and
religious ideas, permitted considerable fluidity of con
ception and latitude of speculation. It was deeply
affected by the regnant forms of earnest religion
especially by ideas from the Mysteries, such as identifica
tion with deity, rebirth, transfiguration into divin
substance. No œcumenical council of astrologists eve
standardized one form of interpretation of the cosmi
problem and anathematized all the others in the interest
of simplicity. Hence we find various conception
running concurrently and often converging.

(1) Of course there was necessarily an eschatologica
conception of union with the blessed gods.

(2) But the astrologists were eminently empiricists i
religion and gave prominence to the actual religiou
experience arising from their faith. In reading thei
works we often meet the facile transition from mathe
matics to mysticism, from science to personal faith, jus
as if in a modern standard work on arithmetic the autho
were to make digressions to convey the *enthousiasmo*
or the religious value of science. Owing to this em
piricism the eschatological communion is by no mean
the most common or most prized. The soul could leav
the body and ascend to heaven not merely at or afte
death, but in certain psychic conditions which could b
experienced by believers. One of these was ascent an
union by ecstasy before death. In such estates the sou

[1] 336c.

could abandon the body on earth and, because of its constitutional kinship with the heavenlies, pay a visit of more or less duration to the stars or become absorbed in *cogitationes divinas,* as in the experience described by Seneca.[1]

Again, we have this ascent in his striking words:[2]

' Then shall our souls have reason to rejoice when released from this darkness in which they roll, they shall have caught sight of the clear light with no feeble vision, but have admitted the full light of day and been restored to their heaven, when they shall have retrieved the place which they occupied at birth. The souls are summoned upward by their origins; they will regain their place even before release from this prison when they shall have put off sin and leaped up in purity and lightness into heavenly thoughts.'

This was an experience attested in various religions, from Paul's visions in 2 Cor. xii. 2 ff. to that so prized in the Hermetic faith by which one could be ' carried away from the body to the enjoyment of the loveliest vision,'[3] or—

' Increase thyself to the immeasurable height, leaping clear of all body and surmounting all time, become eternal, and thou shalt know God. There is nothing impossible in thyself. Deem thyself immortal and able to do all things, . . . become higher than all Height, and lower than all Depth, . . . be everything at the same time in earth and sea and heaven . . . dead and beyond death, . . . perceive all these things together . . and thou shalt know God.'[4]

This ecstatic experience was for astrologists lifted out of the region of speculation as ecstatic elevations were for the Corinthian Christian brotherhood, though only the few contemplatives or the specially strenuous adherents might attain thereto. Vettius Valens[5] tells

[1] E.g. *N.Q.* I, *praef.* 2-3.
[2] *Ep.* 79, 12.   [3] *Corp. Herm.* X. 5.
[4] *Ib.* XI (ii), 20*b*.   [5] *Anth.* p. 241, 13 ff. (Kroll).

how the ancient astrological masters ' attained such a
height of earnestness and virtue that they left the things
of earth to walk in heaven with immortal souls and to
enter into the knowledge of divine and holy love.' Elsewhere,[1] again, ' the writer is overcome with enthusiasm
especially about these things and seems to hold converse
with God.' And such converse is ' an anticipation of
immortality.' [2]

Manilius is eloquent on this uplifting experience: ' A
gladsome thing it is to pass through the air and, stretching oneself out in space, to live in the boundless heaven.'
' The world summons me to hasten my way around all
the stars and to traverse the entire heaven.' [3]

In this exalted condition the ecstatic soul enters into
true *gnosis* of itself and recognizes its kinship and
destiny. It thus satisfies the *natura inest in mentibus
nostris insatiabilis quaedam cupiditas veri videndi*.[4] This
culmination of sidereal, and as it were mediate,
mysticism was a valuable support of that purer and
immediate mysticism of Neo-Platonism which was to
make such a lasting contribution to Christianity and
affirm with Christianity that only the pure in heart
see God.

(3) A kindred method of union often inseparable or
indistinguishable from the condition of ecstasy was that
of intensive cosmic contemplation, to which the ancients
were so responsive. If the intellectual life was cultivated
with intensity under Ionic philosophy, the emotional life
received more attention in the Graeco-Roman period
with the forcing to the front of those intuitive elements [5]
so noted by the greatest of the Ionian philosophers,
Heraclitus, and with the popularizing of Platonism,
which, after the decline of the rationalism of the
Academics, retained with more fidelity its double aspect

---

[1] *Anth.* p. 242, 29.   [2] P. 346, 16.
[3] I. 13 f.; V. 8; cf. also IV. 399 ff., 920 ff.
[4] *Tusc. D.* I. 19, 44.
[5] An interesting study in V. Macchioro, *Eraclito* (Bari, 1922).

of scientific speculation and mystical, poetical presentation of truth.

This cosmic emotion called forth from the ancients seemingly extravagant expression, but it was a fact of experience by which the soul ' united ' with the divine life palpitating throughout the universe and especially in the resplendent heavenly bodies. The acutest scientific spirit of astrology blended with the most responsive mystical spirit. Cicero, reproducing Posidonian mysticism, speaks of the eschatological abode of the soul *in hanc sedem et domum suam* and of that preparation therefor by which the soul still *inclusus in corpore eminebit foras et ea quae extra erunt contemplans quam maxime se a corpore abstrahet.*[1] A scientific writer like Vettius Valens makes a digression to assert his religious interest in astrology and mathematics and his desire for ' a divine and reverent contemplation of the heavenly bodies,' so that ' the divine things seemed to hold converse with me and I had disposed my intellectual faculty for sober inquiry.' [2] The great master, Ptolemy himself, asserts in an epigram,[3] ' That I am mortal and a creature of a day, I well know; but when I gaze upon the innumerable spiral motions of the stars, no longer do I touch earth, but with God Himself I am regaled with the divine food of ambrosia.' The writer of the Pseudo-Aristotelian *On the World* tells at the beginning of his scientific textbook how the soul may leave the body with the aid of philosophy and take Mind as a guide to investigate the wonders of the universe and know things divine.

Seneca is the most eloquent witness to this feeling of cosmic union and the emotion of infinity.

' Whom does the cosmic order [*mundus*], as it nightly pours forth its fires and enkindles such a host of countless stars, not hold in rapture ? . . . Contemplate those

[1] *Som. Scip.* 8, 2 (21).
[2] P. 242, 14 ff.   [3] *Anth. Pal.* IX. 577.

bodies gliding on high in such an assemblage: see how they conceal their swiftness under the appearance of a static and fixed order. How much is transacted in that night by which you mark and measure the days! What a host of things transpire in that silence!' [1]

And:

' This world, the most majestic and lovely product of Nature, and the soul that contemplates and gazes with awe thereon, the most glorious part of the world, are ours and eternal and destined to last as long as we ourselves shall last. . . . Wherefore, while my eyes cannot be wrested from that spectacle, with which they are insatiable, while it is mine to contemplate sun and moon and to follow the other planets, while it is mine to investigate their risings and settings, their periods and the causes of their slow or swift return, while it is mine to gaze upon myriads of stars gleaming in the night, some fixed, some not making their circuit into immense space, but returning within their own orbit, comets suddenly appearing and others blinding the eyes with their diffuse light, . . . while I am united with divine ones, as is man's privilege, while I can keep my mind ever on high in aspirations for the view of kindred stars, what matters it to me which earth I tread? . . . A meagre soul it is whom earthly things delight. The soul must be led away to those things which everywhere have the same appearance and everywhere shine with the same brilliance.' [2]

Truly Seneca could say of this communion, *mihi dulcis est inspectio,* [3] and asseverate, ' I return thanks to Nature, since I see her not merely as everybody does, but because I have entered into her secrets, because I discover the nature of the universe—who is its Maker or Guardian, and what God is. . . . Were I not admitted to such secrets, it had been better for me not to be born.' [4]

[1] *De Benef.* IV. 23, 2 f.   [2] *Ad Helv.* VIII. 6 - IX. 1.
[3] *N.Q.* VI. 4, 2.   [4] *Ib.* I, pr. 2 f.

In a similar strain Cicero explains:

' With what joy, pray, must then the soul of the wise man be thrilled when in such company he spends his life and passes his nights in their study! . . . No wonder the spectacle of all this stimulated those men of old and encouraged them to further search. . . . To the soul occupied night and day in these meditations there comes the knowledge enjoined by the god at Delphi, that the mind should know its own self and feel its union with the divine mind, the source of the fullness of joy unquenchable. For meditation upon the power and nature of the gods of itself kindles the desire of attaining an immortality that resembles theirs, nor does the soul think that it is limited to this short span of life, when it sees that the causes of things are linked one to another in an inevitable chain, and nevertheless their succession from eternity to eternity is governed by reason and intelligence. As the wise man gazes upon this spectacle and looks upward or rather looks round upon all the parts and regions of the universe, with what calmness of soul he turns again to reflect upon what is in man and touches him more nearly! Hence comes his knowledge of virtue.' [1]

A later ' spectator of all time and all existence ' and ' follower of the King-Sun ' testifies:

' From my childhood an extraordinary longing for the rays of the God penetrated deep into my soul; and from my earliest years my mind was so completely swayed by the light that illumines the heavens that not only did I desire to gaze intently at the sun, but whenever I walked abroad in the night-season, when the firmament was clear and cloudless, I abandoned all else without exception and gave myself up to the beauties of the heavens; nor did I understand what anyone might say to me nor heed what I was doing myself.' [2]

This heavenly contemplation yielded to the ancients,

---

[1] *Tusc. Disp.* V. 24, 69 ff., tr. by J. E. King.
[2] Julian, *To the King-Sun*, 130c.d. (W. C. Wright's tr.).

22

sometimes within the same pagan breast, those apparently contradictory or complementary emotions and moods produced to-day in nature-mystics—the crushing sense of annihilation and a consciousness of infinity with the passion for continuity of personality; the insignificance of man beside the welling up of the infinity within him.[1]

(4) To the ancients the gates of heaven stood ajar oftener than to modern scientific mechanism. Dreams to them were not the otiose phenomena which are thoughtlessly cast aside or readily forgotten or offer raw material to psychologists. They conveyed messages from a higher source. Cicero quotes Posidonius as holding that ' there are three ways in which men dream under divine impulse: first, when the soul sees of itself because of its kinship with the divine; secondly, the air is full of immortal souls on which as it were the marks of truth are stamped; thirdly, the gods directly hold converse with the sleepers.' [2] So dream-trances and semiwakeful conditions are means of releasing the soul for special revelation and privileges: ' The souls of men released by sleep are freed from the body, or stirred by the mind move about in freedom of their own volition, and are able to apprehend things which they cannot see when mingled with the body.' [3] Such a condition is that described in the *Dream of Scipio*, the scene of which, according to Macrobius, was in the Galaxy (Milky Way); or that of the recipient of the revelation in the

---

[1] Cf. words of Littré: "Voltaire in his old age writes in one o' his letters that at the sight of a starry night he was wont to say to himself that he was about to lose that spectacle; that through all eternity he should never see it more. Like him, I love to contemplate —with the reflection that it is perhaps for the last time—the starlit night, the greenness of my garden, the immensity of the sea. . . . My room opened upon the beach . . . how often did I sink into contemplation, imagining to myself those Trojan women who *pontum adspectabant flentes*. I did not weep, but I felt that those solemn spondee best harmonized with the grandeur of the night and with the vaguenes of my own meditations."

[2] *De Div*. I. 30, 64.   [3] *Ib*. I. 57, 129.

Poimandres. Before Macrobius launches into his commentary of the *Dream of Scipio* (I. 3) he insists on the preliminary necessity of surveying the various kinds of dreams (*somniandi modos, somnium, visio, oraculum, insomnium*), which are assessed according as they possess divinatory or oracular value or otherwise.

(5) Yet another mode of celestial communion was that of transfiguration or transubstantiation [1] of the material (*hylic*) substance into the *noetic* or *pneumatic* by way of regeneration. As in the Pauline Churches the Christian believer took on the indelible character of *Pneuma* (Spirit), which could not be destroyed even in the fiery assize of the *Parousia* (2 Cor. iii and v), so the ancient astrologist believed that his soul was constitutionally of astral stuff or celestial substance, the quality of which was strengthened by the acquisition of virtue and by contemplation of the heavens.

' This is regeneration, my son, no longer to look upon the body of three dimensions, but upon the incorporeal,' and the body of regeneration ' composed of the divine powers can never suffer dissolution.' [2]

This seems to be the method of ' demortalizing ' so vividly described in the Parisian magical papyrus published by Dieterich as the *Liturgy of Mithra,* in which the mystes ' this day begotten anew by thee, out of so many myriads rendered immortal in this hour,' sees the gates of the spheres open, greets the seven Tychae (goddesses of Fortune), and ' the seven other gods with the faces of black bulls and wearing seven golden diadems ' —the rulers of the poles of heaven—and finally returns thanks that ' begotten of life-producing birth and released for dissolution I go away, as thou hast ordained, as thou hast ordered, as thou hast effected in sacrament.' [3]

In certain circles so realistically was the ascent conceived and so sacramentally, and so close the alliance

---

[1] Cf. Dieterich, *Mithraslit.* p. 185.
[2] *Corp. Herm.* XIII. 3a, 14.
[3] *Mithraslit.* pp. 12, 15 ff., p. 14.

of magic and religion, that the ' demortalizing of the soul ' for its ascent became an important department of theurgy [1] and hastened the degradation of Neo-Platonism into a theurgic system, as represented by Iamblichus.[2]

[1] Cf. Lobeck, *Aglaoph*. p. 105.
[2] E.g. *De Myst.* 8.

CHAPTER XVIII

CHARACTERISTICS OF HERMETICISM AS A RELIGION

THE Hermetic [1] religion is one of the most remarkable products of the syncretistic ferment of the Graeco-Roman world ; a veritable *olla podrida* of the religious, ethical, scientific, and philosophical speculations.[2] It presents, however, less of the abracadabra which we meet so often in its cousin Gnosticism and in some of the Mysteries.

The system is fundamentally Platonic,[3] the *Timaeus* being specially employed, but on this Platonic basis there is built a superstructure of Stoicism from different periods with its different views. Greek thought hesitated between the Platonic conception of God as *Nous* and the Stoic as *Pneuma*. Christianity adopted the latter ; Hermeticism moves rather within the Platonic conception, but it would not be inaccurate to say that for the Hermeticists *Nous* performs most of the functions performed in Christian thought by the Spirit, and has

[1] On the origin of Hermes Trismegistos cf. F. L. Griffith, *Stories of the High Priests of Memphis*, p. 58; P. Boylan, *Thot, the Hermes of Egypt*.

[2] Cf. W. Otto, *Priester u. Tempel im hellenist. Aegypten*, II, p. 218 ff. " L'hermétisme est proprement une tentative poursuivie à travers les siècles pour concilier les traditions religieuses et scientifiques de l'Egypte à la fois avec l'astrologie venue de Babylone et avec la philosophie grecque, et il est impossible de séparer nettement ce qui appartient à l'Orient ou à l'Occident " (Cumont, *J. Rom. Studies*, XV. 1925, p. 273). A " Hellenistic amalgam " (Bevan, *Hellenism and Christianity*, p. 103).

[3] " Cette religion philosophique a emprunté à Platon. Si elle ne le suit pas de tout point, du moins on ne voit rien qui soit nécessairement venu d'ailleurs " (Père Lagrange, *L'Hermétisme* in *Rev. Biblique*, XXXIV, p. 104).

the same, or greater, vagueness and fluidity, and similar subjective and objective aspects.

Some Hermetic writers are more conscientiously loyal to Plato, e.g. *Tractate* II; while others are more imbued with Stoicism, as, e.g., *Tractate* III; others, again, are influenced in cosmogony by Jewish ideas from Genesis, like the writers of the *Poimandres* and *Tractate* III. The Egyptian influence appears strongest in the *Kore Kosmou*.

As might be expected, the Hermetic conception of deity revolves between the poles of Platonic transcendental monotheism and Stoic pantheism in both its varieties of hylozoistic (material) and dynamic. This pantheism receives diverse emphases: it appears very pale in the *Kore Kosmou*, while in the *Asclepius* it is dominant.

No fixed dogmatic system can be discovered in the *Corpus Hermeticum*. No uniform creed or rigid orthodoxy was imposed, and each writer, while drawing on the common sources and ideas, could exercise a selective and assimilative freedom and make his own combinations. We might as well seek a uniform Christianity in the temperaments, experience, and theology of the Church Fathers. The *Hermetica* are all the more interesting as furnishing unexpected nuanciering of some stock doctrine or argument. The Hermetic teachers reveal as wide a variety of outlook as Christian teachers in the interpretation and presentation of a common religion. They attract by a similar variety in unity. The Hermeticist was no more disturbed about inconsistencies as to moral retribution or his own origin than the average Christian by the Christologies of Peter's preaching and of Colossians.

One writer reveals the Augustinian mind in regard to fatalism or predestination; another adopts the Pelagian viewpoint of man's native powers. Thus:

 ' If it is absolutely destined for a man to commit

adultery or sacrilege or some other evil deed, why can one thus compelled of Destiny to commit the deed be punished, for all things are the result of Destiny? My son, nothing either good or bad, having to do with corporeal interest, can happen apart from Destiny, but it has been ordained that the evil-doer should suffer the penalty. Indeed, he does it for this very purpose that he may suffer the penalty for having done it,'[1]

as against another writer who loudly proclaims the 'whosoever will' note 'to the hearts of men' to secure participation in the *Gnosis* (esoteric faith) by dipping in the basin of *Nous* (Mind-Spirit), 'Baptize thyself, O soul that can, into this Basin, and believing thou shalt ascend to him who sent down the Basin by recognizing the purpose of thy being' (IV. 4).

Similarly, the pessimistic dualism that 'the world is the pleroma of evil and God the pleroma of Good' (VI. 4) is not uncontested, for 'the region of evil is the earth, not the cosmos, as some will blasphemously assert in days to come' (IX. 4b). 'The universe is full of God,' but again the cosmos is neither bad nor good, but partly material and partly incorporeal (X. 10b–11). One holds that 'the Good is God and God the Good' (II. 16); to another, 'the Beautiful and the Good are parts of God' (VI. 4b).

Immortality, variously conceived, is the boon of Hermetic faith, but the author of *Tractate* III. 4 offers only the immortality of remembrance, the individual disappearing into the elements and leaving behind only his name. Another (VIII. 5) positively rejects the Platonic hope of individual immortality of the soul, since man does not belong to 'the deathless living beings' (the cosmos and the heavenly bodies), but to 'the dissoluble organisms': he does not 'perish,' but

---

[1] *Tract.* XII (i), 5. For the convenience of readers, references will be given according to Professor Walter Scott's annotation in his ed. of *Hermetica*. The writer cannot at many points accept his drastic treatment of the MS. readings or his rearrangements. When Scott's translation or restored text is used it will be indicated as WS.

is resolved into the imperishable cosmic elements—the
' dear and congenial elements ' of Epictetus' future.[1]

The origin of evil is a vexing but persistent problem.
The general view may be said to be the Platonic one
of the *Poimandres* that *Hyle* (Matter) is the cause.   In
the most uncompromising dualism ' God is good: man
is bad ' (*Exc*. XI. 19), and ' His will is wholly goodness ' (*Asc*. 14*b*, 15) and the *natura materiae* is *maligni-
tatis eadem est aeque fecunda* (*Asclepius*).   The question
was immensely complicated by the regnant doctrine of
Anangké (Necessity), *Pronoia* (Providence), and *Heimar-
mené* (Fate), which were the modes of operation of a
world made by a good God.   Inexorable logic was never
permitted to overleap these barriers between God and
evil and attribute evil to Him either directly or remotely.
Beside a determinism due to Stoicism, to cosmic
mechanism and order, and to astrology, the ways of
God were clearly justified so that man appeared the
originator of evil by free choice.   ' God is blameless, yet
we are to blame for evil by choice ' (IV. 8*a*).   Nevertheless it could also be asseverated ' the good is
voluntary, the evil involuntary ' (*Exc*. XI. 20) ; and
again,[2] ' men choose evil under the illusion of good.'
This choice was partly prenatal, as in the *Anthropos*
(Man) myth of the *Poimandres*, and partly in the incarnate estate.

Astralism made its contribution in various guises ;
e.g. that man took on the seven *passions* or affections
of the soul, one from each planet, on his descent to the
sublunary world, and on its way homeward the soul
will slough off these beguiling *passions* by parting with
them to their respective stellar sources (I. 13, 25).
Another writer derives from the twelve signs of the
Zodiac the view that the operation of the Zodiac produces
the ' manifold forms ' or twelve ' torments ' of evil
passions ' for the purpose of deceiving man,' from
which deliverance comes only through the Ten Powers

[1] *Diss*. III. 13, 1.   [2] *Exc*. XI. 21, according to Meineke's text.

of the Decad.[1] Another holds that evil arises from the gradual degradation of the soul through its increasing separation from the World-Soul and through the increase of the body drawing the soul into matter and producing forgetfulness:[2] ' Having separated itself from the Good and the Beautiful, it no longer shares in these but through forgetfulness becomes evil ' (X. 15). Fatalism in conjunction with a doctrine of divine grace appears in the view that ' the illuminated of God ' receives the seeds of his thoughts from God, whereas bad thoughts and impious deeds springing therefrom come from some demon entering the man and depositing in his mind evil seeds (IX. 3), and this same writer immediately further justifies God for withholding prevenient grace by a different theory that ' God, the Demiurge of all things, makes all things like Himself, good when made, . . . for the movement of the cosmos varies the births of things, giving them this or that quality ; it fouls with evil the births of some and purifies with good the births of others.[3] Demonology was always conveniently to hand to help in this moral impasse. The demons effecting entrance through the body into the two irrational parts of the soul pervert souls in different ways, but have no power over the rational parts of the soul (XVI. 15). A more philosophic view construes evil as rather an accident in God's good work, arising like rust on brass, for ' to the Maker nothing is considered [4] good or evil,' whose glory is to make all things.

Ample provision was made for the punishment of sin, whether prenatal or post-natal. Sometimes the punishment is meted out eschatologically, sometimes here. Sin may be its own punishment, or penal agents may be employed. In the *Kore Kosmou* incarnation in a

[1] XIII. 12; cf. Scott *ad loc.*
[2] Cf. Plotinus, *Enn.* I. 8, 13; IV. 8, 7.
[3] 5 partly WS.; cf. *Asc.* 35.
[4] XIV. 7. The meaning is considerably and unnecessarily altered by WS.'s " correction " of the MS., νομιζόμενον into νομιστέον and σῶμα into οὐσία.

' human organism ' is the penalty of pre-temporal audacity of souls in claiming equality with the heavenly gods and in transgressing their order (*Exc*. XXIII. 24). In *Poimandres* (I. 23) the avenging demon tortures the impious and equips him for lawlessness that he may earn the greater penalty. Elsewhere *Nous* itself entering the impious soul ' torments it with the scourges of its sins,' impelling it to crimes and outrages (X. 21). The childless atone for their ' very great sin ' of dying without issue by being compelled by demons to pass into non-human bodies after death (II. 17*a*). The punishment may be self-inflicted both in the case of the discarnate soul and in its embodied estate. The wicked soul not only fails to become *Nous* while in the body and to become a *daemon* after separation from the body, but ' it remains of its own substance, undergoing self-inflicted retribution and seeking re-entrance into an earthly body ' (X. 19*a*). Yet here and now, Hermes informs Tat—

' What greater punishment can there be, my son, than impiety? What fire burns so fierce as impiety? what ravenous beast has such power to mangle the body as impiety has to mangle the soul? See you not what tortures the impious soul endures? It cries and shrieks, " I am burning, I am all on fire, . . . wretch that I am, I am devoured by the miseries that have hold of me." Are not such cries as these the outcries of a soul that is suffering punishment? ' (X. 20, WS.).

Incarnation was variously viewed, as a reward of excellence or as a punishment for a degrading choice, or as a stage in man's return to the higher world. The *Kore Kosmou* gives the most elaborate statement of penal *ensomatosis,* with which, however, it couples a gospel of release. Again, the discarnate impious soul strives for reincarnation (X. 19*a*). On the other hand, souls undergo all kinds of changes, some gravitating to bestial embodiments, the ' airy ' souls into men, and such souls on attaining immortality are transformed into demons and ' pass into the choir of the gods,' thus reaching ' the most perfect felicity of the soul.' But the impure soul may reverse this career and be subjected to irrational reincarnation. ' If a soul when it has entered a human body persists in evil, it does not taste the sweets of immortal life, but is dragged back again ; it reverses its course and takes its way back to the creeping things ; and that ill-fated soul, having failed to know itself, lives in servitude to uncouth and noxious bodies. To this doom are vicious souls condemned ' (X. 8, WS.).

Asclepius teaches that incarnation is a necessary provision of the ' material integument ' (the Platonic ὄχημα), that man may be in a position to tend both the earthly and the heavenly worlds, for which faithful service and ' co-operation with the will of God ' he will be restored ' pure and holy to the highest divine part of his nature.' Such a ' return to heaven ' is denied to the wicked, for whom is ordained a shameful migration ' into other bodies unworthy of the holy Mind (7c–12a). Again, this Pythagorean-Platonic doctrine of *metensomatosis* is vigorously assailed as ' very grievous error ' ; reincarnation may take place only ' into a human body, for no other kind of body can contain a human soul. It is not permitted that the human soul should sink into the body of an irrational animal; it is God's law that the human souls should be saved from such an outrage. . . . A soul may rise to a higher estate; it cannot sink to a lower ' (X. 19b–22a).

The usual view of the origin of the world is that God is not directly its maker, but that He operates through a Demiurge such as the *Nous,* or the Word (Logos), or the Aeon, or the Sun, or the *Topos-Nous* (Space-Mind) (II), but all such intermediaries are rejected by the writer of *Tractate* XIV as ' vain talking ': God made the cosmos, and so there exist only God and the cosmos. It is striking that the Stoic pantheistic idea of Spirit as a cosmic force has failed to secure a place in this question of cosmogony with its inevitable bearing upon man's salvation.[1]

In the creative and intermediary functions the Logos is not prominent. We read in Cyril's quotations: ' God's Word, who is all-accomplishing and fecund, went forth, and flinging Himself upon the water, which was a thing of fecund nature, made the water pregnant,' and ' the Word presides over and governs the things that have been made through Him ' (the Master of the All) and ' the nature of His intellectual Word is generative,' [2] but such views do not permeate the body of Hermetic writings.

In this connexion arises the problem of the relation of the cosmic theology of the Prologue of the Fourth Gospel and of some of the sayings of Jesus in that Gospel to the Hermetic movement. Reitzenstein,[3] recognizing Egyptian-Hermetic kinship of ideas, posits Hermeticism and Hellenistic mysticism as an origin of Johannine thought. But in the *Cosmogony of Strassbourg* [4] it is Hermes who is commissioned ' to make a very beautiful world,' in the execution of which he is assisted by the Logos, ' his shining Son.' [5] The Demiurge is therefore Hermes, not the Logos, who occupies an inferior position. Hermes is also the civilizer, in which capacity he again employs the services of the Logos.[6]

[1] Lagrange (*Rev. biblique*, July 1925, p. 387) says of the *Perfect Word* (*Asclepius*): " La notion d'esprit ne paraît guère sous la forme stoicienne d'une force qui anime le monde," and of the Hermetic citations in Cyril only " des tentatives assez voisines du gnosticisme, de faire entrer dans l'hermétisme la doctrine du Logos, ou de ramener à la conception du monothéisme platonicien le rôle stoicien de l'esprit dans la nature " (p. 396).

[2] *Con. Julianum*, 552d; 553 A: WS. I, p. 544.

[3] *Zwei relig. Fragen*, p. 47 ff.; *Poim.* p. 247 ff.

[4] Ed. by Reitzenstein in *Zwei rel. Fragen*, p. 53 ff.

[5] *Ib.* p. 56, 1. 6.

[6] " C'est le rôle humain de la raison et de la parole que l'esprit religieux du poète rattache à une généalogie divine " (Lagrange, *ib.* October 1924, p. 497).

On the other hand, Krebs [1] and Lagrange [2] contest Reitzenstein's position. The former relies chiefly on Old Testament parallels and synoptic sayings of Jesus as the line of filiation with the cosmic-mystic conceptions of the Fourth Gospel. But Krebs's source is quite insufficient. Contemporary Judaism would be at least as influential as the Old Testament scriptures and would put forward the *Memre* or the Wisdom of God as cosmic intermediaries, except in philosophic circles where such a conception as the Philonian Logos would find acceptance. Père Lagrange has recourse to a large infiltration of Christian ideas into Hermeticism. He is probably right in asserting the influence of Christian ideas in the Hermetic quotations of Cyril and Lactantius,[3] but these are lacking in the regular *Corpus Hermeticum*, so that we cannot determine with certainty their primitive form. He maintains that the text of the *Perfect Word* (*Asclepius*) has been retouched with Johannine ideas or terms,[4] and that the citations of Lydus suggest a Christian rehandling of the Latin text of the *Asclepius*.[5] His conclusion is: " Mais par ailleurs c'est le Dieu suprême qui est créature dans l'hermétisme tel que nous le connaissons déjà. Il faut dont conclure que le Logos-Demiurge est une innovation qui n'avait pas penétré partout, même là ou l'on faisait une place au *Logos*," and " Par ailleurs le Logos est une surcharge contraire à l'esprit de la religion du *Nous*." [6]

Reitzenstein,[7] on the other hand, denies the presence

---

[1] *Logos als Heiland*, pp. 157-72.

[2] *L'Hermétisme*, in *Rev. Bib.* October 1924, January, April, and July 1925.

[3] *Rev. Biblique*, XXXIV, pp. 388-96.   [4] *Ib.* 381.

[5] *Ib.* pp. 387, 393.   [6] *Ib.* pp. 392, 396.

[7] *Poim.* pp. 247-8: " Das Christentum hatte schon früher (than the writing of the Fourth Gospel) schon als es sich bildete u. seine erste Literatur schuf, diese Mystik u. ihre Literatur am Platz u. in jüdischen Kreisen wirksam gefunden . . . in dem Herm. Corpus mancherlei jüdisches, aber kein christliches Sprachgut nachweisen, wohl aber umgekehrt in der spätjüdischen wie der frühchrist. Literatur viel Hermetisches."

of Christian elements in Hermeticism. It is noteworthy that the latest editor of the *Hermetica* corroborates Reitzenstein: "I have failed to find anything in the doctrines taught that is of Christian origin—with the possible exception of the doctrine of Rebirth in *Corp.* XIII. That is the only extant *libellus* in which the notion of rebirth occurs; and its author . . . *may* have got it from a Christian source; but it cannot be said to be certain that he did,"[1] with the first part of which statement we would agree, but dissent from the unnecessary caution of the second part concerning a doctrine which cannot be attributed exclusively to a Christian source, but was made familiar by the Mystery-Religions of Paganism.

We cannot approach this question with either the *parti pris* of Reitzenstein or that of Krebs and Lagrange. It must be confessed that Paganism, both early and later, exercised a considerable and lasting influence over Christianity, and also that later Paganism, e.g. that of Julian and Porphyry, was influenced by Christianity as also by Jewish literature. It must also be admitted that the influence of Judaism within Christianity waned with the increasing schism between it and Christianity and with the immense preponderance from the second century onward of Gentile membership in the organizing Catholic Church. The assignment of exclusive parentage to an idea in a new and plastic religion in a world of seething religious syncretism is a hazardous task. The greatness of the unknown writer of the Ephesian Gospel (Fourth Gospel) and his inestimable services in presenting an original reinterpretation of Christianity as a timeless religion are not lessened by our recognizing in his guiding Logos conception a parentage stretching from the fruitful guess of the Ephesian mystic philosopher[2] of the sixth century B.C. to the Pauline pre-existent Christ with lines of filiation through Jewish transcen-

---

[1] Scott, *Hermetica*, I, p. 12.

[2] Cf. treatment by V. Macchioro, *Eraclito* (Bari, 1922).

dentalism, Stoic immanence, and the cosmic requirements, which were postulates of every religion in the
Graeco-Roman world.

To claim Hermeticism as the source of Johannine
mysticism, and especially of the Logos functions, is as
unwarranted as to claim Johannine thought as the
main ingredient or even a permeating influence in
Hermeticism. Let it be remembered that the Hermetic
writings are but a torso of a vast literature and of a
movement which Christianity sought to sweep out of
its path, and that if we had the same proportion of
Hermetic literature as of that of early Christianity, the
kinship in thought would probably be more, not less,
striking. Also, the origins of Hermeticism go back to
at least the second century B.C., and so its ideas were
in operation and forming their combinations at the same
time as Christianity was growing to self-consciousness in
literature. Both movements were drawing to a large
extent from the same speculative sources, the Christians
having the decided advantage of possessing also the
historic facts of the life of Jesus and the valued tradition
of His teaching. Both were affected by the atmosphere
of mysticism of their age, and both, seeking to enlist
the serious-minded, operated with the same terms of
Life, Light, Truth, which were catch-words of their
contemporary *Zeitgeist,* and both were deflected by the
same excessive transcendentalism in theology and
religion.

On such a vital question as the perseverance of the
Hermetic ' illuminated ' uniformity was not attained.
Hermeticism permitted within it the same divergences as
to moral miscarriage of its adherents as Christianity
recognized within the New Testament itself and still more
in later days of Church organization. Within the New
Testament we find that Paul makes no reference to
entreaty for forgiveness of sins after conversion or
baptism. Paul neither prays for forgiveness daily nor
commands his Churches to do so. Such forgiveness is

not a recurrent or constant necessity for himself and he does not make it normative for his converts.[1] Christians are ' dead to sin ' and ' living to righteousness.' The ' new creation ' in Christ is so thorough that it cannot be undone or destroyed even by poor workmanship (1 Cor. iii. 13–15) or by gross sin (v. 5). ' If any [i.e. Christian] sin, we have an Advocate,' was a thought quite alien to the mind of Paul and to his conception of the Christian vocation. The *auctor ad Hebraeos* agrees with Paul as to the ideally sinless character (iv. 15) of Christians, but he makes a wide divagation from Paul in holding that ' renewal to repentance ' is impossible for those who ' after having tasted the heavenly gift ' have lapsed (vi. 4–8). A second repentance can cover only involuntary sins: voluntary sin ' after receiving the knowledge of the truth ' can meet only ' a fearful expectation of judgment ' and find even for seeking ' no place of repentance ' (X. 26 ff., XII. 16 f.). The rigorism of Hebrews is firmly supported by another canonical writer, who, while holding that ' if any [Christian] sin, we have an Advocate ' for venial sins, ' there is a mortal sin, and I do not affirm that you should make entreaty concerning this ' (1 John ii. 1; v. 16). Dissenting from both Paul and Hebrews, the Apocalyptist declares expressly for a second repentance (Rev. ii. 5, 16, 21 f.; iii. 3, 15, 19). This practical question of the higher moral life received much attention later among Christians. Justin Martyr[2] declares that there is no other way to salvation than ' that we should know this Christ and be bathed in the laver for forgiveness of sins . . . and lead henceforth

---

[1] " The fact can hardly be disputed that the petition ' Forgive us our debts, as we forgive our debtors,' has no place in the Apostle's teaching. The sins from which the believers are justified are those committed before he became a Christian. The message of forgiveness in Paul's gospel stands at the beginning, and has no reference to lapses in the Christian life. For post-baptismal sins no provision is made " (Morgan, *Religion and Theology of Paul*, p. 152).

[2] *Dial.* XLIV. 263*b*.

a sinless life,' and in the *Shepherd of Hermas* [1] ' there is no other repentance than when we descended into the water and received forgiveness of our former sins.' The stricter view was championed chiefly by the Montanists and later Novatians. The Church officially adopted the milder view of a second repentance, not only for involuntary sins but for deliberate sins and backsliding, on the theory stated by Hermas,[2] ' For the Lord, being a heart-searcher and foreknowing all things, knew the weakness of men and the wiles of the devil. . . . He took pity on His work and established this (second) repentance.'

Among the Jews the same question had caused serious reflexion, and from the days of Ezekiel onwards sins of relapse were treated with increasing severity (Ezek. xviii. 21 ff.). Although there was a liberal view, as represented, e.g., by the *Wisdom of Solomon* (xii. 10, 19), the more rigorous view gained sway, as, e.g., that of Philo, that ' the soul that has been once divorced [from the Good] and has changed its abode, has been cast out for ever as irreconcilable, and unable to return to its previous home,' and ' many souls who desired to avail themselves of repentance were denied by God.' [3]

In view of the uncertainty of Jewish and Christian thought on this moral enigma of the instability of the higher life, we are not surprised to find diversity of outlook among the Hermeticists. The author of the important tractate on *Regeneration* (XIII. 14) holds that ' the body composed of the divine powers,' i.e. the incorporeal reborn man, cannot suffer dissolution, his character being indelible ; and with this teacher agrees *Exc. IIb*, 3:

' He that is religious shall know both where and what the truth is, and having learned it he will be yet more

---

[1] *Mand.* IV. 3, 1.　　　　　　　　　　[2] *Ib.* IV. 3, 4-5.
[3] *Quod Det.* 40, C.-W. 149; *De Legg. All.* III. 213, p. 129. Cf. also *De Cherub.* 10, p. 140. Other references in Windisch's note *Hebräerbrief*, pp. 50-4.

23

religious. For never, my son, can a soul [1] that has raised
itself to the apprehension of that which is really Good
and True slip back to the opposite. For when a soul
has learned its parentage it acquires a strange yearning
and a forgetfulness of all evil, and it can no more fall
away from the Good.'

" We are not informed what happens to those who
have made shipwreck in this struggle: the disciples of
Hermes must all attain victory when once they have
enlisted in the combat." [2]

Yet the prayers for steadfastness in the *Poimandres*
(32) and in the *Asclepius* (41b) (' be pleased that we
be kept in Thy knowledge and love that we may never
fall away from such a life ') imply the disastrous
possibility of ' falling away from that knowledge of
Thee.'

In regard to the divulgence of the revelation the
fascination for the esoteric to which Christianity easily
yielded in establishing an élite or esoteric type, and an
exoteric or popular type of religion, proved even more
attractive to the Hermeticists. The principle of such
secrecy was stated by Strabo [3] as ' the mysterious concealment of holy things adds to reverence for the divine
by imitating the nature of the divine which eludes our
apprehension.' Orthodox Christians condemned secrecy
among heretics, but held it necessary and laudable
among themselves.[4] Origen candidly admits [5] the
existence of esoteric and of exoteric dogmas and justifies
the distinction on the analogy of Greek philosophy and
the Pagan Mysteries. He even asserts that ' it is not
without elements of danger to entrust the plain truth of
such things to writing,' and with this view the cultured
Clement was in agreement.[6]

The Hermeticists faced a similar difficulty about the

---

[1] Adopting WS. text.   [2] Lagrange, *R.B.* XXXIV, p. 104.
[3] X. 3, 9, p. 467.   [4] Hippolytus, *Phil.* I *proem*, p. 4.
[5] *C. Celsum*, I. 7, p. 325.
[6] Cf. references in Hatch, *Influence of Greek Ideas*, p. 293, n. 1.

value of religious secrecy and failed to reach accord. The authors of *Tractates* I and VII outstrip all in their missionary zeal to make known the revealed truth to all: ' Have you not received all to become a guide to the worthy in order that the race of mankind may be saved through thee? ' asks Poimandres [1]; and:

' I began to preach to men the beauty of piety and of the knowledge of God, saying, '' Hearken, ye folk, men born of earth, who have given yourselves up to drunkenness and sleep in your ignorance of God; awake to soberness; cease to be sodden with strong drink and lulled in sleep devoid of reason.'' And when they heard they gathered round me with one accord. And I said, '' O men, why have ye given yourselves up to death, when you have been granted power to partake of immortality? Repent, ye who have journeyed with Error, and joined company with Ignorance; rid yourselves of darkness and lay hold on the Light; partake of immortality, forsaking corruption,'' the experience of one who prayed, '' put power into me, that so having obtained this boon, I may enlighten those of my race who are in ignorance, my brothers and thy sons.'' ' [2]

The other preacher, taking as his text ' The greatest evil among men is ignorance of God,' proclaims: ' Whither are ye carried, O men, in your drunkenness, having drunk the strong word of ignorance? You are not able to bear it and are even now vomiting it forth. Stand up in soberness, gazing upward with the eyes of your hearts, and if you cannot all do this, at least those who can' (VII. 1a), which reminds one of the Oxyrhynchus logion of Jesus, ' I stood in the midst of the world, and in the flesh was I seen of them. And I found all men revelling, but none found I thirsting among them. And my soul grieves for the sons of men, because they are blind in their hearts and (see) not their poverty.'

[1] 26b.   [2] 27, 32 WS.

Another writer encourages proclamation. God, having put *Nous* into the Basin, sent a Herald to announce to the hearts of men, ' Baptize thyself, heart that can, into this Basin. . . . And as many as took notice of the proclamation baptized themselves in the *Nous,* became participators in the *Knowledge* and became perfect men by the reception of the *Nous.'* [1]

But other teachers enjoin secrecy and emphasize the esoteric character of the Hermetic revelation. ' Avoid converse with the multitude, not because of envy, but (1) because you will be laughed at, (2) as like welcomes like, so the Hermeticist cannot be friend to the non-Hermeticist, and (3) these discourses will find few worthy, and (4) because they involve something peculiar which provokes the wicked to greater wickedness.' [2] And Hermes commanded Tat to keep silence on Rebirth ' and not to reveal to any the tradition of the Rebirth lest we be counted as blasphemers ' (XIII, 22*b*), an attitude which the ancient editor commends, ' This discourse about Rebirth I have set down privately in writing, to be read by those to whom God Himself wills it to be known, and not by the many, that we may not be deemed maligners of the universe.' [3] And the writer, or editor, of *Tractate* XIV. 1 professes to ' give a more esoteric exegesis ' of ' the leading doctrines ' of Trismegistus to Asclepius. Egyptian particularism [4]

---

[1] IV. 4*b*, WS.   [2] *Exc.* XI. 4.

[3] XIII. 13*b*, WS. text and tr.

[4] Lagrange says of the Hermetic excerpts from Stobaeus: " Au surplus le caractère concis et parfois énigmatique de ces formules s'explique par cette reflexion que la doctrine ne pas doit être propagée. Et chose étrangère pour une doctrine de salut . . . Car les hommes sont portés au mal, et s'ils viennent à savoir que leurs actions leurs sont imposées par le destin, ils lui laisseront la responsabilité et pécheront davantage. L'hermétisme se révèle ici comme une vérité qui doit être tenue secrète, parce que nuisable au plus grand nombre. . . . L'homme est mauvais et il pèche, mais, c'est involontairement et en exécutant ce que est réglé par le destin. Voilà pourquoi il ne faut pas répandre la doctrine d'Hermes : ce serait encourager les hommes à pécher en excusant leurs manquements " (*Rev. Bib.* XXXIV, pp. 99, 104).

appears in the protest to king Ammon against translation of the sacred writings into Greek, since the Greeks
' have words devoid of conviction ' and their philosophy
is a ' noise of words ' (XVI. 2). The *Perfect Discourse*
of the Asclepius would be profaned by an unauthorized
crowd of listeners: ' Don't invite anyone else besides
Ammon, lest a deeply reverential discourse on matters
of such import be profaned by the appearance and
presence of many ' (1*b*). Yet this same writer rebukes
the envy of those who would deny to men the gift of
immortality by the *gnosis*.

Hermeticism naturally accepted, with every vital
religion of that day, asceticism as a *sine qua non* for
spiritual advance, but not so unqualifiedly [1] as its competitors. With Paul's antithesis, ' the flesh lusteth
against the Spirit, and the Spirit against the flesh ' (Gal.
v. 17) the Hermeticist agrees: ' Unless you first hate
the body, my son, you cannot love your true self; and
if you love your true self, you shall have *Nous,* and
possessing *Nous* you shall partake also of knowledge '
(iv. 6*b*). The renunciation requisite in realizing that
' no man can serve two masters ' is unambiguously
demanded: ' It is impossible, my son, to be concerned
about the things of both worlds, that is about things
mortal and things divine. For there are two classes
of things, the corporeal and the incorporeal, the mortal
and the divine, and the choice of either is left free to
the chooser, but it is impossible to choose both ' (IV. 6*b*).

Again, another teacher affirms:

' It is necessary that you first tear off the garment
that you wear, the web of ignorance, the living death,
the sensible corpse, the portable tomb, the robber in
the house, the enemy who hates the things which you
desire, and who grudges you the things you wish. Such
is the hostile garment in which you have clothed yourself, and which holds you down to itself, lest you should

---

[1] Cf. Kroll, *Lehren des H-Trismeg.* p. 348.

look up and contemplate the beauty of Truth and the Good that abides in yonder world.' [1]

The prize of self-denial is great indeed, no less than the possession of the highest principle of spiritual life, the *Nous*. ' For oftentimes the Nous departs from the soul, and in such an hour the soul neither sees nor hears, but is like unto an irrational animal. . . . Mind cannot endure a torpid soul ; it abandons the soul that is attached to the body and held down by it. Such a soul, my son, has no *Nous,* and consequently such a one is not to be deemed a human being ' (X. 24*a*).

A word of praise should be spoken of the Hermeticists for their wise moderation on the question of procreation of children, on which they stand on common ground with the saner Stoics [2] and with the Jews. Flight from the world's affairs, hatred of the body, and indifference to domestic ties advocated by Platonists, Pythagoreans, and Christians, both orthodox and heretical, resulted in race-suicide which contributed largely to the downfall of ancient Graeco-Roman civilization. This moderation of the Hermetic teachers is all the more astonishing as they never made pretensions to a universal religion as did the Christians. One teacher views childlessness as ' a very great sin ' to be punished hereafter by demons in non-human reincarnations (II. 17). According to *Asclepius,* the bisexual God made both sexes in a *unitas incomprehensibilis* and ' devised and bestowed upon all creatures the mystery of eternal procreation with all its innate endearment, joy, gladness, yearning, and divine love ' of a ' necessary sacrament ' (*ib.* 21).

The dualism of the *Poimandres* compels the writer to

---

[1] VII. 2*b*, an amazing mixture of metaphors to express contempt for the body as ' the tomb of the soul.' I do not follow Scott in his transposition of the words τὸν σκοτεινὸν περίβολον. I observe that Professor E. Riess also regards Scott's transposition as otiose (*Amer. J. Philology,* XLVII. 2, p. 191). I adopt Scott's emendation in the omission of the δι' before ὦν in both cases (I, p. 172).

[2] Cf. Kroll, *Lehren,* p. 348; Scott, III, pp. 138-42.

hold that the first incorporeal Man [1] (15) and his seven
Men (the issue of the first Man and Nature, 16) were,
like God, bisexual and therefore free from Eros or sexual
desire, which effected births and consequently deaths.
Man's orginal position was that to which he shall return
according to the logion of Jesus in the *Gospel according
to the Hebrews* : ' Death shall cease when you shall have
trodden under foot the garment of shame, and whenever
the two [sexes] shall become one, and the male with
the female is neither male nor female.' On this logic,
since Eros prompts to marriage which produces death,
it would seem that marriage is necessarily evil. Yet
since the original androgyne character is lost, the author
represents the Creator as commanding mankind to
' increase and multiply ' (17) with the promise of an
ultimate return to primal conditions. A similar command
to procreate is repeated in another *Tractate,* III. 3*b*.
And God's creative activity is cited as an encouragement
to imitate God by procreation (II. 17*a*). In these sections
we detect the influence of the creation story of Genesis.
Asclepius accounts for the diversity of the sexes and their
procreative powers by the fact that God has endowed
all things with fecundity (20*b* ff.).

The Hermetic religion was never offered as an easy
religion. The Hermetic disciple must be prepared to
suffer persecution and endure calumny.

' Wherefore those who are in *Gnosis* (faith-knowledge)
are neither pleasing to the multitude nor the multitude
to them. Indeed, they appear as madmen and incur
derision ; they are hated and despised and possibly even
put to death. . . . But the godly man will endure all
things, holding fast to his *knowledge* ; for to such a man
all things are good even if they prove evil to others ;
and when he is plotted against, he measures all things
by his *knowledge,* and he alone makes good out of the
evil ' (IX. 4*b*).

And it is probable that the persecutors here were our

[1] Cf. C. H. Kraeling, *Anthropos and Son of Man,* p. 41 ff.

Christian predecessors [1] who in their advocacy of faith (*pistis*) against knowledge (*gnosis*) produced in their victims similar moral results to those so often manifested by themselves under sufferings, for ' transmuting evil into good ' ; the Hermetic believer is like the righteous man of Plato [2] who ' will be scourged, tortured on the rack, bound ; will have his eyes burned out, and finally, after enduring much suffering, he will be crucified.' Again, the Hermetic *religiosus* ' will be deemed insane ' and his cherished articles of faith, such as the divinity of the world and the immortality of the soul, will be turned to mockery or pronounced vanity, by the Christians whose victory he fears and whose laws were suppressing his faith. These writers were striving to encourage the martyr-spirit in their communities as earlier the writers of the Epistle to the Hebrews and of the Apocalypse had done for their co-religionists.

The Hermeticists occupied the position among the ancient religiously minded distinctive of the Quakers to-day, inasmuch as their faith necessitated no fixed cult-forms and dispensed with sacraments and their concomitant sacerdotalism.[3] Considering how sacramentarianism was inseparable from the ubiquitous Mystery-Religions and from the nearest type of religion to Hermeticism, that is, Gnosticism, and how it had taken control of Christianity, this inwardness and independence of Hermetic spiritual life is all the more arresting. Theurgia was as utterly repudiated by them as by Jesus Himself. Gnosis was for the most part *illuminatio* when not intuitive, and initiation was by

---

[1] Cf. Scott, II, p. 204.

[2] *Repub.* II. 362a. Cf. *Phaedr.* 249d; *Gorgias* 521d ff.; *Thaet.* 174a f.; Cicero, *De Repub.* III. 17.

[3] Lagrange's language (*Rev. Bib.* XXXIV, p. 104) must be understood only in connexion with the *Kore Kosmou* fragments; it is inaccurate in the italicized words for Hermeticism as a whole: " C'est une religion, si l'on veux, mais une religion naturelle, sans prêtres, sans sacrifices, et *même sans prière*. C'est une ascèse volontaire en suite de la connaissance, ce qui n'est sans noblesse, mais *exclut le surnaturel.*"

instruction in a ' divine discourse ' ; wherever teacher
and taught met was a holy shrine (*adytum*) in which
' Divine Love spake ' (*Asc.* 1), and ' that shrine was
consecrated by the true religion of four men and filled
with God's own presence ' (19).

Hermeticism was decidedly of the prophetic, not of
the priestly, type of religion, the priest being quite unnecessary either for the exercise of the religion or as an
agent of salvation. The sympathetic spiritual teacher
with his word of saving *knowledge,* or the guide of souls
to the Basin of *Nous,* was in demand. ' Seek a Guide
to lead you to the doors of *Knowledge,* where is the
bright Light pure from darkness, where none is drunken,
but where all are sober, looking with the heart to him
who wills to be seen.' [1]

The sacrifices of God [2] are ' reasonable sacrifices '
(XIII. 21), ' holy and from heart and soul directed
toward thee ' (*Poim.*). ' There is only one worship of
God, not to be wicked ' (XII. (2) 23*b*), since God only
can be called good. ' The love of heaven and of all
herein is the one practice of worship ' (*Asc.* 9), of which
man alone is capable. ' He raises his eyes to heaven '
[*suspicit caelum, Asc.* 6] and only the few endowed
with pure mind can exercise this ' lofty duty of contemplating heaven ' (9). ' Man, united in kinship with
the gods, worships them in religion and with a pure
mind ' (22*b*). Even ' to add the customary incense
and perfume ' to prayer to God is ' the greatest impiety :
these and such gifts are unfit for Him,' which must have
sounded as strange to users of the Orphic Hymn-book

[1] VII. 2.

[2] Seneca's words, which commended themselves to Lactantius, would
have been acceptable to the Hermeticists : ' Will you think of God
as great and placid and a friend to be reverenced with gentle majesty,
and always at hand? not to be worshipped with the immolation of
victims and with much blood . . . but with a pure mind and with a
good and honourable purpose. Temples are not to be built to Him
with stones piled up on high; He is to be consecrated by each man in
his own breast ' (*Div. Inst.* VI. 25; tr. by Fletcher, *Ante-Nicene
Christian Library,* I, p. 419).

or the Liturgies of the Mysteries as a Roman Mass would
to a Quaker to-day. ' Let us adore and give thanks,
since thanksgiving on the part of mortals is the offering
of the supreme God ' (*Asc.* 41*a*), or according to
Lactantius' version, ' praise is His only sacrifice ': ' to
worship God . . . this is philosophy,' [1] which is Hermetic *gnosis*. Hence thanksgiving (*eucharistia*) and
fervid prayer are the highest expression of this religion
and the ' offering acceptable to God the Father of all '
(XIII. 21). Reverential and rapt silence was also an
important element in the worship and practices of
Hermeticism, as of other forms of ancient religion.

Nowhere is the efficacy of sacramental formulae and
acts recognized. Visions of the highest order, securing
henosis with God and revealing the spiritual world, are
vouchsafed by illumination as in the mental concentration or as in the rarer visions of Plotinus, and not
mediately by the stimuli of external suggestion or
tangible symbols or sacral acts. The Hermetic convert
can become *ousiodes,* ' essential,' or spiritual, and cast
off his former *hylic* or material nature,[2] and the soul can
make its ascent to the divine Ogdoad without having
undergone sacramental *catharsis* and without any mystic
password communicated in participation in a sacrament
The *gnosis* which ensures salvation and bestows the
highest bliss is imparted by instruction or intuition or
by a divine revealer, never in cult-acts. It is remarkable
that the boon of *Palingenesia* (rebirth), in protest against
the doctrines and practices of baptismal sacramental
operation in the Mysteries and Christianity, is represented
as effected by God through a ministrant, a ' Son of
God, a Man, acting by the will of God ' by means of a
process of instruction to one prepared ' to alienate his

[1] Cf. Scott, *Asc.* 14*a*.
[2] Philo relates how Moses, ' summoned by the Father ' to put on
mortal being from a double being of body and soul, became a ' single
being, ' transformed wholly into the most sun-like Mind ' (*Nous*) (*D
Vita M*. II. 39, C.-W. 288).

'mind from the deceit of the world' and actually to experience the 'deification' 'into a God, a Son of the One.'

Even when the language or symbolism of a salvation by baptism, as in IV. 4, is employed, it is made plain that no virtue is to be derived from the act,[1] and that there is no sympathy with the popular Pagan and Christian religious usages of the day. The same writer speaks contemptuously of processions 'which can of themselves do nothing but only obstruct other people' (7), as an illustration of the function of those who choose the worse, 'in a similar fashion these merely pass along in procession, conducted by things corporeal.'

And the Hermeticists had the advantage over many modern Christians, to whom the same sacral act with the same liturgy and actions in the evening would be devoid of the virtues emanating therefrom before breakfast. To the Pagan Hermeticist every hour was a holy season: 'at what time shall I sing hymns to Thee? for it is impossible to find an hour or any season apart from Thee' (V. 11). No gesture gives more grace than another, and every place[2] is hallowed ground and pregnant with a mystic presence: 'Where shall I look as I praise Thee? upward or downward? within or without? for Thou art Place[3]; there is no place outside Thee; all things are in Thee' (V. 10b).

Yet though popular sacramentarianism is rudely cast aside, the rich symbolism of tangible things may serve the purpose of bringing nearer the incorporeal realities. The Hermeticists, despite their dualism and the constant irruption of transcendental deism into their Stoic

---

[1] "The figure (i.e. of dipping in the great Basin of *Nous*) must have been suggested to him by some sacramental rite with which he was acquainted; but it seems clear that he himself attached no value and ascribed no efficacy to the sacramental rite of which he was thinking, and that he uses it merely as a figure to illustrate his doctrine of *Nous*" (Scott, II, p. 140).

[2] Cf. XI (2), 21b, WS. text.

[3] Adopting WS.'s correction τόπος for τρόπος.

Pantheism, differed from their Gnostic kin [1] in holding
the world of sense to be an image or copy of the intelligible world, and hence pregnant with sacramental
suggestiveness and parallelisms. The visible sun is an
image of the invisible God. And the visible cosmos is
a symbol of Him who made it.

In *Tractate* XVII Tat discourses to king Ammon on
' the incorporeal images of corporeal things ' and ' the
reflexions of the incorporeal in the corporeal.' Images,
εἴδωλα, are given off by material things, and forms,
ideae, by the intelligible things, τὰ νοητά,[2] on the
principle laid down by Plotinus:[3]

' Now the ancients seem to me to have been wise in
having made shrines and images to induce the presence
of the gods. I think, therefore, that those ancient sages,
who sought to secure the presence of divine beings by
the erection of shrines and statues, showed insight into
the nature of the All; they perceived that, though this
Soul is everywhere tractable, its presence will be secured
all the more readily when an appropriate receptacle is
elaborated, a place especially capable of receiving some
portion of it or phase of it, something reproducing it, or
representing it, and serving like a mirror to catch an
image of it.'

It was enjoined, ' Wherefore worship statues, O King,
inasmuch as they have within them the visible forms of
the intelligible world ' (XVII).

The question of the use of images and sensible objects
in worship is further discussed in the *Asclepius* (24a,
37, 38). As God is the maker of the heavenly gods
(planets), so is man a *fictor deorum* or ' maker of gods.'
' Mankind, ever mindful of its nature and source, persists
in that imitation of the divine . . . so that mankind
makes its gods in its own likeness, . . . I mean statues,
animated with feeling and full of spirit (life), and per-

---

[1] Cf. Kroll, *Lehren*, p. 116.
[2] Cf. Scott, II, p. 459.   [3] IV. 3, 11, Mackenna's tr.

forming mighty works, . . . inflicting diseases and curing them, and bestowing sadness or joy according to merit.' [1]

The Hermeticists were evidently in conflict with some party impugning the usage of images for worship—their Christian opponents. It is a strange fact of history that in the early centuries of Christianity we find cultured Pagans defending idolatry against Christian attacks, and later, with the waning of Paganism, we find Christianity taking over by degrees idolatry,[2] though solicitously discriminating by poor logic between the principle of their idolatry and that of the Pagans, as, e.g., we find in the Roman Catechism. Yet the same arguments which were advanced by Pagans were taken over, *mutatis mutandis,* by the Christians. Thus Maximus of Tyre, in his essay ' Ought images to be erected to the gods ? ' warmly advocates the use of images in their honorific functions as means whereby the deity symbolized is honoured and as a valuable means of overcoming the weakness of the masses to comprehend spiritual things.[3]

Early Christian worship was, like that of its mother-religion,[4] an aniconic cult, and as Christians grew in numbers and self-consciousness they manifested a fanatical hatred toward surrounding idolatry. Then they gradually realized its attraction and its religious advantages. Pictorial art was the first form to be used by them, but apparently only for decorative or edificatory purposes, as in the Catacombs. As late as the fourth century Christians were sharply divided on the permissibility of even pictorial art in churches. The enemy of heretics, Epiphanius, tore down a curtain on

[1] Cf. further references too long to cite, in chs. 37, 38.
[2] Cf. art. *Images* in *Catholic Ency.*, and the excellent article by Ed. Bevan on *Idolatry* in *Edinburgh Rev.* April 1926.
[3] See tr. of passage in Bevan, *Edin. Rev.* p. 267, or *Later Greek Religion,* p. 147.
[4] ' Judaea gens contumelia numinum insignis ' (Pliny, *H.N.* XIII, 4, 9).

which a sacred picture was painted. Pictures were
excluded from churches by a canon of the Council of
Elvira, ' so that that which is worshipped and adored
shall not be painted on walls.'

Christians were long reluctant to avail themselves of
plastic art or sculptured images. The first of such
images of Christ [1] were used by heretics, the Carpocra-
tians. By the end of the second or the beginning of the
third century orthodox Christians were familiar with
statues of Christ as the youthful Good Shepherd. With
the rapid paganizing of the Church after Constantine's
adoption of Christianity as the imperial religion, richly
furnished with a new sacerdotalism, the adoration of
pictorial images grew apace in the Greek East, while in
the Latin West adoration of such was positively forbidden, their use being restricted to mental suggestiveness. As late as the beginning of the seventh century
Serenus, Bishop of Marseilles, destroyed ecclesiastical
pictures to which his flock were offering homage, concerning which the letter of Pope Gregory I stated the
view of the Roman See:

" Old custom, and not without good reason, permits
stories of the saints to be pictorially represented in
sacred places. That you forbade homage to be offered
them, we wholly agree. But we consider that you did
wrong in destroying the pictures. It is one thing to offer
homage to a picture and quite another thing to learn,
by means of a story pictorially told, what the proper
object of adoration is. What a written document is to
those who read, that a picture is to the unlearned who
look at it." [2]

It is interesting to note that the very rationale of
Christian image-worship, as stated in Basil's words ἐπὶ
τὸ πρωτότυπον διαβαίνει, that ' the homage passes
through [the image] to the person whom it represents,'
and adopted officially by the Roman Church in the

[1] Bevan, *Edinburgh Rev*. p. 259.   [2] Cited Bevan, *ib*. p. 268.

Tridentine Catechism as "honos qui imaginibus exhibetur, refertur ad prototypa," [1] is that recognized by the Hermeticists and by the cultured Pagan advocates of images. It is also noteworthy that the moral perils attendant on the use of images did not escape Pagan theologians and are recognized by the Roman Catechism.[2] It was against these abuses that the Christians chiefly inveighed in their attacks upon Pagan idolatry and which led to the discarding of images by the more thoroughly Reformed Churches.

This age-long controversy concerning the relations of the material and the spiritual in worship and of the function of *eidola* and *ideae* (forms) in the apprehension of the spiritual, which agitated Hermetic circles and which divided Christians and Pagans and set Christians in opposing camps, is still unsettled.[3]

Hermeticism was a religion of Revelation; it was revealed rather than natural religion. It was committed to the widespread conception of *henosis* with God through *gnosis*, but that knowledge of God was difficult for man to attain; it must be vouchsafed from above. The Hermeticists therefore ranged themselves with those who, after Aristotle's days, despaired of knowledge by the conceptual methods and analytical processes of the Ionian schools and by the dialectic of Socrates, and looked for a revelation from without, or accepted the intuitions without subjecting them to critical examination, or encouraged mystic experiences.

God is unknown and unknowable, invisible and unmanifest, ineffable and above designation. The Platonic view [4] is asserted, ' It is difficult to apprehend God, and it is impossible even for one who may apprehend Him to describe Him ' (*Exc.* I).[5] Nevertheless, ' God wills to be known and is known to His own ' (I. 31). Indeed

[1] *Pass.* III, Q. 24. [2] Qs. 18-24.
[3] Cf. Ch. Clerc. *Théories rel. au culte des images chez les auteurs grecs du II* siècle après J.-C. (Paris, 1915).
[4] *Tim.* 28c. [5] Cf. XV. 6.

the object of creation is revelation: ' Who is more manifest than God ? He made all things for this very purpose, that through all things you might behold him ' (XI. (ii) 22*a*) ; but according to another view, God ' made the visible things to the end that He Himself might remain invisible,' ' since the things generated are seen, He is unseen ; for this very purpose He made them, that He might be invisible.' [1] Hence the paradox, ' It is not at all difficult to apprehend God, if you will, and to see Him. Look at the order of the world ' (XII. (ii) 20*b*). Thus the Father of all, ' who is too great to be named God,' is through His immanence in the cosmos ' unmanifest, yet most manifest ; He is apprehensible by Mind ; He is visible to our eyes ' (V. 10*a*).

The revelation with its salutary *gnosis* is imparted in the Hermetic religion in three ways :

(1) Mediately by a divine prophet and teacher to a sympathetic and prepared pupil, e.g. by the divine Poimandres, ' the Mind of Sovereignty,' or by Hermes to Tat or Asclepius or Ammon, or by Isis to her divine son Horus (*Kore Kosmou*), or by the Agathos Daemon to Hermes (XII. (1) 8). According to a section of the *Kore Kosmou* (4–6), Hermes was the chief divine mediator between the Maker and later agents of revelation.

' While the Maker of the All did not will to be known, ignorance held all things. But when He decided to reveal Himself, He inspired enthusiastic love in divine ones and He bestowed on their minds a ray greater than had visited their breasts that they should first be willing to seek, and then desire to find and then be empowered to succeed. This, my wondrous son, Horus, would have been impossible for mortal offspring, nor would it have

[1] XIV. 3, which Scott, with his usual attempts to reduce the Hermetic writings to consistency, corrects into conformity with the statement in XI (ii), 22*b* with the translation ' inasmuch as the things generated are seen, the Maker also can be seen ; for to this end He makes them that He may be seen.'

occurred as the soul was not yet endowed with its
sympathy with the divine mysteries. But such a one
was Hermes, who knew all ; who also saw all, and having
seen he understood, and having understood he was able
to reveal and to receive [revelations ?]. . . . He was
succeeded by his son Tat, . . . and all the holy men
who were destined to search out with great accuracy the
things of heavenly study.' [1]

(2) By means of *Nous* [2]; ' the exercise of Nous
[*noesis*] alone beholds that which is unmanifest. . . .
If you are equal to it, He will appear to the eyes of
your Mind ' (V. 2). The ' sober ' can gaze upon Him
' invisible to the eyes, but visible to Mind and Heart '
VII. 2*a*), for he is *mente sola intelligibilis* (*Asc.*).

(3) By converting to religious usages the ancient
commonplace thought that ' like is apprehended by like.'
' Unless you make yourself equal with God, you cannot
apprehend God, for like is apprehensible by like ' (XI
(1) 20*b*) by a cosmic-mystical experience whereby one
expands oneself to be co-extensive with the universe,
leaping clear of the body and transcending the *longe
flammantia moenia mundi* so as to attain to that unity
of subject and object recognized in Aristotle's epistemological dictum, ' In things immaterial thought and its
object are the same.' [3]

As a corollary to a religion of Revelation it follows
that Hermeticism was pre-eminently a religion of grace,
here again betraying Gnostic affinities.[4] The ' hidden '
God, ' by presenting all things to us by the images of

---

[1] *Exc.* XXIII. 4-5. Cf. Kroll, p. 17; Lagrange, *R. Bib.* XXXIV,
p. 83. Scott's drastic rewriting of this passage may be indicated in
his translation: " But when he (Craftsman) determined to reveal himself, he breathed into certain godlike men a passionate desire to know
him . . . that so they might first will to seek the yet unknown God.
But this . . . it would not have been possible for men of mortal breed
to do, if there had not arisen one whose soul was responsive to the
influence of the holy Powers of heaven," etc. (I, p. 459).

[2] On God as *Nous* cf. Diels, *Doxogr. Gr.* p. 301 ff.

[3] *De Anima*, III. 4. Cf. Plotinus, *Enn.* I. 6, 9.

[4] Cf. Liechtenhahn, *Offenbarung im Gnosticismus*, p. 102.

24

sense, manifests Himself through all and in all, and
especially to those to whomsoever He wills to reveal
Himself. Pray therefore . . . that you may find favour
and that but one ray of Him may flash upon your mind '
(V. 2). ' On God's will depend all things ' (*Asc.* 7*c*),
even the knowledge of God (*Divinitatis etenim ratio
divina sensus intentione noscenda,* 3*b*). The boon of
rebirth with its immortalizing is conferred ' by the mercy
of God ' (XIII. 3)—' the bodily senses all depart from
him who has obtained mercy of God ' (7*b*). Rebirth
is wholly ' of the will of God,' even the ministrant
thereof, ' a son of God, a Man,' effecting it ' by the
will of God ' (2).

This religion of grace produced the like problems of
all such systems in the antinomies of predestination and
freedom. As in Christian theology, some emphasized
the divine co-efficient almost to the neglect of the human
(as in phases of Paulinism [1] and Augustinianism) ; others
proudly asserted human freedom and power ; while
others adopted a view equivalent to the Christian
doctrine of synergism. The pessimism of the writer of
Tractate VI on the theme that ' In God alone is Goodness, and nowhere else ' is corrected in the protest of
Tractate X, in which the destiny of the soul lies within
the soul. In IV. 3 *gnosis* is a prize for souls to win and
the choice of the material or the immaterial blessings
' is left to the chooser,' though even in this tractate the
proclamation is ' baptize thyself, the *soul that can* ' (4).

The prevailing view was that, though *Nous,* the
highest potency [2] of spiritual life and practically the
equivalent of the Holy Spirit in Christian thought, is
the organ of *gnosis* (*Asc.* 6*b*), God ' did not impart Mind
[Spirit] to all men ' (IV. 3). ' God said, Let the man
endowed with Spirit recognize himself.' ' Have not all
men Spirit? . . . I, Spirit, come to the holy and good
and pure and merciful ; and My presence is their

---

[1] Morgan, *Religion and Theology of Paul,* p. 246 ff.
[2] Cf. X. 24*a*.

succour ' (*Poim.* 21 f.). Another doctrine is that of the good Mind which selects the pious soul for entry, and an evil Mind which attaches itself to impious souls (X. 19–21). Still again, on another view, Mind or Spirit is the common endowment of humanity differentiating it from beasts, but all men do not avail themselves of the privilege of exercising the Mind, the functions of which are determined in some men, the evil, by the demons who implant the seeds of all their thinking; others, saved by God from such demonic operations, think good thoughts (IX. 5). ' The Mind, thinking good thoughts when it receives its seed from God, and the opposite kind of thoughts when its seed is of demonic origin ' (3).

The Hermetic religion could not properly be designated a communion of the saints, save exceptionally. Elect souls sought their kindred, convinced that few are saved. ' There are not many religious men in the world, or rather so few that they may be counted ' (*Asc.* 22a). The Hermeticists enjoyed on the whole a solitary but comforting religion of the severer type. The use of hymns and thanksgiving in the first person plural suggests some elemental form of united worship. Where four men are gathered together in quest of saving knowledge is a holy shrine (*Asc.* 1b). However élite was their religious society, it would manifest the tendency of all human societies to organize, however unofficially, for the purpose of self-preservation. The Hermeticists did not organize into powerful institutions like the Mystery-brotherhoods, the Synagogues, and the Christian Churches. They were content to occupy a place in the alien religions around them somewhat like that of the Friends or the Plymouth Brethren to-day.

Hermeticism was an aristocratic [1] religion like Gnosticism, but could not vie with the latter in combining its gnostic-mystery character and pretensions to catholicity. The Hermeticists indeed deliberately

[1] Liechtenhahn, *Offenbarung,* p. 84.

eschewed popularity and were satisfied to remain an esoteric and select brotherhood.[1] They believed that their difficult way of life was for the few. All pretence to catholicism is renounced in such a claim as ' without philosophy it is impossible to be religious in the highest stage ' (*Exc.* II B, 2). Even the subsequent modification, ' but the religious man shall know where and what reality [2] is,' hardly brings the religion within reach of the masses to whom the Christian, the Cynic, and the Mystery preachers appealed. Mysticism, unaccompanied by sacraments and cult, deprived Hermeticism of the charm of popularity ; its chances of winning the suffrages of the multitude were further lessened by the unconcealed difficulty attendant on the saving knowledge. Salvation was procurable elsewhere on easier conditions and with more of the outward trappings of impressive cult and spectacular worship. The task of the true Hermetist is ' to recognize himself ' in the religious consummation of the message of Socrates, and on the other hand ' to contemplate the world and God.' Abundant emphasis is laid on the necessity of self-abnegation and escape from hampering selfhood, but not so much for service to the brethren as for victorious transcendence of spatial and temporal bounds in cosmic expansion.

" The writer of XI. (ii), when he bids a man break out of his narrow cell in space and time and ' become eternal,' is at one with what may be called the cosmic side of the religion of Paul and the Fourth Gospel, as distinguished from its ' human ' side ; but he has nothing to say about the brotherhood of men, or the ' love of one's neighbour.' For him, as for most of the Hermetists, human society hardly exists, and the only human relation recognized is that between teacher and pupil. The individual man stands solitary, face to face with the universe at large ; and if he would escape from

---

[1] Cf. Lagrange, *R. Bib.*, pp. 99, 104.

[2] *Ib.* 3. So codd., gratuitously corrected by Scott to ' he who pursues philosophy to its highest pitch,' etc.

his isolation, it is in the life which fills the universe, and
the God whom he sees behind that universal life, that
he must ' lose himself to find himself.' '' [1]

Even martyrdom is to be endured at Christian hands
not primarily for a ' witness ' to the persecutors, but for
its purifying effects in the martyr himself (IX. 4).
Hermetic goodness is religious rather than ethical
(*religio quam sequitur bonitas, Asc.* 11*a*), consisting in
the resisting of desire and in scorning all that is alien to
the true man, including his body and earthly possessions
(*ib.*). True religion is ' to avoid being wicked ' (XII.
(ii) 23*b*), since God only can be called good.[2] In conformity with this is the definition of true religion for
the ' daemonic and divine soul ' as ' to have come to
the knowledge of God and to have wronged no man.'
Being born again is naturally followed by ' the immortal
offspring of truth ' (the Pauline ' fruits of the Spirit '),
but this seems to be of the same religious character for
' you have come to a knowledge of yourself and of your
Father ' (XIII. 22*a*).

The Hermeticists were justified by *gnosis* rather than
by works. But social activities and ' mutual obligations
which is the strongest link binding humanity together '
(*commodationes alternae quae est humanitatis inter se
firmissimus nexus, Asc.* 8) were not overlooked. The
Hermetic Gnostic could not be guilty of the base deeds
which marked the corporeal *hylic* or unregenerate.
That soul which ' the Spirit enters and guides to the

---

[1] Scott, II, p. 304 f.

[2] '' The Hermetist has chosen to write ' not to be bad ' rather than
' to be good,' presumably because he considers that God alone can
properly be called good (VI), and that ' not to be bad ' is the utmost to
which man, while yet in the body, can attain. The ' not being bad '
of which he is thinking is probably not abstinence from wrong-doing
towards one's fellow-men (the *iustitia* which Lactantius, in his comment on the passage, takes this phrase to imply); he would doubtless
have said, like other Hermetists, that the chief and all-inclusive virtue
is not δικαιοσύνη (justice towards men), but εὐσέβεια (piety towards
God) '' (Scott, II, p. 371).

light of knowledge ' ' can never weary praising and
blessing God and doing good in every way in word
and deed to all men, in imitation of its Father '
(XI. 21).

Ample compensation for the meagre realization of
' the communion of the saints ' here was made to the
true Hermeticist in the ineffable and exalted experiences
which it was his privilege to enjoy here, and in the
plenitude of the realization of such communion in the
next world, or to the vigorous soul that has already in
this life made the ascent of heaven, and also in the
unity of all life here with the life of the all. The
Hermetic literature is rich in testimony to the triumphant
character of Hermetic religion. Men may so know God
and themselves that they may be identified with the
All; they may even sometimes leave the body on a
religious quest to enjoy the ecstatic vision.[1] We must,
in estimating the Hermetic communion or comparing it
with that of other religions, remember that Hermetic
fellowship is not only that of man with man, but rather
that of man with God and with the ' heavenly gods '
(celestial ensouled magnitudes) and with every class of
being and order of existence in the cosmos. St. Francis's
Cantico delle Creature with its pervading sympathy with
all natural things and its brotherhood of man and beasts
and birds and plants would have commended itself to
the Hermetic communities. ' There is a communion of
souls. And the souls of the gods hold communion with
those of men, and the souls of men with those of
irrational beings ' (X. 22b). Individual souls, as
separated fragments of the World-Soul, may through
the stages of human souls and demons ' pass into the
choir of the gods, . . . the most complete glory of the
soul ' (X. 7). ' If a man uses these (Mind and Logos)
as he ought, . . . when he leaves the body he will be
guided by them to the troop of other gods and of the
blessed ' (XII. (1) 12). In the *Poimandres* the ascended

[1] Kroll, *Lehren*, p. 355 ff.

soul in ecstasy not only receives its own spiritual powers, but itself becomes identified with the Powers so as to participate in the universal hymn of praise, and ' they that are there [the astral gods and the blessed human souls] rejoice together at his coming ' (26) and ' they become in God.'

CHAPTER XIX

HERMETIC RELIGION AND THE UPWARD WAY

HERMETICISM was a cosmocentric religion of three terms, God, the Cosmos, and Man, and deeply committed to speculation. Tertullian knew Hermes as *magister omnium physicorum,*[1] or cosmogony-writers. We are at once arrested by what seems the excessive attention and religious earnestness with which the origin of things and of man is treated, but this is due not merely to a love of speculation, but to the accepted fact that the life of man is inseparably linked with that of the sun and stars and nature, so that man cannot be known apart from the knowledge of these. If this stern religion was to find a way of escape for man, cosmology and cosmogony must be mastered and his destiny sought in his origin, the Whither explained by the Whence. To lead life aright, man must philosophize, and this includes the knowledge of the nature, order, origin, and purpose of things.[2] These investigators were interested to discover " the Hills where his life rose " that they might trace it to " the Sea where it goes." ' Let the man endowed with Mind recognize himself ' (*Poim.* 21) is a postulate of all Hermetic teachers who would affirm:

> " Know this, O man, sole root of sin in thee
> Is not to know thine own divinity."

Two other causes contributed to this insistent cosmic inquiry: first, the doctrine of man as a microcosm of the macrocosm, the world. The knowledge of each of these was therefore necessary, as well as mutual and complementary. The microcosm stands in alignment

---

[1] *Adv. Valen.* 20. [2] *Exc.* II B, 2; cf. XVI. 17 f.

with the macrocosm. ' First of all is God, . . . the second is the world made by God in His own image, . . . and the third is man made in the image of God ' (VIII. 2, 5). ' There are these three—God the Father of all and the Good ; the World, and Man. God contains the world ; the world contains man : the world is a son of God, man a son of the world and as it were an off-spring of God.[1]

Secondly, the deity was conceived either so transcendentally or so pantheistically that the individual stands solitary in a vast universe the law of which is change. Man's only escape then is into the engulfing All or larger universal consciousness. His only safety is to bring himself into obedience to the laws and divine economy of the cosmos. His isolation can be removed only by deliberate unification with the universal life.[2]

Hermeticism accepted the current ensouled unitary cosmos [3] of the day ; *mundus unus, anima una* (*Asc.* 3*a*). ' All are filled with soul and in motion, things in heaven and things on earth ' (XI. (ii), 8*a*). ' This whole body (the world) in which are all bodies, is full of soul, and soul is full of Mind, and Mind is full of God.' [4] The cosmos received at its creation both sense and thought (*aesthesis* and *noesis*) from God, who is moving all things and in whom are all things (IX. 9). ' The cosmos is made by God and is in God ; man is made by the cosmos and is in the cosmos : but God is the beginning, the circumference, and the constitution of all things ' (VIII. 5). There obtains an all-penetrative *koinonia* or fellowship (X. 22*b*).

' This whole cosmos—which is a great god and an image of him who is greater, and is united with him

---

[1] X. 14*b*. Scott, with more probability than his usual emendations, corrects ἔκγονος (offspring) to ἔγγονος (grandson).

[2] Lagrange (*Rev. Bib.* XXXIII. p. 494) speaks of the Egyptian " confusion traditionelle qui leur permet d'attribuer à chaque dieu, à chaque élément du monde, à chaque partie du corps la même valeur qu'à tout le reste. Tout est tout." Cf. Scott, II, pp. 303-5.

[3] Cf. Kroll, *Lehren*, p. 275. [4] XI (1), 4*b*, Reitzenstein's *v.l.*

and maintains its order in accordance with the Father's will—is one mass of life; and there is not anything in the cosmos . . . that is not alive. There is not, and has never been, and never will be in the cosmos anything that is dead. For it was the Father's will that Kosmos, as long as it exists, should be a living being, and therefore it must needs be a god also.' [1]

Naturally there were gradations of being from the Supreme Father to the Demiurge-Creator, astral gods, demons, men, animals, and plants. And there were also different kinds of souls, the divine, the human, and the irrational (*Exc.* IV*a,* 5).

Though the Hermetic religion was construed on a cosmocentric basis, its object was man, whose origin, nature, and destiny speculation probed relentlessly. Man stands third in order after the Father-Demiurge and the cosmos: [2] ' God, the Lord of eternity is first, the cosmos second, man third ' (*Asc.* 10). He is subject to the cosmos as the cosmos is subject to God (X. 22*b*). The cosmos and man are as son and offspring, or on Scott's emendation, son and grandson of God (X. 14*b*). He is a ' mortal image of immortal being,' the world (IV. 2; VIII. 5). Man is a ' second image of God,' being an image of the cosmos (*Asc.* 10), for *sunt imagines duae mundus et homo.* [3] His place is again between gods and daemonic beings (XVI. 18; *Asc.* 6*a*). The greatness of man appears emphatically in the *Hermetica,* though not without several inconsistencies: ' magnum miraculum est homo, animal adorandum atque honorandum. Hoc enim in naturam dei transit, quasi ipse deus . . . deis cognata divinitate coniunctus est . . . suscipit caelum . . . colit terram . . . omnia illi licent . . . omnia idem est et ubique idem est ' (*Asc.* 6*a*).

Man is a *fictor deorum,* ' a miracle and the greatest of all creatures ' (*Asc.* 23*b*), and ' mankind, ever mindful of its origin and nature, persists in the imitation of

---

[1] XII. 11, 15*b*, WS. tr.

[2] *Exc.* XI. 6; cf. *C.H.* VIII. 5.   [3] *Ib.* Cf. V. 6.

God ' (ib.). God made man to gaze upon the beauty
of His lovely world; He made him incorporeal and
eternal, to tend the things of heaven; but perceiving
that man needed a material integument to tend the
things of earth, He supplied him with a body, that the
terrestrial part of the universe might be kept in order by
man (Asc. 8). God ' sent man down to be an ornament
of the divine body,' the earth,[1] to contemplate the
heavens and their glory (III. 3b; IV. 2; Asc. 8) and to
tend both worlds of heaven and earth. Nature was
entranced at his beauty (I. 14). Along with God he
governs the world (Asc. 10): ' Thou hast delivered to
him all power ' on earth (Poim. 32), and ' omnia illi
licent ' (Asc. 6a). He alone is possessor of Logos (Reason
and Speech) and Nous (Mind and Spirit) (IV. 3; XII. 1,
11 f.; Asc. 4, 1b). Some men (by the Nous) are divine,
and the humanity of such is near to deity; for as the
Agathos Daemon (Good Demon) said, ' Gods are immortal men and men mortal gods ' (XII. i. 1). It is
not to be deemed impossible that ' you should make
yourself equal with God ' (XI. ii. 20b) and ' participate
in immortality.' ' Man is receptive of God and capable
of fellowship with God, for with this being alone God
holds intercourse ' (ib. 19). ' He not only has sympatheia with the second God ' (cosmos), but has ' a
spiritual intuition of the first God ' (VIII. 5) with whom
he is capable of identification (XI. ii. 22a). In short—

' Man is a being of divine nature; he is comparable,
not to the other living creatures upon earth, but to the
gods in heaven (astral deities). Nay, if we are to speak
truth without fear, he who is indeed a man is even above
the gods of heaven or at any rate he equals them in
power. None of the gods of heaven will ever quit
heaven and pass its boundary and come down to earth;
but man ascends even to heaven without quitting the
earth.' [2]

---

[1] IV. 2, with a play on Kosmos.
[2] X. 24b-25, WS. tr.

Yet his weakness is not overlooked and his limitations arising from his twofold nature are too obvious. He sees ' as through a dark mist things of heaven,' for ' when we aspire to such lofty things our power is very limited ' (*Asc.* 32*b*). Man is a creature fallen from high estate (*Poim.*; *Exc.* XXIII. 24); prone to error from birth (*Exc.* VII; XI. 5); and incapable of absolute goodness (II. 6) but relatively good (VI. 2*b*). True, he is not handicapped by original sin (' behold how lovely is the soul of a child as hardly yet separated from the world-soul,' X. 15*b*); he is evil in so far as he is mortal (X. 12); he is imperfect and composite (*Exc.* II A, 2); he is not real because not abiding (*ib.* II ff.). He is weak and blind, choosing evil through illusion, but involuntarily (*Exc.* XI. 20 f.), but the rational part of his soul cannot be devastated by demonic potencies (XVI. 16). Man stands in need of grace; it is because God has endowed us with *sensu, disciplina,* and *intelligentia* that ' we are able to escape the deceptions and traps and corruptions of evil ' (*Asc.* 16*a*). Our twofold nature as participating both in the corporeal and the spiritual worlds is our misery as also our greatness (*Asc.* 7*b*; *Poim.* 15). " Trailing clouds of glory do we come," but through contact with matter there results separation from th , Beautiful and the Good with the evil of oblivion (X. 15*b*), but not an absolute forgetfulness of " God who is our home," for *humanitas semper memor naturae et originis suae* (*Asc.* 23*b*).

Owing to the Hermetic conception of salvation as the return of man to his original home, it was of first importance to inquire whence came this marvellous and composite creature, this *miraculum,* this *animal adorandum atque honorandum* (*Asc.* 6*a*).

As in nearly every department of Hermetic theology, no dogmatic uniformity was attained or imposed in this vital inquiry. We may cite the three most elaborate and characteristic accounts of man's origin and destiny as given in the *Poimandres,* the *Asclepius,* and the *Kore*

Kosmou respectively. These three anthropogonies are different in outlook and would entail differences in the details of salvation. The first is largely an attempted conflation of the widespread idea of an archetypal or Primal Man [1] with the cosmogony of Genesis on a Platonic and Stoic background together with Egyptian suggestions. The second represents Greek conceptions and may be termed roughly Posidonian. Incarnation is neither an accident nor a punishment, but the means of a divine purpose. The third is the most syncretistic and most difficult; it is mostly a variant mingling of Greek, Jewish, and Egyptian elements, the Greek and the Egyptian being the chief ingredients in the amalgam.

From the foregoing account of this ancient faith it is apparent that the Hermetic teachers did not offer either an easy religion or a cheap salvation. As it secured the highest bliss of a ' deified ' life, it imposed hard conditions. Hence the complaint of the prophets of every high religion, that ' few are the chosen.' It is a ' system incredible to the masses ' (*Asc.* I. 10); ' some men, and those few indeed, endowed with a pure spirit (mind), have been appointed the high task of contemplating heaven ' (9). ' In this earthly life souls stand in jeopardy for the hope of the coming eternity ' (12*a*). Man cannot serve two masters: confronted with the incorporeal and the corporeal, ' the choice is free to him who wishes to choose either; it is impossible to choose both . . . and the choice of the better is most glorious to the chooser; it will deify the man.' [2] Health of soul comes only by a severe moral surgery: ' for as a good physician inflicts pain on the body, burning or cutting it, when disease has taken possession of it, even so Mind inflicts pain on the soul, ridding it of pleasure, from

---

[1] Cf. Reitzenstein, *Das iran. Erlösungsmysterium*; C. H. Kraeling, *Anthropos and Son of Man*.

[2] IV. 6*b*–7; reading ἀποθεώσει for codd. ἀποθεῶσαι, contra Scott's ἀποσώζουσα, who here and in XIII unjustifiably removes this ancient catholic doctrine of *apotheosis*.

which springs all the soul's diseases. And godlessness is a great disease of the soul.' [1] True religion is ' the path to the things above ' (IV. II*b*), a path known from the days of Hesiod and the Pythagoreans to be a steep and rugged path. The soul ' having completed the contest of true religion—and this contest of religion is to come to know God and to injure no man—becomes wholly *Nous* ' (X. 19). ' God has willed that Spirit (*Nous*) should be set as a prize in the midst for souls to win ' (IV. 3).

A dignified, but silent and contemptuous, apologetic against Christianity may be detected in the magnifying of man,[2] in warning without a firm hope against the coming of another alien religion, in encouragement to martyrdom, in the rejection of rites, liturgies, and sacraments, in the blessing on the *mysterium* of procreation, and probably in the refutation of the doctrine of incarnation [3] by the denial for the future of the coming of ' immortal offspring ' to mankind and by the declaration that such an advent was that of the great Father Osiris and the great Isis,[4] and in salvation by *knowledge* rather than by faith.

Salvation is by piety based on *gnosis* : ' This alone is man's means of salvation, even the knowledge of God ; this is the ascent to Olympus ; by this alone the soul becomes good ' (X. 15*a*). This gnosis is the circle of self-knowledge, knowledge of the cosmos and of God (*Poim.* 3), and, discounting its pantheism and its mysticism, it approaches Ritschl's requirements of a religion that " three points are necessary to determine the circle by which a religion is completely represented —God, man, and the world." [5] It is the apprehension of Reality, of cosmic processes, and of the Good (X. 8*b*–10*a*). It is initiation into *magna et divina*

[1] XII (1), 3, WS.
[2] Lagrange, *Rev. Bib.* July 1925, pp. 374, 387.
[3] *Ib.* Jan. 1925, p. 96.
[4] *Exc.* XXIII. 64, 1, 32, following cod. contra Scott.
[5] *Justification and Reconciliation* (Eng. tr.), p. 30.

mysteria (*Asc.* 19). Without philosophy it is impossible to be religious in the highest degree; but he who has learned what things are, and how ordered and by whom and to what end, shall give thanks to the Maker of all as to a good Father and gentle fosterer and faithful guardian; and giving thanks, he will be religious.' [1] ' The virtue of the soul is *knowledge*; he who has acquired knowledge is good and religious and already divine ' (X. 9). Thus the Hermetic *gnosis* embraces (1) the cosmic story, (2) man's true origin and dual character and the means of ascent of the soul, (3) the knowledge of God as the means of becoming divine and equal to God (XI (ii), 20b), and (4) the knowledge of things as the corollary or counterpart to the knowledge of God (*Poim.* 3). All this puts man securely on ' the only road leading to Reality ' *Exc.* IIb, 5). ' It is a holy and smooth road, but difficult for the soul while in the body to travel.' [2]

' The light of knowledge ' (X. 21) is ' the knowledge of God ' (15a), ' the vision of the Good ' (4b), ' the knowledge of the Good ' (5), ' the opening of the eyes of the Spirit to contemplate the beauty of Goodness ' which is imperishable and ineffable, ' the presence of the *Nous* ' (*Poim.* 22), and ' the sobriety of soul, and the closing of the eyes, true vision ' (*Poim.* 30). The Hermetic salvation consists in seeing with the eyes of the heart (VII. 1a) and in finding ' the upward way ' (IV. 11b)—a return to Life and Light (*Poim.* 21), whence we came (IV. 9). It is ' the path to Truth ' (*Exc.* IIb, 5), and the one road to the Beautiful (VI. 5). Seeing with the eyes of the Mind we acquire that *noesis* by which we apprehend the invisible (V. 2). It is an estate of light without darkness, where ' all are sober, looking with the heart to Him who wills to be seen ' (VII. 2a).

---

[1] *Exc.* IIb, 2, retaining MS. εὐσεβῶν and ἄκρως, contra Scott: tr. mostly Scott's.

[2] *Ib.*, MS. reading, contra Scott's conjecture.

The Hermetic illuminated face Destiny differently from other mortals (XII (1), 7-9. They are delivered from the power of the demons and from the necessity imposed by astralism (XVI. 16); they may even rise through the gradations of demons to become astral gods (X. 7); the 'most perfect glory of the soul' is to join the choir of the sidereal gods in the Ogdoad, though the Platonic conception that the soul can surmount even the highest heaven on the flight to a higher supracosmic world is the view of the writer of *Poimandres, 26a*. Or, after death the Hermetic may become a daemonic being with a body of fiery substance (X. 19a). By becoming equal with God the Hermetic apprehends God (XI (ii), 20b).

Another boon of Hermetic religion is the attainment of immortality by *apotheosis*. Such *athanasia*, deathlessness, is the privilege of enjoying the state of the gods by seeing the Good and so being secure against all ill. It is more than deliverance from the fear of death, for ' the fear of death frightens the multitude as a great evil,' [1] but Asclepius learns (27e) that ' hope and terror torture the masses ignorant of the true religion,' which holds that after death there is a strict judgment (28) according to deserts (*arbitrium examenque meriti*) which has no dread for the ' pious and righteous soul.'

This immortality may come to a man by the vision of the Good and by conformity therewith, or by the process of *apotheosis*. And apotheosis is conceived by some Hermeticists as effected here, and by others as eschatologically attained. Thus *C.H.* XIII holds to apotheosis by regeneration and by initiatory instruction (3, 5, 7a) and by the abolition of the senses of the body (5, 7, 10b). Asclepius joins in the Hymn of Thanksgiving (41a): ' We rejoice that in our mortal frames thou hast divinized us '; while the writer of *Tractate* X regards apotheosis as taking place at or subsequent to

---

[1] Stobaeus, Wachs. V, p. 1087.

death, ' it is impossible for a human soul to be rendered
divine in the body ' (6).

The enjoyment of the vision was as prized in Hermeticism as in several other phases of Graeco-Roman
religious life.[1] ' The vision of the Good is not like the
ray of the sun that in its fiery nature blazes upon us
and causes the eyes to close; on the contrary, it shines
in proportion as one is able to receive the inrush of its
spiritual radiance.'[2] This vision cannot take place except
' by leaping clear of the body and by the suppression of
all time ' (XI (ii), 20), a condition which may be fulfilled
in two ways: either by ecstasy, in which the soul leaves
the body to return later bearing the secret of the revelation, or at or after death—in either case ' in yonder
world ' of reality. The former experience is that of
Poimandres: ' When my thoughts soared on high and
my physical senses were overcome, like those oppressed
by sleep from surfeit of food or bodily toil, I thought
I saw one of boundless proportions. . . . I beheld a
boundless vision, all things changed to a pleasing and
joyous light, and I greatly rejoiced at the sight ' (1, 4)
—a testimony which recalls the personal experience of
Philo,[3] of the rapt Apostle in the ' third heaven ' unconscious of ' whether in the body or out of the body,'
the ecstasy of Plotinus,[4] or of Monica and her son.[5]
There is no implication that the speaker was dead, but
rather ' having been instructed in the nature of the
universe and having contemplated the highest vision '
(27), he resumes earthly existence ' to enlighten my
brothers thy sons ' (32). He could say, ' My bodily
sleep had become soberness of soul and the closing of
my eyes true seeing ' (30). This was a privilege for
the advanced saints: ' Those who are endowed to draw
somewhat more from that vision are often carried away

[1] Kroll, *Lehren*, p. 357 ff.
[2] X. 4b, following the MS. contra Scott.
[3] *Migr. Abr.* 7; C.-W. 34 f.
[4] E.g. *Enn.* IV. 8, 1.   [5] Augustine, *Conf.* IX. 10.

25

from the body to the supreme vision ' (X. 5). ' Would
that *we too* might enjoy that vision.' But for the
majority—

' We are in this world still unequal to the vision, and
so we are not able to open the eyes of our Mind to
behold the beauty of Goodness which is incorruptible
and incomprehensible. Then shalt thou see it when
thou canst say nothing of it: the knowledge of it is a
reverential silence and a suppression of all the senses.
He who has come to a spiritual apprehension of this
Beauty can apprehend nothing else, nor can he who has
gazed upon it gaze upon aught else, nor can he listen
to aught else, nor can he move his body at all, for
oblivious of all physical sensations and movements he
keeps still. Radiating around his Mind it draws up his
soul and draws it through the body, and transmutes
him into essence.' [1]

Analogous to the visionary apprehension of truth the
Hermetic might attain the realization of a larger cosmic
self, transcending time and space, and, identifying himself with the whole cosmos, escape from the bounds of
isolated individuality. He may lose himself, not to find
himself, but to discover the secret of the world and his
place in its order and the supreme realities of the incorporeal. The writer of XI (2) has entered most deeply
into this experience, of which he has left first-hand
testimony :

' Leap clear of all that is corporeal, and make yourself grow to a like expanse with that greatness which
is beyond all measure; rise above all time and become
eternal; then you will apprehend God. Think that for
you too nothing is impossible; deem that you too are
immortal, and that you are able to grasp all things in

[1] Professor Scott has evidently erred (I, p. 190; II, p. 239 ff.) in
this passage so critical for the understanding of Hermeticism, by failing
to observe (1) that *Poimandres* supplies an instance of a soul leaving
the body in ecstasy, as in death, and having enjoyed the vision takes
up life here again; (2) that the contrast is between οἱ δυνάμενοι and
ἡμεῖς. Therefore, instead of Scott's textual alteration and misleading
translation based thereon, we should adhere to the traditional text.

your thought; . . . find your home in the haunts of
every living creature; make yourself higher than all
heights and lower than all depths; . . . think that you
are everywhere at once, on land, at sea, in heaven;
think that you are not yet begotten, that you are in
the womb, that you are young, that you are old, that
you have died, that you are in the world beyond the
grave; grasp in your thought all this at once, all times
and places, all substances and qualities and magnitudes
together; then you can apprehend God. . . . Everywhere God will come to meet you; everywhere He will
appear to you, at places and times at which you look
not for it.' [1]

The opposite to this realization of the larger and
infinite self is ' to imprison the soul in the body and
abase yourself ' to ignorance and evil. Elsewhere, the
reborn Hermetic can say: ' I perceive that I have
entered an immortal body. . . . I have been begotten
again in Mind. . . . I am in heaven and on earth, in
water and the air; I am in animals and plants; I am in
the womb, not yet begotten and after birth; I am everywhere, . . . it is rebirth when no longer the body of
three dimensions is perceived,' after which experience
' do you not know that you have become divine, and
a son of the One? ' (XIII. 3, 11b, 13a, 14).

These experiences may seem echoes from a far-away
world, but they are merely instances, valuable because
first hand, of a class of mystical experiences which
psychologists and students of religion recognize as valid
and confined to no one type of religion or culture. Poets
like Wordsworth and Walt Whitman would feel at home
with these experiences. The words used by Shelley of
one who was dead would describe a possible experience
for the Hermetic still in this life [2] but ' out of the body ':

> " But the pure spirit shall flow
> Back to the burning fountain whence it came,
> A portion of the Eternal which must glow
> Through time and space unquenchably the same.

---

[1] XI (ii), 20b-21b, WS. text and tr.   [2] Scott, II, p. 333, n. 1.

> He is made one with Nature; there is heard
> His voice in all her music, from the moan
> Of thunder, to the song of night's sweet bird;
> He is a presence to be felt and known
> In darkness and in light, from herb and stone,
> Spreading itself where'er that Power may move.''

Similarly Amiel asks in his *Journal*:

"Shall I ever again have any of those prodigious reveries which sometimes came to me in former years? One day in youth, at sunrise, sitting in the ruins of the castle of Faucigny; and again, in the mountains, under the noonday sun, above Lavey, lying at the foot of a tree and visited by three butterflies; once more at night upon the shingly shore of the Northern Ocean, my back upon the sand and my vision ranging through the Milky Way; such grand and spacious, immortal, cosmogonic reveries, when one reaches to the stars, when one owns the infinite. Moments divine, ecstatic hours; in which our thought flies from world to world, pierces the great enigma, breathes with a respiration broad, tranquil, and deep as the respiration of the ocean, serene and limitless as the blue firmament; . . . instants of irresistible intuition in which one feels one's self great as the universe, and calm as a god. . . . The vestiges they leave behind are enough to fill us with belief and enthusiasm, as if they were visits of the Holy Ghost.''[1]

Tractate XIII deals with Rebirth. ' No one can be saved without being born again ' (1), the doctrine of which cannot be received apart from ' alienation from the world ' and ' from the world's deceit.' ' Spiritual Wisdom is the womb, conceiving in Silence, and the Seed is the true Good ' sown ' by the will of God.' ' The ministrant of Regeneration is the Son of God, a Man working by the will of God.' ' The begotten becomes other than he was,' divine and a son of God, constituted of the Powers of God. Hermes, in reply to Tat's perplexed question, ' Have I become an alien from my

---

[1] Cited by James, *Varieties of Religious Experience*, p. 394. Other interesting instances are cited by Scott, II, pp. 329-31; Inge, *Christian Mysticism*, chs. 7-8.

Father's race?' can only reply, 'I see that by God's
mercy there has come to be in me a form which is not
fashioned out of matter, and I have passed forth out
of myself and entered into an immortal body. I am
not now the man I was; I have been born again in
Mind, and the bodily shape which was mine before
has been put away from me.'[1] This 'change' deceives
the observer who thinks that the features remain as
before (5): 'in this you are mistaken. The mortal
form changes day by day; it is altered by lapse of time,
and becomes larger and smaller; for it is an illusion,'
but the true form is changeless, unbounded, and
luminous (6). 'Cause the physical sensations to cease
working and the birth of the deity will take place' (7a),
after cleansing from the irrational torments of matter
and by the mercy of God (8a). So 'the knowledge of
God has come to us; . . . ignorance has been driven
out.' The reborn man, composed of the divine Powers,
is like the Pauline *pneumatic* and cannot suffer dissolution (14). The pupil learns that he has become
divine, ceasing to be corporeal and therefore mortal,
and gratefully hears the Hymn of Regeneration.[2]

Those saved by the knowledge of God differed from
the unsaved by undergoing a marvellous and sweeping
change,[3] $\mu\epsilon\tau\alpha\beta o\lambda\eta$, by which at once they were delivered
from the bondage of matter and rendered of divine
essence. The conception is so fluid[4] and the language
so ambiguous that it is difficult to reproduce in certain
terminology the details of this mysterious Hellenistic
transfiguration. The nature of the change and when
and how it takes place are left indefinite. It was a

---

[1] WS. text and translation, but with some hesitation as to his
correction of $\theta\epsilon\alpha\nu$ 'vision,' into $i\delta\epsilon\alpha\nu$ 'form.'

[2] Scott's tr., I, p. 251; the writer's tr. *Mystery-Religions*, p. 98.

[3] Cf. Reitzenstein, *Myst.-religionen*, 2nd ed. p. 139 ff.

[4] " Die schillernde, unklare Sprache ist eine Haupteigentümlichkeit
all jener hellenistischen, d. h. unter Einwirkung des Orients griechisch
geformten religiösen Schriften und macht ihre Erklärung so schwer "
(Reitzenstein, *op. cit.* p. 135).

phase of that ancient realism which had become natural-
ized in the Christian Church from the first generation.
Paul's converts with their Greek conceptions of the immortality of the soul had some difficulties in bringing
home to themselves the features of the Jewish conception
of a resurrection, but they had no difficulty in conceiving
themselves as in some mysterious way in process of
metamorphosis from flesh into spirit, which would be
consummated at the *parousia,* when the remaining stages
of the process would be achieved in the twinkling of
an eye.

In the *Poimandres* (24), ' at the dissolution of the
material body you yield the body to change, and the
visible shape (*eidos*) which you had becomes invisible.'
And at the end of complete *gnosis* is deification, but
properly in the Ogdoad (26a). In the tractate on
Regeneration (XIII. 3) Hermes, who belongs to the
incorporeal world, speaks of his change as giving him
a form invisible to the unregenerated eyes of Tat, while
implying that Tat can and will undergo similar change.
He confronts his pupil's confessed inability, ' I cannot,
O Father,' with ' God forbid, my son: draw it into you,
and it will come; will it, and it happens. Cause the
physical senses to cease working and there shall be born
the divinity ' (7a), and finally declares ' you have
become a god ' (14). This Tat while still in the world
is ' in the world of Spirit ' (ἐν τῷ νοητῷ, 21). Tat has
' come to a spiritual knowledge of himself and of our
Father ' (22b), and this involves transformation, since
ὁ νοήσας ἑαυτὸν εἰς θεὸν χωρεῖ (' he who has come to
a spiritual knowledge of himself departs to God ').

Much depends on the passage X. 5-6, the difficulty of
which is accentuated by the textual uncertainty. Both
Reitzenstein [1] and Scott [2] following him take it to refer
to a condition after death. This is wholly unlikely. The
way to the misunderstanding by Scott was opened by
his arbitrary correction of the manuscript in 5 from

---

[1] *Hellenist. Mysterien-religionen,* p. 139 ff.   [2] II, p. 241 f.

words indicating a present experience for the advanced
or eager, into the post-mortem experience for all. In
paragraph 6 Scott holds that the aorist participles and
the language make it—

" equivalent to saying that he is either dead or dying.
It is clear, therefore, that in the writer's view, the θέα,
vision, of which he speaks is incompatible with the
continuance of earthly life. We may hope to see the
beatific vision, but not until the moment of our release
from the body. If a living man attains to it, his earthly
life is then and there at an end; the vision ' draws his
soul up out of the body ' and transforms him into pure
ousia, or in other words, changes him from a man into
a god." [1]

But these are gratuitous assumptions. We know
elsewhere [2] that this condition is possible even here when
the soul in trance or ecstasy or by ' spiritualizing ' [3]
leaves the body, or when a man is ' in knowledge ' (ἐν
γνώσει, IX. 4b). The meaning of the passage is that
the bodily sensations are stayed by the vision of truth
which enlightens the whole Nous and draws the Soul
(Psyche) from the body, so that no longer does Soul
dominate the man, but he becomes wholly Nous or
Ousia (essence). The MS. reading need not be so
violently emended as by Reitzenstein and Scott, but
may read,[4] ' It is impossible, my son, for a soul to
be deified in a human body, but having beheld the
beauty of the Good, deification is possible.'
We may conceive the Hermetic experience and hope
in a fashion similar to the Pauline. The man ' in knowledge ' (IX. 4) could here at least have premonitory
glimpses of the vision and the beauty of Goodness in

---

[1] II, p. 241 f.
[2] Cf. Poim. I, 27, 30.   [3] Cf. Asc. 41b.
[4] Inserting δὲ after θεασαμένην and with Reitzenstein and Scott τὸ
before κάλλος and omitting with Scott τῷ before ἀποθεωθῆναι, δυνατὸν
being quite easily understood from the preceding ἀδύνατον.

mystical conditions when the body's domination was in
abeyance, but, generally speaking, his hope for full
fruition, like the Christian's, was ' in yonder world.'
' He who has not come to a knowledge of these things
cannot adequately apprehend God, or, to speak boldly,
cannot become an actual beholder and so become
blessed. . . . It is impossible for one in the body to
attain this felicity. He must discipline his soul here in
order that on its arrival in yonder world it may not
miss the way ' (*Exc*. VI. 18).

The enemy of the Hermetic was *Hyle,* matter, or
body, as to Paul the flesh was the enemy of the Spirit.
Man must be either ' *hylic,*' ' corporeal,' or *ousiodes,*
'*essential,* spiritual,' as in the Pauline churches he was
either *sarkikos,* ' carnal,' or synonymously *psychikos,*
' psychic,' or on the other hand *pneumatikos*. The
Hermetic was saved by anticipation here, but, like his
Christian contemporary, he would be completely saved
only eschatologically.

The body and matter were too obstinate to deny as
mere illusion, but proper *gnosis* and love of the Good
planted in man ' the seed of God,' and so he was already
of divine substance and had the earnest of that complete
transfiguration which would ensue on the dissolution
of the body. He could confess confidently with the
Christians that he was ' begotten again not of corruptible, but of incorruptible seed ' (1 Peter i. 3, 23).
He could even now on occasion be ' transported out
of the body to the supremely beautiful vision ' (X. 7);
he could ' out of the body ' be ' snatched up ' to his
third heaven, or even to the loftier Ogdoad and hear
the ineffable words ; but the continuity of such experience
was reserved for his ' becoming wholly spiritual ' (*Nous*)
in ' the most perfect glory of the soul ' (X. 7), as his
Christian brother anticipated being ' known ' of God
' face to face ' in the luminous glory of the *Parousia*.
Religious ecstasy linked with religious experience
brought Reality near to him, as to the Christian,

Platonist, or Jewish mystic. The words of Origen are in agreement with the Hermetic standpoint: ' The soul being lifted up, follows the spirit, and departing from the body, not only follows the spirit, but becomes in the spirit.' [1]

The greatness of the salvation procured by this ' true religion ' may be estimated also by the loss entailed in missing this way of Truth. It is ' a drunken sleep in ignorance of God '; it is the tragedy of ' those who have the privilege of partaking of immortality giving themselves up to death ' (*Poim.* 27 f.). ' He who through deceit of carnal desire had loved the body, remains wandering in the darkness of the senses, suffering the lot of death ' (19). He remains under the twelve deadly torments of sin (XIII. 7b) and falls a prey to the avenging demons (*Asc.* 33b). In the absence of the salutary *gnosis* ' all vices increase in strength and wound the soul with incurable vices (?); the soul, infected with this vicious contagion, breaks out as if with tumours, unless those whose souls have the supreme remedy of knowledge and intelligence ' (*Asc.* 22a).

' The evil of the soul is ignorance [2]: the soul that has not come to know reality or the nature of things, nor the Good, but is blind, is tossed about by the passions of the body; and the wretched soul, not knowing itself, is enslaved to monstrous and adulterous bodies; it carries round the body like a load, not controlling it but controlled by it ' (X. 8b). Consequently ' those who have not travelled that path of piety ' are so warped in judgment that they believe evil to be good, and in this delusion are insatiable for evil (VI. 6). Such ' know not for what purpose they have been made, nor by whom they have been made, are held under constraint by anger and incontinence; they admire the things that are not worth looking at; they give heed only to their

---

[1] Gk. text Reitzenstein, *Hellenist. Mysterien-religionen*, p. 140.
[2] Cf. Philo, *De Ebr.* 39, C.-W. 160, ἄγνοια δὲ χαλεπωτέραν τῆς ἐν τῷ σώματι πήρωσιν ἐπιφέρουσα τῇ ψυχῇ πάντων ἁμαρτημάτων αἰτία γίνεται.

bodily pleasures and desires, and believe that man has been made for such things as these.' [1]

Godlessness is a great disease (XII (1), 3). Those without *Nous* are swept along by irrational passions, like beasts in their craving for evil (4); they are even driven by right teaching to greater wickedness (*Exc.* XI. 5). These godless are *hylic* instead of *ousiodeis,* spiritual (IX. 5). They are led and driven by demons (XVI. 16), and compose merely the train of Destiny (*Frag.* 19), whereas ' neither demon nor Fate has power over a religious man ' (*Asc.* 29b).

And hereafter the godless forfeit the hope of immortality (*Asc.* 22b; *Poim.* 28). Barred from returning to heaven, they undergo a shameful migration into menial bodies (*Asc.* 12a) or suffer other commensurate penalty. ' The soul that has once entered a human body, if it continues evil, never tastes deathlessness nor participates in the Good; reversing its course, it reverts back to creeping things ' (X. 8a). It thus misses 'the consummation of religion,' which is, ' Thou shalt live nobly and die in bliss, and your soul shall not fail to know whither it must wing its way upward ' (*Exc.* IIb, 4).

This venerable faith was essentially a religion of salvation, yet without a Saviour.[2] Its salvation is of a high order and comprehensive for the needs of man, but a definite personal Saviour like the Galilean, or the Stoic Wise Man, or the Gnostic Redeemer, or the saviour-gods of the Mysteries, does not emerge. Man has within

---

[1] IV. 5, WS. and tr.

[2] " The Hermetists have no Christ, and no equivalent for Christ. . . . The ' second God ' of the Hermetists differs fundamentally from the Christ of the Christians in this, that he is not a Saviour of mankind. There is in the *Hermetica* no trace of a ' Saviour ' in the Christian sense—that is, of a divine or supracosmic Person. . . . Hermetists might speak of salvation; it was salvation that they sought and held that they had found; but they did not speak of a Saviour such as was worshipped by the Christians. According to their doctrine, it is by the operation of the divine νοῦς in a man that the man is saved; and the divine νοῦς was never incarnated upon earth " (Scott, I, pp. 12, 13. Cf. Lagrange).

himself the potencies of his own salvation [1]; e.g. he can in obedience to the gospel proclamation baptize himself in the Basin of Mind; or he is assisted thereto by the grace of God or the divine Nous; or the Logos or the Son of God may mediate the *gnosis* of salvation.

[1] ' In naturam dei transit quasi ipse sit deus ' (*Asc.* 6a).

CHAPTER XX

MOTIVES AND AIMS OF GNOSTICISM: ITS ENTRY INTO CHRISTIANITY

THE Jews sought visible signs and the Greeks speculative wisdom, and between these two cravings for miracles and for metaphysical formulation early Christianity found it difficult to maintain the highway, especially when it travelled into the larger environment of the Graeco-Roman world.

What is *Gnosis*? The translation ' knowledge ' is wholly inadequate and misleading as suggesting syllogisms and intellectualism or an ancient phase of the Enlightenment.[1] Gnosis was essentially an earnest system of salvation and an heroic attempt to explain man's place in the world—at once a religion and a philosophy. It was one of the two competing schemes of soteriology, salvation by ' faith,' *pistis*, and salvation by ' knowledge,' *gnosis*. As *pistis*, faith, may also

[1] " Es handelt sich nicht um intellektuelles Begreifen des Verstandes, um Philosophie und Spekulation, vielmehr ist die synkretistische Gotteserkenntnis das *Schauen und mystisch-ekstatische Ergreifen Gottes* mit dem ganzen Komplexe von Vorstellungen, . . . wie die Mysterien und die Kosmologie und Soteriologie. . . . Ist sie selbst ihrem Wesen nach nicht intellektuell, so setzt sie doch ein intellektuelles Streben voraus . . . die Religion ist nie reines Schauen und Erleben, sondern begreift ein Weltverständnis in sich. Insofern führt die Gnosis doch—sekundär und als Folgerung—in Philosophie und Spekulation hinein. Immer aber ist sie auf übernaturlichem Wege erworbene Kenntnis " (Köhler, *Gnosis*, p. 11). " Die Gnostiker sind nicht Religionsphilosophen; Gnosis ist nicht verstandesmässige Erkenntnis, sondern Schauen Gottes, Geheimwissen, das durch persönlichen Verkehr mit der Gottheit und durch Offenbarung gewonnen wird " (Wendland, p. 166). Cf. Norden, *Agnostos Theos*, p. 97 f.

appear as belief, and conviction, and degenerate into opinon and credulity, so *gnosis* was a holy saving science, a way of life, heavenly illumination, satisfying the intellect and touching the emotions, the light of Revelation and the communications of spiritual intuition or of spiritually-endowed and specially receptive natures, but *Gnosis* in degeneration might appear as occultism, religious magic, and cabalistic love. Gnosticism adapted a Pagan cosmology into a Christian scheme of redemption. The light of *Gnosis* might be imparted in a vision or theophany or by a revered teacher or superman, or by a divine being familiar with the heavenly region from which man had descended and to which the Gnostic soul returned, or it might arise after the fashion of the Platonic remembrance (*anamnesis*) or by plumbing the depths of the soul. Its content was ' the deep things of God ' and the mysteries of the universe in relation to ' this imprisonment in the body.' *Gnosis* ' is not taught, but when God wills it is brought to remembrance.' [1] The ' word of *Gnosis* ' was to the orthodox and the Gnostics a *charisma* or supernatural endowment.

Gnosticism is a comprehensive term for a phase of religion which appeared in Paganism, Judaism, and Christianity, but it was in Christianity that it grew most aggressive. According to Harnack,[2] Gnosticism was '' the acute secularizing or Hellenizing of Christianity '' ; according to Reitzenstein,[3] it was '' not Hellenizing but a more extensive Orientalizing of Christianity.'' Farnell [4] presents it as '' the doctrine which laboured most zealously to combine the various elements of the Pagan and Christian creeds '' ; Inge [5] as the '' attempt to complete this reconciliation between speculative and revealed religion, by systematizing the symbols of transcendental mystical theosophy '' ; Legge [6] as '' a

[1] *Corp. Herm.* XIII.   [2] *Hist. of Dogma,* I, p. 227.
[3] *Stud. z. ant. Synkretismus,* p. 141.
[4] *Evolution of Religion,* p. 36.   [5] *Christian Mysticism,* p. 81.
[6] *Forerunners and Rivals,* I, p. 96; *Pistis Sophia,* tr. by Horner, p. iii.

belief in the importance of acquaintance with the divine world, its motives, and the influences to which it is subject "; or " the belief that man's place in the next world is determined by the knowledge of it that he acquires in this." Such definitions have at least the merit of throwing into relief some outstanding phase or motive of Gnosticism. But from definitions one can as little understand Gnosticism as Christianity or mysticism. Gnosticism, a glaciation of very different strata, shows as marked varieties [1] and contradictions as any great system of thought or any organized religion. Thus there is as vast a difference between earlier and later Gnosticism as between the Christianity of Paul and of *Hermas*. The weird cosmogonies of the Ophites and the beautiful mysticism of, e.g., Ptolemaeus to Flora claim a similar common denominator as do, e.g., the Epistle of James and the Fourth Gospel. That species of Gnosticism known as Hermeticism, while sharing the general postulates of Gnosticism, stands apart from its congeners in being less ascetic, in having no personal Saviour, in being non-sacerdotal and non-sacramentarian, in neglecting organization, and in assigning to *Nous* the place given by Christian Gnostics to *Pneuma*. Gnostic schools were as divergent as those of Christianity—it is a heterogeneous complex in which, however, there is a certain unity of ideas and motives. As in Christianity, its creators were followed by organizers, its imaginative thinkers by scholastic systematizers. We note this same declination in Gnosticism as in Christianity from its classical prime. As faith declined into assent to creed and dogma, so Gnosticism declined in the third century and subsequently into puerility and phantasies and parted company with reason which had been the pride of Hellenism.

Gnosticism was one of the greatest efforts ever made to satisfy the religious needs by seeking a religion which

---

[1] Cf. de Faye, *Gnostiques et Gnosticisme*, pp. 15, 417, 427.

would conserve the maximum of the past and yet adjust itself to the contemporary outlook. It was the religious reaction of the syncretistic centuries to the intellectual forces of the time. It was a long-sustained attempt to reconcile religion and culture and to make religion at once rational and uplifting and enthusiastic. It was the natural evolution of the persistent Hellenic demand ' Know thyself ' and thereby ' thou shalt know God and the universe ' and obtain salvation.

Scholarship has devoted much attention to the question of the origin of Gnosticism, but, generally speaking, with unsatisfactory results. Anz traces Gnosticism back to remote Babylonian sources; Bousset, to the Oriental mysteries. Legge would find its ultimate source in Orphism, while recognizing three other more general sources: (1) " the decay of the earlier faith, which showed itself in the popular taste for cosmogonical and other myths "; (2) " the great spread of ceremonial magic " ; and (3) astrology. The truth is that we cannot assign the origin of this influential movement to any one cultural, geographical, or racial source. One can easily discover in the Gnostic systems Babylonian mythology, Persian dualism, Egyptian mysticism and occultism, the Orphic cosmology of a fall and the restitution of the soul from the weary circle of reincarnations, Jewish theology, Greek philosophy, especially Platonism and Pythagoreanism, astral ideas and mystical conceptions and practices, together with the idea of a First or Heavenly Man of Eastern provenance.[1] Hegesippus blamed Jewish sects for giving birth to Gnosticism. Tertullian lays the blame on philosophy as the mother of all heresies, in which he is undoubtedly correct, inasmuch as Gnosticism arose from man's asking questions and seeking a solution on the great problems of his Whence and Whither.[2]

---

[1] Cf. Reitzenstein, *Das iranische Erlösungsmysterium*; Kraeling, *Anthropos and Son of Man*; Schaeder, *Studien z. antiken Synkretismus*, pp. 205-305.

[2] Cf. *Excerpta Theod.* 78, 2, in Clem. Alex. (Stählin, III, p. 131).

Gnosticism must needs have come in the conditions of the world from the days of Alexander the Great. It was an inevitable expression of the human spirit in its deepest needs and desire for freedom. It was a pre-Christian product, Oriental and Pagan in its origin, but finding a permanent place in Judaism and Christianity.

While one must refuse to remain unconvinced by attempts like those of Anz or Bousset or Legge to delimit strictly the definite source of Gnosticism, we can clearly discover the motives and beliefs out of which Gnosticism arose and the religious and philosophical conditions which shaped it.

(1) The first of these is Hellenistic-Oriental syncretism,[1] which set in as a mighty tide from the Orient since the day of the marriage of East and West under the Macedonian conqueror. The barriers of nationalism had been thrown down and men were brought together on the basis of a common humanity rather than as Greeks and barbarians. The religious tolerance which Alexander had inherited from Persia inaugurated a new era in the history of religion. In the concurrence of religions and religious philosophies men sought the most practical religious support. Exclusivism in religion became antiquated and an active process of borrowing and assimilation set in. Gnosticism was the maturest expression of the interaction of religious ideas in the Graeco-Roman age. It was a religion of conglomerates decidedly international in character and outlook. There was more disposition to borrow new elements and accept new ideas and to conserve all that each religion or culture offered than to criticise and reject. Hence superstitions and primitive phantasies survive in Gnosticism with ideas of Platonism and Stoicism.

[1] Usener with reason attributes the beginning of the Gnostic movement to the propaganda and syncretism of the Oriental cults (*Weihnachtsfest*, 2nd ed. p. 25 ff.). "Der Anstoss zu den gnostischen Bildungen ist ausgegangen von der religiösen Invasion des orientalisch-hellenistischen Synkretismus" (Wendland, p. 167, cf. p. 165). Cf. Reitzenstein-Schaeder, *Studien z. antiken Synkretismus*, p. 141 ff.

Gnosticism, like early Christianity, found it a difficult problem to maintain its continuity with the past without conserving much that had better been left behind. Gnosticism, being thus the characteristic expression of the interaction of religions, philosophies, and sciences of the time, deals with the great themes that we find in each of the Mystery-religions and in each of the religious philosophical systems, such themes as the origin of the world and of matter, the origin and destiny of man, both as an individual and as a member of the cosmic order, the problem of the origin and the supersession of evil, the descent and ascent of the soul, and the mode of the deliverance of man from Fate and finitude and the means of the acquisition of immortality.

(2) But Gnosticism did not arise merely out of contact of thought with thought, but out of the desperate need of man at the time. The pursuit of Gnosis was by no means speculation for the sake of speculation or with the aim of a disinterested philosophy in search of truth for its own sake, but for practical religious ends. It arose out of the aspiration of the divine in man to return home. De Faye [1] has correctly remarked that Gnosticism was born of the new spirit of aspiration which commenced with the Roman Empire in the universal revival of religious interests. It is only when one places oneself so far as possible in the situation of the earnest men of the Graeco-Roman age and envisages their fears and hopes, their problems and difficulties, that one can fully understand how truly Gnosis or salvation-knowledge was a veritable way of life for cultured men. Astralism seemed to have brought men more hopelessly under the power of *Heimarmene* (Destiny); the prestige of the magicians from the Euphrates and the Tigris had added new terrors to the enchoric magic of Greece and Rome and placed at the disposal of the magicians a power over life and death. Orphism had brought to the West the unwelcome

---

[1] *Gnostiques et Gnosticisme,* p. 445.

doctrine of the fall of the soul from its native high estate and that of the body as the tomb of the soul from which deliverance must be sought at the peril of everlasting punishment. Ignorance was the main hindrance to safety, and this ignorance could only be removed by the divine revelation of Gnosis or holy science for soul and body. Gnosis was one of the two passionate quests of Hellenistic piety and philosophy, the yearning to know God and to acquire deathlessness; it was the striving to knowledge through love to attain the vision of God; ' the will of God is the deeper knowledge (*epignosis*) of God, which is participation in incorruptibility.' [1]

The Gnostics were keen students of philosophy and no learned triflers or dispassionate inquirers. They were grimly in earnest in search for a way of life and for a solution of the great problems of human destiny. It might be said that in them the two elements in Socrates' character and work—the dialectic and the mystical—which fell apart after Plato, were again united. Yet though they did not despise reasoning and even encouraged speculation, their path to *gnosis* was rather by love and imagination and sincere piety and ascetic morality.

(3) Another sure promise of Gnosticism was the cosmic outlook of the time due to a combination of causes, such as Astralism, Oriental mysticism, and the yearning to live comfortably in an intimidating world. As in much Christian thinking the doctrine of Adam's fall is the first postulate in the construction of Christian soteriology, so the dualism of soul and body, spirit and matter, was a postulate for Gnostic salvation to Pagan and Christian. Man had missed his way into his present sphere—he was out of his place in the cosmic order, and hence exposed to all the discomforts of finitude and of cosmic necessity here, the attacks of the demonic powers upon his material and moral progress, and finally exposed to all the perils attending his return

[1] Clem. Alex. *Str*. IV. 6, 27.

upward to the world of light whence he came. The drama of the soul with its incarnation and disincarnation, its primal disobedience and its purification, its dependence on divine grace and sacramental potencies, and its relation to the whole world of spirits constituted the mythos of salvation.[1]

With the universal prevalence of Astralism the outlook of man was widened and his cosmic problem intensified. Hence Gnosticism was a necessity, and may be viewed either as the response of deeply religious spirits to human needs or as a reaction [2] against the fatalism inherent in Astralism. Gnosticism is therefore another interesting example of how in every age the spirit of man discovers a solution—partial and inadequate—for an immediate difficulty.

(4) Metaphysical interests. Even to a serious student of Gnosticism to-day Gnosis assumes such bizarre forms that it is often unintelligible to him—hence the impression that Gnosis is an arid speculation, an aimless excursion of degenerate or overtired minds into the realm of phantasies. Of course we grant that there are many arid stretches in Gnosticism and much febrile guessing and magical puerilities. But we must remember in the first place, that the key of Gnosis has been lost to us, partly through the fanatical destruction of the Gnostic writings by victorious orthodox Christianity and partly because such Gnostic writings as survived were written not for propaganda among outsiders, but for esoteric circles whose catechumenate had furnished them the key to the study of their scriptures; and in the second place, that our concrete Western mind does not naturally express itself in the same metaphysical moulds as that of the

---

[1] " L'aspiration mystique qui rêvait d'un retour à Dieu ou aux dieux de tout ce qu'il y a divin dans l'homme et dans le Cosmos est alors dans l'air " (de Faye, *Gnostiques et Gnosticisme*, p. 444 f.).

[2] " Die gnostischen Religionen sind die Reaktion gegen die Astralreligion, die des Menschen Schiksal unter die Gewalt der Sterngötter stellt. Die Erlösungsreligionen wollen durch ihre theurgischen Mittel diese Bande sprengen " (Wendland, p. 176).

Graeco-Roman world. In fact metaphysics was to the Gnostic age what the scientific spirit is to us. As to-day we demand of our religion conformity with the results of science and with the philosophical ideals of the age, so the ancients demanded of a religion that it should not only furnish a mythos of salvation, but should prove capable of being reduced to a comprehensive and elaborate metaphysic.[1] Further, religion had in those days to fulfil functions which in our more specialized age have been partially taken over by science, art, medicine, and philosophy. This penchant for metaphysical formulation was immensely increased when Hellenic genius interested itself in Oriental revelation and when the competition of religious and philosophical systems furnished a new material for the exercise of speculative inquiry.

In all these tendencies Christianity, after it was carried beyond the boundaries of Judaea, partook wittingly and unwittingly. The new faith could not escape the religious influences so powerful around it: in the new cosmopolitanism it could not remain a sect partitioned off. The points of view shared with its contemporaries were so numerous that they exposed it to the inroads of other ideas. Despite the obvious advantage of Christianity in making a new beginning as a religion, it was soon drawn into the currents of asceticism, dualism, demonology, and the mythologizing of its historic content. Indeed Christianity offered a more promising field than elsewhere to those who sought Gnosis. There were many reasons why the Christian Church should

---

[1] " Religion im Sinne des Orients ist die Erklärung alles dessen was ist, also eine Weltauffassung " (Winckler, *Himmelsbild der Babylonier*, p. 9, cited Cumont, *Or. Religions*, p. 230). " Der Orientale glaubt die Welt zu erkennen, wenn er den Gott in seiner wahren Gestalt schaut. Aber der Gott ist zugleich das Selbst in ihm, in ihm schaut man die Welt, und nur durch Gott selbst kann man ihn schauen, ja er tritt durch diese Schau ganz in uns ein. Das ist der Grundgedanke aller Gnosis, das entscheidende Erlebnis " (Reitzenstein—Schaeder, *Stud. z. antiken Synkretismus*, p. 141).

become the home of the Gnostic movement. (1) It was in the very lands and centres of Hellenistic-Oriental culture and religious ferment, where the intellectual life of the age was most active, that Christianity spread in its missionary career. The apostolic preachers availed themselves of the common language of the *Koiné* to carry the message to the chief centres of population where East and West met and mingled. Christianity kept pace with the penetration of the oriental religions in the West and availed itself of an organization of conventicles after the muster of the Jewish synagogue and the Mystery fraternities. A new religion cannot spread independent of its historic *milieu,* nor can it forge for itself at once new categories of thought and a psychology of its own. Every new religion lives and expands by facing the problems of the age and by offering new incentives towards the realization of its ideals. Religions of redemption were everywhere in request with saviour-gods who guaranteed salvation to their followers by identification with themselves. It was to the religious quests of its age that Christianity addressed itself in enthusiastic earnest, and even if Christian preachers could have overlooked or discredited the ideas of redemption of the age, their converts would not allow those ideas to become sterile.

(2) The laxity of organization in the early Christian conventicles, the fluidity of doctrine, and the unrestricted freedom of teaching facilitated the entry of Gnosticism which could arise only in an age of the Church when teachers and prophets and itinerant evangelists were carrying on their work, not in an age when an episcopal hierarchy with its apostolic claims represented the highest authority. Theological constructions had as yet not crystallized, and the teacher had not yet been sub-jugated to the bishop. It was still the period when the promise of the Spirit to lead men into truth was taken seriously by every member of the Church, when ' where the spirit of the Lord is, there is liberty.' This Spirit

was the representative of Jesus, and continued His work. It showed itself in the revivalistic phenomena, in prophecy, in the application of the example and teaching of Jesus. Every prophet and evangelist claimed this Spirit as their authority, and there was as yet no court of arbitration which could say them nay. Diversity of doctrine did not trouble the primitive conventicles on the obvious theory that all teaching came from the one source—the Spirit.[1] The New Testament itself is the best evidence that during the three generations of its composition there was no stark uniformity of dogma, and this early tolerance of diversity of teaching did not prevent the Church from the second to the fourth centuries from choosing this selection of Christian scriptures, which on such a critical matter as the Person of Jesus contains such divergent christologies as that of Mark, the supernatural birth-stories of Matthew and Luke, the pre-existent descending and ascending divine Being of Paul, the Logos incarnation of the Fourth Gospel, and the mediatorial high-priesthood of Hebrews. Christianity offered a new Saviour which necessitated a new soteriology or story of redemption amid plans of salvation by competing saviours. The formation of the Christian story of redemption could not take place except in contrast to and in contact with concurrent systems of redemption. Christian converts must be instructed in the nature of their scheme of salvation and in its superiority over its competitors. This was the office of the teacher. But Christian converts did not create or accept their story of redemption in a vacuum; they had been familiar with other stories of redemption under otner redeemers and lords before they became Christians. They were also living as a minority in a society where religious interests were being daily discussed and in

[1] In the apostolic age " the moving and controlling power " of life was " the disciples' vivid sense of the presence and activity of the Holy Spirit. It is its spiritual character which distinguishes the age from all subsequent periods in the history of the Church " (McGiffert, *Apostolic Age*, p. 540; cf. Wernle, *Beginnings*, II, pp. 178, 199).

which they were compelled in argument to give a reason for their faith. Their difficulties were brought for further discussion before the brotherhoods in which the teacher was free to speculate without reference to a dogmatic authority over him. Freedom is ever a perilous path, and this primitive freedom and lack of homogeneity exposed the Church to such opposite dangers as ecstatic-prophetic Montanism and the seductive speculations of Gnosticism.

(3) The crude Messianism of the first preachers could not long survive amid the demands of the larger Graeco-Roman world. The Jewish Messiah or Son of Man was not calculated to meet the needs of the Gentile world. The conditions of preaching in a missionary activity in the centres of Graeco-Roman culture were different from the tense apocalyptism of the Jerusalem community. This Messianism could not win the allegiance of a world familiar with such religious conceptions as the Jewish Sophia or Wisdom as an intermediary or agent of the Most High, the Logos conception of the Greek and Alexandrine thought, the pre-existent Heavenly Man, the ascending divine Redeemer of competing religions. Hence theology was called upon to give an adequate explanation of the Messiah in relation to descending redeemers, to hypostases like Wisdom, Memre, and to the Alexandrine Logos. It is noteworthy that when the first theologian of Christianity appeared to adapt the new faith to the larger Gentile world his speculations about the pre-existent Christ and Power of God took a direction which pointed toward later Gnosticism. It is also noteworthy to contrast the Christology of the *Letters* of his imprisonment with that of his first extant Letters, those to Thessalonica. Between the writing of Thessalonians and Ephesians and Colossians Paul had recognized the dangers threatening his Churches from incipient Gnosticism, and from the extravagances of his own doctrine of liberty. He had also recognized the necessity of claiming for his Lord all the cosmic preten-

sions put forth by his adversaries for other lords, without realizing how far his speculations about the origin and nature of the Christian redeemer would carry others who did not share the depth of his religious experience or his conviction that his loftiest speculations were based on a historic personality.

(4) There obtained among Pagans, Jews, and Christians a free treatment of historical facts which it is difficult for us to understand. Historical events were the mere alphabetical symbols of the human story with which one construed the interpretative idea according to his own insight and intelligence. We recognize that history is more than annals, and that the philosophy of history seeks to find the key to the reading of history, but we are not indifferent to the records, nor do we identify our philosophy of history with the events. But to the ancient philosophers the ' idea ' as the reality had the right of way over the historic fact. As phenomena are merely shadows pointing to the substance, so time-events are but shadows of the eternal ideas as Time itself, in Platonic thought, is but ' the moving image of Eternity.' Hence ancient thought tended to move in the sphere of lofty abstractions rather than to drag its slow course attendant on the happenings between sunrise and sunset. History became at an early date for Christians the amalgam of factual events and '' accepted fiction.''

Origen is Plato's truest disciple in his contemplation of ' the moving image of Eternity.' He likens history to a ladder,[1] the first steps of which are time and space happenings leading up to the Mysteries and to the hidden meaning revealed only to those who scale the heights towering above mere history. He is concerned, almost exclusively, with the pre-existent Logos rather than with the historic Galilean. The Christian dispensation is a twofold gospel of progression consisting of an historical or αἰσθητὸν εὐαγγέλιον (external or sensible gospel) and

[1] *In Joh.* I. 20.

a higher νοητὸν καὶ πνευματικὸν gospel. This was part of Origen's defence against the growing literalism and realism which so alarmed his Platonic soul.

Here again the way was prepared by Paul. He was familiar with the outlines of the life of Jesus, but he prefers to treat those historic events as merely the time-appearances of a supratemporal cosmic plan in a transmundane setting. When, for example, he desires to bring home to his beloved Church of Philippi the lesson of humility and to rebuke their self-seeking, he refers not to any example or word of the Prophet of Nazareth, but to a pretemporal divine being who thought not equality with God a thing to be grasped at, but descended to earth, taking upon himself the form of a servant. Again, he refers not to one who said, ' I came not to be served, but to serve,' but to a pre-existent one who, ' though He was rich, yet for our sakes He became poor ' by means of a Kenosis.

Yet more amazing to the modern historian is the attitude of the writer of the Fourth Gospel to facts of history, to whom historical events are symbols and adumbrations of Christian doctrine.[1] It is somewhat surprising to find in this anti-gnostic gospel with its emphasis on the Incarnation how scanty are the traces of that humanity of Jesus which the author wishes to establish. His conception of history has been so recast into the categories of the Logos Christ that his gospel narrowly escapes Docetism, and escapes it in such a way that if the Fourth Gospel alone survived without the Synoptists we could not properly speak of the humanity of Jesus.

Faintly does the Carpenter of Nazareth appear on the pages of the Fourth Gospel. Jesus did not increase in wisdom, for the Logos Christ had learned all things from His Father in His pretemporal existence. Nor did

---

[1] " History is to him merely a setting in time and space of the Divine ideas; and he feels quite at liberty to embody them, not in history but in doctrine " (Gardner, *Ephesian Gospel*, p. 205).

He submit to a baptism of repentance for remission of sins, nor did He pass through a religious crisis at His baptism wherein He received His call—rather, the *Bath Qol* was vouchsafed to the baptizer to announce the incarnation. The experience at the Jordan did not lead to a time of self-testing and of severe temptations in the neighbourhood. He who went around doing good and healing the demonized as at first the herald and then later the inaugurator of the Kingdom of God summons men to believe in Himself. So far from devoutly declining the appellation of ' good,' He defiantly challenges His opponents—' Which of you convinces Me of sin ? ' Instead of spending a night of lonely vigil in prayer before selecting a group of disciples and receiving an answer in the inscrutable ways of God in such a manner that one of the twelve whom He considered specially fitted for the task of ' fisher of men ', proved a traitor, the Logos Christ, acting from His omniscience and from a full knowledge of the future, deliberately chose ' the son of perdition ' to betray Him. He nowhere prays for strength and guidance ; prayer would be impossible and superfluous. He nowhere fails to effect a faith-cure, but rather proves thaumaturgic in a scale far transcending the Synoptic powers in seven stupendous ' signs.' The pathos and the moral grandeur of Gethsemane have been superseded by a scene in which Christ acknowledges without ' loud crying and entreaty to Him who was able to save Him from death,' that there is no struggle but merely that His hour has come. In the Synoptic story surely the poignancy and the real victory lie in the fact that the victory was enacted within, without supernatural intervention. In the story of the arrest we have the legend of one before whom even a band of Roman soldiers fell back in terror. We can understand therefore with what suspicion this ' spiritual gospel ' was looked upon and with what difficulty it secured its place in the canon. Its dualism of God and the world, light and darkness, the children of God and

the born of Satan, is the Gnostic dualism. So also is
its pessimism in regard to the world and the present
reign of the Prince of Darkness. " However great the
vehemence with which St. John engages in the struggle
against the Gnostics, it must be admitted that the
expressions which he employs are often practically indistinguishable from those of his adversaries." [1]

This writer was a vigorous opponent of Gnostic
Docetism, yet it is only in the light of the Synoptic
Gospels that we could form any idea of the humanity
of Jesus. The disciple of Paul, writing this Ephesian
Gospel to a Pauline foundation, has not only sublimated
history to a greater extent than Paul, but while professedly casting his interpretation of Christianity into
the mould of a Gospel has dramatized and reshapen
history. He meets the Gnostic contentions not as we
should have expected by appealing to the historical facts
of the life of Jesus, but in three ways—first, by asserting
that the Logos became flesh in an episodic career in'
Jesus Christ; secondly, by meticulously giving evidences
of the physical reality of his death; and thirdly, by
accentuating the realistic stories of the Resurrection, not
as a return from the dead, but as a reanimation of the
dead body from the tomb with tangibility and visibility.

(5) In the Jerusalem community at the foundation of
the Church there lacked a cosmic or universal outlook
due partly to the imminence of the Parousia, partly to
the stress on individual salvation, and partly to the lack
of contact with the great Hellenistic world outside.
Properly speaking, apocalyptism had no cosmic outlook; its framework was the two-aeon disjunction of
history into this age and that age separated by a
catastrophic definitive event and the rescue of the elect.
The primitive Christians had no idea of cosmic redemption—indeed, " they had no idea of cosmology." [2] This
apocalyptism could not do service in an outside world

[1] Wernle, *Beginnings of Christianity*, II, p. 184.
[2] De Faye, *Gnostiques*, p. 440.

where redemption was cosmically conceived. And this lack of cosmic interest and equipment in the primitive message exposed it more to the speculation necessary to enlarge its redemptive outlook.

(6) Such a personality as Jesus was certain to attract cosmic speculations, as it did the pre-Christian christological elements such as pre-existence, the idea of the archetypal Heavenly Man, the incarnation of a divine being, His descent to the underworld, His ascent to heaven, the conceptions of intermediary beings between God and man. So great was Jesus that He compelled His followers to the task of attempting to explain Him, and until dogmatic uniformity was insisted upon, those approaching the task did so with the ideas to hand and with the conviction that the previous agencies of salvation must yield to Jesus as the supreme agent. Hence Christians, Gnostic and orthodox alike, assigned to Jesus the cosmic and mediatorial functions of the Logos and Wisdom.

Inasmuch as in Gnosticism, properly speaking, there was no need of a personal Redeemer and inasmuch as ' the Logos became flesh ' presented serious difficulties, the central place given to the Christian Redeemer by Gnosticism and His function of saving by disclosing Mysteries is a striking historic testimony to the greatness of Jesus. The Gnostics were quick to perceive the advantages and superiority of a new and vigorous religion with a Founder of the stature of Jesus. He was given a premier place in their cosmic scheme, partly as the Revealer ' from above ' imparting to ' the earthly ones ' the things of heaven, partly by making His descent and ascent the epitome of the Gnostic scheme and symbolic of the history and destiny of the soul, and partly by identifying him with the Ideal or Archetypal Man who had cast off the material elements.

(7) Lastly, Paul himself could be cited by the Gnostics with considerable plausibility as the founder of Gnosis, and it is striking to note the number of parallelisms

between the Gnostic drama of redemption and that of Paul, and also at how many points the Gnostics pursued the Pauline speculative construction beyond the limit at which he had found it unnecessary or impossible to proceed. But Paul was no more the father of Gnosticism [1] than of sacramentarianism, though the germs of both are latent in his system. In a large measure Paul is a Gnostic, though he would have repudiated the Gnostics as his spiritual offspring. In his soteriology we have the preparation for Christian Gnosticism which may be regarded as a hyper-Paulinism with over-statements of his epoch-making positions and distortions or one-sided expressions of his characteristic presentations. " The Gnostics simply carried out consistently the Hellenistic tendency which voiced itself to a limited degree in Paul. . . . The controlling influence of his principles in their thought is not to be mistaken." [2] The Gnostics took literally the bold statements of Paul apart from their context. The Pauline doctrine of the fall of man based on the Adamic theology was akin to the Gnostic scheme of the descent of the Soul.

The Pauline ethical dualism of flesh and spirit, founded on his own experience, became a metaphysical and cosmic dualism which must conduce to asceticism. The ascetic tendency was quite obvious in Paul, especially in his relation to marriage. It was something for the Gnostics that a leader of Paul's rank could be cited as favouring a dualistic asceticism.

His doctrine of Christ-mysticism, founded on his own experience and suffused with Gnosis, enabled the Gnostics to claim that the Resurrection is past already because they had been raised with Christ and already seated in the heavenly places with Him. The Pauline

---

[1] " He could not endure to see the glory of Jesus Christ obscured by the mist and fog of Gnosticism " (A. T. Robertson, *Paul and the Intellectuals*, p. viii).

[2] McGiffert, *Apostolic Age*, pp. 503, 504. In Marcion and the Gnostic schools of the second century " the characteristic views of Paul found their fullest acceptance and their most remarkable development " (*ib.*).

character of Christians through the possession of the Christ-pneuma was the harbinger of the Gnostic proclamation of the superior and indestructible character of those who had received Gnosis. It was the Gnostics also who took seriously Paul's position that Christians were no longer sinners, having done with sin when they died to it in baptism into Christ, and it was against this spiritual idealism as a self-deception that the writer of the First Johannine Epistle protested as delusion on the part of those who say that they have no sin, whereas the orthodox Christians have an Advocate with the Father for those who sin.

Paul's advocacy of Christian freedom could hardly escape proving perilous when dislocated from his practical moral interests. When Paul contended that we are no longer under the law but under grace and that we have ceased to be in the flesh when transferred into the Spirit, he could not foresee how readily this expression of his own experience and interpretation of Christianity as liberty against legalism should by unworthy Gnostics become a justification for immorality on the grounds that the illuminated spirit was indifferent to or untainted by the deeds of the flesh, though the great Gnostics were strict rigorists. Paul's revolutionary attitude to Judaism and his view of the Law as an inferior and interim dispensation suggested that more radical attitude to Judaism and the religion of the Old Testament as represented by Marcion.

In regard to the treatment of history the Gnostics merely carried to its ultimate issue Paul's free treatment of history and of his rendering of it into a cosmic soteriological system. It is in Paul that the greatest problem of early Christianity emerges—the relation of the Man Jesus to the descending and ascending Christ whose home is in the transcendent world from which He comes merely on an episodic visit for the obedience of death, after which He returns to His home in Heaven to acquire higher rank and to receive the Name above every name.

The divine facts of salvation are the Cross and the Resurrection rather than the moral power and spiritual appeal of Jesus' life. Christ is made the centre of a cosmology, and such scanty historical facts as Paul uses he fits within a cosmic plan of a redemption drama amidst transcendent scenery. It is increasingly recognized that Paul's Christian speculations are not to be discovered even in germinal form in Jesus' teachings, and for not one of them does Paul cite any teaching of Jesus as authentication. Of his Christianity as of his gospel he would have claimed with honesty that he ' was not taught,' but that it came ' by an apocalypse of Jesus Christ,' and that it was a product of the new loyalty and sense of spiritual power arising from the ' appearance.' Of course Paul's boldest speculation and his most daring Christology were always and only undertaken in the practical interest of Christian morality and never with a view to a disinterested philosophy of history. But they suggested endless themes and enthralling enigmas to those who had the genius for speculation without Paul's commensurate capacity for obedience. Moreover, to whatever lofty heights Paul's inquiring thought would soar, or into what mysterious abysses it might descend, Paul was always conscious that his speculations and attempted formulations rested ultimately on a solid basis of history. To Paul the Incarnation appeared the necessary and divinely ordained means of redemption, but to the Gnostics the Incarnation presented a problem arising from their dualism of matter and spirit. Gnostic thought, unfettered by historic fact, soared to giddy heights unknown to Paul. Paul's scanty attention to the historic facts of Jesus' life exposed the Church to a real danger heightened by the sweep and fascination of his speculation on an historic basis.

In Paul's transference of Christ's work from mankind to the cosmos the first step was taken to the remodelling of Christianity into a cosmic drama after Hellenistic-

Oriental models. Christ redeemed not merely from sin and the curse of the law, but from the domination of demons and from cosmic necessity. These functions He could perform as the supreme intermediary between God and man, and also as the pre-temporal agent of creation and the present principle whereby the universe is held together. Such thoughts, penned by the Apostle for immediate moral interest, were not likely to remain fruitless. He had indicated directions which were to be followed by those who shared his speculative interests without his moral sobriety.

Lastly, had not Paul himself claimed a Gnosis and indicated it as a privilege for advanced Christians and was not this Gnosis clearly akin to Hellenistic Gnosis? Every Christian had faith, but every Christian had not Gnosis, though—and here Paul differed both from the Gnostics and from the Fourth Gospel, for the psychic man could become spiritual—Gnosis was accessible to every Christian and not merely to certain supernaturally endowed individuals. The nature of Gnosis, the wonder of Gnosis, was a coveted charisma and therefore attainable chiefly in the ecstatic state, wherein divine disclosures were supposedly more immediate and infallible than in everyday consciousness or by the journeyman method of ratiocination. It was akin to wisdom, but a wisdom not of this aeon nor of the doomed demonic authorities; it was something above faith and superadded to faith. It is the privilege of the few, not of the many, for not all men have Gnosis, though all men ought to have Gnosis. It comes by revelation from above, and is impossible to the natural or psychic man who cannot understand the things of the Spirit, to whom they are foolishness. It can be imparted not to babes but to the perfect or Christian initiates. Elementary knowledge suffices for the Christian neophyte, but the superior *Gnosis* characterizes the initiated.

Wide and deep is the content of this Gnosis, nothing less than the things that have been bestowed on us by

God and the full meaning of the Cross and of the cosmic scope of the same. God's wisdom is a mystery hidden from the world-rulers, who in their blindness had crucified the Lord of Glory to their own undoing. It is the apprehension of the ineffable things prepared for those who love God. Only those who have the mind of Christ can understand it. In addition to furnishing the key to the cosmic secrets of redemption and the plans of God for the future, Pauline Gnosis furnished its adepts with an esoteric interpretation of the Old Testament whereby Christian baptism and the Eucharist were discovered in type in the transit of the Red Sea under Moses and in the feeding on manna in the wilderness and in the interpretation of the political enemies of the psalmist, 110, as demons. Gnosis thus is vouchsafed by the Spirit and is fathomable only by the Spirit. It offered the first Christian *Weltanschauung* whereby Christ subjugated all things to God, that God may be all and in all. Thus Paul formulated a Christian Gnosis, but unfortunately in the subsequent generations it was forgotten that there was a more excellent way than even this supernatural Gnosis—the way of love.

CHAPTER XXI

REACTIONS OF GNOSTICISM AND CHRISTIANITY:
GNOSTIC PIETY

GNOSTICISM was the third and perhaps the greatest crisis in the history of early Christianity, the first being the dangers consequent on the waning of the earliest apocalyptic enthusiasm; the second, the controversy about the universalism of Christianity, of which Paul was the champion; and the third, the tides of Hellenistic-Oriental syncretism which threatened to sweep away Christianity as an historic religion. It was a crisis in which the very existence of Christianity was at stake. When Christianity was spreading in the larger and freer *milieu* of the Pagan world and the Gentile influences winning at the expense of the primitive Jewish, it was historically inevitable that Hellenistic-Oriental thought should claim Christianity and adopt it as it had done other Oriental gospels and seek to qualify its character as Judaism had done in its nascent stages. As Paul, after much effort, had vindicated the independence of Christianity from Judaism and his contention had been corroborated by the reception given his universal Gospel by the Greeks, it was not surprising that the severance from Judaism should be carried to extremes by those who were not Jews either by birth or sympathy. Gnosticism was an attempt to dissever all genetic connexion with the mother-religion and to place Christianity under the tutelage of Hellenism. The religious syncretism, eager and aggressive and in search of a new and satisfying religion, laid hold on Christianity and sought to win it from its historical antecedents. Gnosticism was more than " the acute Hellenizing of

Christianity." It was almost as much an Orientalizing [1] of Christianity. At least the Hellenism was strongly diluted with Oriental ingredients, or rather the later Hellenic spirit was operating on Oriental materials [2] though by Greek methods and traditions.

The Church refused to permit Christianity to be absorbed into Hellenism and the content of the Christian message to be dissolved into a theosophical mysticality. If in the confusion of the conflict the Church could not with safety absorb, or consider even the advisability of absorbing, Hellenism into Christianity, it took the safer alternative and averted the immediate danger. " In Christianity, pagan philosophy and mysticism have in a certain measure been absorbed by the Gospel and utilized by it, but in Gnosticism it is rather the Gospel which has been absorbed by pagan philosophy and mysticism." [3]

The conflict was all the more dangerous because of the ground common to Gnostics and the orthodox, between whom the main quarrel was not about the divinity of Christ, but about His real humanity. The rise of the Catholic Church in opposition to Gnosticism was a narrowing process, but it was also a saving process. Notwithstanding the manner in which the conflict was carried on, the defamatory names applied by the orthodox to their opponents, and the misrepresentations of the Gnostic systems, our sympathy must be on the

---

[1] " Nicht Hellenisierung, sondern weitere Orientalisierung des Christentums bietet die Gnosis " (Reitzenstein-Schaeder, *Stud. z. ant. Synk.* p. 141). " Es lässt sich ganz allgemein sagen, dass γνῶσις θεοῦ . . . eine Zentralbegriff war, um den sich die Religionen des Orients in konzentrischen Kreisen bewegten. Von Hellas dahin eine Verbindungslinie zu ziehen liegt ausser dem Bereiche der Möglichkeit; dagegen scheint der umgekehrte Weg . . . eher gangbar " (Norden, *Agnostos Theos*, p. 96).

[2] The result, according to Leisegang, of the operation of Hellenistic metaphysics on Oriental fantasy, imagery, and symbolism (*Die Gnosis*, p. 3 ff.).

[3] Loisy, *Les Mystères païens et le Mystère chrét.* p. 355. Cf. Gardner, *Growth of Christianity*, p. 99 f.

side of the Church. To protect herself against the present danger [1] and such abuses of liberty in the future, the Church surrounded herself with the threefold wall of apostolic authority in the Episcopate, thus ending democratic freedom, the Apostles' Creed, the end of fluid theology, and the New Testament canon.

The gains to the Church were many. The Church was strengthened by a new self-consciousness. It was better equipped for its missionary work in the Graeco-Roman world. Its principles were clarified by developing what was implicit in its teachings. If the conflict deepened and developed clefts within Christianity, it widened its horizon by the presence of speculative beside moral elements and mystical beside legal. Its equipment with the Episcopate, with one credal formula, and with one canonical book enabled it later to undertake the vast work of civilizing the barbarians who were to conquer the ancient civilizations.

The house-churches of early Christianity became the Church. The Catholic Church was largely the product of the Gnostic controversy. The Church won the victory, but at what a cost! It was a Pyrrhic victory. The Church took the *via media* and entered upon her long career of compromise; the hierarchic organization standardized faith, and forbade the former spontaneity. The Spirit was no longer free for individuals and individual communities—it spoke in classical writings and through ecclesiastical organization. Apostolic tradition was enthroned oftentimes at a considerable violence to history. The dangers of subjectivity among Gnostics and Montanists were all too obvious and must be

---

[1] Gnosticism constituted a threefold danger to the Church: (1) doctrinally, especially on the Person of Jesus; (2) morally, in the liability to abuse in the extravagant form of Paul's doctrine of liberty; (3) as imperilling the unity of the Church and encouraging a sectarianism disruptive of organization. Gnosticism would have made it impossible for the house-churches and the later and larger communities to coalesce into the ancient Catholic Church by rendering the Christian fraternities as fissiparous as the Mystery brotherhoods.

prevented, but only by over-emphasizing the opposite principle of objectivity which was later to lead to vast schisms within Christianity. Now for the first time within the circles of those who called themselves Christians the exclusive principle was introduced, the orthodox stood in contrast to the heretics in doctrine. The Church would no longer allow the wheat and tares to grow together until harvest; while attempting to remain a missionary Church it turned persecutor and prepared the way for later defections. As the Catholic Church later, in the throes of the Donatist controversy, formulated a mystic-magical view of baptism which recognized the validity of heretical (Donatist) baptism and so facilitated for numerous Donatists the path of return to the Church, so the earlier Catholic Church was quite willing to accept the sacramentarianism and vicarious value of ecclesiastical rites as held by the Gnostics. Gnostic magic became easily acclimatized in Christianity. Similar ideas appear. The later Gnostics drew the conclusion that the sacraments guarantee salvation and confer immortality just as in Pseudo-Justin the Eucharist secures the incorruptibility of the bodies of believers that they may share in a physical Resurrection. A loftier view appears earlier in Valentinus, who held that we are saved by becoming wholly ' spiritual ' and not by works '; only the ' imperfect ' need works, and with this Origen agrees.

The problem of faith and history was definitely raised and that of the relation of the historical to the eternal. The Church awoke to the dangers of the severance of Christianity from history and of the sublimation of its historical content into mythical abstractions and also of the solvent effects of mysticism upon history. The Gnostics recognized that history limits and necessarily hinders the redemptive ' idea,' especially the limitations inherent in human conditions. The orthodox leaders, asserting that historic facts are in their relations and effects more than mere facts, rightly insisted that speculative reconstruction should not cut the tap-root in history. Yet the conflict between the rights of history and of experience and the formulation of both were inconclusive. The Church made more concessions to Gnosticism than it was aware. It fought for the full and real humanity of Jesus, but on securing this it lifted Jesus out of humanity into a pre-existent divine descending and ascending Being subordinate to God. The very formulation of Christianity in Pauline thought which lifted it above the narrowness and the particularism of Judaism to become the conquering spiritual power in the Gentile world proved a source of danger. The gospel of Jesus was fitted into a cosmology which demanded wholesale remodelling. Gnosticism also raised acutely the question of the human and the divine in Christ which had the lamentable issue in the Church of restricting the unity of human and divine to Christ who had so perfectly lived the unity. In the transposition of the Jesus of history into the metaphysical and semi-mythical figure of the later Christologies and as the Second Person of the Trinity the Gnostic contention triumphed.[1]

As in every controversy, truth suffers by the over-emphasizing of differences and the rigorism of logic, so truth suffered on both sides in this controversy. The unity of the Person of Jesus was rent in twain by a two-nature formula. In opposition to Docetism, the Passion story was retold with increasing realism and materialism. The primitive Resurrection story of an ascent from the world of the dead, which in the evangelistic narratives had been with increasing literalism cast into the form of a reanimation of a physical body from a tomb, retreated almost beyond the ken of orthodox thought. So great was the emphasis on the real humanity of Jesus

---

[1] " The heresy that reduced the humanity of Christ to an illusive appearance was defeated in its direct aim, but it was victorious in so far as the glorified Christ was absolutely separated from and raised above all his fellows, till it became almost a paradox to say that ' He was in all points tempted like as we are ' " (Caird, *Evolution of Theology in the Greek Philosophers*, II, p. 366).

that even the ascended Lord was represented as taking again tangible form and enjoying table fellowship as of old with His followers. The danger to monotheism arising from Gnosticism was averted, but at considerable danger for the future of Christian theology, inasmuch as a Trinity arose which could only by desperate arguments be distinguished from tritheism. In opposition to the Gnostic plan of salvation wherein the soul of man was saved from its materialistic environment, the Church elaborated the literal resurrection of the flesh such as we find in Justin Martyr, Tertullian, and Augustine. The more refined Gnostic view of the ascent of the soul was rejected in favour of an apocalyptic eschatology in crude Jewish terms which has burdened Christianity to this day. Further, the Church so resented the Gnostic attack on the Old Testament that it gave to the Old Testament an influence in Christianity which promoted sacerdotalism and affected the Christian conception of God. Neither the Gnostics nor the orthodox were correct in their extreme attitudes to the Old Testament, the inferiority of which to the Christian message was pointed out by the Gnostic Marcion.

If the Church rescued the humanity of Jesus from being absorbed in His divinity, it rendered a great service by reaffirming the claims of history. But the dissolution of history into ideas did not cease either during or because of the Gnostic controversy. The speculation of Paul and the tendency to allegorize history or to resolve it into metaphysical ideas reached its consummation in the formulation of the Nicene and Chalcedonian Creeds. Origen takes the same stand to history: " His conviction is that when the development of religion has reached its highest level, anything historical or positive becomes of as little value as the idea of redemption and salvation itself." [1] This is borne out by such affirmations as ' Christ crucified is a teaching for babes ' and ' Happy are they who have come no longer to need

[1] Harnack, *Expansion*, I, p. 143.

God's Son as the physician who heals the sick or as the shepherd—people who now need not any redemption but wisdom, reason, and righteousness alone.' [1] It is striking to note how little interest the apologists take in the career of Jesus compared with their speculation in the pre-existent Christ, the two supreme questions of the early Church being the nature of this pre-existent Christ and his relation to God. An appreciation of the mythologizing of history whether in Philo or the New Testament or the Church Fathers is necessary to understand the evolution of Christian dogma, and particularly of Christology. And in this mythologizing of history the Gnostics differ from the orthodox only in the greater degree to which they carried it.

Gnosticism " left the world of thought to be fought for by two powers which joined issue over its corpse," [2] the revived Pagan enthusiasm, especially of Neo-Platonism, and the Christian philosophers of Alexandria, Clement and Origen and their successors, and the conflict has not always been decisive or the issue unambiguous. The Gnostics, conscious both of the worth of Greek culture and the moral power of Christianity, sought to absorb Christianity into Hellenism rather than Hellenism into Christianity. The orthodox, conscious of the dangerous fascination of Hellenism in alliance with nebular theosophy, in their reaction thrust Hellenism out as far as they could, though to a less extent than they imagined, in favour of the cruder and more severely moral and literal Judaistic heritage, and thus impoverished Christianity by closing to it sources of spirituality and idealism to which its greatest teachers ever gratefully return without disloyalty to Jesus or violence to its Jewish beginnings. The orthodox victory, with its over-emphases and its refusal to distribute the spoils of Gnosticism, compels modern Christianity, in the interest of permanence and universality, to reclaim

---

[1] *Com. in. Joh.* I. 22, Lom. I, p. 43, cited Harnack, *ib.*
[2] Gardner, *Growth of Christianity*, p. 100.

as its rightful heritage in the name of Christ the rich message of Hellas as the revelation of divine truth in history. By such a recognition Christianity will not become less Christian, but will incorporate new elements of power and deepen its content in its appeal to man's nature in its entirety.

If the struggle with Gnosticism and with Montanism led as a precautionary measure to the closing or crystallization of Revelation in a book, a tradition, and a holy office, the enemy has been sufficiently vanquished to enable us with safety to recognize to-day the possibility of fresh truth, as in the first generation, and to acknowledge the continued revealing activity of the Spirit of the Father who ' worketh up to the present.' We may also discover a deeper and more intimate content in Revelation by recognizing that it is not something dropped from another world and attested externally by miracle and guaranteed by an hierarchical office, but rather as something arising from and concomitant with all history as the record of those who from the beginning of time have been ' fellow-workers with God ' and in the oracular experiences of the soul through the ages.

There are two ways in which we should estimate Gnosticism:

First, by the remains of the Gnostics themselves. Too long have the Gnostics been condemned unheard at the bar of their ecclesiastical opponents,[1] who rarely understood them and more rarely had the grace to tell the truth dispassionately. The Church Fathers were controversialists—a difficult office in the present constitution of human nature. We should hear what the Gnostics,

---

[1] The Church Fathers " took minor and unimportant details and magnified them and treated them as the essentials of a system or systems. . . . The essential principles were largely the same throughout; the difference was chiefly in regard to details. It is this conduct on the part of the Fathers that gives us such a distorted and often ridiculous view of Gnosticism " (McGiffert, *Proleg. to Church History of Eusebius,* I, p. 179, n. 17, cited in Horner's tr. of *Pistis Sophia,* p. iv).

who were libelled by their opponents ' savage wild beasts,' ' sons of the Devil,' antichrists, mad dogs, liars, atheists, madmen, doomed to unquenchable fire, and were held guilty of nameless obscenities and ludicrous puerilities, have to say, and read their few extant prayers and their hymns. Even Hippolytus finds it difficult to make a good case against the Ophites in the Hymn of the Naassenes expressing the aspiration of the soul, in which they ' hymn all the mysteries of their error ':

> ' Now she weeps (and now) rejoices;
> Now laments (and now) is judged;
> Now is judged (and now) is dying.
> Now no outlet is left or she wandering
> The labyrinth of woes has entered,
> But Jesus said: Father, behold!
> A strife of woes upon Earth
> From thy breath has fallen,
> But she seeks to flee malignant chaos
> And knows not how to win through it.
> For this cause send me, O Father,
> Holding seals I will go down,
> Through entire aeons I will pass.
> All mysteries I will disclose;
> The forms of the gods I will display;
> The secrets of the holy way
> Called Gnosis, I will hand down.' [1]

He quotes a Naassene writer as saying, ' The beginning of perfection is the knowledge of man, but the knowledge of God is completed perfection,' surely an inoffensive tenet.

The *Hymn of the Soul* [2] presents with all the wealth of Oriental imagery the *mythos* of the descent and redemption of the Soul under the symbolism of a king's son gorgeously robed and sent into Egypt to bring a pearl guarded by a serpent. Seduced by the allurement of Egypt, he neglected his mission and forgot that he was

---

[1] *Philosophoumena*, tr. Legge, I, p. 145.

[2] In *Acts of Thomas*, 108-13; Eng. tr. by James, *Apoc. N.T.* p. 411 ff., by F. C. Burkitt as the *Hymn of Bardaisan*, and by G. R. S. Mead as the *Hymn of the Robe of Glory;* German tr. in original metre by Schultz, *Dokumente der Gnosis*, p. 13 ff. Cf. Bevan, *Texts and Studies*, V. 3; Hoffmann, *Zeitschr. f. neut. Wiss.*, IV, p. 273 ff.

a king's son until he received a missive from the homeland declaring—

' Unto our Son that is in Egypt, peace.
Rise up and wake out of sleep, and hearken unto the words of the
      letter,
And remember that thou art a king's son; lo, thou hast come under
      the yoke of bondage.
Remember the pearl. . . .
Remember thy garment spangled with gold. . . .
Thy name is named in the Book of Life.'

He bestirred himself, rescued the pearl from the serpent,
cast off his filthy garments, and ' directed my way
forthwith to the light of my Fatherland.' Laboriously
he made his return, arrayed himself in a resplendent
royal robe, and the father ' rejoiced over me and
received me with him into his palace '—a story of
aspiration and redemption which recalls the parable of
the Prodigal and in which the writer of the *Acts of
Thomas* probably saw [1] the descent of Christ through
the aeons to redeem the soul from the bondage of matter
and restore it cleansed to the Father.

From the *Acts of John* (106–7) may be cited the
admonition of the apostle before administering the
Eucharist:

' Brethren and fellow-servants and coheirs and partakers with me in the kingdom of the Lord, ye know the
Lord, how many mighty works He hath granted you
by my means. . . . Be ye therefore established in Him,
remembering Him in your every deed, knowing the
mystery of the dispensation which hath come to pass
towards men, for what cause the Lord hath accomplished
it. . . . Let not then our good God be grieved, . . .
even our God Jesus Christ, who is above every name
that we can utter or conceive, and more exalted. Let
Him rejoice with us because we walk aright, let Him
be glad because we live purely, let Him be refreshed
because our conversation is sober. Let Him be without
care because we live continently, let Him be pleased

[1] So Preuschen, *Zwei Gnost. Hymnen,* p. 46 ff.; Bousset, *Hauptprobleme,* p. 252 ff.

because we communicate one with another, let Him smile because we are chaste, let Him be merry because we love Him.'

Or his pre-eucharistic prayer (108), which is more in the spirit of Bernard of Clairvaux than the utterance of ' savage beasts ':

' O Jesu, who hast woven this crown with Thy weaving, who hast joined together these many blossoms into the unfading flower of Thy countenance, who hast sown in them these words: Thou only tender of Thy servants, and physician who healest freely: only doer of good and despiser of none, only merciful and lover of men, only saviour and righteous, only seer of all, who art in all and everywhere present and containing all things and filling all things. Christ Jesu, God, Lord, that with Thy gifts and Thy mercy shelterest them that trust in Thee, that knowest clearly the wiles and the assaults of him that is everywhere our adversary, which he deviseth against us: do Thou only, O Lord, succour Thy servants by Thy visitation. Even so, Lord ! '

The final prayer of the dying apostle bears resemblances to the language of Augustine:

' O Thou who hast kept me until this hour for Thyself and untouched by union with a woman: who when in my youth I desired to marry didst appear unto me and say to me, John, I have need of thee: who didst prepare for me also a sickness of the body: who, when for the third time I would marry, didst forthwith prevent me, and then at the third hour of the day saidst unto me on the sea: John, if thou hadst not been Mine I should have suffered thee to marry: . . . who didst save me from the temporal fantasy and lead me into that which endureth always: who didst rid me of the foul madness that is in the flesh: who didst take me from the bitter death and establish me on Thee alone: who didst muzzle the secret disease of my soul and cut off the open deed: who didst afflict and banish him that raised tumult in me: who didst make my love of Thee spotless: . . . now therefore, Lord, whereas I have accomplished the dispensation wherewith I was entrusted, account me worthy of Thy rest, and grant me that end in Thee which is salvation unspeakable and unutterable. . . . And grant me to accomplish the journey unto Thee without suffering insolence or provocation, and to receive that which Thou hast promised unto them that live purely and have loved Thee only.' [1]

In Valentinus' faith there was a cordial acceptance of the beatitude of Jesus (Matt. v. 8): ' There is one Good, whose presence is the manifestation by the Son, and through Him alone can the heart become pure and every evil spirit be banished from the heart. . . . When the only good Father visits the soul, it is sanctified and becomes radiant with light. He who has such a heart is blessed because he shall see God.' [2]

The use of the canonical Psalms and the *Odes of Solomon* [3] in the circles of the *Pistis Sophia* gives some indication of the warmth of Gnostic piety as also Gnostic taste in hymnody. In the section of the *Pistis Sophia* known as *The Books of the Saviour* Jesus instructs His disciples: ' Whenever I should go unto the Light, preach ye to all the world, say unto them, Desist not in the day with the night seeking, and hold not yourselves back even until ye find the mysteries of the kingdom of the Light '; and then to the refrain ' that ye may be worthy of the mysteries of the Light ' follow the Renunciations: ' Renounce all this world with all the matter which is in it, with all its cares, and with all its sins,' together with ' the murmuring,' ' the listening,' ' litigiousness,' ' false calumny,' ' false witnessings,' ' the boastings with the prides,' ' the gluttony,' ' the garrulity,' ' the wiles which are evil,' ' the lovings of the greater portion,' ' the lovings of the world,' ' the robberies,' ' the

---

[1] *Acts of John,* 112-14; tr. by James.

[2] Cited by Clement, *Strom.* II. 20; 114, 3; reading παρουσία for παρρησία.

[3] Cf. Gunkel, in *Zeit. f. d. neutest. Wiss.* IX. 1910.

words which are evil,' ' the wickednesses,' ' the angers,'
' the curse,' ' the blasphemy,' ' the thievings,' ' the
slander,' ' the fightings and the quarrellings,' ' the
ignorance,' ' the villanies,' ' the senselessness,' ' the
adulteries,' ' the murders,' ' the unmercifulnesses with
the impiousnesses,' ' the godlessnesses,' ' the witchcraft,'
' the blaspheming,' ' the teaching of error.'   Then
follow exhortations and promises: ' do love of man,'
be meek, be peaceable, be merciful, do alms, ' minister
unto the poor with those that are sick,' ' do love of
God,' be righteous, be good, and ' receive the mysteries
of the Light.' [1]

In view of the many calumnies of the morality of the
Gnostics, many citations could be given to prove that
the peril to morality was the excessive chastity or encratism which was also practised by their orthodox
brethren.

Secondly, Gnosticism should be judged also by
observing that it was the strongest and sanest opponents
of Gnosticism who felt its power and recognized the
rights of *Gnosis* besides *Pistis,* especially the writer of
the Fourth Gospel, Ignatius, Clement, and Origen.

The writer of the Fourth Gospel made even greater
concessions to the Gnosis,[2] which he recognized as

---

[1] *Pistis Sophia,* 235a-239b; tr. by G. Horner, pp. 128-31.

[2] Schaeder's brilliant attempt to construe the Prologue of the Fourth
Gospel as the Christianizing re-working of a Gnostic hymn in conjunction with later Jewish Gnostic material seems unconvincing
(*Studien z. ant. Synkretismus,* pp. 306-32, 350). He summarizes:
" Die mandäische und die evangelische Überlieferung schöpfen gemein-
sam aus einer älteren Tradition, die von Johannes aufgenommen und
von seinen Jüngern auf ihn selber bezogen wurde, und die dann von den
Johannes-jüngern einerseits an die Verfasser der Evangelienquelle Q
und des IV. Evangeliums, anderseits—durch unbekannte Zwischen-
glieder—in das Chaos der mandäischen Überlieferung gelangte " and
" Der Prolog des IV. Evangeliums ist, wie die Rekonstruktion seiner
aramäischen Urgestalt lehrt, die christianisierende Bearbeitung eines
gnostischen Hymnus, der mit Hilfe der—bei den Mandäern fortlebenden
—Hauptsymbole der spätjüdischen Gnosis die Einheit des in Welt
kommenden göttlichen Gesandten Enos mit dem Lichte der göttlichen
' Wortes ' (Memra) feiert."

endangering Christian truth, than he did to the regnant sacramentarianism. His scheme of salvation is one of illumination and of revelation by the eternal Logos rather than one of redemption by the historic transactions of the passion-history. The glorified Son draws men to Himself and grants participation in the heavenly glory. This salvation, as against Paul, was accessible only to those spiritually endowed, a striking aspect of the writer's strong predestinarianism. Life and Light are the highest boons bestowed by the Logos Christ. The means of the acquisition of this eternal Life and its content consist in ' knowing the only genuine God and His Apostle Jesus Christ.'

The dualism between God and the World, Light and Darkness, is almost as pronounced as in the system He was combating. God is transcendent as in Gnosticism, but the gulf is bridged by one divine though subordinate Being who fulfils all the functions of the aeons. Jesus' ' works ' and ' powers ' become ' signs,' the inner meaning of which is disclosed in discourses.

Ignatius, who was conversant with Gnostic pretensions in Asia Minor and cognisant of the dangerous fascination of Gnosis, likewise used Gnostic methods and offered Gnostic satisfaction to overcome the Docetism he so dreaded. In emphasizing the incarnation and the reality of the sufferings of Christ, in the corporeity of the eucharistic presence, in his opposition to excessive allegorism and to the rigours of asceticism, he stood resolutely apart from Gnosticism. But he did not hesitate to employ its mysticism, or to speak of ' the Logos proceeding forth from the Silence ' (*Magn.* 8). Christians may ' always partake of God ' (*Eph.* 4) and be ' filled with God ' (*Magn.* 14). In the ' three mysteries of crying ' which deceived ' the Archon of this aeon ' and the ' star above all stars ' (*Eph.* 19) there appears a " Gnostic colouring " as detected by Lightfoot. Similarly the cosmic elements in Paul are enlarging toward Gnosticism in the sure judgment awaiting ' the heavenly existences ' and ' the visible and invisible principalities ' which do not believe in the blood of Christ (*Smyr.* 6).

Clement is the most striking example of how advantageously Christianity might have been presented so as to satisfy the legitimate demands of the Gnostic for a philosophy of history and for a comprehensive theology. He understood Gnosticism and he welcomed philosophy and mysticism in the interpretation of the facts of Christian history. To Clement the true Christian is the true Gnostic, and the true Gnostic is ' the Lord's brother and friend and son.' [1] The Gnostic ' practises being God ' and ' has already become God.' [2]

Similarly, to Origen, Christianity was Gnosis, but the true and only Gnosis. Though he recognized the dangers of an aristocratic religion [3] in which salvation was rather the rescue of the spiritual moiety of men out of the general class of natural, in holding that only the ' imperfect ' require works [4] he stood not far apart from Valentinus' teaching that men are saved by becoming wholly spiritual [5] rather than by works.

And no Christian philosopher elaborated a more comprehensive philosophy of history than did Origen in his *Principia*. A devoted Platonist, a sympathetic and shrewd critic of extravagant Gnosticism, a daring metaphysician, a thorough Biblical scholar, his range of speculation was vaster than that of the only other three Christian thinkers who might be compared with him, John of Damascus, Aquinas, and Calvin. For him Christianity must embrace more than personal salvation and forgiveness within the limits of an apocalyptic scheme. It must give some definite guidance on the great problems on which earnest minds were engaged —the origin of the world and of orders of spiritual being,

---

[1] *Str.* III. 10.   [2] *Ib.* IV. 23.
[3] *C. Celsum*, VII. 60.
[4] *In Ezech. Hom.* III. 4, IV, p. 47, Lomm.
[5] Cf. Irenaeus, *Adv. Haer.* I. 6.

of deliverance from finitude and the attainment of deathlessness. Hence in this first Christian *Summa* there
appears a comprehensive world-view—angels, reprobate
and faithful, demons, planets and ensouled stars, men,
and a descending Redeemer execute the will of a
Supreme God.

Had Origen secured a hearing or had successors to
him arisen, the Church's victory over Gnosticism would
have proved less perilous and would have issued in a
liberalizing and expansive tendency rather than in a
narrowing and codifying process with anathemas of
excommunication.

CHAPTER XXII

RELIGION AS A THERAPEUTIC IN PAGAN AND CHRISTIAN CIRCLES

RELIGION and Healing were closely associated in the Graeco-Roman world. *Soteria* connoted to both Pagans and Christians more than its special meaning to us; it connoted health of body and of soul, for neither Christians nor Pagans distinguished rigidly between physical ills of body and maladies of soul. The philosopher, the Christian teacher, and the medical practitioner were all *healers*. The word *soteria* meant *safety, health* in fullest human sense, and alleviation of pain to which individualism had rendered people more sensitive. Medical language was used in moral teaching and preaching, religious language in the work of medicine. Vices were diseases in the eyes of Christian teachers and Stoic and Platonic moralists. Even sacraments were spoken of as medicine, baptism being ' medicinal water ' and the Eucharist ' medicine of immortality,' and penance a *vera de satisfactione medicina*. Philosophy is to Porphyry ' the *salvation* of the soul,' and ' the medicine of our doctrine ' [1] is the cure of every rational soul. Clement, using the same medical language, says:

' Censure is like a surgical operation on the passions of the soul. The latter are abscesses on the body of the truth, and they must be cut open by the lancet of censure. Censure is like the application of a medicine which breaks up the callosities of the passions, and cleanses the impurities of a lewd life, reducing the

---

[1] Origen, *C. Celsum*, III. 54.

swollen flesh of pride, and restoring the man to health and truth once more.' [1]

' Even as the physician secures health for those who co-operate with him to that end, so does God secure eternal salvation for those who co-operate with Him for knowledge *and good behaviour.*' [2] This ancient alliance of religion and medicine, which has been ratified afresh in the various forms of psychotherapy in ministering to minds diseased and in the general recognition that the physician must know the inner history of his patient to minister to his physical diseases, is quite explicable in the conditions of the Graeco-Roman age.[3] The break-up of collectivism and the dominance of individualism with a deepening inwardness and a new emotionalism produced a keen sensitiveness to suffering. '' The refinements of material civilization and mental culture made people more sensitive to the element of pain in life. . . . There was a real demand for *purity, consolation, expiation,* and *healing,* and as these could not be found elsewhere, they began to be sought in *religion.*'' [4] Men faced suffering in the same twofold fashion of to-day, desiring an escape (*soteria*) or seeking support in it from a fellow-being or a supernatural being —a desire for *sympathia* which made ' man a sacred thing to man ' (Seneca), and which heightened the prestige of the Mystery-gods, who each and all offered *sympathia* in a communion or identification, and this was a fellowship of deities who had themselves been previously either ' men of sorrows ' or divine sufferers.

Moreover, beside a fairly advanced science of medicine, as witnessed by the works of Hipparchus and Galen, and the surgical finds in Pompeii, and numerous

---

[1] *Paed.* I. 8, 64 f., cited Harnack, *Expansion of Christianity,* I, p. 140 f., whence tr.

[2] *Strom.* VII. 7, 48, tr. *ib.* p. 142.

[3] Cf. C. R. Simboli, *Disease-Spirits and Divine Cures among the Greeks and Romans* (New York, 1921).

[4] Harnack, *op. cit.* p. 127.

medical practitioners, there was still a strong belief, not
only among the populace but among the enlightened, in
what was regarded as supernatural or faith-healings.
When physicians failed, sufferers had still the temple-
hospitals to visit. Hospitals were not as numerous and
as accessible as to-day and medical practitioners were
not such a numerous brotherhood.

In a less scientific age than our own there were
abundant opportunities for the religious cultivation of
the healing art. We must remember that it took the
highly efficient medical science of to-day centuries to
sever its original connexions with magic and alchemy,
and the identity of the barber and the dentist belongs
to no remote antiquity. Mediaeval London of six centuries ago stood nearer to this ancient period in the
practice of calling in the priest rather than a doctor in
cases of severe wounds. There were also psychopathic
conditions in the ancient world, as to-day, which could
not be assigned exclusively to either the medical
or to the religious department, and common sense
wisely assigned them to both. Such was demon-
possession, which covered a large number of
modern nerve-derangements and abnormal psychic
states.

In the origins of our own faith we find the same
alliance of religion and healing, an alliance which
obtained throughout centuries and has left the ' Good
Physician ' as one of the titles of the Christian Saviour.
Jesus, despite the fact that He looked upon cures as
generally interruptions to His main work and the cause
of deceptive popularity, occasionally exercised the
healing virtues that were usually expected from prophets
and men of God, and with such success that He was
probably the most popular physician in Galilee. He
used the language of medicine (Mark ii. 17, Luke v. 31),
and admitted that the popular proverb ' Physician, heal
thyself,' might be applied to Himself, whose motto was
to find life by laying it down. Like His contemporaries,

He did not strictly differentiate between physical and spiritual ailments. Like His contemporaries, He regarded various form of mental disturbances and nervous diseases as due to demon-possession, which He on occasion, by His commanding authority, expelled, and proved an efficient exorcist even in cases that baffled His disciples, though in others He failed through the absence of concomitant faith (Mark vi. 5, 6).

The Gospels portray Jesus as physician both of body and of soul, but that the emphasis laid by the Gospels, especially by Mark, on Jesus' miracles of healing and exorcisms and their evidential value is much exaggerated and represents rather a rescript of the popular beliefs of the early Church and the demand for signs, the Gospels themselves give evidence. No professed wonderworker or healer would have left a crowd of sick people, after healing some of them, and fled before dawn from his usual abode to a quiet place outside the town and not only refused to return at the entreaty of his disciples, who were sensitive to their Master's popularity and to the appeal of physical sufferings, but affirmed that he must go elsewhere to *preach,* a mission which was threatened by the healings which Jesus' compassion rendered a temptation to Him.

That He claimed no monopoly of the performance of exorcisms or any exclusive method is also clear, as He admitted that even His critics could do the same. He sternly rebuked His disciples for their attempt to hinder others in the exercise of exorcisms.

The words whereby Jesus describes His work in Luke vii. 18, Matthew xi. 2 ff. are the symbolic expressions of a prophet describing the religious revival of his people in the language of healing, as Hosea described such a revival as a ' raising up again.' If taken literally, as physical signs, they would render pointless the Baptist's mission as they exhibit all the exterior signs that could be wished for. And Luke's attempt to render the words into physical acts by bringing certain classes of diseases on the spot to be dealt with as outward evidences is only partially successful inasmuch as the lepers and the dead are absent. Further, this array of faith-healings culminating in ' dead men are being raised ' leads to an anti-climax in ' the outcastes are receiving the good news.'   Finally, if this were a catalogue of such outward signs as Luke states, it renders otiose the clause, ' Blessed is he whosoever is not offended in Me,' as even the most sign-seeking age or prophet would be satisfied and find no cause of ' offence ' in such a list.

Jesus' consistent attitude toward sign-seeking, which he characterized as the expression or symptom of an ' adulterous and sinful generation ' and which He refused to satisfy, would be stultified if His miraculous works bulked so largely in His mission as they do on the pages of the Gospels, to the writers of which ' wonders ' and ' powers ' and ' signs ' were buttresses of Messianic faith.   Jesus realized that in His day, as in our advanced age, crowds are more actuated by the *Wundersucht* than by love of the eternal things; such gatherings are no evidence that there are more physical invalids than spiritual invalids in the world.

It is questionable whether Jesus commanded His followers to carry on a practice of the disadvantages of which He was acutely aware, but it is certain that in the early Church, with its popular character, healings and preaching were looked upon as conjoint missionary work.   When a member of the Christian society grew ill, it would have been a breach of faith to call in a professional physician; the non-scientific elders were to be summoned, who by their prayers and the age-long beneficent custom of massage or unction with oil were to restore the sick.   The Christians thus acted like their fellow-townsmen in the Jewish synagogue, who called in the rabbi instead of the doctor.[1]   The explanation offered in case of the decease of the sick believer we

1 Cf. Wetstein, *Ad Jac*. V. 14; Mayor, *Ep. of St. James*, pp. 169-73.

are not given, and as the mortality rates among Christians would be approximately the same as among non-Christians, the situation must sometimes have been delicate. The dangerous epidemic in Corinth was not to be arrested by medical prophylactics, but by a proper observance of the Love-feast, the abuses of the elements of which had caused the epidemic resulting in the deaths of several members. *Charismata,* or gifts of healings, were among the more spectacular gifts which abounded in the same community, causing envy and being rated by its apostolic founder as inferior to the ' more excellent way ' of love.

In the early Christian propaganda the Gospel was presented as a therapeutic of body, mind, and soul. The preacher was a physical healer, and such ' powers of healings ' were greatly prized as a boon to sufferers and as corroborating the truth of the message. He also preached a Lord who was *Saviour,* and this Saviour meant Redeemer-Healer, the potency of whose Name was above the potency of His competitor *saviours,* whose saving-acts could not be denied but were merely treated as inferior or performed for ulterior evil ends, or inspired by demons.

Jesus was preached as the Redeemer-Healer, as the Great Physician who saves and restores life. A Church historian [1] describes Jesus, in language taken from a medical textbook of pseudo-Hipparchus, as: ' Like some excellent physician, in order to cure the sick, Jesus examines what is repulsive, handles sores, and reaps pain Himself from the sufferings of others.' The vogue of the term ' physician ' in reference to Jesus in the early centuries indicates not only how widely human was the conception of His functions, but also testifies to the deep sense of need of the centuries when Paganism and Christianity stood face to face. A prayer from that afflicted age was restored to us in an inscription found at Timgad in 1919: ' Come Thou to our help, O Christ;

[1] Eusebius, *H.E.* X. 4, 11; tr. Harnack, *Expansion,* I, p. 136.

way it does not follow that he who can foretell the
future is on that account an honest and upright man.
One is not in a position to prove the virtuous character
of those who heal diseases and foretell the future. Many
instances may be adduced of people being healed who
did not deserve to live, people who were so corrupt and
led a life of such wickedness that no sensible physician
would have troubled to cure them. . . . The power of
healing diseases is no evidence of anything specially
divine.'

The work of the Church embraced the functions of
the medical profession, the nursing profession, and the
ministry of preaching. Care of the sick of body was its
duty as much as soul-culture, and people devoted their
lives to Christ the Healer as others did to Aesculapius
the Healer. Its inspiration was ' the kindness and
philanthropy of God our Saviour.' Christianity—

" did more than set up the actual Jesus against the
imaginary Aesculapius of dreamland. Deliberately and
consciously it assumed the form of ' the religion of
salvation or healing,' or ' the medicine of soul and body,'
and at the same time it recognized that one of its cardinal
duties was to care assiduously for the sick in body." [1]

The associations of medicine cling to the ideals of the
Church. Reference has been made to the summoning
of the elders and unction with oil in James, which is
not mentioned as something novel in the life of the
community. The words on the return of the disciples
to Jesus, ' they anointed with oil them that were sick,'
depict rather the condition of the Church in the days
when the evangelist wrote. Elders are charged to care
for the sick and neglect no poor person.[2] The presiding
officer (bishop) is to dispense from the weekly offerings
of the local ecclesia to those who are in want through
sickness.[3]

---

[1] Harnack, *Expansion*, I, p. 131.
[2] Polycarp, VI. 1.   [3] Justin, *Apol.* I. 67.

In the developing organization of the Church the bishop [1] became the centre of supervision of the sick and poor relief, and under him were deacons and female assistants or deaconesses. The bishop is himself compared to a physician or surgeon. The deacons are to be ' the eyes of the bishop,' inquiring not only into the conduct of Church members, but ' let them find out the physically sick and tell the congregation who are in ignorance of them that they may be visited, and let them supply the wants [of the sick] according to the decision of the president.' [2] The following description from the *Apostolic Constitutions* of the duties and qualifications of a ' widow ' sounds very modern : ' She is to be obliging and sober, she is to report cases of need to the elders, she is not to be greedy or addicted to drink, in order that she may be able to keep sober for calls to service during the night.' [3]

So insistent was the Church on its duty of caring for the sick that none was exempted on the ground of not being a trained nurse or skilled in medicine : ' The sick are not to be overlooked, nor is anyone to say that he has not been trained to this mode of service. No one is to plead a comfortable life, or the unwonted character of the duty, as a pretext for not being helpful to other people.' [4]

Pagans were in agreement with Christians in making healing a part of religion, and though Christians were on the whole conspicuous in the exercise of love, the virtues of loving-kindness and care for the sick were not neglected by their Pagan contemporaries. The ideal of humanity of the ancient physicians is attested by the instruction given in the *Parangeliae* of Pseudo-Hipparchus :

---

[1] Probably in many cases himself a physician; cf. Harnack, *Expansion*, I, p. 149.
[2] Ps.-Clem. *Ep. ad Jac.* XII; tr. Harnack, *op. cit.* p. 150.
[3] Cited Harnack, *op. cit.* p. 149.
[4] Harnack, *op. cit.* p. 150.

' I charge you not to show yourselves inhuman, but to take the wealth or poverty [of the patient] into account, in certain cases even to treat them gratis and to consider future gratitude more than present fame. If, therefore, the summons for aid happens to be the case of an unknown or impecunious man, he is most of all to be assisted; for wherever there is love to one's neighbour, it means readiness to act.' [1]

The unscientific and popular view predominated in the early Church. Christians, convinced that Christ was ' Healer ' in the double sense, were inclined to despise [2] the medical profession as the possession of heathendom and as identical with magical operations, and to trust to their own methods of cure by fasting, prayer, the use of the potency of the Name of Jesus, and by unction with oil. Yet the leading Church Fathers did not accept this rejection of the use of recognized medical means, but the popular view proved more tenacious, and in the first conflict of science and religion in Christianity, science was denied its rights, only to claim them in later centuries, after the science of medicine had passed through its dark ages of neglect of inquiry and experiment.

Another evidence of the persistence of the unscientific popular spirit and the contact of religion and disease was the widespread belief that God used diseases and plagues to punish the unbelievers and the enemies of Christianity. Both Pagans and Christians stood on the same footing, the former accusing Christians of the calamities and sufferings which fell thick and fast upon the Mediterranean world in the third and fourth centuries. This argument must often have proved as broken a reed in Christian hands as that of matching Pagan

---

[1] Harnack, *Expansion*, I, p. 128.

[2] '' Muss man sich freilich erinnern, dass die Medicin mit Zauberei, Astrologie, und dem ganzen Apparat des Heidentums zusammenhing, und dass die Christen ihre eigene Methode der Heilung hatten. Dennoch verwarfen die grossen Kirchenväter die Medicin als solche nicht '' (Harnack, *Medicinisches aus der ältesten Kirchengeschichte*, p. 56).

miracle with Christian miracle,[1] and Pagan exorcisms with Christian exorcisms. But it offered a crude exhibition of justice and satisfied the popular clamant demand for visibility in the operations of deity. If the apocalyptist John, somewhat forgetful of the dying prayer of Jesus, exercises his imagination in inventing tortures for the majority of mankind who have persecuted the elect, and if the Christian jurist Tertullian can represent part of the bliss of Christians hereafter as the contemplation of their opponents in torture in hell, it need not astonish us that some premonitory examples of this retribution were enacted here, despite the view that the victims of the collapse of the tower of Siloam are not necessarily thereby adjudged sinners beyond the survivors. The writer of Acts represents Judas as dying not by his own hand, as in Matthew, but by an accident on his own farm.

As we journey to-day from the ruins and museum of Epidaurus to the Roman Cathedral with its black Virgin overlooking Algiers in the ancient province of Mauretania and on to Lourdes, it is difficult to realize that one has traversed such distances in miles or in era. After all that time and Christian fanaticism have done to Epidaurus,[2] the personal testimony still graven on stones and the *vota* of the limbs or portions of the body healed by the great Healer belong to the same world of ideas [3]

---

[1] E.g. both Pagans and Christians turned to their respective apologetic purposes the legend of the Thundering Legion and the providential rainfall, the Christians by attributing the happy issue to their prayers, and the Pagans with equal conviction assigning it to their prayers, directed to the Immortal Gods, especially to Jupiter Pluvius, as on the Antonine column. Cf. Dio Cassius, LXXI. 8; Tert. *Apol.* 5; Orosius, VII. 17; Eusebius, *H.E.* V. 5.

[2] For account of the excavations by the Greek Archaeological Society, vide *Ephemeris Archaeol.* 1883, p. 197, 1887.

[3] Consult Frazer's note, *Pausanias,* III, p. 248 ff. The cures include Thyson, a blind boy; Cleon, a woman with child five years; Arata's daughter for dropsy; an Aristagora of Troezen with a worm in her stomach, whose head was cut off by the sons of Aesculapius, the worm removed, and then she was sewed up; Gorgias, for an arrow wound received in battle in one lung.

as the votive offerings crowding the walls in the modern
Catholic cathedral of Algiers or in its shrine of Lourdes.
They are alike attestations of the reality of faith-cures
and the potency of expectation and suggestion and the
control of spirit over body. Of course as a weapon of
religious apologetic such cures lose their force as also
taking place daily on those who have little or no religious
sympathies and at the hands of " unordained " doctors.
Exorcisms are being performed to-day both without and
within the Church.

Pagans and Christians alike turned to religion for
healing of mind and body, and the boundaries between
religious ritual, magical incantations, and medical
prescriptions were somewhat fluctuating.[1] Serapis early
added to his popularity by taking over the functions of
Aesculapius or by being through *theocrasia* identified [2]
with him, and at least in one of his shrines there is
evidence of a chapel of Aesculapius being attached.[3] At
Serapis' shrine of Canopus, Strabo [4] found multitudes
of patients of all ranks of society attracted by the
miraculous cures of the god. His consort Isis was
equally celebrated for her miraculous cures [5] ; even
hopeless cases of inveterate disease were successfully
treated by her deity, so that her priests could confidently
point to the walking testimonies of her divine healing.[6]
In the National Museum of Naples to-day may be seen
the *vota* once offered by her grateful clients in the local

---

[1] " The conditions of health and disease are so obscure, the influences of will and imagination on our bodily states are so marked, that, in all ages, the boundaries between the natural and the unknowable are blurred and may be easily crossed. The science of medicine, even down to the age of Hipparchus or the age of Galen, had not abandoned all faith in the magical and mysterious. Incantations long held their ground beside more scientific remedies " (Dill, *Rom. Society from Nero*, p. 459).

[2] Bouché-Leclercq, *Rev. de l'hist. des relig.*, 1902, p. 30.

[3] Cf. De Preslé, *Le Sérapeum de Memphis*, p. 261 ff.

[4] XVII. 17. For other miracles of Serapis, cf. *Oxyrh. Papyri*, 1242, and O. Weinrich, *Neue Urkunden zur Serapis-Religion*, pp. 12, 19, 31.

[5] Cf. *C.I.G.* 2304; *C.I.G.* II. 3386.

[6] Diod. Sic. I. 25.

temple. In her temples painted representations [1] of cures prompted prayers from expectant sufferers, as in Tibullus: [2]

> ' Nunc Dea, nunc sucurre mihi, nam posse mederi
> Picta docet templis multa tabella tuis.'

The institutions of religion extended their organization to embrace the medical functions, and by this means undoubtedly increased their endowments and their clientele. If our modern cathedrals had physicians enrolled on their staffs and also managed the hotels in which their patients resided, it would give us some idea of the condition of affairs in important centres of the Graeco-Roman world. *Incubatio*,[3] the practice of sleeping by proxy or personally within the consecrated precincts of the temple, was much in vogue, and on the site of Epidaurus to this day the ground-plans both of accommodation for tourists and of a dormitory for inquiring sleepers-in are traceable. The chief object of the *enkoimesis* was to be vouchsafed a dream-oracle of directions as to the curative treatment.[4] As in every beneficent institution, there was opportunity in *incubatio* to impose on credulity and to practise charlatanry for the profit of a religious centre. Also from the constitution of our nature all patients would not be alike psychically responsive and their imagination would require artificial aid or even deception from the temple acolytes. No doubt, in many cases robed human beings did service for the theophany and human lips whispered to the occupants of the *incubatio* ward the generally wholesome directions and dietary. But after discounting liberally for all such imposture and for the greed of grasping

---

[1] Cf. Caton, *Temples and Ritual of Asklepios*, p. 36 f.

[2] I. 3, 27.

[3] Cf. Hamilton, *Incubation, or Cure of Disease in Pagan Temples and Christian Churches* (London, 1906); Walton, *Cult of Asklepios*, pp. 57-66; Deubner, *De Incubatione*.

[4] In Greece to-day the practice of patients sleeping in the shrine of a favourite ikon or saint is still known. In Southern Italy and Sicily to-day the sick often prefer a local patron saint or madonna to physic.

priesthoods, there is abundant evidence [1] that to faith and psychically-predisposed patients such salutary dream-oracles were granted and such ' appearances ' vouch-safed. To understand adequately the hold of Aesculapius on his worshippers, or indeed to put ourselves *en rapport* with ancient religious possibilities, we must keep in mind that divine epiphanies and the reception of supernatural messages belonged to the accepted creeds of Pagans and Christians. [2] It did not occur to Christian contemporaries to set down the therapeutic appearances of their healing rivals to fraud, but rather to attribute them to demons or to demon-infected statues of the gods. Origen did not seek to evade the difficulty of Celsus' appeal to the numerous and even contemporary ' appearances ' of Aesculapius by denying them. Nor did Jerome deny such divine visits of Aesculapius at Epidaurus in the first half of the fifth century. [3] Christians in Rome could not dispute the testimony, engraved on stone, of Roman officials who had personally experienced the salutary vision. Besides, if there were shrewd priests there were also shrewd patients, all of whom could not be deceived. Psychology also renders it unnecessary to appeal to fraud. The tense expectancy of relief on the part of acute sufferers, the medical treatment with drug and herb, the infectious faith of the ministrant priests, and the evidence in stone and clay and lead and on painted canvas of those who had received their desires with the additional testimony from the lips of convalescent or restored friends and acquaintances, the prescribed religious-dietary fasting, the overwrought brain and racked nerve, the vesper prayers and promises of religion, the injunction of silence, and the catholic belief in mysterious interven-

---

[1] Cf., e.g., *Oxy. Pap.* 1381, 102 ff.

[2] Cf. L. Weniger, *Theophanien; altgriechische Götteradvente (Archiv f. Religionsw.* XXII, pp. 16-57): Pfister, in Pauly-Wissowa, IV, Supp. p. 277 ff.; epiphany of the God and healings, *ib.* 295.

[3] *In Is.* 55 (p. 482).

tions—these and other conditions all contributed toward the end sought by the patients.[1]

Apart from the dream-oracles of *incubatio,* the whole religious-medical régime was calculated to work for the restoration of numerous worshipper-patients. If the ancients were shrewd enough to advertise their demonstrable cases of successful miraculous healing to attest their science-faith and to be reticent on their failures, they merely used the discretion observed among faith-healers to-day. But similar conditions would produce similar results then and now. The change to a bracing and beautiful spot, the regulation of diet, the complete rest, gymnastic exercises,[2] the comforts of religious ritual, lecture-rooms [3] to divert or occupy the mind, the virtues of naturally or artificially medicated springs, the assiduous attendance of nurses, produced results similar to those at numerous spas to-day.

The vogue of the comprehensive idea of *soteria* as physical-spiritual, and the universal inclination to seek healing in religion are attested by the extraordinary growth of the cult of Aesculapius,[4] who from being a local Thessalian earth-demon became the great œcumenical Saviour-God [5] in the second and third centuries. Not without reason was it believed by the ancients,

' To mortals Apollo [6] gave Aesculapius and Plato;
  The One a healer of the body, the Other a healer of the soul.'

He had established his reputation in Rome as early as 290 B.C., when, summoned from Epidaurus, he stayed a great pestilence. His shrines multiplied with wonderful rapidity through the lands of the Mediterranean basin.

---

[1] Cf. Dill, *Roman Society from Nero,* p. 460 f.
[2] E.g. Dittenberger, *Sylloge,* 3rd ed. III. 1170, 9; cf. Allbutt, *Greek Medicine in Rome,* p. 462.
[3] Cf. Traemer, in Roscher, *Ausführ. Lex.* I, col. 631.
[4] Cf. A. Walton, *The Cult of Asklepios,* in *Cornell Studies in Class. Phil.* III.
[5] Cf. Farnell, *Higher Aspects of Greek Religion,* p. 123.
[6] Apollo himself is the Physician (e.g. Aristophanes, *Birds,* 584).

29

He attracted sufferers under the name of religion to each
of his shrines, as to-day does Lourdes. He was so
helpful and granted such gracious appearances of
himself, that he proved one of the last of the competitors
of Christ to yield. And when he yielded he bequeathed
to his more successful rival a salvationist terminology
and sound rules of health which were to carry men on
through many centuries. He won from sincere hearts
such titles as ' Saviour of the world,' [1] ' the great Joy
to all mortals,' [2] Lord,[3] Healer, ' Gentle One,' ' the
greatest lover of men.' By his miracles of healing he
evoked enthusiasm such as expressed in the following
prayer: [4]

' These are the words of thy loving servant, O
Asklepios, child of Leto's son. How shall I come into
thy golden house, O blessed one, O God of my longing,
unless thy heart is favourable to me and thou art willing
to heal me and establish me again in thy shrine, that
I may behold my God who is brighter than the earth
in springtime? Thou alone, O divine and blessed one,
art mighty. Thee, that lovest compassion, the Supreme
Gods have granted as a mighty boon to mortals, as a
refuge from their sorrows.'

In his sanatoria men acquired health of body and
restoration of mind. The evidences of his humane
services are abundant both from inscriptions and
archaeological remains and from literature. ' His
oracles are everywhere on earth.' [5] His sanatoria were
found in Ephesus, Pergamum, the island of Cos, Tricca,
in Corinth, in Athens, in Rome on an island of the
Tiber, Tarentum, Aegae, and elsewhere.

Pausanias,[6] the archaeologist, records of the temple of
Epidaurus: ' Inside the enclosure pillars had been

---

[1] Julian, *Orat.* IV. 153*b*.
[2] Pausanias, II. 26, 6 (171).   [3] Aristides, 72.
[4] *C.I.A.* III. 171. Farnell's tr., *Greek Hero-Cults,* p. 277.
[5] Julian, *Against the Galileans,* 235*c*.   [6] II. 27, 3; cf. 36, 1.

erected: of old there were many, but in my day six still remain, and on these are inscribed the names of the men and women who had been cured by Aesculapius with the addition of the disease from which each patient suffered and the means of the cure.' Strabo,[1] the geographer, records that Aesculapius ' has his temple always full both of the patients and of those engaged in erecting votive tablets inscribed with the cures effected, as in Cos and Tricca.'

Aristides' eulogy on Aesculapius is based on personal testimony. It is too long to cite, but extracts may give an idea of this first-hand testimony: ' Both great and many are the powers ($\delta\nu\nu\acute{a}\mu\epsilon\iota\varsigma$, miracles) of Aesculapius, or rather of all kinds.' ' He it is who disposes and guides all things, the saviour of all and guardian of the immortals.' ' I have heard several who told how in the straits of sea-voyages the god appeared and reached out his hand.' ' O my Master ($\delta\acute{\epsilon}\sigma\pi\sigma\tau a$) Aesculapius, many and various are the blessings that have accrued to me from thee and thy kindness.'[2]

To Julian, ' Aesculapius does not heal men from the hope of a reward, but in the fulfilment of his peculiar function everywhere to benefit mankind.'[3] Julian also speaks of the kindness of Helios in ' begetting Aesculapius to be the saviour of all,'[4] and in his *Against the Galileans* he contrasts Aesculapius with the Christ as ' the greatest gift of Helios and God.'[5] ' Zeus begot Aesculapius from himself among the intelligible gods,' and ' Aesculapius multiplied himself, and by his visitations stretched out over the whole earth his saving right hand . . . he is present everywhere on land and sea. He visits no one of us separately, and yet he raises up souls that are sinful and bodies that are sick '; and he too adds his personal testimony: ' At any rate ofttimes Aesculapius healed myself by prescribing remedies, and of this God is witness.'[6]

---

[1] VIII. 6, 5, p. 324.   [2] 37, 39, 40.   [3] *Ep.* 40 (78), 419b.
[4] *Orat.* IV. 153b.   [5] 200b.   [6] 235c.

Equally eloquent and indisputable is the archaeological evidence. Numerous *vota* are extant representing the parts of the body healed by this ' saviour ' and inscriptions erected in his honour by the cured.

A glance through the inscriptions from Epidaurus collected by Kabbadias in his *Fouilles d'Épidaure* or the selection in Dittenberger's *Sylloge* or in Weinreich's *Antike Heilungswunder* or Besnier's *L'île Tibérine* will show that Aesculapius was *par éminence* the ' Healer.' Or a visit to his chief shrine of Epidaurus will bring home in a vivid fashion to the modern student the genuine faith evoked by this ' Saviour ' as attested by evidence of a vast concourse of worshippers and the abundant remains of their thanksgiving. As one sits in the local theatre, which is one of the best-preserved and impressive remains of the Graeco-Roman world, with a selection of the often rude Doric inscriptions of long-silent visitors seeking and finding healing, and with the picture of the many *vota* of cures in one's memory, the past seems to return and to make one contemporary with many generations of patients and worshippers.

Only a few examples may be cited. An inscription [1] from Epidaurus has preserved to us a list of forty-eight cures of men and women from the most diverse ailments, slight and serious, most of which present no difficulty to modern readers, though others obviously bear marks of the ancient *Wundersucht* dear to both Pagans and Christians. Repeated reference is made to the ' sleeping-in,' *incubatio,* and to the visionary visitation. To one lady, Sostrata, Aesculapius ' manifested the *Parousia* of himself and ordered her to send her gift for the cure to Epidaurus.' [2] Another patient, Alketas,[3] ' although blind, saw the dream-vision ; the God seemed to come to him and to open his eyes with his fingers, and he first saw the trees that were in the temple. At daybreak

---

[1] Dittenberger, *Syl.* 3rd ed. III. 1168-9.
[2] *Op. cit.* 1169, 26-36.
[3] *Op. cit.* 1168, 120 ff.

he went away cured.' Another patient,[1] M. Julius Apellas, suffering from several ailments, records, ' I prayed the God to discharge me more quickly '; and again, in language parallel to that of Paul's prayer concerning the thorn in the flesh, he records of severe headache after the cure, ' For concerning this also I besought the God.'

Of Aesculapius' success at Rome there is the same ample evidence. A certain blind Gaius,[2] obeying the divine instructions, ' received his sight in the presence of the people, who congratulated him because living virtues had operated.' A Lucius,[3] ' suffering from pleurisy and despaired of by all,' ' was cured [ἐσώθη] and gave thanks publicly to the God, and the people rejoiced with him.' ' To Julianus who was spitting blood and was given up as hopeless by everyone the God vouchsafed a dream-oracle to come, and from his triple altar to take grains of *strobilos* and eat them with honey for three days, and he was cured [ἐσώθη], and he came and returned thanks publicly before the people.' [4]

Similarly emphatic is the testimony of a Roman soldier from the same shrine on an island in the Tiber: ' To Valerius Aper,[5] a blind soldier, the God gave an oracle to come and take blood of a white cock with honey and to mix them into a salve and anoint his eyes for three days, and he received sight and came and gave thanks publicly to the God.'

These instances justify the hold which the gracious figure of Aesculapius had on the imagination and loyalty of his grateful worshippers and interpret something of the yearning with which sufferers turned to the Healer. They also indicate some of the practical difficulties in

---

[1] Dittenburger, *Syl.* 3rd ed. III. 1170. Cf. Deissmann, *Light from East*, p. 311; *Licht*, 4th ed. p. 261; Fiebig, *Antike Wundergeschichten*, p. 20.

[2] *Sylloge*, III. 1173; Weinrich, *Heilungswunder*, p. 64.

[4] *C.I.G.* 5980; Dittenberger, III. 1173; Besnier, p. 214 f.

[5] Besnier, *L'île Tibérine*, p. 216.

strict line between exorcisms in the name of Jesus and
those by other formulae, and endeavoured to prevent
Christian charlatans.

It is indubitable that Jesus shared with His contemporaries a belief in the existence of demons and
their malefic influences on men, and also that He performed exorcisms like the rabbis of His day.   It is
certain that in the days of the writing of the New
Testament and in the subsequent age the practice had
assumed a large place and official importance.   Even
as early as the composition of Mark (circ. 70) exorcism
had such an apologetic value that Mark, writing for
the Roman Church, unduly magnifies exorcism in the
ministry of Jesus and advances it even as evidential
for Jesus' Messiahship, to which the demons are forced
to give testimony.

The Church did not deny the reality of the miraculous
cures of Paganism or of the repeated exorcisms, but it
attributed such cures to magic, whereas Christian
exorcisms were by fasting and prayer or, imitating their
Master's inconsequent critics in the self-stultifying
argument of expelling demons through collusion with the
Prince of Demons, Christians assigned such exorcisms
to demons whose names were less potent than the name
of Jesus, just as Celsus attributed Christian exorcism
to demons ;[1] or, shifting to safer ground, they attributed
' possession ' which called for expulsion to malign
demons, to break whose power was one end of the
Incarnation of the Son of God.[2]

But after the first creative outburst Christianity yielded
more and more to the unscientific outlook and readily
accepted current superstitions.   From the middle of the
second century onwards Christians saw in exorcism a
popular apologetic and sought to claim a monopoly of
it by a practical denial of exorcism to Pagans and
heretics, a dangerous step which a scholar like Origen

---

[1] *C. Celsum*, I. 6.   [2] Justin, *Apol.* II. 6.

could not take in the face of facts. Thus Tertullian [1] bases the truth of Christianity on the truth and antiquity of the Christian Scriptures, and on the confession of defeat from demons in Christian exorcisms. The Christian Church equipped itself with exorcists to outstrip its competitors. Demonology took up its home in the Church in the second century to supply the legions of devils throughout mediaevalism,[2] and, though it was based on a moral perception of the conflict of good and evil, it tended to externalize that conflict by making the protagonists supernatural beings other than men rather than man and God, and by shifting the scene of conflict from the moral and inner life of man to transmundane regions.

The association of magic with religion [3] and the use of magic for purposes of healing and the general practice of exorcism in Pagan and Christian antiquity is too large a topic for the end of a chapter. We have magical recipes for cures very akin to the directions given by Aesculapius in his sanatoria, and no difference can be detected between exorcism in Paganism, Judaism, and Christianity save in ' the name.' Indeed the general trend of the later Graeco-Roman world, Pagan and Christian, was toward the mediaeval mentality of credulity and emotion and the acceptance of authority and the substitution of miracle for argument. In Iamblichus and Proclus we find a similar decline of virile spiritual Neo-Platonism into theurgy [4] as

---

[1] *Apol.* 46.

[2] Cf. Tambornino, *De Antiq. Daemonismo*, pp. 106-10.

[3] Cf. L. Thorndike, *Place of Magic in the Intellectual History of Europe* (New York, 1905).

[4] Cf. Halliday, *Pagan Background*, p. 233: " It is a characteristic feature of the time that the less intelligent influences tended to become increasingly dominant. The magical element became more and more prominent in religion, and this in turn affected philosophy. . . . Finally in Neo-Platonism, in which mystical apprehension supplemented or even supplanted rational perception, philosophy was to claim a perilous kinship with theosophy and theurgy. . . . Plotinus, Porphyry, Iamblichus, Maximus: how swift and abysmal a descent! "

we find in Christianity its creative sanity and spontaneity yielding to a popular identification of science, philosophy, and magic, especially from the throwing open by edict of the gates of the Church by Constantine.

INDEX OF NAMES

INDEX OF SUBJECTS

Printed in Great Britain by
Hazell, Watson & Viney, Ltd., London and Aylesbury.